BIBLE DOCTRINE

for Teens and Young Adults

God's Word, inspired, infallible,
The only source of truth,
Must be the center of our lives
Already in our youth.

Its doctrines, the pure truths therein,
With dogma as its core,
Are searched out in theology
From early days of yore.

May God then bless the study of
His great eternal Word,
That in the hearts of young and old
Its truths may e'er be heard.

BIBLE DOCTRINE
for Teens and Young Adults

BOOK I
CHAPTERS 1–10

James W. Beeke

Illustrated by Ben De Regt

Reformation Heritage Books
Grand Rapids, Michigan

Bible Doctrine for Teens and Young Adults, Book I
© 1987 by James W. Beeke

Reprinted 2020

Reformation Heritage Books
2965 Leonard St. NE
Grand Rapids, MI 49525
616-977-0889 / Fax 616-285-3246
orders@heritagebooks.org
www.heritagebooks.org

ISBN #s for *Bible Doctrine for...*

...Younger Children: Book A	978-1-60178-048-5
...Younger Children: Book B	978-1-60178-049-2
...Older Children: Book A	978-1-60178-050-8
...Older Children: Book B	978-1-60178-051-5
...Teens and Young Adults: Book I	978-1-60178-291-5
...Teens and Young Adults: Book II	978-1-60178-292-2
...Teens and Young Adults: Book III	978-1-60178-293-9

For additional Reformed literature, request a free book list from
Reformation Heritage Books at the above regular or e-mail address.

TABLE OF CONTENTS
Book I
Chapters 1-10

For a complete index of doctrinal standard references, catechism questions, and source credits throughout the thirty chapters in this series, refer to Book III.

ACKNOWLEDGEMENTS

The publication of *Bible Doctrine for Teens and Young Adults, Books I, II, and III* would not have been possible without the assistance of the following persons and groups, whom I wish to sincerely thank for their help in the following ways:

Administrative, proofreading, and layout assistance	Mrs. Jennie Luteyn and Mr. Bob Menger
Artwork	Mr. Ben De Regt
Title page poetry	Mrs. Jennie Luteyn
Critical reading and approval of scriptural and doctrinal content	Rev. J. R. Beeke, Rev. J. Spaans, Rev. A. W. Verhoef, Rev. C. Vogelaar; Evangelist B. Elshout; Elders: J. Beeke, Sr., J. R. Beeke, H. Bisschop, J. De Bruine, L. Den Boer, J. den Bok, B. Harskamp, G. Kanis, G. Moerdyk, J. Neels, H. Van den Dorpel, and W. Van Voorst; and Mr. A. Slootmaker and Mr. S. Van Grouw
Creation Chapter review	Dr. D. E. Chittick, Mr. D. Maljaars, Mr. B. Van der Weide, and Mr. T. Van de Weg
Instructional format review	Dr. H. Van Brummelen
Typesetting	Miss Marlene Les
Layout and paste-up work	Mrs. Arlene Hoefakker
General proofreading	The secretarial staff and teaching faculty of Timothy Christian School
Support, cooperation, and approval	The NRC Synodical Education Committee The NRC Book and Publishing Committee The Timothy Christian School Board
Understanding, patience, self-sacrifice, and loving assistance	My wife, Ruth

Above all may we acknowledge the Lord who has graciously provided the opportunity and means to produce this and the previous series of Bible doctrine textbooks.

May it please the Lord, in His sovereign good pleasure, to richly bless this means of instruction to many high school students and other younger and older adults reading and studying it "that we henceforth be no more children, tossed to and fro, and carried about with every wind of doctrine, by the sleight of men, and cunning craftiness, whereby they lie in wait to deceive; but speaking the truth in love, may grow up unto Him in all things, which is the Head, even Christ" (Ephesians 4:14-15).

Further may the Holy Spirit graciously apply the eternal truths of His Word, studied in this series, to our hearts that increasingly we may be led to "love the Lord thy God with all thy heart, and with all thy soul, and with all thy mind, and with all thy strength" (Mark 12:30a). He is most worthy to be praised and worshipped.

— James W. Beeke

INTRODUCTION

TO: All high school students, other young people, and adults reading this book

Dear Friends,

Can you read what is written on the chalkboard in the photograph pictured on the title pages — pages 2 and 3? It is reproduced for you here:

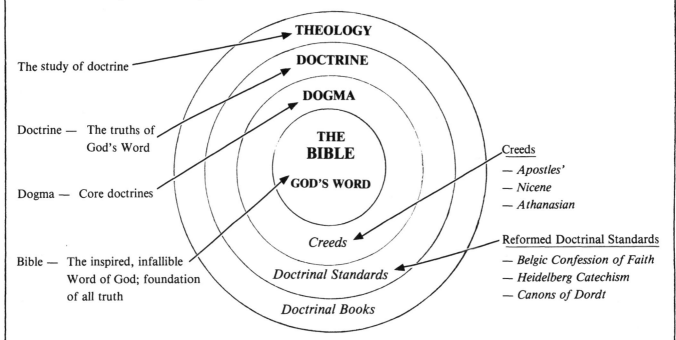

What does this sketch mean? What is in the center of this drawing? The *Bible* is God's Word. It proclaims God's eternal and unchanging truths. The truths of the Bible are called *doctrine*. In this series of books, *Bible Doctrine for Teens and Young Adults, Books I, II, and III,* you will study Bible doctrine — the truths of God's Word. The core doctrines, those necessary to believe for salvation, are called *dogmas*. The explanation of Bible doctrine is called *theology*.

Theology is the attempt to properly understand that which the Bible is teaching regarding a certain doctrine. To do this, it is necessary to read all of the references to this truth found throughout the entire Bible. These references must be carefully studied and compared, and then placed into statements and explanations of belief. This is needed in order to properly summarize that which the Bible teaches about sin, salvation, death, baptism, and all other Bible doctrines. The course of study contained in this series of books is a beginning course in theology.

No person is as important to know as God, no book as necessary to read as the Bible, and no truths as crucial to understand as the doctrines of Scripture. Therefore, as you study Bible doctrine, do so seriously and prayerfully. God can bless your study by applying these truths in your heart and life. To personally and increasingly come to know, love, and follow God and His truth is the most important purpose of human life; it is the reason why man was created. Through salvation in Jesus Christ, sinners can be restored into a loving relationship and communion with God to God's glory and their joy.

May God personally bless your study of Bible doctrine, through the means of this series of books.

1

God's Essence
God's Names
God's Attributes

Majestic is the Lord our God
Who sits enthroned on high,
As providence and conscience and
Creation testify.

God's Word declares His essence and
Exalts His holy Name.
Unfailing love and pardon both
His faithfulness proclaim.

The rainbow of His attributes
Like prismed rays of sun,
Perfected in diversity,
Yet perfectly are one.

FROM OUR REFORMED DOCTRINAL STANDARDS

Belgic Confession of Faith

*Article 1 — That there
is one only God*

We all believe with the heart, and confess with the mouth, that there is one only simple and spiritual Being, which we call God; and that He is eternal, incomprehensible, invisible, immutable, infinite, almighty, perfectly wise, just, good, and the overflowing fountain of all good.

1

GOD'S ESSENCE

The Bible begins with God: "In the beginning God" (Genesis 1:1a). God is the central point of all things. As we start our study of **Bible doctrine**, we too will begin by speaking and learning about God.

God's essence is His nature, or who and what God is.

No person can fully explain God for He is **infinite** — limitless and immeasurable. As human beings, we are not infinite, but are limited to being in only one place at a time. God, however, is everywhere at the same time. Our strength is measurable, but God's power is immeasurable; He is almighty. We are limited by time, but God is eternal.

There are many things which we do not fully understand because our intelligence is also limited. Therefore, we cannot fully explain God who is infinite.

● **Bible doctrine** — The truths taught in God's Word, the Bible

● **God's essence** — God's nature; who and what God is

● **Infinite** — Limitless; without end or measure

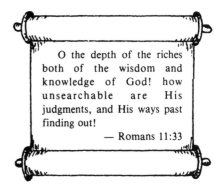

O the depth of the riches both of the wisdom and knowledge of God! how unsearchable are His judgments, and His ways past finding out!
— Romans 11:33

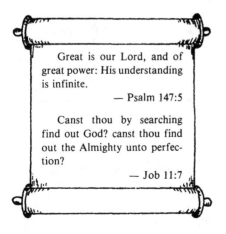

Great is our Lord, and of great power: His understanding is infinite.

— Psalm 147:5

Canst thou by searching find out God? canst thou find out the Almighty unto perfection?

— Job 11:7

A king of Syracuse once asked Simonides, his most famous poet, "What is God?"

The poet asked for a day to think about this question and the king gave his permission.

The following day Simonides returned and asked the king for another two days. After this, he desired four additional days. When this time had past, he requested eight more days.

The king expressed his surprise and asked, "Why do you keep asking for more time to answer this question?"

Simonides answered, "The more I think of God, the more I realize how little I know of Him."

We, too, know that there is a God, but can we fully answer this king's question: "What is God?" Why not?

Mr. Sawyer is very interested in automobile engines. He spends many hours studying engines and working on his car.

Mr. Sawyer has a three-year-old son named Robert. Imagine Mr. Sawyer speaking with his son and saying, "Now, Robert, this is the carburetor. The carburetor mixes the gasoline from the fuel lines with air. This fuel and air mixture is drawn down into the cylinders when the pistons move down. This mixture is compressed as the piston rises again and is ignited by a spark from the spark plug which forces the piston back down and..."

Why will Robert not fully understand his father's explanation of how a car operates? Will Robert, however, still know that his father's car exists and runs?

The difference in understanding between man and God is greater than that between Robert and his father. We cannot fully explain God. Can we, however, still know that God exists and acts?

Although it is impossible to fully understand or explain God, it is possible to know Him. Human beings can know, love, honor, and serve God.

To rightfully know and love God is most important for each of us; it is the purpose for which we were created. We need to know God for the following three reasons:

1. As our Creator, God created us for the purpose of knowing, loving, serving, glorifying, and enjoying Him forever. Therefore He has the right to expect this from us.

2. We will never find true peace, satisfaction or fulfillment apart from God. We were created to love an infinite and perfect God, and therefore, finite and imperfect things will never satisfy us.

3. After death, we must give an account of our lives to God. To have despised our Creator's communion, rejected His purpose, and rebelled against His Person will be most terrible.

How can we know that God is true? We may know this from God's Word (the Bible), creation, **providence**, and our consciences. Yet, we cannot fully understand or explain Him.

? Why can you not fully answer the question that the king of Syracuse asked Simonides, "What is God?"

? Why is the difference in understanding between man and God greater than that between Robert and his father? Can we know that He works, even though we cannot fully understand Him?

Know ye the LORD He is God: it is He that hath made us, and not we ourselves.
— Psalm 100:3a

And Jesus answered him, The first of all the commandments is, Hear O Israel; the Lord our God is one Lord:
And thou shalt love the Lord thy God with all thy heart, and with all thy soul, and with all thy mind, and with all thy strength: this is the first and great commandment.
— Mark 12:29-30

Vanity of vanities, saith the preacher; all is vanity.
Let us hear the conclusion of the whole matter: Fear God, and keep His commandments: for this is the whole duty of man.
For God shall bring every work into judgment, with every secret thing, whether it be good, or whether it be evil.
— Ecclesiastes 12:8,13-14

● **Providence** — God's caring for, upholding of, and ruling over all things

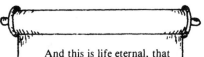

And this is life eternal, that they might know Thee the only true God, and Jesus Christ, whom Thou hast sent.
— John 17:3

The heavens declare the glory of God; and the firmament sheweth His handywork.
— Psalm 19:1

Nevertheless He left not Himself without witness, in that He did good, and gave us rain from heaven, and fruitful seasons, filling our hearts with food and gladness.
— Acts 14:17

Because that which may be known of God is manifest in them; for God hath shewed it unto them.

Which shew the work of the law written in their hearts, their conscience also bearing witness, and their thoughts the mean while accusing or else excusing one another;
— Romans 1:19; 2:15

● **Friar** — A traveling preacher

The fool hath said in his heart, There is no God.
— Psalm 14:1a

● **Atheists** — Those who deny that there is a God

A certain young man went to trap a **friar** with the following three questions:

1. How can you say there is a God, when I cannot see Him and you cannot show Him to me?
2. How is it right to punish man for his crimes if everything he does is according to God's will?
3. How can God punish Satan with fire since that is his natural element?

With a confident smile, he waited for the friar's answer.

The friar asked him to return the following day. When the young man did so, the friar took a large clod of dirt and hit him over the head with it.

A stunned and angry young man immediately went to the town judge. He explained what he had asked the friar and the friar's response. He complained of his pain to the judge.

The judge sent for the friar and asked him why he had done this.

The friar replied, "I did this to answer his three questions:

1. He complains of his pain — let him show me his pain. How can I believe in something I cannot see?
2. Why is he complaining to you if he believes that it is wrong to punish a man for only doing what is in God's will?
3. How could I punish him with earth since that is his natural element?"

A confounded young man and a pleased judge both listened with surprise to the friar's clear answer.

Atheists are people who deny that there is a God. They try to believe and convince others that there is no God. The Bible speaks of atheists as being both foolish and wicked.

Atheists deny the following reasonable **evidences** of the **existence** of God found in nature:

1. *Evidence in Creation (Cosmological Evidence)* — All existing things in the universe require a cause for their existence and activity. The original cause for all things must be powerful enough to produce them. This evidence **testifies** of an "**Ultimate** Power" — of God.

2. *Evidence in Perfection (Ontological Evidence)* — All human beings are born with the idea of an absolutely perfect being. Since absolute perfection is not found in any observable, created things, this evidence testifies of an "Ultimate Perfection" — of God.

3. *Evidence in Design (Teleological Evidence)* — The design, order, and **synchronization** found in all things speaks of an intelligent, planned, and coordinated purpose. This intelligence must be **sufficient** to plan and coordinate such harmony. This evidence testifies of an "Ultimate Wisdom" — of God.

4. *Evidence in Morality (Anthropological Evidence)* — All human beings have a **consciousness** of right and wrong, of being held accountable for their actions, and of law. This evidence testifies of an "Ultimate Righteousness" — of God.

5. *Evidence in History (Ethnological Evidence)* — History reveals that the knowledge and worship of "god(s)" have been found among every tribe and nation on earth. This evidence testifies of an "Ultimate Being" — of God.

We do not need to prove God's existence; but, we need to believe, by faith, God's testimony of Himself in His Word. The Bible not only tells us that there is a God, but also who God is, and how we can come to know, love and serve God. Atheists deny the existence of God both as taught in His Word and as seen in the evidences of nature.

- **Evidences** — Signs; testimonies; indications
- **Existence** — The state of having being and reality
- **Cosmological** — That which pertains to the material universe (cosmos), its parts, elements, and laws
- **Testifies** — Speaks; gives evidence of
- **Ultimate** — Highest; last; final; beyond which there can be no advance
- **Ontological** — That which pertains to the nature of reality or being
- **Teleological** — That which pertains to design and purpose in nature
- **Synchronization** — Various parts fitting and operating together in harmony
- **Sufficient** — Enough; as much as is needed
- **Anthropological** — That which pertains to the study of man
- **Consciousness** — The state of knowing, experiencing, or being aware
- **Ethnological** — That which pertains to the study of different groups or cultures of people

A minister once entered an auditorium to preach to a large crowd on the subject of "God." As he entered, a man rushed forward and handed him a folded note. Supposing it to be an announcement, he opened it as he stepped onto the stage. The note contained one single word — "Fool!"

Despite his surprise, the minister made an excellent application from this note. He addressed the crowd and said, "Something just happened which is very unusual. Someone just handed me a message which consists of only one word — the word 'Fool!' I have often heard of those who have written letters and forgotten to sign their names — but this is the first time I have ever heard of anyone who signed his name and forgot to write the letter!"

The minister then proceeded to preach on Psalm 14:1, "The fool hath said in his heart, There is no God."

Why were this minister's remarks not only fitting, but also true?

What would life be like if you tried to believe that there was no God? If a person denied the important biblical doctrines of God, and the possibility of knowing Him, why would he be missing the most important reason for, and purpose of, his life?

Can a person live without any "gods"? Many people in our society claim to be atheists today. They have turned away from the true God, and yet, they live for other "gods." Can you name some "gods" people live for, care most about, and "worship" in our society?

What is a "god"? Who or what is your "god"? How can your "god" be seen in your life?

What do the following two stories teach us about atheism?

A certain famous atheistic lecturer once addressed a large crowd. He spoke for an hour, using highly educated terms and deep philosophical arguments, attempting to prove that God does not exist.

When he concluded his speech, an older woman stood up and asked simply and politely, "Sir, may I ask you two questions?"

? If a person does not believe in God, why is he yet missing the most important reason for, and purpose of, his life?

? Why can a person not live without having any gods? Can you name several false "gods" that non-church people live for in our society today? Can you name any false "gods" for which church people live?

16

"Certainly!" the lecturer responded.

"Sir, I have known, loved, and served God for many years. I have received great joy from His salvation and deep comfort from His Word. He has graciously kept me from many sins and enabled me to lead a calm and contented life. If, when I die, I come to learn that there is no God — can you please tell me what I have lost by believing in God during my life?"

The room became completely silent as the audience grasped the simple logic of the woman's question. The lecturer, however, had not expected this and did not know what to answer.

After a lengthy pause, the woman spoke again. "Sir, my second question is this — If, when you come to die, you discover that there is a God, and that the Bible is true; can you please tell me, Sir, what you will lose?"

? Why would it be a very difficult task for an atheist to answer the two simple questions asked by the old, Christian woman?

During a church meeting in a small town in Parker County, Texas, a man professed to be an atheist. His confession created a tremendous shock throughout this small, religious community.

The next morning, the atheist went to the post office, which was located in a store. The storekeeper was not at the meeting the night before and the following conversation took place:

"Say, what is this I hear? I heard that you said publicly in the meeting last night that you do not believe in a God."

? In what sense is a church person who believes with his mind that there is a God, but neither loves nor serves Him with his whole heart, a greater fool than the complete atheist?

? What effect would such "mind-believing," but not "heart-living" Christians have upon our society?

17

> God is a Spirit: and they that worship Him must worship Him in spirit and in truth.
>
> — John 4:24
>
> Thou shalt not make unto thee any graven image, or any likeness of anything that is in heaven above, or that is in the earth beneath, or that is in the water under the earth:
>
> Thou shalt not bow down thyself to them, nor serve them: for I the LORD thy God am a jealous God, visiting the iniquity of the fathers upon the children unto the third and fourth generation of them that hate Me;
>
> And shewing mercy unto thousands of them that love Me, and keep My commandments.
>
> — Exodus 20:4-6

"Yes, I said that."

"Why, man, you are a fool. Nature and everything proves that there is a God."

"Do you believe in God?" asked the atheist.

"Certainly I do," said the storekeeper. "I have always believed there is a God."

"Do you serve Him?" asked the atheist.

"No, I don't really serve Him; but I am not an atheist! I believe in God."

The atheist answered, "Man, *you* are a fool. If I believed there was a God, I would not lose an hour serving Him. How can you believe there is a God and not serve Him? That is the most foolish thing any man could possibly do."

Why are both men foolish, the atheist and the person who believes there is a God but does not truly serve Him? Why? Do you love and serve God with all your soul, mind, and strength?

God is a Spirit; He does not have a physical body as we do. The second of God's Ten Commandments forbids trying to picture God. We may not picture Him in the likeness of anything we see in the sky, on land, or in the ocean.

- **Pantheists** — People who believe creation is God and God is creation; There is no personal God who reigns over creation; the universe is God

Pantheists are people who believe that God and creation are the same thing. The universe is God and God is the universe. Pantheists do not believe in a God who previously created and presently upholds creation. They do not acknowledge a God who is separate from and above His creation.

Pantheists make a serious mistake. God created all things and rules over His creation; He is a Spirit who is separate from and above His creation.

? What deep comfort and sense of purpose are missing in the lives of those who deny the biblical doctrine of a personal God?

People who deny the biblical truth that God is a Person — One who lives and reigns over all His creation — do so at a great price. They have no personal God to turn to with their needs and cares nor to thank for received blessings. They have no personal God to whom they can pray nor in whom they can trust. The universe and its impersonal laws are their "god."

? Why does the pantheist miss the comfort expressed in Romans 8:28, "And we know that *all* things work together for *good* to them that love God"?

There are many people in our society today who believe that

they receive their life from, and live at the mercy of, "Mother Nature." To these people, science provides the "key" to the truth of their "universe god." What deep comfort and sense of purpose are missing in the lives of those who deny the biblical doctrine of a personal God?

Science can provide useful knowledge about God's creation, but what deeper "key" to truth has God given us? When man's ideas about truth and scientific **theories** contradict God's revealed truth in His Word, which is in error — man's theory or God's truth? Can you give some examples of this conflict in our society today?

Read Question and Answer 28 in the *Heidelberg Catechism.* How does this answer describe a rich comfort that is missed by those who deny the biblical truth of a living, reigning, personal God?

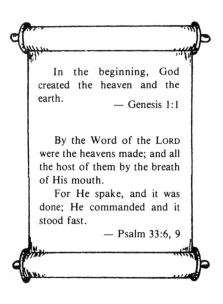

In the beginning, God created the heaven and the earth.
— Genesis 1:1

By the Word of the LORD were the heavens made; and all the host of them by the breath of His mouth.
For He spake, and it was done; He commanded and it stood fast.
— Psalm 33:6, 9

● **Theories** — Possible explanations of how or why certain events happen

? What is the most accurate and deepest source of truth we have today?

HEIDELBERG CATECHISM

Q.28.   What advantage is it to us to know that God has created, and by His providence doth still uphold all things?
A.   That we may be patient in adversity; thankful in prosperity; and that in all things, which may hereafter befall us, we place our firm trust in our faithful God and Father, that nothing shall separate us from His love; since all creatures are so in His hand, that without His will they cannot so much as move.

God is an eternal Spirit; He is without beginning or ending. Angels and men also have spirits, but their spirits have been created. They have a beginning when God forms their spirits. Only God is an eternal spirit; One without beginning.

There is only one God, for there can only be one who is almighty, supreme, and everywhere present. Two "supremes" or two "almighties" would be impossible.

Do you know, love, and serve this one, only true God? Thomas Watson wrote, "It is little comfort to know there is a God, unless He be ours." Is the only true God, your God?

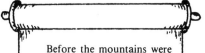

Before the mountains were brought forth, or ever Thou hadst formed the earth and the world, even from everlasting to everlasting, Thou art God.
— Psalm 90:2

For as the Father hath life in Himself; so hath He given to the Son to have life in Himself.
— John 5:26

Thus saith the LORD the King of Israel, and his Redeemer the LORD of hosts; I am the first, and I am the last; and beside Me there is no God.
— Isaiah 44:6

That all the people of the earth may know that the LORD is God, and that there is none else.
— I Kings 8:60

GOD'S NAMES

? Can you name some conflicts in our present society between faith in God's Word and in man's theories?

God does not need names to distinguish Himself from others as we do. God cannot be compared with any other being, for there is only one God.

God's names are given for a different purpose; they reveal something of Himself to us. Biblical names often have special meanings — they reveal truths about a person or place. Study the examples in the box below:

> To whom then will ye liken God? or what likeness will ye compare unto Him?
> To whom then will ye liken Me, or shall I be equal? saith the Holy One.
> — Isaiah 40:18, 25

BIBLICAL NAMES AND MEANINGS	
Name	Meaning
Eve	*Mother of Life*
Noah	*Rest or Comfort*
Babel	*Confusion*
Melchizedek	*King of Righteousness*
King of Salem	*King of Peace*
Solomon	*Peaceful*
Bethel	*House of God*
Jesus	*Savior*
Christ	*Anointed*

? Why is it important to know the meanings of biblical names? How do the names and meanings listed help us to understand the biblical stories and lessons connected with them? What should these examples teach us about God's names?

How do these names reveal certain truths concerning each person or place?

Biblical names for God are also rich in meaning for they reveal various truths about Him. How do the following verses refer to the importance of God's names?

? How do the texts in the box speak of the importance of God's names?

> And they that know Thy *name* will put their trust in Thee.
> — Psalm 9:10a
>
> I have manifested Thy *name* unto the men which Thou gavest Me out of the world.
> — John 17:6a
>
> And I appeared unto Abraham, unto Isaac, and unto Jacob, by the *name* of God Almighty, but by My *name* JEHOVAH was I not known to them.
> — Exodus 6:3
>
> Our Father which art in heaven, Hallowed be Thy *name*.
> — Matthew 6:9b

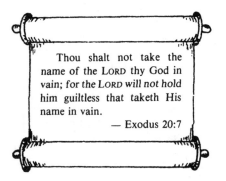

> Thou shalt not take the name of the LORD thy God in vain; for the LORD will not hold him guiltless that taketh His name in vain.
> — Exodus 20:7

God's names are far more important than human or location names, for they reveal something of God's Being, of who He is.

A deep love for God's name can be seen so beautifully in the following story:

Is a deep love for God's name or your own witnessed more often in your life?

> Polycarp was a very old man who had served as a minister in the early church at Smyrna for many years. During a time of Christian persecution, old Polycarp was captured and brought to trial before the Roman governor.
>
> A large crowd had gathered to witness his trial. The governor spoke to Polycarp and said, "Curse Jesus Christ and I will set you free." It became breathlessly quiet as all listened intently for Polycarp's answer.
>
> Polycarp answered, "For eighty-six years I have served Him and He has never done me any wrong. How then could I curse my King and Savior?"
>
> The Roman governor threatened him with death by wild animals or fire, but Polycarp remained firm. He would not dishonor or blaspheme his Lord, and consequently died a Christian martyr's death.
>
> Can you see the deep love for God's name in the life of Polycarp? Which did Polycarp love more — God's name or his own life? Which means more to you — God's name or your own?

The Old Testament was first written in the Hebrew language. The most commonly used Hebrew names of God are:

1. *El or Elohim (God)* — The name "El" or "Elohim" means "the Mighty One." It reveals something of God's great power and speaks to us of the greatness of the almighty God. The name "El" or "Elohim" is written as "God" in our English Bible.

2. *Adonai or Adon (Lord)* — "Adonai" or "Adon" means "Ruler" or "Possessor." The name "Adonai" testifies of God as the possessor of, and ruler over, all things, including man. It speaks of God's power over nature and creation. In our Bible this name is printed as "Lord."

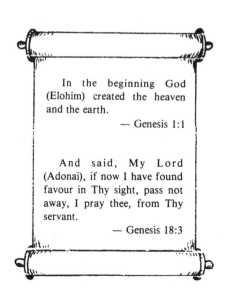

In the beginning God (Elohim) created the heaven and the earth.

— Genesis 1:1

And said, My Lord (Adonai), if now I have found favour in Thy sight, pass not away, I pray thee, from Thy servant.

— Genesis 18:3

3. **Shaddai (Almighty)** — "Shaddai" means "Almighty" or "All-sufficient." This name differs from "Adonai" in both manner and degree. "Shaddai" refers to God using His power to graciously deliver, comfort, and bless His people. "Shaddai" is read as "Almighty" in our English Bible.

4. **Elyon (The Most High God)** — The name "Elyon" refers to the most high God who is exalted far above all creatures in perfection, dwelling place, and dominion. Our Bible writes this name as "the most high God."

5. **Sabaoth (The LORD of hosts)** — "Sabaoth" means "the Unconquerable One." This name refers to God who is mighty in battle to conquer His enemies and preserve His chosen. "Sabaoth" is translated as "the LORD of hosts" in our English Bible.

6. **Yahweh or Jehovah (LORD)** — The name "Yahweh" or "Jehovah" means "I am that I am." This is the most personal and special name of God for it speaks of God as being unchangeable and eternally faithful. This is true for all of creation, but this name especially points to God's remaining faithful to His people and unchangeable in His mercy toward them. God remains true to His covenant promises — He will deliver His people. He will save them from their sins. He is what He is, and will be what He is forever. "I am that I am." The name "Yahweh" or "Jehovah" is written as "LORD" with all capital letters in the King James Version of the English Bible.

In Exodus 3:13-15 we read of God's special name when He appeared to Moses in the burning bush and called him to lead Israel out of Egypt. "And Moses said unto God, Behold, when I come unto the children of Israel, and shall say unto them, The God of your fathers hath sent me unto you; and they shall say to me, What is His name? what shall I say unto them? And God said unto Moses, I AM THAT I AM: and He said, Thus shalt thou say unto the children of Israel, I AM hath sent me unto you. And God said

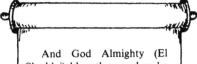

And God Almighty (El Shaddai) bless thee, and make thee fruitful, and multiply thee, that thou mayest be a multitude of people.
— Genesis 28:3

And Melchizedek king of Salem brought forth bread and wine: and he was the priest of the most high God (Elyon).
— Genesis 14:18

Except the LORD of hosts (Sabaoth) had left unto us a very small remnant, we should have been as Sodom, and we should have been like unto Gomorrah.
— Isaiah 1:9

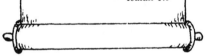

I am the LORD (Jehovah): this is My name: and My glory will I not give to another, neither My praise to graven images.
— Isaiah 42:8

And to Seth, to him also there was born a son; and he called his name Enos: then began men to call upon the name of the LORD (Jehovah).
— Genesis 4:26

For I am the LORD (Jehovah), I change not; therefore ye sons of Jacob are not consumed.
— Malachi 3:6

moreover unto Moses, Thus shalt thou say unto the children of Israel, The LORD God of your fathers, the God of Abraham, the God of Isaac, and the God of Jacob, hath sent me unto you: this is My name for ever, and this is My memorial unto all generations." "I am" is the name "Yahweh" or "Jehovah." How did God prove to Israel, "I am" an unchanging, covenant-keeping God?

The name Jehovah is frequently joined to a second name in the Old Testament, for instance:

Jehovah-jireh (Genesis 22:14) — *The LORD will provide*
Jehovah-nissi (Exodus 17:15) — *The LORD our Banner*
Jehovah-shalom (Judges 6:24) — *The LORD our Peace*
Jehovah-roih (Psalm 23:1) — *The LORD my Shepherd*
Jehovah-shammah (Ezekiel 48:35) — *The LORD is there.*

The New Testament was originally written in the Greek language. The most commonly used Greek names of God are:

1. *Theos (God)* — "Theos" is the Greek name for God which replaces the Hebrew titles of "El," "Elohim," and "Elyon." This is the most commonly used name for God in the New Testament and is printed as "God."

2. *Kurios (Lord)* — "Kurios" is the New Testament name used for "Yahweh," "Jehovah," or "Adonai." This title, used for both God and Christ, is written as "Lord" in our English Bible.

3. *Pantokrator (The Almighty)* — "Pantokrator" replaces the Hebrew name "Shaddai"; it is translated into English as "the Almighty."

4. *Sabaoth (Sabaoth)* — The name "Sabaoth" is not translated in the King James New Testament, but is printed in its Hebrew form as "Sabaoth."

5. *Pater (Father)* — The Greek name "Pater" is a special name for God in the New Testament. This name means, and is written in our English Bible as, "Father." The name "Father" was also used for God in the Old Testament, but its use became more frequent and **predominant** in the new Testament.

And think not to say within yourselves, We have Abraham to our father; for I say unto you, that God (Theos) is able of these stones to raise up children unto Abraham.
— Matthew 3:9

Prepare ye the way of the Lord (Kurios), make His paths straight.
— Matthew 3:3b

I am the Alpha and the Omega, the beginning and the ending, saith the Lord, which is, and which was, and which is to come, the Almighty (Pantokrator).
— Revelation 1:8

And as Esaias said before, Except the Lord of Sabaoth had left us a seed, we had been as Sodoma, and been made like unto Gomorrha.
— Romans 9:29

He shall cry unto Me, Thou art my Father (Pater), my God, and the rock of my salvation.
— Psalm 89:26

Be ye therefore perfect, even as your Father (Pater) which is in heaven is perfect.
— Matthew 5:48

● **Predominant** — Important; noticeable

God is a "Father" in the following three ways:

THE FATHERHOOD OF GOD	
As Father of:	Example Text:
1. His Son	And lo a voice from heaven saying, This is My beloved son, in whom I am well pleased. — Matthew 3:17
2. His creation and all creatures	Have we not all one Father? hath not one God created us? — Malachi 2:10a
3. His saved, adopted children	For ye have not received the spirit of bondage again to fear; but ye have received the Spirit of adoption, whereby we cry, Abba, Father. — Romans 8:15

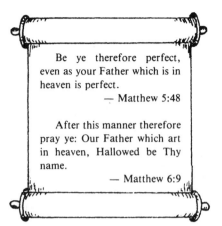

Be ye therefore perfect, even as your Father which is in heaven is perfect.
— Matthew 5:48

After this manner therefore pray ye: Our Father which art in heaven, Hallowed be Thy name.
— Matthew 6:9

? How is knowing God as our personal Father through adoption different from only knowing Him as our Creator? Why is it important to emphasize this distinction? Are you God's child only through creation or also by His gracious adoption? What fruits reveal themselves in the lives of God's truly adopted children?

The name "father" speaks of tender and abiding love. "Fatherly love" is illustrated very touchingly in the following story:

There was a shipwreck on Lake Pontchartrain, a considerable distance from shore. No lifeboats were on board and the ship was slowly sinking. A father and mother with six children were on board.

The father told his children not to be afraid. He promised to return for them, as he jumped into the waves with his wife. After bringing her safely to shore, he plunged back into the rough waves and returned for his children. One by one he brought them safely to shore.

Only one child remained. The loving father's strength was spent; he could not even stand on his feet and yet — he had promised his last son that he would return. He partly swam and partly floated back to the ship. He told his son to jump to him. As he grasped his boy in his arms, his spent strength totally collapsed and they both drowned in the waves.

How can this touching story of a father's love picture the love of God for His children? How would the outcome be different from the sad ending to this story, however? A helpless, human father is very different from the almighty God!

The well-known parable of the **Prodigal** Son is a beautiful example of the unfailing, forgiving love of God the Father. Read this parable as it is recorded in Luke 15:11-24:

● **Prodigal** — One who foolishly spends his possessions; a great waster

Luke 15:11-24

And He said, A certain man had two sons:

And the younger of them said to his father, Father, give me the portion of goods that falleth to me. And he divided unto them his living.

And not many days after the younger son gathered all together, and took his journey into a far country, and there wasted his substance with riotous living.

And when he had spent all, there arose a mighty famine in that land; and he began to be in want.

And he went and joined himself to a citizen of that country; and he sent him into his fields to feed swine.

And he would fain have filled his belly with the husks that the swine did eat: and no man gave unto him.

And when he came to himself, he said, How many hired servants of my father's have bread enough and to spare, and I perish with hunger!

I will arise and go to my father, and will say unto him, Father, I have sinned against heaven, and before thee,

And am no more worthy to be called thy son: make me as one of thy hired servants.

And he arose, and came to his father. But when he was yet a great way off, his father saw him, and had compassion, and ran, and fell on his neck, and kissed him.

And the son said unto him, Father, I have sinned against heaven, and in thy sight, and am no more worthy to be called thy son.

But the father said to his servants, Bring forth the best robe, and put it on him; and put a ring on his hand, and shoes on his feet;

And bring hither the fatted calf, and kill it; and let us eat, and be merry:

For this my son was dead, and is alive again; he was lost, and is found. And they began to be merry.

? How can we observe the father's great love in the following expressions:
— "his father saw him"
— "and had compassion"
— "and ran"
— "and kissed him"
— "the best robe, a ring, and shoes"
— "killing the fatted calf"
— "let us eat and be merry"

How is the prodigal son a picture of a lost sinner, and the father a type of God the Father, in this parable? Why is the love of God the Father so unbelievable when experienced by a lost sinner? Why is the sinner's departure from God so foolish and terrible?

GOD'S ATTRIBUTES

God is perfect. He is one perfect being who does not have various parts, for He is one. Yet as creatures, we see the perfections of God in different ways when viewing His Word and works.

The perfections of God's being are named His "virtues" or "attributes." **God's attributes** are the various ways in which His glory is witnessed by man. God's attributes are God Himself. God is all His attributes at all times. God is, and forever will remain, perfectly true to Himself.

God's being perfectly one and yet being seen by us in various perfections can be illustrated by using sunlight as an example:

Sunlight is a miraculous and glorious gift which enriches our daily lives. Sunlight is one bright, clear light.

However, let this light pass through a prism and it separates into a beautiful rainbow of colors. This spectrum includes the colors of red, orange, yellow, green, blue, indigo, and violet, in that order.

Sunlight contains this full spectrum of colors within the wavelengths of light visible to the human eye. Yet, in actuality, there is such a perfect blending of these seven colors in natural sunlight that there are no distinct colors — sunlight is one, pure, clear light. We can observe and study this miracle, but we cannot fully understand it.

● **God's attributes** — The perfections of God's being as perceived by man

? How can the example of sunlight help picture the truth of God's oneness, and yet His being observed by us in various perfections?

Our personal conditions and situations can produce very different reactions to God's attributes. The following story can help to illustrate this truth:

A store is being robbed by four thieves. The owner of the store, held by two men, watches helplessly as several expensive items are being thrown into sacks by the other two burglars.

Suddenly, several policemen race into the store through both doorways. The storeowner and the thieves see the same policemen. Yet, the sight of the policemen causes opposite reactions — joy to the storeowner, and terror to the thieves. Why?

God is one — He is one perfect, glorious Being. Yet, His appearance will cause opposite reactions in various people. Why will God's presence be the cause of the greatest joy to some, and of the greatest terror to others? Will God's appearance produce great joy or fear within you?

? Read the following Scripture verses:

Luke 21:27-28
And then they shall see the Son of man coming in a cloud with power and great glory.
And when these things begin to come to pass, then look up, and lift up your heads; for your redemption draweth nigh.

Revelation 6:15-17
And the kings of the earth, and the great men, and the rich men, and the chief captains, and the mighty men, and every bondman, and every free man, hid themselves in the dens and in the rocks of the mountains;
And said to the mountains and rocks, Fall on us, and hide us from the face of Him that sitteth on the throne, and from the wrath of the Lamb:
For the great day of His wrath is come; and who shall be able to stand?

The appearance of Jesus Christ as God and King will result in the greatest difference ever witnessed between people. Why will the appearance of the same Judge strike the deepest cords of joy in some, and terror in others?

27

God's attributes are usually divided into two groups:

1. Incommunicable attributes

2. Communicable attributes

- **Incommunicable** — No likeness or resemblance found in man

God's **incommunicable** attributes are the perfections of God in which there is no likeness or resemblance to be found in man. They are not "communicated" to man at all. The five incommunicable attributes are:

- **Independence** — God's self-existence; His not needing anything outside of Himself

- **Simplicity** — God's perfect oneness

- **Eternity** — God's being without beginning or ending

- **Omnipresence** — God's being in all places at all times

- **Immutability** — God's being eternally the same; His unchangeableness

1. **Independence** or Self-sufficiency

2. **Simplicity** or Oneness

3. **Eternity**

4. **Omnipresence** or Everywhere-presence

5. **Immutability** or Unchangeableness

We, as human beings, are not independent; we need other people and things in order to live. We are made from many parts, but God is perfectly and entirely one. We have a beginning, but God does not; He is eternal. We can only be at one place at a time, but God is omnipresent; He is everywhere all the time. We change, but God is immutable; He never changes.

These attributes are called "incommunicable" because there is no trace or likeness of them to be found in man.

- **Communicable** — A faint trace or likeness found in man

God's **communicable** attributes are the perfections of God in which some faint likeness can be found in man. They are "communicated" to man in a limited degree. God's communicable attributes are His:

1. Knowledge

    a. **Omniscience** or All-knowingness

    b. Wisdom

    c. Truth

- **Omniscience** — God's perfect knowledge of all things

2. **Sovereignty** (Will)

    a. Goodness (Love, Grace, Mercy, and Longsuffering)

    b. Righteousness or Justice

    c. Holiness

- **Sovereignty** — God's supreme ruling authority over all things

3. Power (**Omnipotence**)

- **Omnipotence** — God's being almighty and all-powerful

Some trace of these qualities can be found in man, but not at all in the same degree, glory, or perfection. There is only a *faint* trace of these characteristics in man. For this reason, these perfections of God are termed God's communicable attributes.

Carefully study the chart on the following pages which clearly summarizes God's attributes. When studying, however, keep in mind that God is all His attributes at all times. Together, they shine with one brilliant, radiant light — full of beauty and perfection. God's knowledge, will, and power are all infinitely wise, loving, righteous, and holy.

Do you know, love, and worship this glorious and almighty God? Do you worship Him with deep reverence? There is no greater joy or deeper satisfaction to be found than honoring, glorifying, and serving this wonderful God. By nature, we do not know or love the Lord, but through God's regenerating grace, this is possible. If we love God in truth, then we love to walk in ways which are pleasing in His sight. Is this true in your life?

? What were the reactions of Job and Isaiah when God revealed something of His majesty to them?

Job 42:5-6
I have heard of Thee by the hearing of the ear: but now mine eye seeth Thee.
Wherefore I abhor myself, and repent in dust and ashes.

Isaiah 6:5
Then said I, Woe is me! for I am undone; because I am a man of unclean lips, and I dwell in the midst of a people of unclean lips: for mine eyes have seen the King, the LORD of hosts.

The knowledge of self and God deepen together. The more God is exalted in our lives, the more we are humbled. Why would this be true?

A SUMMARY OF

GOD'S INCOMMUNICABLE ATTRIBUTES

Name	Description	Sample Text
1. *Independence*	God's perfect existence; His being entirely self-sufficient, not dependent upon anything or anyone outside of Himself	Neither is worshipped with men's hands, as though He needed any thing, seeing He giveth to all life, and breath, and all things. —Acts 17:25
2. *Simplicity*	God's perfect oneness; His perfect unity of being totally complete without containing various parts in His composition	Hear, O Israel: The Lord our God is one Lord. —Deuteronomy 6:4
3. *Eternity*	God's perfect eternalness; His being without beginning or ending	Before the mountains were brought forth, or ever Thou hadst formed the earth and the world, even from everlasting to everlasting, Thou art God. —Psalm 90:2
4. *Omnipresence*	God's perfect presence in all places at all times	Can any hide himself in secret places that I shall not see him? saith the Lord. Do not I fill heaven and earth? saith the Lord. —Jeremiah 23:24
5. *Immutability*	God's perfect unchangeableness; His being eternally the same	For I am the Lord, I change not; therefore ye sons of Jacob are not consumed. — Malachi 3:6

30

GOD'S ATTRIBUTES

GOD'S COMMUNICABLE ATTRIBUTES		
Name	Description	Sample Text
1. *Knowledge* a. Omniscience	God's perfect knowledge of all things	Great is our Lord, and of great power: His understanding is infinite. —Psalm 147:5
b. Wisdom	God's perfect use of His omniscience to reach His purpose in the wisest manner	O LORD, how manifold are Thy works! In wisdom hast Thou made them all: the earth is full of Thy riches. —Psalm 104:24
c. Truth	God's perfect truth. His being the infallible source of all truth	For His merciful kindness is great toward us: and the truth of the LORD endureth forever. Praise ye the LORD. —Psalm 117:2
2. *Will (Sovereignty)*	God's perfect self-determination and supreme ruling authority over all His creation	The LORD hath prepared His throne in the heavens; and His kingdom ruleth over all. —Psalm 103:19
a. Goodness — *Love*	God's perfect goodness in granting blessings to *all* His creatures	He that loveth not knoweth not God; for God is love. —I John 4:8
— *Grace*	God's perfect goodness in granting blessings to *guilty* sinners	The LORD is gracious, and full of compassion; slow to anger, and of great mercy. —Psalm 145:8
— *Mercy*	God's perfect goodness in granting blessings to *miserable* sinners	The LORD is good to all: and His tender mercies are over all His works. —Psalm 145:9
— *Longsuffering* *(Patience)*	God's perfect goodness in *delaying* just punishment due to *all* sinners	The LORD is not slack concerning His promise, as some men count slackness; but is longsuffering to us-ward, not willing that any should perish, but that all should come to repentance. —II Peter 3:9
b. Righteousness *(Justice)*	God's perfect devotion to that which is right; His will by which He rewards the righteous and punishes the unrighteous	He cometh to judge the earth: He shall judge the world with righteousness, and the people with His truth. —Psalm 96:13
c. Holiness	God's perfect devotion to the highest good; His nature which results in a perfect separation from, and hatred of, all sin.	Holy, holy, holy, is the LORD of hosts: the whole earth is full of His glory. —Isaiah 6:3b
3. *Power* *(Omnipotence)*	God's perfect and unlimited power; His being almighty and all-powerful	But Jesus beheld them, and said unto them, With men this is impossible; but with God all things are possible. —Matthew 19:26

? To believe in *some* but not *all* God's attributes is dangerous. Why? If people believe that God is only "love" or only "justice," how will they both be mistaken in opposite ways?

? Are there any "good" or "innocent" people in the world? When some people experience sicknesses, deaths, or disasters, why should we not question God's justice by wondering why these "innocent" people are suffering?

Why is the following statement true: "The fact that some people do not presently experience just punishments upon their sins speaks of God's great mercy and patience"?

? Can you describe any biblical examples in which God's actions of love were misinterpreted as acts of His displeasure and judgment? Can you describe some present-day situations which would be examples of this same truth?

Due to our lack of understanding of God and His dealings, we often misread and mistrust His actions. Our sinful hearts naturally underestimate both God's attributes of justice and mercy. We do not properly understand the depth of punishment our sins deserve, nor the depth of gracious love required to save sinners. The following two stories illustrate these truths:

As Robert left the hospital after visiting his sick and suffering grandfather, he thought to himself, "God is not good. If there was a good God, why does my grandfather, as well as do so many other good people, have to suffer?"

This thought bothered Robert. The next time he visited his suffering grandfather, he told him his thoughts. "Robert," his grandfather answered, "I am not good. I am a sinner and so are all the other people in this hospital. I would like to give you a different thought to think about. Since all people are guilty sinners before God, why doesn't God cause every person to suffer in hospitals and torment them with far worse sufferings?"

Why is Grandfather's answer true? Why should we be amazed that some people are healthy, without severe pains; not destroyed in disasters, and still living? Do we deserve any of the blessings which the Lord gives us? What do we deserve instead? Is God good, also to us?

Years ago, a woman was traveling in a stagecoach in Western Montana on a bitter winter day. She was not properly dressed for the cold, and the driver was worried that she would freeze to death. He went as fast as he dared and kept calling down to her to make sure that fatal drowsiness was not overtaking her.

When she no longer answered, he stopped, seized the woman, and roughly dragged her over the frozen ground. His violence partially awakened her. He then climbed back onto the stagecoach and drove away, leaving the woman lying by the side of the road.

Fear gripped the woman. Screaming and yelling, she began to run after the stagecoach. After a few minutes, the driver stopped and let the woman back inside. The healthy recirculation of her blood helped save her life.

Did the driver's actions look like loving actions? Were they? How can this be true in the lives of God's children? Do God's actions always look like loving actions to them? How can the harshest treatment sometimes be the best for a person?

CATECHISM MEMORIZATION

Questions from Rev. A. Hellenbroek's *Divine Truths* — Chapter III: Parts 2 and 3

1. Does God need names as men do?
   No, because there are none like Him (Gen. 32:29; Judges 13:18).

2. Are all the names of God significant?
   Yes, for each name reveals something of His divine essence.

3. What is God's most significant name?
   The name of Jehovah or LORD.

4. Why is the name of Jehovah so significant?
   Because it signifies the self-existence, immutability and faithfulness of God (Ex. 3:14). "And God said unto Moses, I AM THAT I AM" (Ex. 6:2).

5. Are the attributes of God distinct from God Himself?
   No, they are God Himself; therefore He is said to be Light (I John 1:5), Life, Truth, Love (I John 4:8), and Holiness. Thus, to swear by God's holiness is to swear by God Himself (Amos 4:2; Heb. 6:13).

6. Are the attributes of God different and distinct from each other?
   Not in God, for in Him every thing is infinitely perfect; they are only distinct in our manner of comprehending them and in the different ways that God manifests His perfections to His creatures.

7. How are God's attributes usually distinguished?
   Into incommunicable and communicable attributes (Gen. 1:26; I John 3:2; Peter 1:4).

8. What are the incommunicable attributes?
   The independency, simplicity, eternity, omnipresence, and immutability of God.

9. Why are these attributes called incommunicable?
   Because there is no resemblance of them in any creature.

10. What is the independency of God?
    His self-existence and self-sufficiency. "I am the Almighty God; walk before Me and be thou perfect" (Gen 17:1).

11. What is the simplicity of God?
    The oneness of God. God is not composed of different parts or matters. "Hear, O Israel; the Lord our God is one Lord" (Deut. 6:4).

12. What is the eternity of God?
    That He is: (1) without any beginning; (2) above any succession or distinction of time; and (3) without end. "Before the world was, from everlasting to everlasting Thou art God" (Ps. 90:2).

13. Where is God?
    God is everywhere present. "Am I a God at hand, saith the Lord, and not a God afar off? Do I not fill heaven and earth? saith the Lord" (Jer. 23:23-24).

14. Is God changeable or unchangeable?
    God is unchangeable. "I am the Lord, I change not" (Mal. 3:6).

15. What are the communicable attributes of God?
    The knowledge, will, justice, power, goodness, grace, mercy, patience and sovereignty of God.

16. Why are these attributes called communicable?
    Because there is a remote resemblance of them in men, although as they are in God, they are infinite, and thus incommunicable.

17. What is God's knowledge?
    That perfection in God whereby He knows everything from eternity in the most perfect manner. "Known unto God are all His works from the beginning of the world" (Acts 15:18).

18. How is the will of God distinguished?
    Into (1) the will of His decree and (2) the will of His command, or into (1) His secret and (2) His revealed will.

19. Which of these aspects of God's will must we follow?
    We must obey the will of God's command, for the will of His decree is unknown to us. "The secret things belong unto the Lord our God; but the things which are revealed belong unto us, and to our children forever, that we may do all the words of this law" (Deut. 29:29).

20. What is the justice of God?
    That divine perfection by which God hates and punishes all sin.

21. What is God's power?
    A power of omnipotence. "With God all things are possible" (Matt. 19:26).

22. What is God's goodness?
    God's goodness is (1) His kindness towards all creatures (Ps. 4:7-8); (2) the manifestations of His benevolence and love toward all men (Ps. 36:7); and above all, (3) His saving love towards His saints (John 3:16).

23. What is God's grace?
    That goodness of God whereby He shows mercy unto man irrespective of his worthiness.

24. What is God's mercy?
    God's mercy is His goodness toward a miserable, elect sinner, by which He daily restores him in the state of grace through the Mediator Jesus (Eph. 2:4; Ex. 34:6).

25. What is God's longsuffering?
    God's longsuffering is His goodness in delaying well-deserved punishment in order to bring the elect to repentance and to convince the reprobate (Rom. 2:4).

26. What is God's sovereignty?
    God's sovereignty is His supreme authority over all creatures (Jer. 10:6-7, Rom. 9:18,20).

CHAPTER 1

Part I. Chapter Review

1. What is God's essence? _____
   _____

2. What is meant by the statement: "God is infinite"? _____
   _____
   _____

3. Considering the reasonable evidences of the existence of God found in nature, complete the following sentences.
   a. A native from a remote, uncivilized tribe knowing that it is wrong to steal is an example of an evidence found in _____
   b. A form of religious worship being found in all tribes and cultures throughout the world is an evidence found in _____
   c. The life-giving relationship between bees and flowers, sunlight and plants, and male and female, are examples of evidences found in _____

4. What is believed by:
   a. Atheists? _____
      _____
   b. Pantheists? _____
      _____
      _____

5. God is a Spirit and man has a spirit. How are they different in their origin or beginning? _____
   _____
   _____

6. God's names serve a different purpose from our names. Explain how this is true.
   _____
   _____

7. List the most commonly used names of God and explain their meanings:
   a. In the Hebrew Old Testament:
      1. _____ — _____
      2. _____ — _____
      3. _____ — _____
      4. _____ — _____
      5. _____ — _____
      6. _____ — _____

b. In the Greek New Testament:

   1. _____ — _____

   2. _____ — _____

   3. _____ — _____

   4. _____ — _____

   5. _____ — _____

8. Describe three ways in which God is a ''Father'':

   a. _____

   b. _____

   c. _____

9. What is meant by the term: ''God's attributes''? _____

_____

_____

10. Name and define God's attributes.

   a. God's incommunicable attributes:

      1. _____ — _____

      2. _____ — _____

      3. _____ — _____

      4. _____ — _____

      5. _____ — _____

   b. God's communicable attributes:

      1. _____

         a. _____ — _____

         b. _____ — _____

         c. _____ — _____

      2. _____

         a. _____ — _____

         b. _____ — _____

         c. _____ — _____

      3. _____

CHAPTER 1

Part II. Deepening Your Insight

1. a. Why can a person not live without having any "god"? _____
    _____
    _____

    b. Name several false "gods" that people live for today in our society: _____
    _____
    _____

2. Describe the rich comfort found in Romans 8:28 and Question and Answer 28 of the *Heidelberg Catechism,* which the pantheist misses in his daily life: _____
    _____
    _____

3. Why has God forbidden us to try to picture Him in any way? _____
    _____
    _____

4. a. What do biblical names often reveal about various persons and places?
    _____
    _____

    b. Why is this fact important when we view God's names? _____
    _____
    _____

5. Why is the name "Jehovah" full of rich meaning for His children?_____
    _____
    _____

6. How can light and its seven principal colors be compared with God and His eight attributes? _____
    _____
    _____
    _____

7. Define the following terms:
    a. Independence — _____
    b. Simplicity (of God) — _____
    c. Omnipresence — _____
    d. Immutability — _____
    e. Omniscience — _____
    f. Sovereignty — _____
    g. Omnipotence — _____

8. Describe two possible present-day situations in which God's actions of love could easily be misread and misinterpreted by people to be actions of His displeasure and judgment:
    a. _____
    _____

    b. _____
    _____

QUESTIONS

Part III. Biblical Applications

1. What truth is taught about God in Elihu's speech in Job 36:26-33?

   _____

   _____

2. Name the attribute of God most clearly portrayed in the following verses:
   a. Psalm 41:13 — _____
   b. Psalm 68:19 — _____
   c. James 1:13 — _____
   d. I Samuel 15:29 — _____
   e. Hebrews 10:30-31 — _____
   f. Genesis 18:14 — _____
   g. Psalm 139:7-10 — _____
   h. Psalm 147:5 — _____
   i. Daniel 6:26 — _____
   j. Mark 12:29 — _____

3. a. Read Genesis 42:36. Why was Jacob mistaken when he spoke these words?

   _____

   b. What lesson does this teach about how we can often mistake God's actions in our lives? ___

   _____

   _____

Part IV. From the Writings of our Church Forefathers

In your own words, explain the meaning of the following quotations:

1. "The little word 'Father,' pronounced in faith, has overcome God" (Thomas Watson). _____

   _____

   _____

2. "There can be but one Infinite" (Elisha Coles). _____

   _____

   _____

   _____

3. "It is visible *that* God is, it is invisible *what* He is" (Stephen Charnock). _____

   _____

   _____

   _____

CHAPTER 1

Part V. From the Marginal Questions

1. Why can we not fully answer the question, "What is God?" How can we know that God works even though we cannot fully understand Him? _____
   _____
   _____
   _____
   _____

2. Can you name some conflicts in our present society between faith in God and His Word, and faith in man and his theories? _____
   _____
   _____
   _____
   _____

3. If a person does not believe in the true God, why is he yet missing the most important reason for, and purpose of, his life? _____
   _____
   _____
   _____
   _____

4. What effect do "mind-believing," but not "heart-living," Christians have on society? _____
   _____
   _____
   _____

5. To believe in *some* but not *all* God's attributes is dangerous. Why? _____
   _____
   _____
   _____
   _____

EXTRA CHALLENGE QUESTIONS

Part VI. Your Selection from the Marginal Questions

Write out and respond to two marginal questions that interest you which have not been previously asked in this chapter's question section.

1. Question: _____
    _____

    Response: _____
    _____
    _____
    _____
    _____

2. Question: _____
    _____

    Response: _____
    _____
    _____
    _____
    _____

Part VII. Project Ideas

1. Search for additional names of God. Make a poster with these names and their respective meanings.

2. How can we know from God's creation and providence that there is a God? Draw a chart, including as many reasons as you can find.

3. Design a clear, attractive display of God's communicable and incommunicable attributes.

4. Write a report on one or more of God's attributes. Include several scriptural texts which illustrate this attribute.

5. Pretend that you are speaking to a pantheist. Write out your conversation with him to show how you would try to convince him of his error.

2

God's Revelation
- General
- Special

God's Word
- Inspiration
- Completion

God's twofold revelation shows
The fallen race of man:
His work—in all creation, and
His Word—salvation's plan.

His general revelation can
Be seen and felt by all,
But conscience and creation don't
Proclaim the gospel's call.

God's special revelation is
His Word—inspired, complete;
Containing law and gospel, 'tis
A lamp unto our feet.

FROM OUR REFORMED DOCTRINAL STANDARDS

Belgic Confession of Faith

Article 2 — By what means God is made known unto us

We know Him by two means: first, by the creation, preservation and government of the universe; which is before our eyes as a most elegant book, wherein all creatures, great and small, are as so many characters leading us to contemplate the invisible things of God, namely, His power and divinity, as the apostle Paul saith, Rom. 1:20. All which things are sufficient to convince men, and leave them without excuse. Secondly, He makes Himself more clearly and fully known to us by His holy and divine Word, that is to say, as far as is necessary for us to know in this life, to His glory and our salvation.

Article 3 — Of the written Word of God

We confess that this Word of God was not sent, nor delivered by the will of man, but that holy men of God spake as they were moved by the Holy Ghost, as the apostle Peter saith. And that afterwards God, from a special care, which He has for us and our salvation, commanded His servants, the prophets and apostles, to commit His revealed Word to writing; and He Himself wrote with His own finger, the two tables of the law. Therefore we call such writings holy and divine Scriptures.

Article 4 — Canonical Books of the Holy Scripture

We believe that the Holy Scriptures are contained in two books, namely, the Old and New Testament, which are canonical, against which nothing can be alleged. These are thus named in the Church of God. The books of the Old Testament are, the five books of Moses, viz.: Genesis, Exodus, Leviticus, Numbers, Deuteronomy; the books of Joshua, Ruth, Judges, the two books of Samuel, the two of the Kings, two books of the Chronicles, commonly called Paralipomenon, the first of Ezra, Nehemiah, Esther, Job, the Psalms of David, the three books of Solomon, namely, the Proverbs, Ecclesiastes, and the Song of Songs; the four great prophets Isaiah, Jeremiah, Ezekiel and Daniel; and the twelve lesser prophets, namely, Hosea, Joel, Amos, Obadiah, Jonah, Micah, Nahum, Habakkuk, Zephaniah, Haggai, Zechariah, and Malachi.

Those of the New Testament are the four evangelists, viz.: Matthew, Mark, Luke, and John; the Acts of the Apostles; the fourteen epistles of the apostle Paul, viz.: one to the Romans, two to the Corinthians, one to the Galatians, one to the Ephesians, one to the Philippians, one to the Colossians, two to the Thessalonians, two to Timothy, one to Titus, one to Philemon, and one to the Hebrews; the seven epistles of the other apostles, namely, one of James, two of Peter, three of John, one of Jude; and the Revelation of the apostle John.

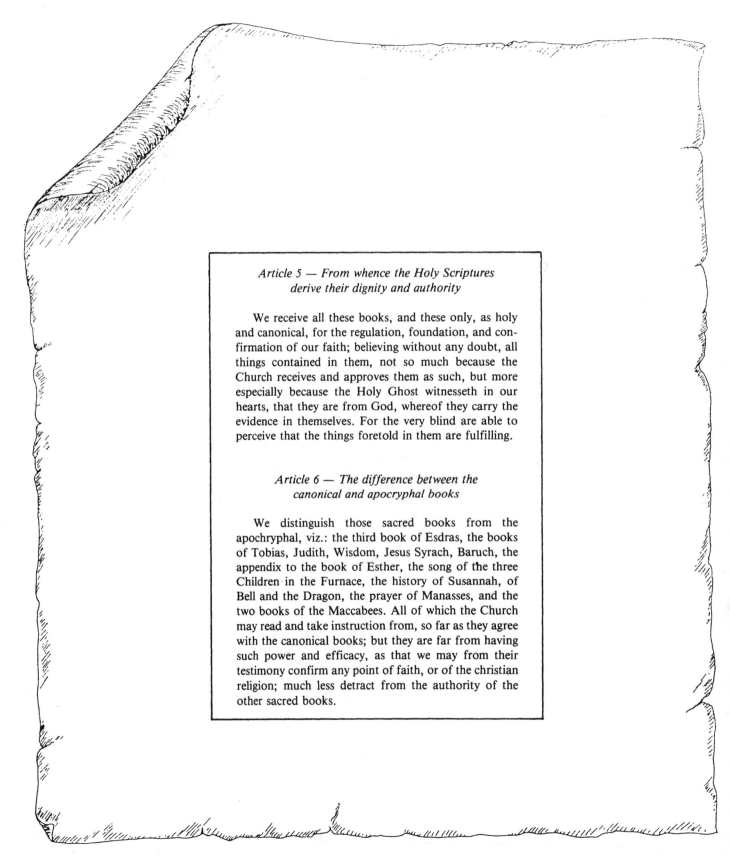

*Article 5 — From whence the Holy Scriptures
derive their dignity and authority*

We receive all these books, and these only, as holy
and canonical, for the regulation, foundation, and confirmation of our faith; believing without any doubt, all
things contained in them, not so much because the
Church receives and approves them as such, but more
especially because the Holy Ghost witnesseth in our
hearts, that they are from God, whereof they carry the
evidence in themselves. For the very blind are able to
perceive that the things foretold in them are fulfilling.

*Article 6 — The difference between the
canonical and apocryphal books*

We distinguish those sacred books from the
apochryphal, viz.: the third book of Esdras, the books
of Tobias, Judith, Wisdom, Jesus Syrach, Baruch, the
appendix to the book of Esther, the song of the three
Children in the Furnace, the history of Susannah, of
Bell and the Dragon, the prayer of Manasses, and the
two books of the Maccabees. All of which the Church
may read and take instruction from, so far as they agree
with the canonical books; but they are far from having
such power and efficacy, as that we may from their
testimony confirm any point of faith, or of the christian
religion; much less detract from the authority of the
other sacred books.

2

GOD'S REVELATION

God is perfect, complete, and entirely self-existent and self-sufficient. He does not need anyone or anything outside of Himself. God does not need man, nor is He required to reveal Himself to man in any mannner. The great wonder is, however, that God has freely and sovereignly desired to reveal Himself to man.

After man's deep fall in Paradise, the wonder of God's gracious willingness to reveal Himself to sinful mankind is even greater! God would have been perfectly just to never reveal Himself to sinful people and to leave them completely and entirely in the sin and misery into which they had brought themselves.

Has this thought ever amazed you? Has God's grace to still reveal Himself to sinners ever melted your heart? David felt something of this truth when he wrote, "What is man that Thou art mindful of him? and the son of man, that Thou visitest him?" (Psalm 8:4).

God has chosen to reveal something of Himself in a two-fold manner. These two forms of **revelation** are known as:

1. God's *general* revelation

2. God's *special* revelation

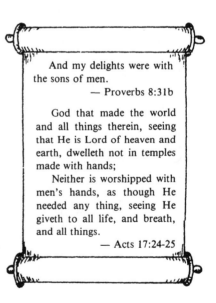

And my delights were with the sons of men.
— Proverbs 8:31b

God that made the world and all things therein, seeing that He is Lord of heaven and earth, dwelleth not in temples made with hands;
Neither is worshipped with men's hands, as though He needed any thing, seeing He giveth to all life, and breath, and all things.
— Acts 17:24-25

● **Revelation** — The act of showing, uncovering, making known

? Why is it a great wonder that God is willing to reveal something of Himself to us?

45

Each of these two forms includes two items. These forms and aspects of God's revelation are portrayed in the following diagram:

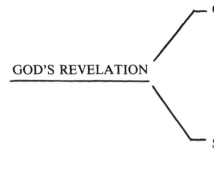

- **Innate** — Inborn

- **Acquired** — Learned; gathered; gained

GOD'S REVELATION
- GENERAL (OR NATURAL)
  1. *Man's Conscience* (**innate** or internal knowledge)
  2. *God's Creation* (**acquired** or external knowledge)
- SPECIAL (OR SUPER-NATURAL)
  1. *The Bible* (learning its truths mentally)
  2. *The Bible savingly applied by the Holy Spirit* (experiencing its truths spiritually)

What is meant by each of these forms and aspects of God's revelation?

GENERAL REVELATION

God's **general** (or natural) **revelation** is given by God to all people on earth — it is "general." It reveals to all that there is a God. God's general revelation includes:

1. Man's **conscience** (innate or internal knowledge)
2. God's creation (acquired or external knowledge)

All people are born with a conscience. God has planted within each person an inborn knowledge that there is a supreme being — a god — and a basic concept of "right" and "wrong." Each person knows that he is responsible and accountable to do the right and avoid the wrong.

This is true not only of people raised in Christian homes or societies, but also of heathen persons. All have a conscience.

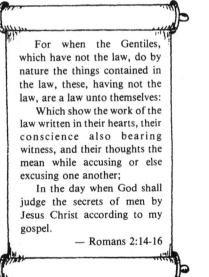

For when the Gentiles, which have not the law, do by nature the things contained in the law, these, having not the law, are a law unto themselves:

Which show the work of the law written in their hearts, their conscience also bearing witness, and their thoughts the mean while accusing or else excusing one another;

In the day when God shall judge the secrets of men by Jesus Christ according to my gospel.

— Romans 2:14-16

- **General revelation** — God's revealing something of Himself to all people through their consciences and His creation

- **Conscience** — A basic, inborn knowledge of God and of right and wrong

A native once received some provisions from a missionary at a newly-opened mission station. On reaching his hut, he found some money among the things he had received. At first he was delighted, but during the night he became restless. He could not sleep; thoughts about the money kept troubling him.

Early the next morning the native returned to the missionary and said, "I found money in the things I got from you. Here it is."

The missionary was amazed and asked, "Why didn't you keep the money?"

The native pointed to his chest and said, "Two voices talk in here. One voice says, 'Money is yours — you found it. Keep it.' Other voice says, 'Money not yours. Give it back.' These talk inside me all night. I not sleep. They trouble me very bad. Now I bring money back. Now I feel good."

What "voice" kept telling the native to return the money? The mission station had just opened; the missionary had not had an opportunity to instruct the natives from the Bible. How did this man have the knowledge that it was wrong to steal?

A person's conscience is a precious gift from God. However, its voice can be quieted or distorted through wrong teachings or practices. The following story is an example of this:

? Can our consciences always be our guide? How are our consciences influenced as we mature? Are our consciences infallible (without error)? What dangers can you foresee if people base their decisions upon their consciences instead of God's Word?

Michael had always attended church each Sunday morning with his parents for as long as he could remember. Weather permitting, after church, they always

● **Infallible** — Without any mistake

The heavens declare the glory of God; and the firmament showeth His handiwork.

Day unto day uttereth speech, and night unto night showeth knowledge.

There is no speech nor language, where their voice is not heard.

Their line is gone out through all the earth, and their words to the end of the world. In them hath He set a tabernacle for the sun.

— Psalm 19:1-4

Because that which may be known of God is manifest in them; for God hath shown it unto them.

For the invisible things of Him from the creation of the world are clearly seen, being understood by the things that are made, even His eternal power and Godhead; so that they are without excuse.

— Romans 1:19-20

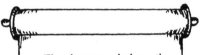

How does creation testify of its Creator? How do atheists and evolutionists deny God's revelation of Himself in their consciences and creation?

packed a picnic lunch, and spent the afternoon at the city's swimming beach. Now that Michael was thirteen years old, this practice had become a regular Sunday custom to him.

Once when discussing how to lead a Christian life, Michael's best friend, Robert, told him that spending Sunday afternoons at the beach was wrong. Michael disagreed.

"When I do something wrong, my conscience tells me," Michael argued, "and I can honestly say that I do not feel that I am doing anything wrong on Sunday afternoon."

"The Bible teaches: 'Remember the Sabbath day to keep it holy,' and can you honestly say that spending the afternoon swimming helps you to worship God and keep His Sabbath day holy?" Robert retorted.

Which should be the **infallible** basis and guide for our lives — our consciences or the Bible? Why? Both Michael and Robert were sincere; but one was sincerely mistaken. Why?

All people see something of God, especially of His wisdom, greatness, and majesty — in God's *creation*. The order, complexity, beauty, vastness, power, and interrelatedness of creation reveal to everyone that there is a master creator, a supreme being, a god, who planned and created all things.

There are people in our society today who deny the revelation of God in creation. They believe that creation developed by itself, by chance, over long periods of time.

Herman once toured an art gallery with a group of his fellow employees. He had previously spoken with some of them who did not believe that there was a God.

As the group was admiring and commenting on the excellence of a beautiful oil painting of a mountain and lake landscape scene, Herman saw an opportunity to teach a fitting lesson.

As they were speaking, he stepped forward and said seriously, "The painting you are admiring was actually never painted by an artist." As the group looked at him rather strangely, he continued, "This painting developed entirely by itself over a period of many years. Let me tell you its story. A person once built a cabin overlooking the lake that you see in this painting. One morning he set out a painting canvas, paints, and brushes on his picnic table, planning to paint this scene. However, before he could begin, a severe earthquake shook the area, which totally destroyed the cabin, and the owner never returned to the property. The remarkable thing is, however, that the earthquake also shook the picnic table which toppled the various paint jars and unscrewed their lids. During the years that followed, various winds blew the colors of paint over the canvas; and various rains blended the colors as you see them in the painting. Twigs, leaves, and other wind-blown objects caused the various brush-like marks we see today. Of course this process required many years, but over time, the different processes described produced this beautiful painting. Years later, it was discovered by a hiker in the area.''

The group stared at Herman in shocked silence. Finally one said, ''Herman, you are not serious, are you? You're not expecting us to believe that, are you?''

''Why not?'' Herman replied. ''There are some here who believe that the *actual* mountains, sky, trees, and lake painted on this canvas, developed entirely on their own, so why not believe the much simpler story regarding this small painting?''

The resulting silence testified that Herman's lesson was understood by all.

How does creation speak of its Creator? Why would it be more difficult to believe in a ''creatorless'' creation than a ''painterless'' painting?

? Is believing in a ''creatorless'' creation reasonable or unreasonable? Why?

Not only does God's initial creation testify of His work, but His daily upholding, preserving, and governing of creation also speak of God's presence, wisdom, and power. The following examples illustrate this truth:

''When I drop this book, why does it fall to the floor?'' Audrey's teacher asked her.

''Because of gravity,'' she answered.

''What is gravity?''

''The force of one mass pulling on another mass.''

''What generates this force or gives one mass power to pull on another? Does the earth have a great power source at its center which generates a strong force to pull all objects towards its center? If not, how does it have this power?''

Audrey did not know how to answer these questions.

''We are touched by, and witness, God's power in creation in many ways,'' the teacher answered.

? Is our universe governed by scientific laws or do scientific laws help us describe the orderly way in which God is upholding and governing His creation?

? There are people in our society today who deny the testimony of God's presence in creation and providence. They believe that all things are controlled by impersonal, natural forces. What price do they pay for denying God's general revelation?

What other examples can you name where God's power can be seen in the daily operation and upholding of creation? Can you name any examples where God's power cannot be seen? Why not?

He giveth to all life, and breath, and all things;
— Acts 17:25b

Who being the brightness of His glory, and the express image of His person, and upholding all things by the word of His power.
— Hebrews 1:3a

For in Him we live, and move, and have our being.
— Acts 17:28a

Thou visitest the earth, and waterest it: Thou greatly enrichest it with the river of God, which is full of water: Thou preparest them corn, when Thou hast so provided for it.
— Psalm 65:9

"I don't see God," stated an atheist to an elderly man. "Give me a proof that God exists."

The older man paused and replied, "Every day for seventy years I have seen the sun rise and set on time. Every night I see the North Star in its place. The moon, planets, and stars have kept their exact schedules and paths in the sky. Show me a human clock that has run perfectly for thousands of years if you want proof! I observe God in everything around me. I'm amazed that you cannot see Him."

How does **God's providence** testify of His existence and care?

● **God's providence** — God's caring for, upholding of, and governing over all things

God's general revelation speaks to all people; both creation and conscience testify to everyone that there is a God. But general revelation does not reveal who God is nor how we may be saved. General revelation is not sufficient for salvation.

SPECIAL REVELATION

To be saved, we need God's special revelation. Special revelation is not given to all people, but it is graciously given to some. Due to our sinfulness, God could justly never reveal Himself or His truth to anyone; but He has mercifully chosen to reveal this to some.

God's special revelation is His Word, the Bible. Only God's Word reveals to man:

1. Who God is — the Trinity
2. How God is to be worshipped — in spirit and in truth
3. God's plan of salvation — Jesus Christ.

In order to know, worship, and be saved by God, we need His special revelation; we need God's Word.

These three important distinctions between God's general and special revelations are denied by some today. The following story is an example of this:

> "I am in church each Sunday," answered a young man when being asked by his minister why he had been absent from several church services. "I attend a 'nature church' on Sundays. I love hiking, and when I find a quiet place, I sit down and enjoy God's creation. My conscience and nature testify of God and I worship God just as well in my 'church' as you do in yours!"
>
> After a short pause, the minister asked, "What do you learn about the Trinity and the way of salvation in your church?"
>
> Why could the young man not give a satisfactory answer to the minister's question? How does this example illustrate the important difference between God's general and special revelations?

In ancient times, before the Bible was completed, the Lord revealed His Word to man through dreams, visions, appearances of angels or of God Himself, direct communication, casting of lots, or the use of the **Urim and Thummim.** Can you provide an Old Testament example of each of these forms of revelation being used?

As time progressed, God graciously inspired various persons to perfectly write and record His Word of revelation in order to preserve His Word for every age. This written Word of God is the Bible.

How then shall they call on Him in whom they have not believed? and how shall they believe in Him of whom they have not heard? and how shall they hear without a preacher?

So then faith cometh by hearing, and hearing by the Word of God.
— Romans 10:14,17

Search the Scriptures; for in them ye think ye have eternal life: and they are they which testify of Me.
— John 5:39

? Those believing that one can worship God equally through studying nature or the Bible are mistaken. Why?

? Can you give an Old Testament example of God's revealing His Word through a dream, vision, angelic appearance, divine appearance, direct communication, casting of a lot, and use of the Urim and Thummim?

● **Urim and Thummim** — Objects carried in the breastplate of the Old Testament high priest, by which Israel could learn God's will regarding various important matters (Ex. 28:30; Num. 27:21)

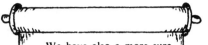

We have also a more sure word of prophecy; whereunto ye do well that ye take heed, as unto a light that shineth in a dark place, until the day dawn, and the day star arise in your hearts:

Knowing this first, that no prophecy of the Scripture is of any private interpretation.

For the prophecy came not in old time by the will of man: but holy men of God spake as they were moved by the Holy Ghost.

— II Peter 1:19-21

God, who at sundry times and in divers manners spake in time past unto the fathers by the prophets,

Hath in these last days spoken unto us by His Son.

— Hebrews 1:1-2a

Since the Scriptures have been completed, God does not reveal new truths. His written Word is His complete revelation to man. Since the completion of the Bible, God's normal manner of working is to reveal Himself and His truths through the means of His Word. If God should speak through a vision or dream today, the lesson taught would illustrate and agree with the truths revealed in Scripture. God will not reveal additional or different truths from those proclaimed in His eternal Word.

God's *special revelation* may be spoken of in two ways:

1. Learning the truths of God's Word in our *minds*.

2. Learning the truths of God's Word in our *hearts* through personal application by the Holy Spirit.

To hear the gospel message, or possess a copy of the Bible is a great privilege. We are not better than many others who have never heard God's Word; God has graciously given us this priceless gift. Without His Word, we cannot properly know or worship God. Only through the Bible can we hear the call of the gospel, the message of salvation in Jesus Christ for lost sinners.

The great value of possessing a Bible is illustrated in the following stories:

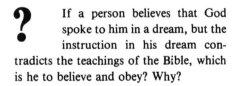 If a person believes that God spoke to him in a dream, but the instruction in his dream contradicts the teachings of the Bible, which is he to believe and obey? Why?

God revealed His Word both in *language* and in *Person*. What is meant by this statement?

Moon Pyung Chan was a young Korean boy who longed to have a Bible, but his parents were too poor to buy one for him. Moon was very sad about this.

One day at church Moon's pastor said, "The 'Bible-men' are coming to our village with many Bibles. They will accept farm produce for a Bible if you are not able to pay for one."

Moon was very happy and exclaimed, "Now my chance to get a Bible has come. I will make a straw rope to buy my Bible."

He ran home as fast as he could and began to make a straw rope. Every day from early morning until late at night, Moon worked at his task. By the time the 'Bible-men' reached his village, he had made 455 feet of rope.

It was a large load for Moon, but he carried and dragged the rope to the 'Biblemen' who gave him a beautiful New Testament in exchange. Tears of joy ran down Moon's cheeks as he pressed his precious Book to his heart.

Do you treasure your Bible as Moon did his? Is your Bible becoming increasingly more valuable—or are you taking this precious gift for granted?

A young man once dreamed that when he opened his Bible to read, every page was blank! In amazement, he found that all copies of the Bible in his home were blank. He rushed to his neighbor's house, only to find his Bibles also blank. His fear grew yet stronger as he discovered that every Bible he found was entirely blank!

He decided to begin reassembling a copy of the Bible by gathering textual quotations found in other books, but he found only blank spaces wherever any Scripture quotation had been previously.

The young man awoke from his dream in a cold sweat. What a relief it was to discover that this was only a dream!

How would our personal, family, and church life be different if there were no Bible? What would our nation and the world be like without God's Word?

? What happened to Old Testament Israel when it departed from God's Word? What lesson has history revealed about nations that depart from God's law? What will happen to our nation if we reject the Bible and do not follow God's law?

Do you treasure your Bible above all other possessions? Are you actively reading and prayerfully studying your Bible?

We must pray and work to bring the Word of God to all people, for hearing, reading, and learning the truths of the Bible is a great privilege. God calls to us in His Word to repent from our sins and to seek our salvation in Jesus Christ. All those who have heard God's Word are responsible for obeying it; God will ask each of us what we have done with His Word and invitation.

> And that servant, which knew his lord's will, and prepared not himself, neither did according to his will, shall be beaten with many stripes.
>
> But he that knew not, and did commit things worthy of stripes, shall be beaten with few stripes. For unto whomsoever much is given, of him shall be much required: and to whom men have committed much, of him they will ask the more.
>
> — Luke 12:47-48

While it is a great blessing to hear and read God's Word and to learn the truths of the Bible in our mind, we need more than this to be saved. Due to our sinful fall in Paradise and our continual sinful desires, we are not interested in loving and serving God. As sinners, we are interested in serving ourselves, sin, and the lusts and desires of this world. Therefore, we need God the Holy Spirit to irresistibly apply the truths of God's Word in our hearts.

The difference between "knowledge" and "experience" is illustrated in the following story:

For our gospel came not unto you in word only, but also in power, and in the Holy Ghost.
— I Thessalonians 1:5a

For it is God which worketh in you both to will and to do of His good pleasure.
— Philippians 2:13

But the Comforter, which is the Holy Ghost, whom the Father will send in My name, He shall teach you all things, and bring all things to your remembrance, whatsoever I have said unto you.
— John 14:26

Peter presented a report on car accidents in his country. He studied various accident statistics, causes, and costs. He knew and spoke a great deal about automobile accidents.

However, a few years later he experienced the reality of a serious car accident. Lying critically injured in a hospital, with the doctors fearing that he might die, Peter experienced the pains, sorrows, and fears of car accidents. He felt his deep need for the best of doctors; but he also experienced sincere feelings of thankfulness as he gradually recovered and was restored to health.

How can this story help picture the difference between only mental knowledge and heartfelt experience of the truths of God's Word? Have you experienced the reality of your sinful condition (your dying condition), your need for salvation in Jesus Christ (the best of physicians), and thankfulness to God for His wonderful deliverance?

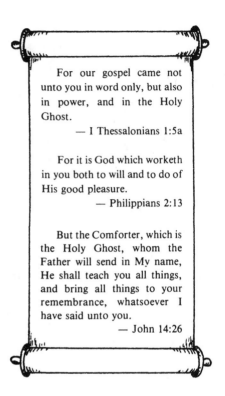

If a person reasons in the following way, "I was born into a Christian home, I attend a Christian school, and I read the Bible; therefore, I must be a true Christian," why is he sadly mistaken? How is head-knowledge different from heart-experience?

We need the Holy Spirit to plant new spiritual life in our spiritually dead hearts — to awaken within us a saving need and interest in the truths of the Bible. God the Holy Spirit is able to do this for He is Almighty; He can regenerate sinners and convert them from a deep love of self, sin, world, and Satan to God. He has promised to bless His Word in this saving manner.

The Holy Spirit can savingly apply the truths of the Bible in remarkable ways. Can you see the power of the Holy Spirit at work in the following stories?

A diamond merchant in England chose some expensive gems to send to a trader in India and wrapped each diamond with great care. When he came to the last one which was the largest of all, he wrapped it with some soft paper from the wastebasket in his office. It was paper which had been torn from an old Bible. On the paper were written the first three chapters of John. When the trader in India received the precious gems, he carefully unwrapped each one. As he took the wrapping from the largest diamond, he read these words, "For God so loved the world, that He gave His only begotten Son, that whosoever believeth in Him should not perish, but have everlasting life" (John 3:16).

The Indian trader was astonished and read these words over and over. He then read and reread the chapters contained in the pages he had received. As the Holy Spirit applied the truths he read to his heart, he told others of them and began to read these chapters to them.

Sometime later, a missionary arrived at this village in India. He expected to find only heathens, but instead found a large gathering of Christian Indians.

How can the power of the Holy Spirit, working through and applying the truths of the Bible, be clearly seen in this story?

Some years ago a sales representative for a New York company arrived in Chicago. He had been stealing money from his company until the amount totaled several thousands of dollars. The man had worked out a plan by which he thought to stifle his conscience; he would work hard all day and go to places of amusement at night, remaining there until a late hour. In this manner, there would be no time for his conscience to speak.

One day in a Chicago hotel, he was shaving with an old-fashioned razor, and, looking for a piece of paper to wipe the blade on, he tore out a page from the Gideon-placed Bible. As he wiped the blade, his eye caught these words, "The wages of sin is death." This struck his heart, and smoothing out the page, he read, "For the wages of sin is death; but the gift of God is eternal life through Jesus Christ our Lord."

The startled salesman began to read further, and read

For as the rain cometh down, and the snow from heaven, and returneth not thither, but watereth the earth, and maketh it bring forth and bud, that it may give seed to the sower, and bread to the eater.

So shall My Word be that goeth forth out of My mouth: it shall not return unto Me void, but it shall accomplish that which I please, and it shall prosper in the thing whereto I sent it.

— Isaiah 55:10-11

? Some "Christian" people deny the truth of the necessity of the Holy Spirit's saving application of biblical truths to a sinner's heart. If this doctrine were not true, no sinner would ever be saved. Why not? What rich truths about God's grace and man's salvation are missed by people who deny this doctrine?

? When God the Holy Spirit savingly applies His Word and converts a sinner, is the length of time or unusualness of circumstances the most important? What is most important?

● **Irresistible** — That which cannot be stopped or resisted; all-powerful

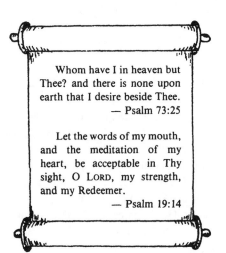

Whom have I in heaven but Thee? and there is none upon earth that I desire beside Thee.
— Psalm 73:25

Let the words of my mouth, and the meditation of my heart, be acceptable in Thy sight, O LORD, my strength, and my Redeemer.
— Psalm 19:14

the Bible for two hours. Then, falling on his knees beside the bed with the open Bible before him, he pleaded with the Lord for forgiveness. Day after day, he continued to read, and the Holy Spirit powerfully applied the truths of God's Word to his heart and life. He phoned the firm in New York to say that he was returning and confessed having stolen the money. He was not prosecuted and did not even lose his job, but was allowed to repay part of the stolen amount each month from his wages. His life continued to reflect the fruits of a renewed heart and he remained living in New Jersey where he faithfully and lovingly served the Lord.

How can the **irresistible** power of the Holy Spirit applying God's Word to a person's heart be clearly seen in these remarkable stories? Does the Holy Spirit always work this suddenly and quickly?

Has God the Holy Spirit savingly applied His Word to your heart? What are your deepest desires? Whom do you serve in your life? Is your name, honor, and will still your god — the idol that you worship? If God has savingly applied the truths of His Word to your heart, then your deepest longings and strivings have changed. Do you know something of your deepest desires being changed to know, love, and serve God? Do you value and strive to live according to God's Word? Do you most deeply desire to walk in a manner pleasing to God in all things and to avoid all sin?

INSPIRATION OF THE BIBLE

The word "Bible" means "book." The Bible is the "Book" of all books. It is a letter, a book written by God to us as human beings.

Something of its great value as a letter from God to us can be compared to the following example:

David possessed a letter from his father which was written to him before his father passed away several years before. In this important and treasured letter, David's father had written several loving instructions and warnings to guide him as he grew up. This letter reminded David of his father's love and concern for him; therefore, he treasured it very dearly. He read and reread it often.

How can the Bible be compared to a letter? Who is its Author and to whom was the Bible written? What instructions and warnings does it contain to guide its readers through life? How does the Bible reveal God's love and concern for sinful people? Why should the Bible be the most important and treasured letter we possess?

? How can the Bible be compared to a letter? Who wrote it, and to whom was it written? Why should the Bible be the most treasured "letter" we possess?

The entire Bible was written by the **inspiration** of God; God the Holy Spirit was its Author. He used different human writers as means and inspired them to write His Word. God the Holy Spirit prompted these people to write, informed them of what to write, and perfectly guided them in the exact words to write.

● **Inspiration** — God's influence and direction by which He guided each human writer of the various biblical books to perfectly write His Word

57

Different explanations are given regarding the *nature* and *extent* of divine inspiration. The following three beliefs concerning the *nature* of inspiration are taught:

1. Mechanical inspiration
2. Dynamical inspiration
3. Organic inspiration

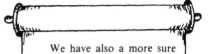

We have also a more sure word of prophecy; whereunto ye do well that ye take heed, as unto a light that shineth in a dark place, until the day dawn, and the day star arise in your hearts.

Knowing this first, that no prophecy of the Scripture is of any private interpretation.

For the prophecy came not in old time by the will of man: but holy men of God spake as they were moved by the Holy Ghost.

— II Peter 1:19-21

And without controversy great is the mystery of godliness: God was manifest in the flesh, justified in the Spirit, seen of angels, preached unto the Gentiles, believed on in the world, received up into glory.

— I Timothy 3:16

Mechanical inspiration can be compared to God the Holy Spirit using the human writers of the various Bible books as one would use a typewriter. God told them a word and they wrote it, another word and they wrote it. The writers' minds and personalities were inactive in the process. They were used "mechanically," as one would use a typewriter, to type out God's desired message.

Dynamical inspiration believes that God inspired the writers as persons. He did not inspire them to only write certain scriptural books, but as inspired people everything which they wrote throughout the remainder of their lives was also inspired.

These explanations regarding the nature of divine inspiration are not correct. Each biblical book reflects the different language usage, personality, and background of its human writer; therefore, mechanical inspiration would not be accurate. Many of the biblical writers wrote additional letters and articles which were not inspired and not included in the Bible; therefore dynamical inspiration is not true.

Organic inspiration most accurately defines the nature of divine inspiration. God used the different personality, experience, language development, educational background, and peculiar talents of each writer. Each writer was intimately connected to the message and book he was instrumental in writing. Yet the Holy Spirit carefully and perfectly directed each writer's thoughts and guided their hands that each word written in the Bible was inspired by Him. Not a single word was written which God did not want. Each word in the Bible is God's Word.

The following three explanations are believed today by different groups of people concerning the *extent* of divine inspiration in Scripture.

1. Thought inspiration
2. Partial inspiration
3. **Verbal-plenary** inspiration

Thought inspiration is a belief that God only inspired the thoughts of the human writers of the biblical books. The words and expressions used to describe these thoughts were entirely the person's.

Partial inspiration is a teaching that only portions of the Bible are divinely inspired — not all.

Both of these views are incorrect. Both deny the truth that every word, expression, and portion of Scripture is divinely inspired.

Verbal-plenary inspiration proclaims the truth. "Verbal" means "word"; "plenary" refers to "fully" or "entirely." It means that the Bible is fully inspired by God; every word is God's. The entire Bible is infallible, for each word is a word of God.

The importance of each word can be illustrated with the following example:

> A man once purchased a large shipment of goods from a New York business firm, giving a signed promissory note for future payment. He listed a large dealer in Chicago as personal reference and a telegram was sent to the Chicago company to confirm the man's credit.
>
> A reply telegram was received which stated, "*Note* good for any amount." Based on this reply the New York Company delivered all the ordered goods. However, no payment was ever received and the firm lost thousands of dollars.
>
> Upon investigation it was discovered that an error of one letter was made in the reply telegram. It was meant to state, "*Not* good for any amount." This one letter made a significant and costly difference.
>
> When we speak of the Bible as being inspired by God, why is each sentence, word, and letter very important?

- **Verbal** — Word

- **Plenary** — Fully; entirely; completely

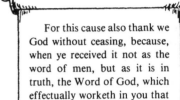

> For this cause also thank we God without ceasing, because, when ye received it not as the word of men, but as it is in truth, the Word of God, which effectually worketh in you that believe.
> — I Thessalonians 2:13
>
> For I testify unto every man that heareth the words of the prophecy of this book, If any man shall add unto these things, God shall add unto him the plagues that are written in this book:
> And if any man shall take away from the words of the book of this prophecy, God shall take away his part out of the book of life, and out of the holy city, and from the things which are written in this book.
> — Revelation 22:18-19

? Some "Christian" people deny the truth that *every* word in the Bible is divinely inspired. Some deny the first chapters of Genesis; others, some of the biblical miracles, and some other parts which they believe to be outdated. What great danger is there in believing parts of the Bible to be not inspired by God?

? What eternal strength and comfort is missed by those who deny the doctrine of the inspiration of Scripture?

COMPLETION OF THE BIBLE

God inspired more than forty different persons to write His Word over a time span of nearly two thousand years. The first writer was Moses; and the last, the Apostle John.

The Bible includes two **testaments**—the Old and the New Testaments. The word "testament" means "will," "covenant," or "agreement." The Old Testament was God's *promise*, and the New Testament His *fulfillment* of the Covenant of Grace; His testimony and will concerning salvation through Jesus Christ. These two testaments form one complete book, the Book of books — the Bible.

The Old Testament was originally written in the Hebrew language with a few verses or portions in Jeremiah, Daniel, and Ezra in **Aramaic** (a **dialect** which developed during the Jewish captivity and gradually took the place of Hebrew as the common language of the Jews). The New Testament was originally written in the Greek language.

The Old Testament contains thirty-nine books, and the New Testament, twenty-seven books. In total, the Bible includes sixty-six divinely-inspired books. These sixty-six books are placed in the order described in the following charts:

- **Testament** — A will, covenant, or agreement

? Some religious groups today only believe in the Old Testament; others only in the New Testament. Why are both of these beliefs seriously wrong? Why is there perfect agreement between both the Old and the New Testaments?

- **Aramaic** — The language commonly used by the Jews during their captivity in Babylon

- **Dialect** — A form of speech spoken by a group of people in a certain district; a slightly different but closely related language

---

OLD TESTAMENT BOOKS

Groupings		Books
Books of the Law (Pentateuch)		Genesis, Exodus, Leviticus, Numbers, Deuteronomy
Books of History		Joshua, Judges, Ruth, I Samuel, II Samuel, I Kings, II Kings, I Chronicles, II Chronicles, Ezra, Nehemiah, Esther
Books of Poetry		Job, Psalms, Proverbs, Ecclesiastes, The Song of Solomon
Books of Prophecy	*Major Prophets*	Isaiah, Jeremiah, Lamentations of Jeremiah, Ezekiel, Daniel
	Minor Prophets	Hosea, Joel, Amos, Obadiah, Jonah, Micah, Nahum, Habakkuk, Zephaniah, Haggai, Zechariah, Malachi

NEW TESTAMENT BOOKS

Groupings	Books		
The Gospels	Matthew, Mark, Luke, John		
Historical Book	Acts		
Doctrinal Books (The Epistles)	*Pauline Epistles*	To Gentile churches	Romans, I Corinthians, II Corinthians, Galatians, Ephesians, Philippians, Colossians, I Thessalonians, II Thessalonians
		To Individuals	I Timothy, II Timothy, Titus, Philemon
		To the Jews	Hebrews
	General Epistles		James, I Peter, II Peter, I John, II John, III John, Jude
Prophetical Book	Revelation		

These sixty-six books are termed the "**Canonical books**" or the **Canon** of Scripture. The word "canon" is derived from a Greek word meaning "a measuring rod or standard." The scriptural canon refers to those books which have been measured and passed by the standard (or test) of divine inspiration. The Canon is a listing, then, of all divinely-inspired writings. The sixty-six books which are included are therefore called "canonical" books.

Article VI of the *Belgic Confession of Faith* lists several additional books which, at times, have been included with the sixty-six canonical books as books of the Bible. These books are referred to as the "**Apocrypha**." The Apocrypha is a group of fourteen books which were written by Jews between the close of the Old Testament and the opening of the New Testament canon. The Roman Catholic Church includes eleven of the fourteen apocryphal books in its Bible.

The apocryphal books may be read and instruction received from them in so far as they do not contradict the canonical books. But they must never be treated as divinely-inspired writings, for they are not divinely-inspired.

- **Canonical books** — Books that are included in the *Canon* of Scripture

- **Canon** — The complete list of the sixty-six divinely-inspired books

- **Apocrypha** — Fourteen books that were written by Jews between the closing of the Old and the opening of the New Testaments

61

● **Cult** — Religious devotion to a person, ideal, or thing. A belief which denies the doctrine of the Trinity

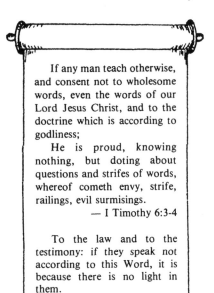

If any man teach otherwise, and consent not to wholesome words, even the words of our Lord Jesus Christ, and to the doctrine which is according to godliness;

He is proud, knowing nothing, but doting about questions and strifes of words, whereof cometh envy, strife, railings, evil surmisings.

— I Timothy 6:3-4

To the law and to the testimony: if they speak not according to this Word, it is because there is no light in them.

— Isaiah 8:20

? What security is lost by those who deny the truth that the divinely-inspired Canon is closed?

? How does the Mormon belief regarding *The Book of Mormon* contradict the closing verses of Scripture (see Revelation 22:18)?

? Some people today reject God's Word and trust in their own knowledge and will. How can this story be used as an example to picture their sad condition?

Other **cults** and groups have attempted to add other writings, revelations, and visions to the sixty-six canonical books. How do the closing verses found in the final chapter of the Bible clearly teach that God's written Word is complete, that the Canon of Scripture has been closed, and that no additional divinely-inspired writings will be given? "For I testify unto every man that heareth the words of the prophecy of this Book, If any man shall add unto these things, God shall add unto him the plagues that are written in this Book: And if any man shall take away from the words of the Book of this prophecy, God shall take away his part out of the book of life, and out of the holy city, and from the things which are written in this Book" (Revelation 22:18-19).

The *Book of Mormon* is one example of a non-biblical book which people claim and believe to be divinely inspired. Read the following information about this book and its history:

In 1830, Joseph Smith organized a new religious movement in the United States called The Church of Jesus Christ of the Latter-day Saints. Today this large group is known as the Mormons.

Joseph Smith claimed to have discovered and translated the *Book of Mormon* from several golden plates which he found buried in the earth. An angel directed him to these plates which revealed new revelations of truth given by Jesus Christ when He physically appeared to North American Indian people and established His church among them.

The *Book of Mormon* contains fourteen books which are believed to be: inspired by God, additions to the Bible, and equal with the Old and New Testaments in authority.

Does the Bible teach us that God's Word of truth and way of salvation is not complete? Does it proclaim that more books will be added in the future? How does the final chapter of the Bible contradict this belief of the Mormons?

One afternoon little Sally wandered away from her family to look for wild flowers in the woods near her family's picnic spot.

Sally was so involved in her search for flowers that it was quite some time before she realized that she had become lost in the woods.

After walking first in one direction and then in another, Sally started to call for help. After receiving no answer, she began to panic. By now it had become dark — very dark — in the woods. Shouting and screaming hysterically, she tried to dash through the dark. Her panic increased as she stumbled over rocks, fell into unseen holes, and crashed into trees. At last, completely exhausted, she fell to the ground where she lay weeping in despair.

After some time, however, she noticed a light moving in the distance. With renewed courage, she arose and ran toward the light, which proved to be her approaching father's lantern.

Sally was happy and thankful beyond words as she safely walked out of the woods with her hand in her father's. The lantern in the hand of her father provided a clear light upon her path; she could now walk safely in the direction she should go.

Psalm 119:105 states, "Thy Word is a lamp unto my feet, and a light unto my path." Why is the "lamp" of God's Word so valuable on our journey through life? What will happen if we try to walk without this "light"? Why would the "light" of God through His Word be deeply valued by those who have experienced something of their sinful and lost condition? Is God's Word your "lamp" and "light"?

? Why are those who walk in the light of Scripture, through the application of the Holy Spirit, the most blessed people on earth?

CATECHISM MEMORIZATION
Questions from Rev. A. Hellenbroek's *Divine Truths* — Chapter I and II

1. How do we know that there is a God?
From nature, and from the Holy Scriptures.

2. How can we know from nature that there is a God?
In two ways: (1) by an internal or innate knowledge, and (2) by an external or acquired knowledge.

3. What is internal or innate knowledge?
The knowledge of God which is born in the hearts of all men by nature. "Because that which may be known of God, is manifest in them" (Rom. 1:19).

4. How can we say that there is an innate knowledge, seeing there are fools who say in their hearts that there is no God? (Ps. 14:1).
Their opinion is a desire rather than an actual belief that there is no God.

5. What is external or acquired knowledge?
The knowledge of God which can be derived from the visible creation. "The heavens declare the glory of God, and the firmament showeth His handywork" (Ps. 19:1).

6. How can we conclude from creation that there must be a God?
Because the creation cannot exist or continue of itself, but must be created and sustained by God Himself. "Who knoweth not in all these that the hand of the Lord hath wrought this?" (Job 12:9).

7. Is the knowledge of God from nature sufficient to save us?
No, because it does not teach us of Christ, the Savior.

8. Is the knowledge of Christ absolutely necessary for salvation?
Yes. "And this is life eternal, that they might know Thee, the only true God, and Jesus Christ whom Thou has sent" (John 17:3).

9. Where must we obtain this saving knowledge of Christ?
From the Holy Scriptures (2 Peter 1:19).

10. What are the Holy Scriptures?
The written Word of God (John 5:39; 2 Tim. 3:15).

11. Who ordered the Holy Scriptures to be written?
God. "All Scripture is given by inspiration of God" (2 Tim. 3:16).

12. Whom did God inspire to write the Holy Scriptures?
The Old Testament was written by the Prophets, and the New Testament by the Evangelists and Apostles (Ex. 17:14; Rev. 1:19).

13. Who inspired them to write the Holy Scriptures?
The Holy Ghost. "The holy men of God spake as they were moved by the Holy Ghost" (2 Pet. 1:21).

14. Could these men err in their writing?
No, the Holy Spirit led them into all truth (John 16:13).

15. How many Testaments are there in the Holy Scriptures?
Two, the Old and the New Testaments (2 Cor. 3:14; Heb. 9:15).

16. What is the original language of the Old Testament?
Hebrew. A small part was written in the Chaldean language.

17. What is the original language of the New Testament?
The Greek language.

18. Is the entire Bible a divine book?
Yes, because it contains truths which could come only from God.

19. Are the Apocryphal books part of the inspired Word of God?
No, because they contain fictitious things contrary to the Word of God; therefore they were never acknowledged as divine by the Jewish Church although the oracles of God were committed to them (Rom. 3:2).

CHAPTER 2

Part I. Chapter Review

1. Name the two-fold manner in which God has chosen to reveal something of himself to man:

   a. _____

   b. _____

2. God's general revelation includes man's _____ and God's _____.

3. List three important truths which are only revealed through God's special revelation and not by natural revelation:

   a. _____

   b. _____

   c. _____

4. God's special revelation includes the following two items:

   a. _____

   b. _____

5. Before the Bible was completed, God revealed His Word to man through:

   a. _____   d. _____

   b. _____   e. _____

   c. _____   f. _____

6. Why is it insufficient for salvation to only read the Bible? What else does a person need? Why?

   _____

   _____

   _____

   _____

7. What is meant by the terms:

   a. Canonical books? — _____

   _____

   b. Apocryphal books? — _____

   _____

8. Name the four main groupings of Old and New Testament books:

   Old Testament   *New Testament*

   a. _____   e. _____

   b. _____   f. _____

   c. _____   g. _____

   d. _____   h. _____

9. The Old Testament is God's _____ and the New Testament God's _____ of His plan of salvation.

10. The Old Testament books were originally written in the _____ language with a few portions in _____. The New Testament books were written in the _____ language.

11. The Old Testament contains _____ and the New Testament _____ books. In total, the two testaments number _____ canonical books.

12. Define the following terms:

    a. God's revelation — _____
        _____

    b. Man's conscience — _____
        _____

    c. Bible — _____
        _____

    d. Pentateuch — _____
        _____

    e. Divine inspiration — _____
        _____

CHAPTER 2

Part II. Deepening Your Insight

1. After man's fall in Paradise, why is God's revelation of Himself to man a *gracious* revelation? _____
   _____
   _____

2. How do the following testify of God to all people on earth?
   a. Man's conscience — _____
   _____

   b. God's creation — _____
   _____

3. Since everyone has a knowledge of God through his conscience and observance of creation, why is it necessary to bring the Bible to all people? _____
   _____
   _____
   _____

4. Why can observing nature never replace Bible study and church attendance?
   _____
   _____
   _____

5. Explain how only mental knowledge of misery, deliverance, and thankfulness differs from experiential knowledge of these matters: _____
   _____
   _____

6. The importance of each written letter, word, and sentence can be seen in numerous examples from daily life. Explain how the importance of this truth is magnified when we speak of the Bible:
   _____
   _____

7. How does Psalm 119:105 illustrate the experiential needing and valuing of God's Word in the life of a truly lost sinner?
   _____
   _____
   _____
   _____

QUESTIONS

Part III. Biblical Applications

1. What truths concerning God's general revelation are taught in:
   a. Romans 2:14-16? _____
   _____

   b. Romans 1:19-20? _____
   _____

   c. Acts 14:17? _____
   _____

2. Read the following two parables. Explain how they teach the truth of a person's greater responsibility after hearing God's Word and living in God's church:
   a. The Parable of the Marriage of the King's Son (Matthew 22:1-10) — _____
   _____
   _____

   b. The Parable of the Wicked Husbandmen (Matthew 21:33-46) — _____
   _____
   _____

3. Explain how Revelation 22:18 clearly teaches that the scriptural canon is closed, and warns us against believing in any additional divinely-inspired books. _____
   _____
   _____
   _____

Part IV. From the Writings of our Church Forefathers

In your own words, explain the meaning of the following quotations:

1. "No flattery can heal a bad conscience, so no slander can hurt a good one" (Thomas Watson).
   _____
   _____
   _____
   _____

2. "The Spirit of God rides most triumphantly in His own chariot" (Thomas Manton).
   _____
   _____
   _____

3. "The two testaments are the two lips by which God hath spoken to us" (Thomas Watson).
   _____
   _____
   _____

CHAPTER 2

Part V. From the Marginal Questions

1. What danger can you foresee if people base their decisions only upon their conscience — letting "their consciences be their guide"? _____
   _____
   _____
   _____
   _____

2. Is believing in a "creatorless" creation reasonable or unreasonable. Why? _____
   _____
   _____
   _____
   _____

3. What great difference is there between believing that all things are controlled by a personal God or by impersonal, natural forces? _____
   _____
   _____
   _____
   _____

4. If a person believes that God spoke to him in a dream, but the instruction in his dream contradicts the teachings of the Bible, which is he to believe and obey? Why? _____
   _____
   _____
   _____
   _____

5. What security is lost by those who deny the truth that the divinely-inspired canon is closed? _____
   _____
   _____
   _____
   _____

EXTRA CHALLENGE QUESTIONS

Part VI. Your Selection from the Marginal Questions

Write out and respond to two marginal questions that interest you which have not been previously asked in this chapter's question section.

1. Question: _____
   _____

   Response: _____
   _____
   _____
   _____
   _____
   _____

2. Question: _____
   _____

   Response: _____
   _____
   _____
   _____
   _____
   _____

Part VII. Project Ideas

1. Research and write a report on each of the apocryphal books.

2. Design a poster which clearly displays the various aspects of God's revelation. Clearly distinguish the teaching and value of both God's general and special revelations.

3. Write a story which would illustrate the same truth displayed in the example, *A "Painterless" Painting*.

4. Construct a poster containing a poem that illustrates the truths of Psalm 19:1-4.

3

The Bible's
- **Ancient History**
- **Translations**
- **Infallibility**
- **Qualities**

False Religions

In days of yore the Lord inspired
The writing of His Word
By men of various time and place,
And yet one truth is heard.

His Word is indestructible
And shall forever stand;
Sent forth, it shall accomplish all
His will at His command.

Our sinfulness, reflected in
The Scriptures' holy mirror,
Shows who we are but also who
Alone our guilt can clear.

FROM OUR REFORMED DOCTRINAL STANDARDS

Belgic Confession of Faith

Article 7 — The sufficiency of the Holy Scriptures, to be the only rule of faith

We believe that those Holy Scriptures fully contain the will of God, and that whatsoever man ought to believe, unto salvation, is sufficiently taught therein. For, since the whole manner of worship, which God requires of us, is written in them at large, it is unlawful for any one, though an apostle, to teach otherwise than we are now taught in the Holy Scriptures: nay, though it were an angel from heaven, as the apostle Paul saith. For, since it is forbidden to add unto or take away anything from the Word of God, it doth thereby evidently appear, that the doctrine thereof is most perfect and complete in all respects. Neither do we consider of equal value any writing of men, however holy these men may have been, with those divine Scriptures, nor ought we to consider custom, or the great multitude, or antiquity, or succession of times and persons, or councils, decrees or statutes, as of equal value with the truth of God, for the truth is above all; for all men are of themselves liars, and more vain than vanity itself. Therefore, we reject with all our hearts, whatsoever doth not agree with this infallible rule, which the apostles have taught us, saying, Try the spirits whether they are of God. Likewise, if there come any unto you, and bring not this doctrine, receive him not into your house.

3

THE BIBLE'S ANCIENT HISTORY

When viewing the history of the world in relationship to the Bible, we may observe three different time periods. These three stages are times when there:

1. Was *no written* Word of God. (From Adam to Moses)

2. Was a *partially-written* Word of God. (From Moses to the Apostle John and the closing of the New Testament)

3. Is a *fully written* Word of God. (From the close of the New Testament to the end of the world)

As explained in the previous chapter, after the completion of His Word, God's normal manner of revealing Himself and His truth is through His Word. Claims of additional or contrary "inspired truths" to those revealed in the Bible are not to be accepted. This makes every word in the Bible very special; it makes its history and translation very important.

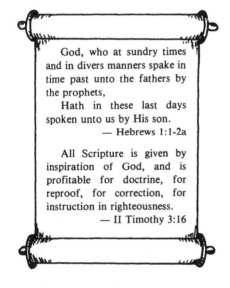

God, who at sundry times and in divers manners spake in time past unto the fathers by the prophets,
    Hath in these last days spoken unto us by His son.
    — Hebrews 1:1-2a

All Scripture is given by inspiration of God, and is profitable for doctrine, for reproof, for correction, for instruction in righteousness.
    — II Timothy 3:16

? Why are we living in the "richest" time period of the world's history? Why is the New Testament time referred to as the "fullness of time" or the "last time" in the Bible?

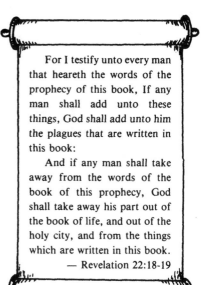

For I testify unto every man that heareth the words of the prophecy of this book, If any man shall add unto these things, God shall add unto him the plagues that are written in this book:

And if any man shall take away from the words of the book of this prophecy, God shall take away his part out of the book of life, and out of the holy city, and from the things which are written in this book.

— Revelation 22:18-19

? How would Galatians 1:7-9 contradict a person who claimed that new truths (not found in the Bible) were revealed to him by an angel, dream, special person, or another unusual means? Can you name some groups which believe and teach that this has happened after the Bible was completed or that it is still happening today?

What deep security would these people be missing in their lives regarding God's truth?

- **Manuscripts** — Ancient, handwritten copies of the Bible in its original languages (Hebrew, Aramaic or Greek)

- **Codex** — A manuscript written on sheets of "paper" (papyrus or animal skin) and tied in a book format, having pages rather than being fastened together in scroll form.

- **"Aleph"** — The first letter ("A") in the Hebrew Alphabet

- **Mt. Sinai** — The Mount upon which Moses received the Ten Commandments from God

No originally written copies of any Bible books have been preserved. All the original scrolls have been recopied by carefully-trained and accurately-working scribes until they were worn beyond further use. Under the guiding hand of God, scribes, who devoted their lives to precise copying work, reproduced exact handwritten copies from generation to generation, until the printing press was invented.

Thousands of partial, ancient copies, written in the original languages of both Testaments have been found and carefully studied and preserved. The three most ancient and well-known, complete Bible **manuscripts** (ancient, handwritten, original-language copies) containing all or most of the books of both the Old and New Testament are:

1. *Sinaitic Manuscript or* **Codex "Aleph"**

The Sinaitic Manuscript, written in the fourth century A.D., contains numerous changes and corrections made by later scribes. Some pages from the codex were discovered by Constantin Tischendorf in a wastebasket in the Monastery of St. Catherine on **Mt. Sinai**. After fifteen years of trying, he finally secured the entire codex in 1859. This manuscript is presently stored in the British Museum in London.

2. *Alexandrian Manuscript or Codex "A"*

The Alexandrian Manuscript, written in the fifth century A.D., was obtained by the **Patriarch** of Constantinople in **Alexandria**, who presented it to King

Charles I of England in 1627. This manuscript is presently displayed next to the Codex Aleph in the British Museum.

3. *Vatican Manuscript or Codex "B"*

The **Vatican** Manuscript is the oldest, complete manuscript of the Bible. Written in the middle of the fourth century A.D., it also includes several books of the **Apocrypha**. This codex has been known to be stored in the Vatican library in Rome since 1481.

There is little **controversy** regarding the original Old Testament **text** of the Bible for there is nearly identical wording in all ancient copies. A fairly recent discovery of several very ancient Old Testament scrolls, called the "Dead Sea Scrolls," illustrates this truth in a remarkable way:

In March, 1948, an Arab shepherd boy was looking for a lost goat and stumbled into one of the Qumram caves (located about seven miles south of Jericho near the Dead Sea), which contained a large number of jars holding ancient leather scrolls.

Since this discovery, more than 350 scrolls have been found—most in **fragmentary** condition. These scrolls date back to approximately 50-200 years before Christ, when a deeply religious community of **Essene** Jews lived there.

Hebrew and **Aramaic fragments** from every Old Testament book except Esther have been found. The most famous find was a complete Hebrew manuscript of the entire Book of Isaiah. This manuscript, copied in approximately 125-100 B.C., was one thousand years older than the oldest previously discovered Hebrew manuscript copied by scribes in approximately A.D. 900! The excitement generated by finding a Bible manuscript of a complete book 1,000 years older than any previously-known copy was tremendous!

After careful and **precise** comparison work was completed on the entire Book of Isaiah, thirteen very minor differences were noted, but not one change of meaning was found after one thousand years of copying by ancient scribes! This type of accurate copying was also observed when comparing other scrolls and fragments.

How do the results from examinations of the Dead Sea Scrolls help confirm the truth of the accuracy of scribes' copying?

- **Patriarch** — A bishop (head minister) over a large city; an archbishop
- **Alexandria** — A famous, historic city located in Egypt on the coast of the Mediterranean Sea
- **Vatican** — An independent state within the city of Rome which is the world center of the Roman Catholic Church
- **Apocrypha** — Fourteen books which were written by Jews between the closing of the Old, and the opening of the New Testaments
- **Controversy** — Debate; argument; difference of opinion
- **Text** — The actual, original words of Scripture
- **Fragmentary** — Incomplete; partial
- **Essenes** — A Jewish religious community that lived in a colony near the Dead Sea before, during, and after the time of Christ
- **Aramaic** — The language commonly used by the Jews during and after their captivity in Babylon
- **Fragments** — Parts; incomplete portions; sections
- **Precise** — Exact; careful attention given to each detail

- **Partial** — Incomplete; containing part(s) but not all

- **Papyri** — Ancient writings on "paper" made from the stems of the papyrus plant

- **Uncial** — Written with capital letters

- **Minuscule** — Written with small or cursive letters

- **Lectionary** — A book containing portions of Scripture to be publicly read on various occasions

- **Traditional Text** — The standard New Testament text that is found in 96 percent of all Greek manuscripts

- **Westcott and Hort** — B.F. Westcott (1825-1901) was an Anglican bishop and theologian who served as a Professor of Divinity at Cambridge University.
F.J.A. Hort (1828-1892) was also an Anglican priest and professor at Cambridge University.
Together, in 1882, Westcott and Hort developed a new text of the Greek New Testament based upon the argument that the oldest complete manuscripts, Codex "Aleph" and "B," are the most reliable

- **Translation** — The writing of an author's words in another language

? Why is the translating of the Bible very necessary and important? Why must a translation of the Bible be as accurate as possible?

Unlike the Old Testament text, however, there is debate concerning various New Testament textual wordings. Of the more than 4,500 **partial** or complete Greek New Testament manuscripts known today, approximately 170 are **papyri** fragments dating from the second to seventh centuries; more than 210 are **uncials** (capital letter manuscripts) from the fourth to tenth centuries; approximately 2,500 are **minuscules** (small letter or cursive manuscripts) dating from the ninth to sixteenth centuries; and more than 1,650 are **lectionaries** (Scripture portions used for public reading).

Approximately 96 percent of all known Greek New Testament manuscripts agree together so closely in reading that they are classified as one textual reading. This reading is known as the "Textus Receptus" or the **Traditional** (Majority, Received, or Byzantine) **Text**. Codex A, the Alexandrian Manuscript, is in the Traditional Text group.

After the discovery and possession of Codex Aleph (or the Sinaitic Manuscript) in 1859, a different opinion regarding the original text of the New Testament was developed by two scholars named **Westcott and Hort.** These men researched and published a theory which stated that "oldest" meant "most accurate and reliable." Upon this basis they taught that the two oldest complete manuscripts, Codex B and Codex Aleph were more reliable than the Traditional Text.

This debate between the "oldest" (Westcott and Hort) and the "majority" (Traditional Text) readings, as to which is more reliable, will be very important when we study the reasons for various English versions of the Bible later in this chapter.

THE BIBLE'S TRANSLATIONS

Ancient Translations

Two of the most important ancient **translations** of the Bible were the:

1. Septuagint
2. Vulgate

The **Septuagint** was a translation of the Old Testament from Hebrew into the Greek language. The word "Septuagint" means "seventy." This translation is named "The Septuagint" (or "The LXX") because tradition teaches that *seventy* Jewish elders completed this Old Testament translation in Alexandria in the third century B.C. This translation of the Old Testament was used by most Jews living in the Roman Empire when Jesus was on earth. It provided the possiblity for gentile people to read the Old Testament when Paul was undertaking his missionary labors.

- **Septuagint** — An ancient translation (third century B.C.) of the Old Testament from Hebrew into the Greek language

As Latin began to be accepted as the official language throughout the western world, various Latin translations of Bible books and portions began to appear. To **eliminate** confusion arising from differing translations, Pope Damasus I authorized **Jerome** to complete a Latin translation of the entire Bible in A.D. 382. Jerome used the Septuagint, Hebrew Old Testament and Greek New Testament manuscripts, as well as other Latin translations as sources for his work.

- **Eliminate** — To end; to cut away; to reduce
- **Jerome** — (348-420 A.D.) A great scholar and famous early church father

Jerome's Latin translation of the Bible became known as the **Vulgate** ("Vulgate" means "common"). His translation was more accurate and precise in some parts of Scripture than in others, but considerable freedom was taken in translating the text. **Numerous** changes and **variations** continued to multiply through the more than 8,000 variations of the Vulgate known to have been made during the Middle Ages.

- **Vulgate** — Jerome's translation of the Bible into the Latin language
- **Numerous** — Several or many in number
- **Variations** — Different forms; alterations; changes

English Translations

The translation of the Bible into English is of primary interest to us. Numerous English translations have appeared over the past centuries.

Study the charts on the following two pages which summarize the most important past and present English Bible translations. Versions based upon the Traditional Text are clearly distinguished from those based upon the Westcott and Hort Text.

? Why could it be misleading to use the Vulgate, or an English translation based on the Vulgate, as one's Bible?

MAJOR ENGLISH BIBLE TRANSLATIONS

THE TRADITIONAL TEXT

Tyndale Version (1525, 1534)

Translating and publishing during times of persecution in England, Tyndale often had to flee and work on his translation in other countries. Tyndale died as a martyr in 1536 leaving his Old Testament translation incomplete. This translation, based squarely upon the Traditional Text, served as a solid English base for later translations in content, freshness of style, and richness of language.

Coverdale Version (1535)

Coverdale used Tyndale's English and Luther's German translations as primary sources for his version. While Tyndale's incomplete Old and complete New Testaments were published separately, Coverdale's was the first complete, printed English Bible. (Wycliffe's version was written before the age of printing.)

Geneva Version (1560)

The Geneva Version was translated by several English scholars in Geneva during the persecution under Mary in England. Difficult verses and doctrines were clarified in lengthy explanations.

King James (Authorized) Version - KJV (1611)

The KJV translation was completed from the original Hebrew and Greek Traditional Text by fifty appointed language scholars and devout church leaders, who also used the previous English translations as examples. King James I endorsed this translation and had it printed for use in all churches throughout England. It contains no marginal notes or comments.

The KJV has historically been used by all Protestant churches and seminaries and it is the most widely-circulated and read English Bible today.

THE WESTCOTT AND HORT TEXT

English Revised Version - RV (1881, 1885)

The RV was translated by sixty-five English and thirty-two American scholars from various denominations, primarily sponsored by the Church of England. The New Testament follows Westcott and Hort's teachings, (both were members of the translation team), relying primarily on the two oldest, complete manuscripts, rather than on the Traditional Text.

American Standard Verson - ASV (1901)

The American Committee serving on the RV translation team promised to refrain from publishing an American version for fourteen years. In 1901 the ASV was published favoring the word choice preferences of the American Committee.

Revised Standard Version - RSV (1952)

A revision of the RV and ASV, this version attempted to maintain the dignified literary style of the KJV. The liberal views of the men involved in this translation can be observed in several places.

New English Bible - NEB (1961, 1970)

Unlike the ASV and RSV, the NEB is not a revision of previous translations, but a return to the original Hebrew and the two oldest complete Greek manuscripts. Obscuring of words which speak of man's sinful, fallen nature and Christ's divinity takes place frequently.

New International Version - NIV (1979)

The NIV is a new translation completed by one hundred scholars from many different denominational backgrounds sponsored by the New York Bible Society International. While this translation was completed in a very scholarly fashion, it follows the Westcott and Hort theory, and the nature of widely interdenominational translation teams raises serious doubts regarding the understanding of the content being translated on the part of many of its translators.

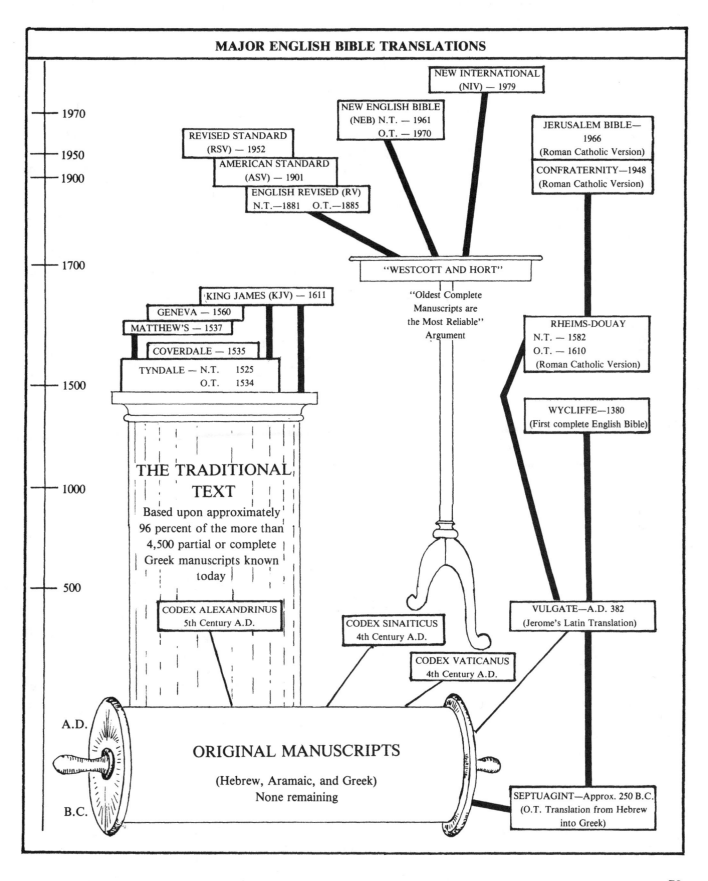

MAJOR ENGLISH BIBLE TRANSLATIONS

NEW INTERNATIONAL
(NIV) — 1979

NEW ENGLISH BIBLE
(NEB) N.T. — 1961
O.T. — 1970

REVISED STANDARD
(RSV) — 1952

AMERICAN STANDARD
(ASV) — 1901

ENGLISH REVISED (RV)
N.T.—1881   O.T.—1885

JERUSALEM BIBLE—
1966
(Roman Catholic Version)

CONFRATERNITY—1948
(Roman Catholic Version)

"WESTCOTT AND HORT"

"Oldest Complete
Manuscripts are
the Most Reliable"
Argument

KING JAMES (KJV) — 1611

GENEVA — 1560

MATTHEW'S — 1537

COVERDALE — 1535

TYNDALE — N.T. 1525
O.T. 1534

RHEIMS-DOUAY
N.T. — 1582
O.T. — 1610
(Roman Catholic Version)

WYCLIFFE—1380
(First complete English Bible)

THE TRADITIONAL TEXT

Based upon approximately
96 percent of the more than
4,500 partial or complete
Greek manuscripts known
today

CODEX ALEXANDRINUS
5th Century A.D.

CODEX SINAITICUS
4th Century A.D.

CODEX VATICANUS
4th Century A.D.

VULGATE—A.D. 382
(Jerome's Latin Translation)

A.D.

ORIGINAL MANUSCRIPTS

(Hebrew, Aramaic, and Greek)
None remaining

B.C.

SEPTUAGINT—Approx. 250 B.C.
(O.T. Translation from Hebrew
into Greek)

1970
1950
1900
1700
1500
1000
500

How different are the various ancient manuscripts and present English Bible translations? The vast majority of differences between ancient manuscripts deal with matters such as spelling, grammar, word order, and other copying items which do not affect the meaning of the text.

There are, however, several verses or sections of the new Testament left out, placed in brackets, or footnoted in the newer Bible versions which follow Westcott and Hort's departure from the Traditional Text. Some examples of "left-out" portions of Scripture include:

John 7:53-8:11	The story of the adulterous woman brought to Jesus.
Acts 8:37	"And Philip said, If thou believest with all thine heart, thou mayest. And he answered and said, I believe that Jesus Christ is the Son of God."
I John 5:7	"For there are three that bear record in heaven, the Father, the Word, and the Holy Ghost: and these three are one."
Mark 16:9-20	The closing verses of the Gospel of Mark.

Some examples of different translation readings are as follows (KJV — King James Version; ASV — American Standard Version; NIV — New International Version; RSV — Revised Standard Version):

Luke 2:14	*KJV*	"and on earth peace, good will toward men."
	ASV	"and on earth peace toward men of goodwill."
John 3:13	*KJV*	"even the Son of man *which is in heaven*."
	RSV	"the Son of man."
Luke 24:40	*KJV*	"He shewed them His hands and His feet."
	ASV	(Dismissed to a marginal note.)
Tim. 3:16	*KJV*	"And without controversy great is the mystery of godliness: *God* was manifest in the flesh, justified in the Spirit."
	NIV	"Beyond all question; the mystery of godliness is great: He appeared in a body, was vindicated by the Spirit."
Matt. 6:13	*KJV*	'And lead us not into temptation, but deliver us from evil: For Thine is the kingdom, and the power, and the glory, for ever. Amen."
	RSV	"And lead us not into temptation, but deliver us from evil."
I Cor. 15:47	*KJV*	"The second man is *the Lord* from heaven."
	ASV	"The second man is from heaven."

? Study the changes made in the newer English translations (based upon the Westcott and Hort text) in these examples. Which changes refer to the divinity of Jesus Christ? Are references to Jesus being God added or taken away in the new translations? Why is this dangerous?

Gal. 3:24	*KJV*	"Wherefore the law was our schoolmaster to bring us unto Christ, that we might be justified by faith."
	NIV	"So that the law was our custodian until Christ came, that we might be justified by faith."
John 6:47	*KJV*	"He that believeth *on me* hath everlasting life."
	NIV	"He who believes has eternal life."

Are the newer "Westcott and Hort" translations different from the older "Traditional Text" translations? Can you see how each change is significant?

Paraphrased "Bibles" are different from translated versions. A Bible translation attempts to translate Scripture word by word. A paraphrase attempts to translate "meanings" — to retell stories in today's language.

Examples of modern paraphrase "Bibles" would include: *The New Testament in Modern English* (1958), *The New Testament in Plain English* (1963), *Good News for Modern Man* (1966), and *The Living Bible—TLB* (1972). Of these *The Living Bible* has gained the greatest popularity. Below are various textual comparisons between the KJV (King James Version) and the TLB (The Living Bible) paraphrase:

Judges 7:20b	*KJV*	"And they cried, The sword of the Lord, and of Gideon."
	TLB	"All yelling for the Lord and for Gideon."
Judges 19:2	*KJV*	"And his concubine played the whore against him."
	TLB	"But she became angry with him and ran away."
II Sam. 16:4b	*KJV*	"And Ziba said, I humbly beseech thee that I may find grace in thy sight, my lord, O king."
	TLB	"Thank you, thank you, sir, Ziba replied."
II Cor. 5:21	*KJV*	"For He hath made Him to be sin for us, Who knew no sin; that we might be made the righteousness of God in Him."
	TLB	"For God took the sinless Christ and poured into Him our sins. Then in exchange He poured God's goodness into us."
I Tim. 3:16a	*KJV*	"And without controversy great is the mystery of godliness: God was manifest in the flesh."
	TLB	"It is quite true that the matter to live a godly life is not an easy matter, but the answer lies in Christ who came to earth as a man."

? Why is it wrong to retell God's Words in my own and call it the "Bible"? What dangers can you see in using a paraphrased "Bible"after reading the comparison examples listed?

? Is a paraphrased "Bible" truly *God's* Word?

We favor remaining with the King James or Authorized (Traditional Text-based) Version of the English Bible instead of using one of the newer (Westcott and Hort-based) translations for the following reasons:

1. *Volume* — The King James Version is based upon the Traditional Text. Approximately 96 percent of the more than 4,500 known partial and complete Greek manuscripts follow this textual reading.

2. *Church History* — The Traditional Text has been used by the church historically. The English, French, Dutch, and German Reformation churches all used Bibles based on the Traditional Text. (The Dutch "Statenvertaling," 1618-1619, is also based upon the Traditional Text.)

3. *God's Providence* — Would God, after carefully inspiring each word in the Bible, permit 96 percent of all the Greek manuscripts and all the Bible translations of the Reformation to be based upon corrupted copies, only to bring to light the "truer text" in 1882 through Westcott and Hort? God's providential dealings support the Traditional Text or King James Version.

4. *Church Acceptance* — Of all English translations, only the King James Version has passed the tests of time and of **universal** Protestant church acceptance.

5. *Oldest Does Not Mean Best* — The Westcott and Hort arguments that "the oldest manuscripts are the most reliable" and that "age carries more weight than volume" are not necessarily true. It could well be that the two oldest, complete manuscripts were found to be in such unusually excellent condition because they were already recognized as faulty manuscripts in their time and therefore were placed aside and not recopied until worn out as were the reliable manuscripts. This is further supported by numerous existing differences between the Vatican and Sinaitic Manuscripts.

6. *Word-for-Word Translation* — The translators of the King James Version were filled with such deep respect for each word of Scripture, that when any word had to be added in order to produce a grammatically correct sentence in English, the added word was printed in *italics*. In this way,

● **Universal** — Worldwide; general

? Why would the large number of differences between the Vatican and Sinaitic manuscripts provide additional support to the argument proposed in Reason Five?

the English reader knows which English words were not in the original, but had to be added to form proper English sentences.

Newer translations use a wider and freer form of translation, known as the "dynamic equivalence theory." This theory believes that not only the words but also the form or manner of explaining something differs from one language to another; therefore, the Bible should not only be translated word for word, but it should be re-told or re-explained according to the English way of reasoning. This theory has produced newer versions which are supposedly "easier for the English mind to understand," but in doing this, they depart from a word-for-word translation method.

Believing that each word of Scripture is very important, because each word was inspired and chosen by God, a strictly word-for-word translation of the Bible is crucial. The newer translations all reflect a further departure from the original words and message forms than found in the King James Version.

Read the highlight box below entitled "A Good Translator Must Understand His Subject." In addition to an excellent knowledge of both languages, what "knowledge" must a good translator of the Bible possess? Why?

? Besides an excellent knowledge of both needed languages, what other "knowledge" must a translator possess? Why?

? Some people believe that it does not matter which English translation of the Bible a person uses. Why is this not true?

A GOOD TRANSLATOR MUST UNDERSTAND HIS SUBJECT

To effectively translate from one language to another, the translator must not only have a good knowledge of both languages, but he must also understand the material he is translating. For instance, if two people were asked to translate a book on truck engine repair from German into English and both were fluent in both languages, but one was an experienced diesel mechanic and the other person knew little or nothing about truck engines, which translator's work would convey the true meaning of the German author more clearly in English? Why?

G.S. Paine in his book, *The Men Behind the KJV*, has researched the lives of the translators of the KJV. Not only were they fluent in the required languages, but the majority were also devout, God-fearing people who knew, loved, and served God in spirit and truth. They upheld the core doctrines of Scripture both in their talk and walk. They knew from experience the matters they were translating.

Their deep awareness of and high regard for the Bible's being profoundly sacred and each word's being divinely inspired can be seen in their use of italicized words. Every time additional words were required in English to convey the original meaning, these words were printed in italics.

This deep love for God — evidenced by love for scriptural truths, leading of God-fearing lives, and deep reverence for God's Word — is a necessary characteristic of translators of God's Word.

Why would deep love and reverence for God and His Word be very important requirements for a translator of the Bible?

7. *The Character of the Translators* — The fifty men appointed to translate the King James Version, were not only well-known scholars, but were also men of sound religious faith. They were strong believers in every word of the Bible being inspired by God and in all the central doctrinal truths of Scripture. Many lived lives which testified of a saving knowledge of these truths.

   This same testimony cannot be made of all translators serving on modern translation teams.

8. *Language Usage* — The King James Version is a classic in the English-speaking world, not only for its clearness of translation, but also for its excellent language usage. The King James Version is written in a noble and dignified style; and its simple, yet beautiful, majestic, and powerful Elizabethan English has made it a literary masterpiece of the English language for several centuries.

THE BIBLE'S INFALLIBILITY

● **Infallible** — Without error; absolutely trustworthy and sure

● **Inerrant** — Without any mistake; every detail being correct

? Some people deny that the Bible is inspired by God and infallible. Why would these people live in an uncertain world when speaking of absolute truths?

● **Crucial** — Of greatest importance; critical; decisive

As *God's* Word, as the only divinely-inspired Book, the Bible is **infallible** and **inerrant**. What a wonderful and valuable truth this is! In a world full of uncertainties, doubts, differences of opinion, and errors, there is an infallible and inerrant truth—God's own Word, our Bible.

Have you come to recognize and value the Bible as God's infallible and inerrant Word in your heart? Is it the rule for your life? When God's grace is worked and His love shed abroad in our hearts by the Holy Spirit, then we love to live according to God's Word—to do that which is pleasing in His sight.

Today, many people do not believe that the Bible is infallible or inerrant; they do not believe that the Bible is the actual inspired Word of God. This matter is of **crucial** importance. If the Bible is truly the Word of God, then it is infallible; if it is not, then each person's ideas of right and wrong are as valid as anyone else's because there are no final absolute values—no infallible and inerrant Word of God.

The Bible states more than three thousand times that its words are not the words of men, but of God. As the Word of God, the Bible gives a clear testimony of its divine authorship. This claim of

Scripture is supported by the following eleven truths as *evidences* that *the Bible is the Word of God.*

1. *The order and completeness of the Bible* — The Bible contains sixty-six different books, written by over forty different writers. Among its writers were judges and tentmakers, kings and herdsmen, priests and soldiers, prophets and doctors, presidents and fishermen. Parts of the Bible were written in tents, parts in deserts, parts on mountains, parts in cities, parts in palaces, and parts in dungeons. The last writer lived more than two thousand years after the first. Yet, despite all of these differences, the Bible has a perfect unity throughout — it is one book. From Genesis through Revelation it teaches one code of **ethics**, one system of doctrine, one plan of salvation, and one rule of faith. It is clearly one book. Where else can we find forty different authors, practicing different occupations, coming from different backgrounds, living under different circumstances, writing in different periods of history, whose writings form one book with perfect **unity**, a book with no differences of opinion or disagreements concerning the **core** issues of life? We, as human beings, can never make what the Bible is, because *the Bible is the Word of God.*

? "Humanism" is a popular belief and religion in our society today. It believes that each person can decide what is true or false, right or wrong, important or unimportant for himself. Whom does a person have faith in when believing this religion? Who is his "god"? Are the "gods" in this belief-system infallible? Why is humanism an insecure and comfortless religion?

● **Ethics** — A system of proper conduct, morals, and principles for daily living

● **Unity** — Agreement; oneness

● **Core** — Central; most important

Young Tommy watched intently as his grandfather carefully removed the back cover of his gold pocket-watch. Tommy sat spellbound as he observed thirty to forty different gears all interlocking and turning to move the hands of the watch in the right direction and at the proper speed.

"All the wheels work together," he whispered in amazement to his grandfather.

There are sixty-six different books and more than forty different writers interlocking and forming one Bible—one message of salvation.

What comparisons can be made between Grandfather's watch and the Bible? How do the order and completeness of the Bible testify of its one Author? When reading the Bible, have you ever experienced the awe and amazement felt by Tommy when he observed that "all the wheels work together"?

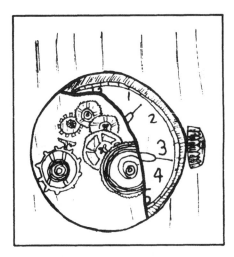

? How does this example help illustrate the truth that the Bible's order and completeness testify of its divine authorship?

2. *The **indestructibility** of the Bible* — Who can count the number of Bibles which have been burned in countless persecutions? Emperors have made all-out wars to destroy the Bible. People have been burned, thrown to wild animals, and tortured to

● **Indestructibility** — The quality of being unable to be destroyed

85

death in many different ways for possessing a Bible or confessing to believe in its truths. Yet, the Bible has survived and has continually spread its influence over the world. Historically, the Bible has always been the most widely read book. Since the day of the printing press, it has consistently been the best-selling book in the world. Never has there been a book so hated and so loved in the entire history of mankind. Why? Because *the Bible is the Word of God.*

A hotel owner in Western Canada became very angry when he found that someone had placed Bibles in all his hotel rooms. He gathered all the Bibles and threw them on a garbage heap for later burning.

A poor girl, who often visited the spot looking for thrown-away food, saw the large heap of Bibles and took some copies home with her.

She soon began to read God's Word, and God blessed its truths to her heart. The seed fell upon prepared ground and brought forth fruits of love to God and others.

Her life was changed and she spoke to others about the truths of God found in the Bible. Her words had impact upon others, for they saw how the Bible had changed her life.

The hotel owner had thought to destroy God's Word but he was actually a means of spreading it. Can you think of examples from the Bible and church history which illustrate the same truth?

? How do these two examples help illustrate in two different manners the truth that the Bible's indestructibility testifies of its divine authorship?

In Armenia, an entire village of sixty families became Mohammedans. They did so under the threats of torture and death from well-armed Mohammedan soldiers.

One woman, more than one hundred years of age, refused. Holding her Bible to her heart, she confessed, "I am too old to deny my Lord!"

The fierce Mohammedans snatched the Bible from her, but she calmly replied, "You can tear of the Bible out of my hands, but you can never tear it out of my heart."

Can you relate other examples which illustrate the Bible's inward indestructibility?

● **Contrasting** — Differing

● **Sundry** — Several; various; many

3. *The Bible's ability to speak to all types of people* — The Bible has spoken to people from different cultures, **contrasting** backgrounds, various occupations, **sundry** ages, and from

dissimilar periods of history. Despite all these differences, thousands have found, through the application of the Holy Spirit, that the Bible spoke personally to them. It revealed to them the true God, their own hearts, and the purpose of their lives. Why could it do this? Because *the Bible is the Word of God.*

A minister once addressed his congregation with the following example:

"If I had a very expensive and complicated lock, and there was only one known key which would fit and unlock it, I would feel very sure that the key was made by the one who built and knew the lock.

So, congregation, when I see all the complexities and mysteries of the human heart and find that there is only one Bible which fits and unlocks human hearts, I am sure that the Bible was written by the same God who created us and knows us so perfectly."

How does this story illustrate the truth that the Bible's ability to speak to all types of people is an evidence of its divine authorship?

? How does this example help illustrate the truth that the Bible's ability to speak to all types of people testifies of its divine authorship?

? What will happen to our nation if it continues to depart from God's truth? If God's Word, blessed by His Spirit, turns savagery to civilization; will civilized nations become more savage when they depart from the truths of the Bible?

4. *The power and influence of the Bible* — Think of the work of Bible missionaries. They enter a new territory with neither weapons to force the people nor with money to bribe them, but only with the Word of God. In many areas, when blessed by God, the Bible has changed savagery to civilization, cruelty to kindness, and lust to purity. Think of all the nations throughout the history of mankind, from the children of Israel to our nation today—when they followed the teachings of the Bible, they prospered; but when they left its truths, they declined. Why? Because *the Bible is the Word of God.*

One day a woman bought a Bible at the village marketplace. After bringing it home, she began reading, and God blessed its truths to her heart. Her husband, however, was a very rough man who hated religion. One evening he came home drunk, and found her again reading her Bible. After snatching it from her, he threw it into the burning stove and angrily shouted, "Now we'll see what will be left of your new religion!"

The next morning, as he opened the stove door and began to stir up the ashes, he saw a half-burned page left from the Bible. He took it out and read these words:

? How does this example help illustrate the truth that the Bible's power and influence testify of its divine authorship?

- **Inexhaustibility**— The quality of being limitless; incapable of reaching an end

- **Finite** — Limited; bounded; measurable

? Can you think of examples in our society where people "continually insist upon choking on the bones"? In doing so, what "meat" do they miss?

? How does this example help illustrate the truth that the Bible's inexhaustibility should not be a stumbling block but that it testifies of its divine authorship?

"Heaven and earth shall pass away, but My Word shall not pass away."

The truth of these words arrested him. He felt a deep sorrow that he had tried to destroy God's Word and told his wife to buy another Bible. He began to prayerfully read with his wife, and God also blessed this in his life.

How was this man "burned" by the Bible he was burning? Why and how does the Bible have power to do such things?

5. *The inexhaustibility of the Bible* — Hundreds of commentaries have been written on the Bible. Countless sermons have been preached on single texts over thousands of years; and yet, there is always something new. We have a **finite** mind. We cannot reach the limitless depths of the Bible. The Bible contains the infinite wisdom of its Author, because *the Bible is the Word of God.*

A bold young man, who frequently boasted of being a confirmed atheist, sat at a table in the dining car of a passenger train. A minister also seated himself at the same table.

As they were enjoying their delicious fish dinners, the young man looked at the minister and said, "I guess you are a minister!"

"Yes," the minister answered, "I am in my Master's service."

"I thought so. Preach out of the Bible, don't you?"

"Yes, I do."

"Find quite a few things there that you don't understand, I'll bet!"

"Yes, there are things I do not fully understand."

"I thought so. What do you do then, Minister—still go on believing in your book even when you don't understand it?"

The minister paused before answering and then responded, "My friend, I simply practice what we are presently doing with our fish dinner. When I come to a bone I quietly lay it aside and continue enjoying the delicious meat. I feel sincerely sorry, however, for anyone who continually insists upon choking on the bones."

What important lesson regarding Bible reading and studying is taught by this example? While this minister used an immediate example to effectively illustrate his point, we must also observe that bones are worthless, but passages of Scripture that are harder to understand are not. Are you praying and trying to increase your biblical knowledge?

6. *The honesty of the writers of the Bible* — When we read a humanly-written **biography** the author often tries to **idolize** the person about whom he is writing. This is done by smoothing over his faults and enlarging his achievements. But this is not so with the Bible; we read openly and honestly about Noah's faith and his sin, David's trust and his doubt, Solomon's wisdom and his foolishness, and so we could continue with all of the biblical heroes of faith. The Bible is totally honest throughout, because *the Bible is the Word of God.*

- **Biography** — A book written about the life of another
- **Idolize** — To adore; to view another as nearly perfect or without fault

John's teacher asked each student to write the names of ten well-known Bible heroes on a blank sheet of paper. John listed the following:

1. Noah
2. Abraham
3. Jacob
4. Moses
5. Samson
6. Gideon
7. David
8. Solomon
9. Hezekiah
10. Peter

"Now, write next to each name that you listed, a sin or failure of that person spoken of in the Bible," instructed his teacher.

What sins could John list next to each of the names he chose? Does the Bible falsely idolize its champions of faith? Why not?

? How does this example help illustrate the truth that the Bible's honesty testifies of its divine authorship?

7. *The biblical teachings concerning God and man* — All non-biblical early forms of religion had gods similar to human beings. These gods had bodies and were not infallible. But, the teachings of the Bible concerning God are different. God is One, a Spirit, who is perfect in all His attributes. The books of other religions also speak differently of man: either man is good, or he is somewhat sick, and with proper attitudes and good works he can improve and eventually earn salvation. These ideas testify of their human authors, for these themes are to man's liking. We prefer to help ourselves, for this appeals to our pride. But the Bible, and only the Bible, teaches differently. The Bible proclaims that man is spiritually dead in sin. It states that man cannot save himself. It declares that

- **Exalted** — Honored; glorified; elevated or raised on high

- **Abased** — Humbled; lowered; reduced

? How does this example help illustrate the truth that the Bible's teachings concerning God and man are not human, but that they testify of its divine authorship?

- **Bible critics** — People who question, doubt, and try to find fault with the Bible

- **Archeologists** — Scientists who study the ancient history of various civilizations by uncovering and examining their past belongings, homes, customs, etc.

- **Bitumen** — An asphalt-type material that evaporates very rapidly

- **Verified** — Proven; confirmed

man stands in total need of God to deliver him. Only the Bible, in distinction from the writings of other religions, teaches the truth concerning God and man. Only in the Bible is God **exalted** to the highest and man **abased** to the lowest. Why? Because *the Bible is the Word of God.*

> A native of India was once shown, by looking through a microscope, the germs in the water from the Ganges River. He was then told, for health reasons, not to drink river water any longer.
> The sight of the germs wriggling around in the water deeply bothered him. In hatred and anger he took his club and smashed the microscope. He then returned to drinking river water.
> The Bible's clear uncovering of our total sinfulness often stirs within us a similar reponse as the Indian's to the microscope. How is this true? Why is this reaction so very foolish?

8. *The historical exactness of the Bible* — Many historical places and occurances, long doubted by many **Bible critics**, have been brought to light today through the work of **archeologists**. Stories about the flood have been found in myths from many different countries throughout the world. Writings tablets of children attending school in Ur of the Chaldees at the time of Abraham have been unearthed. The former site of Sodom and Gomorrah has been determined; lying under huge quantities of sulfur, **bitumen**, and volcanic rock, the large amounts of sulfuric gases yet in the soil point back to the disastrous overthrow of these cities. The captivity of the children of Israel in Egypt has been **verified** in Egyptian records. Solomon's large stables and copper furnace at Ezion-geber have been uncovered. Hezekiah's pool and conduit have been discovered, still intact. So we could continue throughout the Old and New Testaments; but to summarize, let us quote a concluding statement of Dr. Nelson Glueck, one of the greatest authorities on Israeli archeology: "No archeological discovery has ever disproved a biblical record. Scores of findings have been made which confirm in clear outline, or in exact detail, historical statements in the Bible." Many errors and exaggerations have been found in the ancient records of the Assyrians, Egyptians, and other nations living during biblical times; but never has a mistake been found with the historical facts of the Bible; because *the Bible is the Word of God.*

Sennacherib's palace in Nineveh has been unearthed by archeologists. This King of Assyria's palace and records speak of his great pride as taught in the biblical story of Hezekiah. The proud speech and letter of Sennacherib and his general, Rabshekeh, are noted several times in scriptural history (II Kings 18-19, II Chronicles 32, Isaiah 36-37).

Sennacherib built several palaces in Nineveh with "trophy rooms." Here he proudly displayed, in stone-carved pictures and writing, exaggerated reports of his war victories. One large room, of special interest to us, is called the "Lachish Room." Twelve stone slabs, covering three of the four walls in this room, show scenes of Sennacherib's conquering of Lachish, *but none display his conquering of Jerusalem.*

The translated, engraven records of Sennacherib speak in boastful language about his attacks upon Judah and Hezekiah as follows:

"As for Hezekiah, the awful splendor of my lordship overwhelmed him and all kinds of valuable treasures he sent me...Hezekiah the Judean, I shut up in Jerusalem, his royal city, like a bird in a cage."

Following this there is no further record of King Sennacherib's victory; only silence! Why was there no glorious victory account recorded as found on all of his other records? Because there was no Assyrian victory over Jerusalem as the Bible tells us in II Kings 19:35-36. The angel of God destroyed Sennacherib's army and he returned in shame to his own country. The completion of this history would not "fit" into King Sennacherib's "trophy room," but it does fit in the historically accurate, infallible Word of God.

? How does this example help illustrate the truth that the Bible's historical accuracy testifies of it divine authorship?

? Have you ever read any ancient myths or histories? If so, how is the Bible remarkably different from other ancient writings?

● **Environment** — The world in which we live with its various properties and qualities

9. *The scientific knowledge of the Bible* — When we read other books, at times only a few years old, we frequently find mistakes due to a lack of scientific knowledge concerning some aspect of our **environment**. Especially when reading books written several hundreds of years ago, we often encounter strange explanations and beliefs regarding scientific matters. However, no proven scientific fact disagrees with the teachings of the Bible, which was written thousands of years ago. In fact, several scientific facts discovered rather recently were previously spoken of in the Bible. How could the Bible speak of these facts thousands of years before man "discovered" them? There is only one answer: the Author of the Bible was not human but divine, because *the Bible is the Word of God.*

For centuries man was occupied with trying to count the number of stars. Each time a more powerful telescope was produced, the number of the stars increased. Not until recently were galaxies beyond our own discovered; with this knowledge man realized the impossibility of ever counting the number of stars. But Jeremiah wrote already 2,500 years ago that the stars of heaven cannot be numbered (Jeremiah 33:22).

During the past ages, men had various ideas about the shape and foundation of the earth. The earth was generally believed to be flat and built upon a solid foundation. Later, man began to realize that the earth was round. Even later, man learned that the earth is in space which means that it rests upon nothing. However, the Bible previously testified of these facts. Isaiah proclaimed 2,700 years ago that the Lord "sitteth upon the circle (sphere) of the earth" (Isaiah 40:22). Approximately 3,500 years ago, Job testified that the Lord "hangeth the earth upon nothing" (Job 26:7).

The Bible testified thousands of years ago of a water cycle, wind circuits, and the circuit of the sun in our galaxy. These also have only been recently discovered by man.

? How do these examples help illustrate the truth that the Bible's scientific knowledge testifies of its divine authorship?

How could the Bible testify of these scientific facts, thousands of years before people "discovered" them? How is this an evidence of the Bible's being God's infallible Word?

● **Vague** — Unclear; uncertain; general; doubtful

● **Self-acclaimed** — Declared by one's own self

10. *The prophetical accuracy of the Bible* — Biblical prophecies are not **vague** predictions as the "prophecies" of **self-acclaimed** "prophets." False prophets state *vague* predictions for which they later try to claim fulfillments. The prophecies of the Bible are different; they are very clear and plain. The Bible is full of prophecy. Think of the prophecies against Samaria, Jericho, Jerusalem, Moab, Ammon, and Babylon; think of the prophecies of Daniel and many more. Above all, think of the more than three hundred prophecies concerning the birth, life, death and resurrection of the Lord Jesus. Every one of these prophecies has been fulfilled exactly. Why is the prophecy of the Bible so accurate? There is only one answer: *the Bible is the Word of God.*

The following is an example of specific biblical prophecy and its fulfillment:

In Ezekiel 26 we can read the following seven prophecies against the city of Tyre, written in 590 B.C.:

1. *Nebuchadnezzar shall take the city.*
2. *Other nations shall also participate in the fulfillment of this prophecy.*
3. *The city will be made flat like the top of a rock.*
4. *It will become a place for the spreading of fishing nets.*
5. *Its stones and timbers will be laid in the sea.*
6. *Other cities will greatly fear at the fall of Tyre.*
7. *The old city of Tyre shall never be rebuilt.*

Historically, the fulfillment of this prophecy took place in the following manner. In 586 B.C. Nebuchadnezzar laid siege to Tyre. He captured it thirteen years later in 573 B.C. However, when he finally captured the city, the inhabitants had secretly moved, with their valuables, to an island approximately one-half mile from the shore. Nebuchadnezzar could not conquer them on this island without a navy, and therefore, only captured an empty city.

Tyre continued in this manner for 251 years, with only the first prophecy of the seven fulfilled. However, in 322 B.C., Alexander the Great wished to capture the city of Tyre because of its strategic location. He felt that he could not conquer the island city with only his navy, and therefore ordered his army to construct a **causeway** from the mainland to the island. In making this causeway, his soldiers took all the stones and timber from the old city and pushed it into the sea. They scraped away all of the soil, literally transforming the old city into a flat rock. With this causeway, Alexander's army attacked by land, and his navy by sea. In this manner, he captured the city. The neighboring cities were so frightened after hearing of the manner in which Alexander had conquered Tyre that they surrendered to him. Today, visitors to this place find that this flat rock area is a popular place for fishermen. They spread out their nets to dry them on this very spot. Despite its excellent location, the city has never been rebuilt.

If God did not infallibly inspire the writing of the Bible, how could Ezekiel have prophesied so exactly what would happen to Tyre more than 250 years later?

? How does this example help illustrate the truth that the Bible's prophetical accuracy testifies of its divine authorship?

● **Causeway** — A solid, raised roadway that rises above a normally watery or marshy area

? How does this example show that biblical prophecy is not vague or general but very clear and specific?

? Can you name any biblical, historical, or present-day example of any person that truly experienced God's saving power in his heart and did not believe the Bible to be God's Word? Why would this never happen? If experienced, why is the person totally convinced that the Bible is God's infallible Word?

Heaven and earth shall pass away; but My Word shall not pass away.
— Mark 13:31

Forever, O LORD, Thy Word is settled in heaven.
— Psalm 119:89

? How are those that build their purposes, plans, goals, and lives upon their own ideas, like the foolish builder in Matthew 7:26-27?

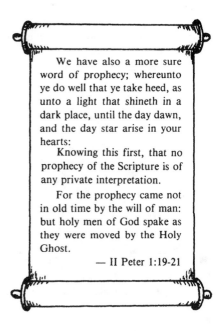

We have also a more sure word of prophecy; whereunto ye do well that ye take heed, as unto a light that shineth in a dark place, until the day dawn, and the day star arise in your hearts:

Knowing this first, that no prophecy of the Scripture is of any private interpretation.

For the prophecy came not in old time by the will of man: but holy men of God spake as they were moved by the Holy Ghost.
— II Peter 1:19-21

11. *The powerful and personal application of the Bible to one's heart by the Holy Spirit* — This evidence establishes the truth that the Bible is the infallible Word of God in the deepest manner. It is this application of divine power, when experienced in one's life, which removes all doubt. This divine power is a power which produces a great change in a person's life. It is a power which implants a new birth, a new spiritual life. It is a power which convicts of sin. It is a power which teaches what sin is and what one's condition is without God in this world. It is a power which convinces a person that God is righteous in His demands upon him. It is a power which reveals a personal way of escape—a way of deliverance. It is a power which works faith to believe and hope in a Savior, outside of himself, in the Lord Jesus Christ. It is a power which turns the heart from a love of sin and self to God and His truth. It is the power of a sovereign, sinner-electing God. In short, it is the power of God the Holy Spirit blessing His Word unto salvation. This is the proof, which when engraven in one's heart, will establish forever the truth that *the Bible is the Word of God.*

Do you know something of this saving conviction in your life? Is the Bible the infallible Word of God to you? If so, then its words and truths will be most precious to you, and the fruits of faith, hope, and love will be seen in your life. Are they?

Would you dare to walk across a frozen lake if you did not know that the ice under your feet was solid? Would you cross a deep ravine by walking on a plank if you were not certain that the board would hold your weight? Of course not! Likewise, you should not build your thoughts, values and spiritual hopes on unstable human ideas. But you must, by God's sovereign grace, build the house of your hope on a solid, proven, and unmovable foundation. The Bible testifies through its *order and completeness, indestructibility, power and influence, ability to speak to all types of people, inexhaustibility, honesty, teachings concerning God and man, historical exactness, scientific knowledge, prophetical accuracy,* and above all, through its *power when applied in the heart by the Holy Spirit* that it is truly the inspired, infallible *Word of God.* Pray that you may, by God's grace, base your thoughts, ideas, values, purposes, hopes; in short — your entire life — on the absolute and infallible truths of God's Word. The Bible shall stand forever as the one and only God-given Word because *the Bible is the Word of God.*

THE BIBLE'S QUALITIES

As the one, only, infallible, inspired Word of God, the Bible — and only the Bible — has the following four qualities:

1. *The Authority of the Bible* — The Bible is the absolute and final authority for all matters of faith and practice. The church with its doctrinal standards, rules, and practices only has authority from the Bible. The church does not stand alone nor next to Scripture, but under it.

2. *The Necessity of the Bible* — The Bible is necessary for salvation. God the Holy Spirit must apply the truths of the Bible within the soul of a person; without this he is lost.

3. *The Clearness of the Bible* — The Bible is clear and plain in all matters necessary unto salvation.

4. *The Sufficiency of the Bible* — The Bible provides all things necessary for the moral and spiritual needs of all people. It contains the complete revelation needed for man's salvation.

What qualities of Scripture are illustrated in the following story?

After the Reformation, a Roman Catholic priest was condemning an Irish farmer for trying to read and understand the Bible on his own. He said, "The Bible is for the church — for the priests to read and understand — not for individual people."

"I was just reading in Psalm 78 that God commanded fathers to explain His Word to their children," the farmer answered. "This cannot mean only priests because they have no children."

"Mike, the church will teach you. It has received God's Word and it will give you the milk of the Word," the priest explained.

"Yes," replied the farmer, "but I would rather keep the cow and milk her myself!"

What did Mike mean with his final answer?

So then faith cometh by hearing, and hearing by the Word of God.
— Romans 10:17

And that from a child thou hast known the Holy Scriptures, which are able to make thee wise unto salvation through faith which is in Christ Jesus.
— II Timothy 3:15

Search the Scriptures; for in them ye think ye have eternal life: and they are they which testify of Me.
— John 5:39

For whatsoever things were written aforetime were written for our learning, that we through patience and comfort of the Scriptures might have hope.
— Romans 15:4

To the law and to the testimony: if they speak not according to this Word, it is because there is no light in them.
— Isaiah 8:20

Ye shall not add unto the Word which I command you, neither shall ye diminish aught from it, that ye may keep the commandments of the LORD your God which I command you.
— Deuteronomy 4:2

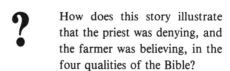

? How does this story illustrate that the priest was denying, and the farmer was believing, in the four qualities of the Bible?

? Has the Roman Catholic Church changed its view toward the private reading of Scripture? Has it changed its four views regarding the Bible's qualities, however, as explained in the chart on the following page?

Study the following chart which displays the four differing views concerning the Bible's qualities as they are taught by the Roman Catholic and Protestant churches.

? Why would the Roman Catholic Church teach that the Bible is not necessary while the Protestant churches teach that it is necessary for salvation?

? How would the following groups deny the four qualities of Scripture?
- Roman Catholics
- Quakers
- Christian Scientists
- Mormons
- Jehovah's Witnesses

? While Protestants confess to believe in the four qualities of Scripture, how can they deny these truths in practice?

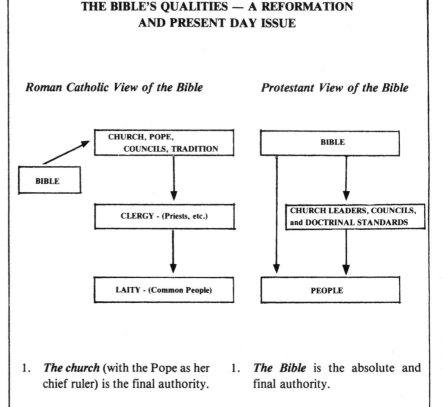

THE BIBLE'S QUALITIES — A REFORMATION AND PRESENT DAY ISSUE

Roman Catholic View of the Bible

CHURCH, POPE, COUNCILS, TRADITION

BIBLE

CLERGY - (Priests, etc.)

LAITY - (Common People)

Protestant View of the Bible

BIBLE

CHURCH LEADERS, COUNCILS, and DOCTRINAL STANDARDS

PEOPLE

1. *The church* (with the Pope as her chief ruler) is the final authority.

2. *The church* is necessary for salvation.

3. *The church* must clarify and teach all matters necessary unto salvation.

4. *The church* and its sacraments, teachings, and blessings are sufficient for salvation.

1. *The Bible* is the absolute and final authority.

2. *The Bible* is necessary for salvation.

3. *The Bible* is clear and plain in all matters necessary unto salvation.

4. *The Bible* is sufficient for salvation.

In the summer we see many insects moving among colorful flowers. The two we see most often are the butterfly and the bee. How different are these two insects! The butterfly flutters from flower to flower, and gets a drop of nectar here and a drop of nectar there. But the bee is a hard worker, it goes down deep into the heart of the flower and gets all the nectar from it. Then it flies to the beehive where it stores away the nectar in the form of honey, to be used as food in the wintertime.

Are you a "butterfly" or "bee" type of Bible reader?

A young lady was reading a book; however, she found it quite boring and uninteresting. In disgust, she threw the book onto a shelf in her closet where it lay forgotten for some months. One evening, she met a young man, whom she immediately liked and in whom she became very interested. When he told her his name, she exclaimed, "Why, I have a book whose author's name and initials are exactly the same as yours!"

When she mentioned the title of the book that she had previously thrown onto her closet shelf, the young man said, "I wrote that book. It's mine!"

That night, the young lady sat up until early-morning hours reading this book. The once "boring book" was now very interesting because she knew and loved the author.

Some people view the Bible as quite boring and uninteresting, but if they come to know and love God, why would this completely change? Why do God's true children love His Word?

? The Scriptures contain an infinite depth of instruction. How does this require "bee" type studying of the Bible? If a person does not diligently search the Scriptures, what price will he pay in his life?

FALSE RELIGIONS

All people have a general knowledge of God and a need to worship Him. This knowledge stems from their consciences and their viewings of creation. Due to man's sinful fall, the hardening of his conscience, and his lack of scriptural understanding, however, man's general knowledge often reveals itself in mistaken, twisted, and corrupt religious ideas and practices. This has led to the development of numerous false religions in the world. The main false religions in the world today are:

1. Judaism
2. Mohammedanism
3. Heathenism

Study the following descriptive charts which explain the basic teachings of the main false religions in the world today.

? Is it possible to love God and not to love His Word? Why not? If a person continually finds the Bible to be uninteresting, of what deeper problem is this an indication?

- **Monotheistic** — Believing in only one god

❓ Does the Old Testament speak of Jesus Christ and salvation through Him? Do the Orthodox Jews truly believe the truths taught in the Old Testament? Can a person believe in one Testament and not in the other?

- **Mecca** — The birthplace of Mohammed and headquarters of Islam

❓ Can you name several basic principles of Christianity that are missing in Mohammedanism? Which basic principles are found in both?

❓ How does Acts 4:12 apply to Judaism and Mohammedanism? To us?

MONOTHEISTIC FALSE RELIGIONS

JUDAISM

Judaism is the religion of the Jews. It is one of the oldest religions in the world and has as its basis the Old Testament law and prophets. It has always been monotheistic, believing in only one God.

The rejection of the Lord Jesus Christ as the Messiah, the Savior, and the denial of the books of the New Testament have turned Judaism into a false religion.

Today, Judaism is divided into three main branches:

1. Orthodox — Strict followers of the Old Testament laws and the interpretations of the scribes who yet expect the Messiah to come

2. Reformed — Believers in the nation of Israel as the Messiah prophesied in the Old Testament

3. Radical — Deniers of all special revelation from God

MOHAMMEDANISM or ISLAM

Mohammedanism is based on the teachings of its founder Mohammed who lived from 570 to 632 A.D. in Arabia. As a merchant traveling in caravans to the east, Mohammed became familiar with various forms of heathenism, Judaism, and Christianity. After marrying a rich widow, he retired and devoted his time to the development of Islam. ("Islam" means "submission to God.") He wrote the Koran, the "Bible" of all Moslems (also known as "Muslims," or "followers of Islam").

Islam requires submission to the following "Five Pillars of the Faith":

1. Profession of faith — All Moslems believe that there is only one god, or Allah, that Mohammed was his greatest and last prophet, and that there will be a final judgment.

2. Prayer — Islamic custom requires the performance of five ritual prayers daily. These may usually be performed wherever the Moslem is, but preferably in a mosque. He must bow in the direction of **Mecca**.

3. Almsgiving — The regular giving of alms, in the amount of one fortieth of a man's annual revenue, is required.

4. Fasting — Abstinence from food and drink from sunrise to sunset, is required during the holy month of Ramadan. Those sick or on a journey may be exempted from fasting if they make up for the lost days by fasting at a later time.

5. Pilgrimage — Every Moslem must, if at all financially possible, make a pilgrimage to Mecca once in his lifetime.

Belief in "jihad," or the obligation of waging holy war for Allah, has often made Moslem nations a fierce and fearful power.

MAIN POLYTHEISTIC FALSE RELIGIONS

EASTERN RELIGIONS

HINDUISM

Hinduism began in India in approximately 1500 B.C. The oldest Hindu scriptures are the "Vedas," written from approximately 1,000 B.C. to the time of Christ. To find peace, a person must overcome sense and feeling through sincere devotion in numerous ways. If successful, a person will be **reincarnated** at a higher level of life and finally escape human levels to become a god in Brahman—the **cosmic** soul. Hinduism believes in a strong **caste system**.

BUDDHISM

A split from Hinduism, Buddhism was founded by Gautama Buddha, "The Enlightened One," in the late 500s B.C. Buddhism rejects the Hindu: caste system, belief in thousands of gods, and special powers of the priestly class. Buddha taught four noble truths: **1.** Life is suffering. **2.** The cause of suffering is desiring. **3.** The end of suffering is to eliminate all desiring. **4.** To eliminate all desiring one must follow an eight-fold path. This will bring a person to "nirvana," a state of perfect peace and happiness.

CONFUCIANISM

Confucianism is a Chinese religion based upon the teachings of Confucius, a philosopher in the 400s B.C. Confucianism does not believe in an eternal God nor eternity. It stresses good morality, dedication to public service, and respect for authority. Its teachings are based upon the Five Classics and the Four Books of Conduct.

TAOISM

Taoism, like Confucianism, is a Chinese religion. It became organized around 100 B.C. Taoism strongly believes in spirits which must be **pacified** through communication with the spirit world via fortune-telling, witchcraft, and astrology. Taoism is a highly superstitious religion. Its goals are to become happy and immortal.

SHINTOISM

Shintoism is the native religion of Japan. Japan and the Japanese people were specially created by gods. These gods are to be worshipped in various mountains, rocks, trees, etc., in Japan. Until the mid 1900's, the Japanese Emperor was worshipped as a direct descendant of the sun goddess, the most important god.

TRIBAL RELIGIONS

HEATHEN TRIBAL RELIGIONS

Hundreds of different primitive tribal religions exist in the world. In general they include the following characteristics: the belief in many gods and spirits (both good and evil); the constant fear of, and need to pacify, evil spirits; the worshipping of self-made gods (idols); the ability to communicate with the spirit world through various mystical practices, and the religious use of fire or fire worship.

- **Polytheistic** — Believing in more than one god

- **Reincarnated** — The soul of a person being returned to earth after death to live in a new life form — either animal or human

- **Cosmic** — Pertaining to the universe; the system of order and harmony in the universe

- **Caste system** — An unchangeable class of established social orders of people in society

? Can you discover any common characteristics found in all false religions? How is true Christianity different from all false religions?

- **Pacified** — Made peace with; subdued; appeased

? Why are all people in the world "religious"? What false gods are worshipped by educated, civilized "heathenism" today?

The following chart reflects the numbers of people believing in each of the major religions of the world.

? It was estimated that in 1985 one-half of the world was Christianized, the world population being approximately 4.7 billion. Why is Christianity the most rapidly growing religion in the world today?

? Why should this chart stir mission desires within us? Do you pray for and support world-wide mission work? Are you active in local mission activities?

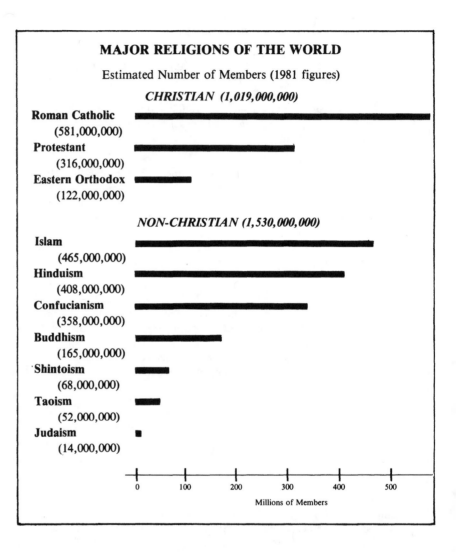

MAJOR RELIGIONS OF THE WORLD

Estimated Number of Members (1981 figures)

CHRISTIAN (1,019,000,000)

Roman Catholic (581,000,000)
Protestant (316,000,000)
Eastern Orthodox (122,000,000)

NON-CHRISTIAN (1,530,000,000)

Islam (465,000,000)
Hinduism (408,000,000)
Confucianism (358,000,000)
Buddhism (165,000,000)
Shintoism (68,000,000)
Taoism (52,000,000)
Judaism (14,000,000)

0   100   200   300   400   500

Millions of Members

With so many false religions in the world today, how can we be sure that Christianity is the true religion?

Christianity is different from false religions in the following four important respects:

1. Only Christianity is *based on God's infallible Word*. Only the Bible is God's infallible Word, as evidenced by the eleven reasons explained previously in this chapter.

2. Only Christianity *presents man's sin as totally* **abominable** *and man as a totally lost sinner* who cannot earn or merit his own salvation.

- **Abominable** — Terrible; loathsome; detestable; awful

3. Only Christianity *proclaims a perfect and complete salvation by God's free* **grace** *through a perfect substitute,* the God-man, Jesus Christ.

? Why are Points 2 and 3 inseparably connected?

- **Grace** — A one-sided love to persons totally undeserving of it

4. Only Christianity *presents a perfect God;* one who is infinitely **transcendent** and perfect in all His attributes and yet who is most personal and approachable through Jesus Christ.

- **Transcendent** — Far above and beyond all human abilities and powers of natural creation

These four points of truth also apply to false teachings within Christianity. When errors occur within Christianity, they generally involve:

1. Departing from the truths of God's Word.

? Re-examine the false religions listed on the previous pages. Do all of them miss these four marks of true, biblical religion? Which is closer than the others to some of these marks? Why?

2. Giving some credit to man, enabling him to earn a part of his salvation through his works or faith.

3. Denying that salvation is entirely based on God's grace and that Jesus accomplishes everything in the salvation of a sinner, as a full and complete Savior.

? How do each of these four points relate to the previous four?

4. Lowering God and His perfections to some degree.

The following two examples help illustrate how false opinions enter all religions, even Christian teachings:

Materially, Howard Hughes was one of the richest men that ever lived. He died a billionaire. After his death, numerous properly registered and documented wills of Howard Hughes appeared. Obviously only one was true and the others were **counterfeit**.

- **Counterfeit** — The quality of not being genuine but having a true or real appearance in order to deceive others

- **Resolve** — To settle; to decide

- **Forgery** — The act of producing a false imitation and claiming that it is real or genuine

? Using the truth illustrated in this story, what clear signs of "counterfeiting" can you see in the false religions described on the previous pages?

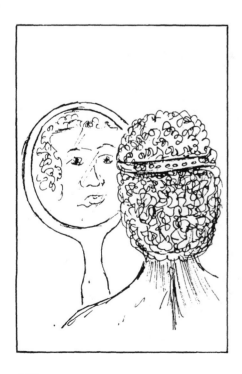

In attempting to **resolve** the confusion regarding this matter, the lawyers and judges working on this case examined each will for tell-tale signs of **forgery**. What did they look for? Did the will claim more for the person or group presenting it than what could be realistically expected? If so, this would provide evidence of the will's counterfeitness.

There are numerous writings today which claim to be the one, true, infallible Word of God. Obviously only one is true and the others must be counterfeit.

In attempting to resolve this confusion, we may proceed along the same line of thought as the judges in the previous case. Does the book or religion presented give undue honor, credit, or merit to those presenting it—to man? Does it bear this telltale sign of forgery?

The true Word of God exalts God to the highest, but abases man to the lowest; man is a totally lost and spiritually dead sinner who needs to be completely and graciously saved by God. Man's being totally lost, totally responsible, and needing total salvation by God is not to man's natural liking. Certainly, no man would ever forge this type of book or religion!

Study each of the false religions presented in the previous charts. How does man earn, or partially earn his own salvation in each one? What telltale signs of counterfeitness can you detect?

A missionary in Africa once carried a few mirrors. The natives had never seen their own faces, except unclearly in the water of a lake or stream. Soon news of this wonderful instrument, which clearly showed people their own features, was spread abroad.

The missionary was invited to visit tribe after tribe. Deep in the interior lived a princess in one of the tribes who had been told that she was the most beautiful woman in the tribe. When she heard of this wonderful glass, she sent for the missionary, telling him to bring one of his mirrors.

The princess was not a beautiful woman. In actuality, she was the least attractive woman in the tribe. When she received the mirror, she went into her hut alone to take a long look at her "beauty." She held up the glass and clearly saw how unattractive she really was. With great anger, she dashed the mirror to pieces, banished the missionary from her tribe, and made a law that no such glass could ever be brought into the tribe again.

Why did the princess hate the mirror? What truth did it tell her? Why do so many people hate the Bible? What truth does the Bible tell us about ourselves? Why are we not attractive in the eyes of God?

Due to its speaking the truth about our sinfulness and misery, the true Word of God and true religion are often despised and cast away.

While the Bible and true religion may be compared to a mirror when God shows us our sinfulness or misery, it is different in another respect. It not only shows us who we are, but whom else does it reveal?

? Does the biblical "mirror" reveal each of us as an "attractive" person? Why not? Why is it natural for each of us to hate the "mirror of biblical truth" as the princess hated the missionary's mirror?

? Why is it to man's natural liking to change God's truths regarding his sinful condition?

> Yea doubtless, and I count all things but loss for the excellency of the knowledge of Christ Jesus my Lord: for whom I have suffered the loss of all things, and do count them but dung, that I may win Christ,
>
> And be found in Him, not having mine own righteousness, which is of the law, but that which is through the faith of Christ, the righteousness which is of God by faith.
>
> — Philippians 3:8-9

Have you discovered enmity against God and His way of salvation in your own heart? Our sinful nature and pride cannot endure the true teachings of Scripture — our total sinfulness and God's total free grace. We would be willing to work hard to earn our salvation and keep our pride, but to be freely saved as a lost sinner and beggar by another stirs our proud hearts to rebellion.

Those who have experienced the truths of true Christianity in their hearts have surrendered to God through the conquering love of His Spirit. They now love to proclaim and live true religion—God exalted to the highest and self abased to the lowest. Is this your life?

CATECHISM MEMORIZATION
Questions from Rev. A. Hellenbroek's *Divine Truths* — Chapter II

1. Are the Holy Scriptures perfect?
   Yes, "The law of the Lord is perfect" (Ps. 19:7).

2. Was any part of the Holy Scriptures lost or falsified?
   No. They are as entire and pure as they ever were (Matt. 5:18).

3. Are human traditions necessary for salvation in addition to the Holy Scriptures?
   No, the Holy Scriptures alone are sufficient. "In vain do they worship Me, teaching for doctrines the commandments of men" (Matt. 15:9).

4. Are the Holy Scriptures plain or obscure?
   The Bible is plain in all things necessary for salvation. "Thy Word is a lamp unto my feet, and a light unto my path" (Ps. 119:105).

5. What then does Peter mean when he says that in the epistles of Paul there are some things that are hard to understand (II Peter 3:16)?
   That the truth of a thing may be clearly revealed although we cannot comprehend the matter in itself, as is true of all scriptural mysteries, such the Triune existence of God, etc.

6. Must we read the Holy Scriptures?
   Yes. "Search the Scriptures, for in them ye think ye have eternal life, and they are they which testify of Me" (John 5:39).

7. How must we search the Scriptures?
   (1) In the fear of God (Ps. 111:10); (2) with a praying heart (Ps. 119:18); (3) reverently (Isaiah 66:5); (4) attentively and with spiritual judgment (I Cor. 2:13).

CHAPTER 3

Part I. Chapter Review

1. Concerning the completion of the Bible, name three different time periods in the history of the world, and name the condition of Bible completion for each:

   Time period   *Condition*

   a. _____   _____
   b. _____   _____
   c. _____   _____

2. Name the three most ancient and well-known, complete Bible manuscripts:
   a. _____
   b. _____
   c. _____

3. The _____ Text is the text found in approximately _____ percent of the more than _____ known Greek New Testament manuscripts. Codex _____ , or the _____ Manuscript is a Traditional Text manuscript.

4. Describe the following two ancient translations of the Bible:
   a. The Septuagint — _____
   _____
   _____
   b. The Vulgate — _____
   _____
   _____

5. Why do we favor the King James or Authorized Version of the Bible in English?
   a. _____
   b. _____
   c. _____
   d. _____
   e. _____
   f. _____
   g. _____
   h. _____

6. List four qualities of, or truths concerning, the Bible which are denied by the Roman Catholic Church:
   a. _____
   b. _____
   c. _____
   d. _____

7. List eleven evidences which testify of the Bible's being God's true and infallible Word:
   a. _____
   b. _____
   c. _____
   d. _____
   e. _____
   f. _____
   g. _____
   h. _____
   i. _____
   j. _____
   k. _____

8. How are Judaism and Islam different from heathen religions?_____
   _____
   _____

9. Describe four ways in which true Christianity differs from all false religions:
   a. _____
   b. _____
   c. _____
   d. _____

10. List the name of the false religion described below:

    a. _____ A highly superstitious Chinese religion which believes in communication with the spirit world

    b. _____ A belief in reincarnation at various levels of life and a human caste system

    c. _____ A native Japanese religion

    d. _____ A belief based on the Old Testament, but rejecting Jesus Christ as the Messiah

    e. _____ A religion which stresses good morality, dedication to public service and respect for authority

    f. _____ Hundreds of primitive religions motivated by fear of, and a need to pacify, evil spirits

    g. _____ A strict religion based on the Koran

    h. _____ Peace and happiness can only be found through understanding the "four noble truths" and by following the "eight-fold path"

CHAPTER 3

Part II. Deepening Your Insight

1. How did the discovery and examination of the Dead Sea Scrolls serve:
    a. As a clear and powerful proof of the scribes' copying accuracy? _____
    _____

    b. As strong evidence for the copying accuracy of the Traditional Text?_____
    _____

2. Explain how the more recent English Bible translations (the RV, ASV, RSV, NEB, and NIV) have departed from the Traditional Text. _____
    _____
    _____
    _____

3. Explain why the argument of Westcott and Hort that ''The oldest manuscripts are the most reliable'' is not necessarily true. _____
    _____
    _____
    _____

4. Why is a paraphrased ''Bible'' very dangerous? _____
    _____
    _____

5. What important lesson regarding Bible reading is taught in the example of ''eating the meat'' rather than ''choking on the bones''?_____
    _____
    _____

6. If the Bible were not divinely inspired, how would the history of the kings of Israel and Judah be more like the kingly records of Sennacherib? _____
    _____
    _____

7. What is the *main* difference between the Roman Catholic and Protestant views concerning the Bible and the Church? _____
    _____
    _____

8. Explain how the principle taught in the example of Howard Hughes' will can be used when examining religions and books which claim to be from God._____
    _____
    _____
    _____

Part III. Biblical Applications

1. How does Revelation 22:18-19 condemn those who try to deny parts of the Bible or add new teachings to it? _____
   _____
   _____
   _____

2. Write out the verses in Isaiah 55 which beautifully describe the power and life-giving influence of God's Word:_____
   _____
   _____

3. Which lengthy psalm in the Bible describes the wonderfulness of the Word of God in every verse, almost without exception? Psalm: _____. Name the eight different words used for God's "Word" in this psalm:

   a. _____   e. _____
   b. _____   f. _____
   c. _____   g. _____
   d. _____   h. _____

4. Write out the verses in Psalm 78 to which "Farmer Mike" was referring when answering the priest's objections to his personal use of the Bible:
   _____
   _____
   _____

Part IV. From the Writings of our Church Forefathers

In your own words, explain the meaning of the following quotations:

1. "The Scripture is both the breeder and feeder of grace" (Thomas Watson). _____
   _____
   _____

2. "We say not that the Spirit ever speaks to us *of* the Word, but *by* the Word" (John Owen). _____
   _____
   _____

3. "The Scriptures teach us the best way of living, the noisiest way of suffering, and the most comfortable way of dying" (John Flavel). _____
   _____
   _____
   _____

CHAPTER 3

Part V. From the Marginal Questions

1. Concerning God's revelation, why are we living in the "richest time period of world history"? ___
   _____
   _____
   _____
   _____

2. Why should the large number of differences between the Vatican and Sinaitic manuscripts decrease the reliableness of using them as a primary basis for Bible translation? _____
   _____
   _____
   _____
   _____

3. Besides an excellent knowledge of languages, what other "knowledge" must a good translator of the Bible possess? Why? _____
   _____
   _____
   _____
   _____

4. Why is "humanism" an insecure and comfortless religion? _____
   _____
   _____
   _____
   _____

5. Can you discover any common characteristics found in all false religions? How does true Christianity differ from all false religions? _____
   _____
   _____
   _____
   _____

EXTRA CHALLENGE QUESTION

Part VI. Your Selection from the Marginal Questions

Write out and respond to two marginal questions that interest you which have not been previously asked in the chapter's question section.

1. Question: _____

    _____

    Response: _____

    _____

    _____

    _____

    _____

2. Question: _____

    _____

    Response: _____

    _____

    _____

    _____

    _____

Part VII. Project Ideas

1. Prepare an oral presentation on why we believe the King James Version to be the safest and soundest English Bible version to use.

2. Examine several different modern Bible versions. Write a report or draw a large chart explaining important changes of meaning you found in the same verse in various versions.

3. Write a report on the men who translated the KJV, especially the leaders in this work.

4. Construct a mural on evidences that the Bible is the Word of God. Try to illustrate each point with as many different examples as you can find.

5. After reading some archeological reports or books, share some of the discoveries you read about that confirm the historical accuracy of the Bible.

6. Describe one of the false religions in detail and illustrate some of its religious practices. What "evidences of counterfeiting" did you find?

4

The Trinity
God's Decree
Predestination

As in its course the sun completes
Its ordered daily race,
Likewise predestination sets
Man's final dwelling place.

The doctrine of the Trinity
Mankind cannot perceive;
That God is one and yet is three
In faith we may believe.

His sovereign will He has decreed,
And by His mighty hand,
His counsel shall be carried out
And shall forever stand.

FROM OUR REFORMED DOCTRINAL STANDARDS

Belgic Confession of Faith

Article 8 — That God is one in Essence, yet nevertheless distinguished in three Persons

According to this truth and this Word of God, we believe in one only God, who is the one single essence, in which are three Persons, really, truly, and eternally distinct, according to their incommunicable properties; namely, the Father, and the Son, and the Holy Ghost. The Father is the cause, origin and beginning of all things visible and invisible; the Son is the Word, wisdom, and image of the Father; the Holy Ghost is the eternal power and might, proceeding from the Father and the Son. Nevertheless God is not by this distinction divided into three, since the Holy Scriptures teach us, that the Father, and the Son, and the Holy Ghost, have each His personality, distinguished by their properties; but in such wise that these three Persons are but one only God. Hence then, it is evident, that the Father is not the Son, nor the Son the Father, and likewise the Holy Ghost is neither the Father nor the Son. Nevertheless these Persons thus distinguished are not divided, nor intermixed: for the Father hath not assumed the flesh, nor hath the Holy Ghost, but the Son only. The Father hath never been without His Son, or without His Holy Ghost. For they are all three co-eternal and co-essential. There is neither first nor last: for they are all three One, in truth, in power, in goodness, and in mercy.

Article 9 — The proof of the foregoing article of the Trinity of Persons in one God

All this we know, as well from the testimonies of holy writ, as from their operations, and chiefly by those we feel in ourselves. The testimonies of the Holy Scriptures, that teach us to believe this Holy Trinity are written in many places of the Old Testament, which are not so necessary to enumerate, as to choose them out with discretion and judgment. In Genesis 1:26- 27, God saith: Let Us make man in Our image, after Our likeness, etc. So God created man in His own image, male and female created He them. And Genesis 3:22. Behold, the man is become as one of Us. From this saying, let Us make man in Our image, it appears that there are more Persons than one in the Godhead; and when He saith, God created, He signifies the unity. It is true He doth not say how many Persons there are, but that, which appears to us somewhat obscure in the Old Testament, is very plain in the New. For when our Lord was baptized in Jordan, the voice of the Father was heard, saying: This is My beloved Son: the Son was seen in the water, and the Holy Ghost appeared in the shape of a dove. This form is also instituted by Christ in the baptism of all believers: Baptize all nations, in the name of the Father, and of the Son, and of the Holy Ghost. In the Gospel of Luke the angel Gabriel thus addressed Mary, the mother of our Lord: The Holy Ghost shall come upon thee, and the power of the Highest shall overshadow thee, therefore also that holy thing, which shall be born of thee, shall be called the Son of God: likewise, the grace of our Lord Jesus Christ, and the love of God, and the communion of the Holy Ghost be with you. And there are three that bear record in heaven, the Father, the Word, and the Holy Ghost, and these three are one. In all which places we are fully taught, that there are three Persons in one only divine essence. And although this doctrine far surpasses all human understanding, nevertheless, we now believe it by means of the Word of God, but expect hereafter to enjoy the perfect knowledge and benefit thereof in heaven. Moreover, we must observe the particular offices and operations of these three Persons towards us. The Father is called our Creator, by His power; the Son is our Savior and Redeemer, by His blood; the Holy Ghost is our Sanctifier, by His dwelling in our hearts. This doctrine of the Holy Trinity, that hath always been defended and maintained by the true Church, since the time of the apostles, to this very day, against the Jews, Mohammedans, and some false Christians and heretics, as Marcion, Manes Praxeas, Sabellius, Samosatenus, Arius, and such like, who have been justly condemned by the orthodox fathers. Therefore, in this point, we do willingly receive the three creeds, namely, that of the Apostles, of Nice and of Athanasius: likewise that, which, conformable thereunto, is agreed upon by the ancient fathers.

Article 10 — That Jesus Christ is true and eternal God

We believe that Jesus Christ, according to His divine nature, is the only begotten Son of God, begotten from eternity, not made nor created (for then He should be a creature), but co-essential and co-eternal with the Father, the express image of His Person, and the brightness of His glory, equal unto Him in all things. He is the Son of God, not only from the time that He assumed our nature, but from all eternity, as these testimonies, when compared together, teach us. Moses saith, that God created the world; and John saith, that all things were made by that Word, which he calleth God. And the apostle saith, that God made the worlds by His Son; likewise, that God created all things by Jesus Christ. Therefore it must needs follow, that He, who is called God, the Word, the Son, and Jesus Christ, did exist at that time, when all things were created by Him. Therefore the prophet Micah saith: His goings forth have been from of old, from everlasting. And the apostle: He hath neither beginning of days, nor end of life. He therefore is that true, eternal, and almighty God, whom we invoke, worship and serve.

Article 11 — That the Holy Ghost is true and eternal God

We believe and confess also, that the Holy Ghost, from eternity, proceeds from the Father and Son; and therefore neither is made, created, nor begotten, but only proceedeth from both; who in order is the third person of the Holy Trinity; of one and the same essence, majesty and glory with the Father, and the Son: and therefore, is the true and eternal God, as the Holy Scriptures teach us.

Article 16 — Of Eternal Election

We believe that all the posterity of Adam being thus fallen into perdition and ruin, by the sin of our first parents, God then did manifest Himself, such as He is; that is to say, merciful and just: Merciful, since He delivers and preserves from this perdition all, whom He, in His eternal and unchangeable counsel of mere goodness, hath elected in Christ Jesus our Lord, without any respect to their works: Just, in leaving others in the fall and perdition wherein they have involved themselves.

Heidelberg Catechism

Questions and Answers 24, 25 and 53

Q. 24.   How are these articles divided?

A.   Into three parts; the first is of God the Father, and our creation; the second of God the Son, and our redemption; the third of God the Holy Ghost, and our sanctification.

Q. 25.   Since there is but one only divine essence, why speakest thou of Father, Son, and Holy Ghost?

A.   Because God hath so revealed Himself in His Word, that these three distinct persons are the one only true and eternal God.

Q. 53.   What dost thou believe concerning the Holy Ghost?

A.   First, that He is true and co-eternal God with the Father and the Son; secondly, that He is also given me, to make me by a true faith, partaker of Christ and all His benefits, that He may comfort me and abide with me forever.

Canons of Dordt

FIRST HEAD OF DOCTRINE
OF DIVINE PREDESTINATION

Article 1

As all men have sinned in Adam, lie under the curse, and are deserving of eternal death, God would have done no injustice by leaving them all to perish, and delivering them over to condemnation on account of sin, according to the words of the apostle, Rom. 3:19, "that every mouth may be stopped, and all the world may become guilty before God." And verse 23: "for all have sinned, and come short of the glory of God." And Rom. 6:23: "for the wages of sin is death."

Article 2

But in this the love of God was manifested, that He sent His only begotten Son into the world, that whosoever believeth on Him should not perish, but have everlasting life (I John 4:9; John 3:16).

Article 3

And that men may be brought to believe, God mercifully sends the messengers of these most joyful tidings, to whom He will and at what time He pleaseth; by whose ministry men are called to repentance and faith in Christ crucified. Rom. 10:14-15. "How then shall they call on Him in whom they have not believed? And how shall they believe in Him of whom they have not heard? And how shall they hear without a preacher? And how shall they preach except they be sent?"

Article 4

The wrath of God abideth upon those who believe not this gospel. But such as receive it, and embrace Jesus the Savior by a true and living faith, are by Him delivered from the wrath of God, and from destruction, and have the gift of eternal life conferred upon them.

Article 5

The cause or guilt of this unbelief as well as of all other sins, is no wise in God, but in man himself; whereas faith in Jesus Christ, and salvation through Him is the free gift of God, as it is written: "By grace ye are saved through faith, and that not of yourselves, it is the gift of God." Eph. 2:8. "and unto you it is given in the behalf of Christ, not only to believe on Him," etc. (Phil. 1:29).

Article 6

That some receive the gift of faith from God, and others do not receive it proceeds from God's eternal decree, "For known unto God are all His works from the beginning of the world," Acts 15:18. "Who worketh all things after the counsel of His will" (Eph. 1:11). According to which decree, He graciously softens the hearts of the elect, however obstinate, and inclines them to believe, while He leaves the non-elect in His just judgment to their own wickedness and obduracy. And herein is especially displayed the profound, the merciful, and at the same time the righteous discrimination between men, equally involved in ruin; or that decree of election and reprobation, revealed in the Word of God, which though men of perverse, impure and unstable minds wrest to their own destruction, yet to holy and pious souls affords unspeakable consolation.

Article 7

Election is the unchangeable purpose of God, whereby, before the foundation of the world, He hath out of mere grace, according to the sovereign good pleasure of His own will, chosen, from the whole human race, which had fallen through their own fault, from their primitive state of rectitude, into sin and destruction, a certain number of persons to redemption in Christ, whom He from eternity appointed the Mediator and Head of the elect, and the foundation of salvation.

This elect number, though by nature neither better nor more deserving than others, but with them involved in one common misery, God hath decreed to give to Christ, to be saved by Him, and effectually to call and draw them to His communion by His Word and Spirit, to bestow upon them true faith, justification and sanctification; and having powerfully preserved them in the fellowship of His Son, finally, to glorify them for the demonstration of His mercy, and for the praise of His glorious grace; as it is written: "According as He hath chosen us in Him, before the foundation of the world, that we should be holy, and without blame before Him in love; having predestinated us unto the adoption of children by Jesus Christ to Himself, according to the good pleasure of His will, to the praise of the glory of His grace, wherein He hath made us accepted in the beloved" (Eph. 1:4-6). And elsewhere: "Whom He did predestinate, them He also called, and whom He called, them He also justified, and whom He justified, them He also glorified" (Rom. 8:30).

elected, while others are passed by in the eternal decree; whom God, out of His sovereign, most just, irreprehensible and unchangeable good pleasure, hath decreed to leave in the common misery into which they have wilfully plunged themselves, and not to bestow upon them saving faith and the grace of conversion; but permitting them in His just judgment to follow their own ways, at last for the declaration of His justice, to condemn and perish them forever, not only on account of their unbelief, but also for all their other sins. And this is the decree of reprobation which by no means makes God the author of sin (the very thought of which is blasphemy), but declares Him to be an awful, irreprehensible, and righteous judge and avenger thereof.

Article 8

There are not various decrees of election, but one and the same decree respecting all those, who shall be saved, both under the Old and New Testament: since the Scripture declares the good pleasure, purpose and counsel of the divine will to be one, according to which He hath chosen us from eternity, both to grace and glory, to salvation and the way of salvation, which He hath ordained that we should walk therein.

Article 9

This election was not founded upon foreseen faith, and the obedience of faith, holiness, or any other good quality or disposition in man, as the pre-requisite, cause or condition on which it depended; but men are chosen to faith and to the obedience of faith, holiness, etc., therefore election is the fountain of every saving good; from which proceed faith, holiness, and the other gifts of salvation, and finally eternal life itself, as its fruits and effects, according to that of the apostle: "He hath chosen us (not because we were) but that we should be holy, and without blame, before Him in love" (Eph. 1:4).

Article 10

The good pleasure of God is the sole cause of this gracious election; which doth not consist herein, that out of all possible qualities and actions of men God has chosen some as a condition of salvation; but that He was pleased out of the common mass of sinners to adopt some certain persons as a peculiar people to Himself, as it is written, "For the children being not yet born neither having done any good or evil," etc., it was said (namely to Rebecca): "the elder shall serve the younger; as it is written, Jacob have I loved, but Esau have I hated" (Rom. 9:11-13). "And as many as were ordained to eternal life believed" (Acts 13:48).

Article 15

What peculiarly tends to illustrate and recommend to us the eternal and unmerited grace of election, is the express testimony of sacred Scripture, that not all, but some only are

Article 16

Those who do not yet experience a lively faith in Christ, an assured confidence of soul, peace of conscience, an earnest endeavor after filial obedience, and glorying in God through Christ, efficaciously wrought in them, and do nevertheless persist in the use of the means which God hath appointed for working these graces in us, ought not to be alarmed at the mention of reprobation, nor to rank themselves among the reprobate, but diligently to persevere in the use of means, and with ardent desires, devoutly and humbly wait for a season of richer grace. Much less cause have they to be terrified by the doctrine of reprobation, who, though they seriously desire to be turned to God, to please Him only, and to be delivered from the body of death, cannot yet reach that measure of holiness and faith to which they aspire; since a merciful God has promised that He will not quench the smoking flax, nor break the bruised reed. But this doctrine is justly terrible to those, who regardless of God and of the Savior Jesus Christ, have wholly given themselves up to the cares of the world, and the pleasures of the flesh, so long as they are not seriously converted to God.

Article 18

To those who murmur at the free grace of election, and just severity of reprobation, we answer with the apostle; "Nay, but O man, who art thou that repliest against God?" (Rom. 9:30), and quote the language of our Savior: "Is it not lawful for Me to do what I will with Mine own?" (Matt. 20:15). And therefore with holy adoration of these mysteries, we exclaim in the words of the apostle: "O the depth of the riches both of the wisdom and knowledge of God! how unsearchable are His judgments, and His ways past finding out! For who hath known the mind of the Lord, or who hath been His counsellor? or who hath first given to Him, and it shall be recompensed unto him again? For of Him, and through Him, and to Him are all things: to whom be glory for ever. Amen."

(For the unprinted articles, see the First Head of Doctrine: Of Divine Predestination)

4

THE TRINITY

We know from God's general revelation (His creation and our consciences) that there is a god; but only through God's special revelation (His infallible Word) do we learn who God is. Only the Bible reveals the truth of the **Trinity**.

The word "trinity" is an abbreviation for the word "tri-unity." "Tri" means "three" and "unity" refers to "oneness." "Trinity," therefore, means "three-in-one."

Scripture reveals that there is one God and that God is **indivisible**. Yet in this one God there are three distinct Persons:

1. God the Father
2. God the Son
3. God the Holy Spirit (Holy Ghost)

In God there is one eternal Being. There is one intelligence and one will; and yet the three divine Persons exercise this one intelligence and will. The three divine Persons are distinct from, and communicate with, one another. The divine Being is not divided among the three Persons, but is fully, with all its perfections, in each of the Persons. Yet, there are not three Gods, but one — one eternal, divine Being. There are three divine Persons in one Godhead — three in one.

● **Trinity** — The three distinct divine Persons in one divine Being; three Persons in one Godhead; one God revealed in three Persons

● **Indivisible** — Cannot be divided or separated

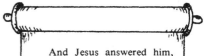

And Jesus answered him, The first of all the commandments is, Hear O Israel; the Lord our God is one Lord.
— Mark 12:29

For there are three that bear record in heaven, the Father, the Word, and the Holy Ghost: and these three are one.
— I John 5:7

The grace of the Lord Jesus Christ, and the love of God, and the communion of the Holy Ghost, be with you all. Amen.
— II Corinthians 13:14

- **Essential** — Core, central, basic; pertaining to the particular nature of a person or thing

- **Comprehend** — To understand; to grasp with one's mind

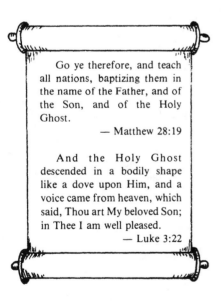

The truth of something may be so clearly revealed that we believe it to be true, although we cannot fully understand the matter itself. Some examples of this would be electricity, gravity, fear, and love. Can you add others to this list? How does this relate to believing in the truth of the Trinity?

> Go ye therefore, and teach all nations, baptizing them in the name of the Father, and of the Son, and of the Holy Ghost.
> — Matthew 28:19
>
> And the Holy Ghost descended in a bodily shape like a dove upon Him, and a voice came from heaven, which said, Thou art My beloved Son; in Thee I am well pleased.
> — Luke 3:22

Why is it more "understandable" to have a God that we cannot fully understand, than to believe in a god that can be completely comprehended by the human mind?

This teaching of the Bible is a mystery to us. How these three divine Persons are distinct and yet in one **essential** Being remains a truth which we cannot fully understand nor explain. As human beings, we cannot fully **comprehend** God's Being.

While we cannot fully understand this mystery, we are called to believe it, for God has revealed this truth in His infallible Word.

The following examples help to illustrate our incapability of fully understanding the Trinity:

One Sunday a minister announced to his congregation that he would explain the Trinity the following Sunday.

As he was walking home later that week, he stopped in surprise. Kneeling by a river, which the minister usually crossed on his way home, was one of his elders. As the minister observed, the man kept scooping water from the river with a spoon, and dumping it into a small hole nearby.

The minister approached him and asked, "What are you doing?"

"Emptying the river with a spoon," he answered.

"You can never do that."

"I can succeed in emptying this river as well as you will succeed in being able to explain the Trinity next Sunday, Reverend," the elder replied.

What true comparison was the elder making, and in what important truth was he instructing his minister?

Six-year-old Tommy once asked, "Mother, where did God come from?"

His mother took off her wedding ring, handed it to him, and asked, "Where does this ring begin and where does it end?"

After examining the ring carefully, Tommy answered, "There is no starting or stopping place on the ring."

Then his mother said, "That is the same for God. There is no beginning nor ending to God. He always has been and always will be!"

How can this story be used to illustrate certain truths about God which we cannot fully understand?

? Is the Trinity the only aspect of God that we cannot fully understand, but by grace can learn to know and adore? Can you name others? Are there any attributes of God which we can fully understand?

Alice's father watched her plant her last row of corn. When she finished, he asked her, "Do you believe that corn plants will actually grow from the kernels you planted?"

"Of course!" she answered somewhat surprised.

"Explain to me, then, how those little kernels you buried in the ground will develop into full-grown corn plants."

"I don't know; I can't explain it," Alice replied, puzzled by her father's questions.

"That's ridiculous! How can you believe in something you can't explain?"·

"I can't explain it, but I know I'm right," Alice responded, "and if you don't believe it — you wait and see! Corn plants will be here!"

Her father laughed. "I like your answer, Alice. I questioned you in this way in order to teach you an important lesson. Some people laugh at us for believing in a God whom we cannot fully understand. When you hear this kind of reasoning, just remember your corn. We believe, and have faith in, many things which we cannot fully understand."

How does this story illustrate an important truth concerning the Trinity?

God revealed His Triune Being in an ever-clearer manner throughout His Word. We may find the revelation of the Trinity already in the first chapter of the Bible. Increasingly throughout the Old Testament, but especially in the New Testament after God the Son lived upon earth and the Holy Spirit was poured out, God clearly revealed His Triune Being.

? How did God reveal in the first chapter of the Bible that He is both singular and plural (see Genesis 1:26)?

In the Old Testament, the doctrine of the Trinity was revealed in:

● **Plural** — More than one

● **Singular** — One

1. Texts in which God spoke of Himself as both **plural** and **singular**

> And God said, Let Us make man in Our image, after Our likeness: and let them have dominion over the fish of the sea, and over the fowl of the air, and over the cattle, and over all the earth, and over every creeping thing that creepeth upon the earth.
> — Genesis 1:26

> And the LORD God said, Behold, the man is become as one of Us, to know good and evil: and now, lest he put forth his hand, and take also of the tree of life, and eat, and live for ever.
> — Genesis 3:22

2. Texts in which God and God, and Lord and Lord are distinguished from each other

? Who did David mean by "The LORD" and by "my Lord" in Psalm 110?

> Thy throne, O God, is for ever and ever: the sceptre of Thy kingdom is a right sceptre.
> Thou lovest righteousness, and hatest wickedness: therefore God, Thy God, hath anointed Thee with the oil of gladness above Thy fellows.
> — Psalm 45:6-7

> The LORD said unto my Lord, Sit thou at My right hand until I make Thine enemies Thy footstool.
> — Psalm 110:1

● **Expressly** — Clearly; plainly; directly

3. Texts in which the three Persons are **expressly** mentioned

? In Psalm 33:6, who is referred to as:
— The Word?
— The LORD?
— The Breath?

Were God the Son and God the Holy Spirit also active in creating the heavens and earth? How can you prove your answer from Scripture?

> By the Word of the LORD were the heavens made; and all the host of them by the Breath of His mouth.
> — Psalm 33:6

> Come ye near unto me, hear ye this; I have not spoken in secret from the beginning; from the time that it was, there am I: and now the Lord GOD, and His Spirit, hath sent me.
> — Isaiah 48:16

In the New Testament, the Trinity is revealed more directly in numerous references.

THE TRINITY IN THE NEW TESTAMENT

For there are three that bear record in heaven, the Father, the Word, and the Holy Ghost: and these three are One.
— I John 5:7

Go ye therefore, and teach all nations, baptizing them in the name of the Father, and of the Son, and of the Holy Ghost.
— Matthew 28:19

The grace of the Lord Jesus Christ, and the love of God, and the communion of the Holy Ghost, be with you all. Amen.
— II Corinthians 13:14

Elect according to the foreknowledge of God the Father, through sanctification of the Spirit, unto obedience and sprinkling of the blood of Jesus Christ: Grace unto you, and peace, be multiplied.
— I Peter 1:2

And the Holy Ghost descended in a bodily shape like a dove upon Him, and a voice came from heaven, which said, Thou art My beloved Son: in Thee I am well pleased.
— Luke 3:22

But when the Comforter is come, whom I will send unto you from the Father, even the Spirit of truth, which proceedeth from the Father, He shall testify of Me.
— John 15:26

Now He which stablisheth us with you in Christ, and hath appointed us, is God;
Who hath also sealed us, and given the earnest of the Spirit in our hearts.
— II Corinthians 1:21-22

For Christ also hath once suffered for sins, the Just for the unjust, that He might bring us to God, being put to death in the flesh, but quickened by the Spirit.
— I Peter 3:18

? Why does the Bible speak more clearly of God the Son after His birth in Bethlehem and of God the Holy Spirit after His outpouring on Pentecost? Why are they spoken of more by prophecies and pictures (types) in the Old Testament?

● **Universal** — Including and involving all; worldwide

● **Creeds** — Official statements and confessions of belief

Each of the three **universal creeds** (the *Apostles', Nicene,* and *Athanasian*) that are confessed by all Christian churches in the world, speak clearly of the Trinity. Read each one carefully, especially noting its teaching regarding the Trinity.

THE TRINITY IN THE APOSTLES' CREED

1. I believe in God the Father Almighty, Maker of heaven and earth.
2. And in Jesus Christ, His only begotten Son, our Lord;
3. Who was conceived by the Holy Spirit, born of the Virgin Mary;
4. Suffered under Pontius Pilate; was crucified, dead, and buried; He descended into hell;
5. The third day he rose again from the dead;
6. He ascended into heaven, and sitteth at the right hand of God the Father Almighty.
7. From thence He shall come to judge the quick and the dead;
8. I believe in the Holy Ghost.
9. I believe an holy **catholic** Church; the communion of saints;
10. The forgiveness of sins;
11. The resurrection of the body;
12. And the life everlasting. Amen.

? State which articles in the *Apostles' Creed* speak about the Person and work of:
— God the Father
— God the Son
— God the Holy Ghost

● **Catholic** — General; universal; worldwide

? How are the divinity of God the Son and God the Holy Spirit more clearly mentioned in the *Nicene* than in the *Apostles' Creed?*

● **Incarnate** — Christ taking on our human nature in his being conceived by the Holy Ghost and born of the Virgin Mary

? State which articles in the *Nicene Creed* speak about the personal work of:
— God the Father
— God the Son
— God the Holy Spirit

? Find the expressions used in the *Athanasian Creed* to teach that:
— God is One in Being
— God is Three in Persons
— Each Person is distinct
— No one Person excells another in greatness or importance

● **Verity** — Truth; fact; reality

? What type of "believing" is meant in the closing statement of this creed?

THE TRINITY IN THE NICENE CREED

I believe in one God, the Father Almighty, Maker of heaven and earth, and of all things visible and invisible.

And in one Lord Jesus Christ, the only-begotten Son of God, begotten of the Father before all worlds; God of God, Light of Light, very God of very God; begotten, not made, being of one substance with the Father by whom all things were made.

Who, for us men for our salvation, came down from heaven, and was **incarnate** by the Holy Spirit of the virgin Mary, and was made man; and was crucified also for us under Pontius Pilate; He suffered and was buried; and the third day He rose again, according to the Scriptures; and ascended into heaven, and sitteth on the right hand of the Father; and He shall come again, with glory to judge the quick and the dead; whose kingdom shall have no end.

And I believe in the Holy Ghost, the Lord and Giver of life; who proceedeth from the Father and the Son; who with the Father and the Son together is worshipped and glorified; who spake by the prophets.

And I believe one holy catholic and apostolic Church. I acknowledge one baptism for the remission of sins; and I look for the resurrection of the dead, and the life of the world to come. Amen.

THE TRINITY IN THE ATHANASIAN CREED
(Articles 1 - 28)

1. Whosoever will be saved, before all things it is necessary that he hold the catholic faith; 2. Which faith except every one do keep whole and undefiled, without doubt he shall perish everlastingly. 3. And the catholic faith is this: That we worship one God in Trinity, and Trinity in Unity; 4. Neither confounding the Persons, nor dividing the substance. 5. For there is one Person of the Father, another of the Son, and another of the Holy Spirit. 6. But the Godhead of the Father, of the Son, and of the Holy Spirit is all one, the glory equal, the majesty co-eternal. 7. Such as the Father is, such is the Son, and such is the Holy Spirit. 8. The Father uncreate, the Son uncreate, and the Holy Spirit uncreate. 9. The Father incomprehensible, the Son incomprehensible, and the Holy Spirit incomprehensible. 10. The Father eternal, the Son eternal, and the Holy Spirit eternal. 11. And yet they are not three eternal, but one eternal. 12. As also there are not three uncreated nor three incomprehensibles, but one uncreated and one incomprehensible. 13. So likewise the Father is almighty, the Son almighty, and the Holy Spirit almighty. 14. And yet they are not three almighties, but one almighty. 15. So the Father is God, the Son is God, and the Holy Spirit is God; 16. And yet they are not three Gods, but one God. 17. So likewise the Father is Lord, the Son is Lord, and the Holy Spirit Lord; 18. And yet they are not three Lords, but one Lord. 19. For like as we are compelled by the Christian **verity** to acknowledge every Person by Himself to be God and Lord; 20. So are we forbidden by the catholic religion to say; There are three Gods or three Lords. 21. The Father is made of none, neither created nor begotten. 22. The Son is of the Father alone; not made nor created, but begotten. 23. The Holy Spirit is of the Father and of the Son; neither made, nor created, nor begotten, but proceeding. 24. So there is one Father, not three Fathers; one Son, not three Sons; one Holy Spirit, not three Holy Spirits. 25. And in this Trinity none is afore, or after another; none is greater or less than another. 26. But the whole three persons are co-eternal, and co-equal. 27. So that in all things, as aforesaid, the Unity in Trinity and the Trinity in Unity is to be worshipped. 28. He therefore that will be saved must thus think of the Trinity...

While God is one in Being, each divine Person is distinct. Each is distinct in His personal properties and work.

The personal properties of the divine Persons are shown in the following chart.

PERSONAL PROPERTIES OF THE DIVINE PERSONS		
God the Father	*Exists* of Himself.	For as the Father hath life in Himself; so hath He given to the Son to have life in Himself. — John 5:26
God the Son	Is eternally *begotten* of the Father.	No man hath seen God at any time; the only begotten Son, which is in the bosom of the Father, He hath declared Him. — John 1:18
God the Holy Spirit	*Proceeds* forth from the Father and the Son.	But when the Comforter is come, whom I will send unto you from the Father, even the Spirit of truth, which proceedeth from the Father, He shall testify of Me. — John 15:26

? In the Triune God, how does His church have a God that is above, with, and in them?

? Is Jesus' divine or human nature *eternally* begotten of the Father? Did Jesus always have His human nature? When did He receive it?

These properties are called personal properties or attributes because they belong to one divine Person in particular and not to the whole Being of God.

The Bible also attributes different works to each of the three divine Persons. This does not mean that each work mentioned will be done **exclusively**, but rather **primarily**. The primary emphasis in each work is on one of the three divine Persons.

• **Exclusively** — Only; solely; by one only — all others being excluded

• **Primarily** — Mainly; principally; chiefly

The following charts display the works that are primarily the works of God the Father, God the Son, and God the Holy Spirit:

GOD THE FATHER

1. Planning the way of salvation for lost sinners	But when the fulness of time was come, God sent forth His Son, made of a woman, made under the law. To redeem them that were under the law, that we might receive the adoption of sons. And because ye are sons, God hath sent forth the Spirit of His Son into your hearts, crying, Abba, Father. — Galatians 4:4-6
2. Electing sinners to salvation	Elect according to the foreknowledge of God the Father, through sanctification of the Spirit unto obedience and sprinkling of the blood of Jesus Christ: Grace unto you, and peace, be multiplied. — I Peter 1:2
3. Creating all things	But to us there is but one God, the Father, of whom are all things, and we in Him. — I Corinthians 8:6a
4. Providing for all things	Behold the fowls of the air: for they sow not, neither do they reap, nor gather into barns; yet your heavenly Father feedeth them. Are ye not much better than they? — Matthew 6:26
5. Maintaining divine justice toward sinners	My little children, these things write I unto you that ye sin not. And if any man sin, we have an advocate with the Father, Jesus Christ the righteous. — I John 2:1

GOD THE SON

1. Purchasing salvation through His human birth, suffering, and death	Neither by the blood of goats and calves, but by His own blood He entered in once into the holy place, having obtained eternal redemption for us. — Hebrews 9:12
2. Pleading for His children as their advocate, upon His own merits	Who is he that condemneth? It is Christ that died, yea rather, that is risen again, who is even at the right hand of God, who also maketh intercession for us. — Romans 8:34
3. Being the Word through whom the Father created all things and will judge all creatures	For we must all appear before the judgment seat of Christ; that every one may receive the things done in his body, according to that he hath done, whether it be good or bad. — II Corinthians 5:10

? What would have happened to the entire human race if God the Father had not planned the way of, and elected sinners to, salvation?

? What would have happened to the entire human race if God the Son had not purchased salvation through His suffering and death?

GOD THE HOLY SPIRIT	
1. Applying Christ's benefits of regeneration, justification, sanctification, and glorification to the elect	Not by works of righteousness which we have done, but according to His mercy He saved us, by the washing of regeneration, and renewing of the Holy Ghost. — Titus 3:5
2. Dwelling in the hearts of all true believers	Know ye not that ye are the temple of God, and that the Spirit of God dwelleth in you? — I Corinthians 3:16
3. Giving life; both spiritually and naturally	And the earth was without form, and void; and darkness was upon the face of the deep. And the Spirit of God moved upon the face of the waters. — Genesis 1:2
4. Calling and equipping men for special service	As they ministered to the Lord, and fasted, the Holy Ghost said, Separate Me Barnabas and Saul for the work whereunto I have called them. — Acts 13:2
5. Gathering and leading the church	In whom ye also are builded together for an habitation of God through the Spirit. — Ephesians 2:22
6. Inspiring the writing of the Scriptures	For the prophecy came not in old time by the will of man; but holy men of God spake as they were moved by the Holy Ghost. — II Peter 1:21
7. Preparing the human nature of Christ	And the angel answered and said unto her, The Holy Ghost shall come upon thee, and the power of the Highest shall overshadow thee: therefore also that holy thing which shall be born of thee shall be called the Son of God. — Luke 1:35

? What would happen to the entire human race if God the Holy Spirit did not apply salvation to the hearts of elected sinners?

The primary work of each divine Person in the salvation of sinners is often remembered through the following three rhyming words:

1. *Thought* by God the Father in heaven.

2. *Bought* by God the Son on earth.

3. *Wrought* (worked) by God the Holy Spirit in the hearts of the saved.

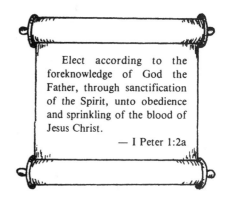

Elect according to the foreknowledge of God the Father, through sanctification of the Spirit, unto obedience and sprinkling of the blood of Jesus Christ.
— I Peter 1:2a

We know from the Bible that God the Son and God the Holy Spirit are actual, divine Persons because Scripture gives to both the following four characteristics:

1. Divine names
2. Divine attributes
3. Divine works
4. Divine honors

Example texts from these four headings regarding God the Son are given in Chapter Ten when dealing with the divine and human natures of Christ.

The following chart provides scriptural proof that the Holy Spirit is a divine Person by **ascribing** divine names, attributes, works, and honors to Him.

? How do the texts listed here regarding the Holy Spirit and those in Chapter Ten regarding Jesus Christ, teach that the doctrine of the Trinity is a core truth of Scripture?

- **Ascribing** — Assigning; giving; crediting; attributing

- **Omnipresence** — Everywhere-present; being in all places at all times

- **Omniscience** — All-knowing; having a perfect knowledge of all things

---

THE HOLY SPIRIT IS A DIVINE PERSON
for the Bible ascribes to Him:

1. DIVINE NAMES — Names that can only be given to God

Know ye not that ye are the temple of God, and that the *Spirit of God* dwelleth in you? — I Corinthians 3:16	But Peter said, Ananias, why hath Satan filled thine heart to lie to the Holy Ghost... thou hast not lied unto men, but unto *God.* — Acts 5:3-4

2. DIVINE ATTRIBUTES — Attributes of God alone

a. **Omnipresence**	Whither shall I go from Thy Spirit? or whither shall I flee from Thy presence? If I ascend up into heaven, Thou art there: if I make my bed in hell, behold, Thou art there. — Psalm 139:7-8
b. **Omniscience**	But God hath revealed them unto us by His Spirit: for the Spirit searcheth all things, yea, the deep things of God. For what man knoweth the things of a man, save the spirit of man which is in him? even so, the things of God knoweth no man, but the Spirit of God. — I Corinthians 2:10-11

c. **Omnipotence**	And the angel answered and said unto her, The Holy Ghost shall come upon thee, and the power of the Highest shall overshadow thee. — Luke 1:35a
d. **Sovereignty**	But all these worketh that one and the self-same Spirit, dividing to every man severally as He will. — I Corinthians 12:11
e. **Eternity**	How much more shall the blood of Christ, who through the eternal Spirit offered Himself without spot to God, purge your conscience from dead works to serve the living God? — Hebrews 9:14

- **Omnipotence** — All-powerful; having unlimited power; almighty

- **Sovereignty** — Supreme authority; having perfect self-determination and ruling authority

- **Eternity** — Everlasting; being without beginning or ending

3. DIVINE WORKS — Works that only God can do

a. Creation	The Spirit of God hath made me, and the Breath of the Almighty hath given me life. — Job 33:4
b. Regeneration	Not by works of righteousness which we have done, but according to His mercy He saved us, by the washing of regeneration, and renewing of the Holy Ghost. — Titus 3:5
c. Inspiration of the Scriptures	For the prophecy came not in old time by the will of man: but holy men of God spake as they were moved by the Holy Ghost. — II Peter 1:21
d. Working of miracles	But if I cast out devils by the Spirit of God, then the kingdom of God is come unto you. — Matthew 12:28
e. Providence	Thou sendest forth Thy Spirit, they are created: and Thou renewest the face of the earth. — Psalm 104:30
f. Resurrection	But if the Spirit of Him that raised up Jesus from the dead dwell in you, He that raised up Christ from the dead shall also quicken your mortal bodies by His Spirit that dwelleth in you. — Romans 8:11

? If God the Son or God the Holy Spirit were not God, why would the salvation of a sinner be impossible?

4. DIVINE HONORS — Honors that can only be given to God	
a. Go ye therefore, and teach all nations, baptizing them in the name of the Father, and of the Son, and of the Holy Ghost. — Matthew 28:19	b. The grace of the Lord Jesus Christ, and the love of God, and the communion of the Holy Ghost, be with you all. Amen. — II Corinthians 13:14
c. Wherefore I say unto you, All manner of sin and blasphemy shall be forgiven unto men: but the blasphemy against the Holy Ghost shall not be forgiven unto men. — Matthew 12:31	d. For there are three that bear record in heaven, the Father, the Word, and the Holy Ghost: and these three are one. — I John 5:7

? Can you name some religious groups which deny the truths of the Trinity and the personhood of God the Holy Spirit?

Some who deny the scriptural truth of the Holy Trinity claim that the Holy Spirit is only a power or an influence which flows forth from God. The Bible, however, speaks of the Holy Spirit as a divine *Person* in the following five ways:

1. God the Holy Spirit is spoken of as a *Comforter*, not a comfort (John 14:26, 15:26, 16:17).

2. The *characteristics of a person* are given to God the Holy Spirit:
   a. Intelligence (John 14:26, Romans 3:16).
   b. Will (Acts 16:7, I Corinthians 12:11).
   c. Affections (Isaiah 63:10, Ephesians 4:30).

? Do you know the difference between a church and a cult? Churches believe in the Trinity and cults do not. Can you name some cults in your area?

3. God the Holy Spirit *performs the actions of a person*:
   a. Creates (Genesis 1:2).
   b. Strives (Genesis 6:3).
   c. Teaches (Luke 12:12).
   d. Testifies (John 15:26).
   e. Reproves (John 16:8).
   f. Commands (Acts 13:2).
   g. Resurrects (Romans 8:11).
   h. Searches (I Corinthians 2:10-11).

? What should we do to possibly help deniers of the Trinity in our society? Would having photocopies of these pages at home be of help, if some came to your door?

4. God the Holy Spirit *stands in relation to others as His own person* (Acts 15:28, Matthew 28:19, I Peter 1:1-2, John 16:14, II Corinthians 13:14, Jude: 20-21).

5. God the Holy Spirit is *distinguished as a person from His own power* (Luke 1:35, Acts 10:38, I Corinthians 2:4, Luke 4:14, Romans 15:13).

It is necessary for each of you to know the Triune God, not only mentally as you study this biblical doctrine, but also spiritually in your personal life's experience.

The difference between mental and **experiential knowledge** is illustrated in the following example:

Sandy served many years as a registered nurse in the recovery room of a hospital. She had extensively studied the human nervous system and knew much about pain.

Hundreds of times she told her patients, who were recovering from operations, "Do not worry. Don't let the pain bother you. Pain is only a sign that the anesthetic is leaving your body. Pain is only a message to your brain that your body is beginning the healing process. You should not ask for painkillers. Learn to cope with your pain. Breathe in deeply when your worst pains begin."

After being a nurse for many years, Sandy had to undergo an operation. In the recovery room, for the first time in her life, she experienced the pains she mentally "knew" about. Experiencing pain was certainly different from reading, studying, and talking about it!

How can this story serve as an example to us when we speak about "knowing" God? How must we "know" Him? Why is an experiential knowledge of God necessary in our lives?

? How would only the mental knowledge of sin and pain be different from the experiential knowledge of them?

? Why must a person experience: His lost condition before he cries out to be found? His sickness before he needs a physician? His misery before seeking deliverance? His sins before needing the Savior?

A saving knowledge of God is possible through the gracious work of the Holy Spirit. When God the Holy Spirit begins His saving work in a sinner's heart, He starts by revealing and convicting him of his sin.

And the commandment, which was ordained to life, I found to be unto death.

For sin, taking occasion by the commandment, deceived me, and by it slew me.

Wherefore the law is holy, and the commandment holy, and just, and good.

Was then that which is good made death unto me? God forbid. But sin, that it might appear sin, working death in me by that which is good; that sin by the commandment might become exceeding sinful.

— Romans 7:10-13

For the good that I would I do not: but the evil which I would not, that I do.

— Romans 7:19

For I delight in the law of God after the inward man:

But I see another law in my members, warring against the law of my mind, and bringing me into captivity to the law of sin which is in my members.

O wretched man that I am! Who shall deliver me from the body of this death?

I thank God through Jesus Christ our Lord.

— Romans 7:22-25a

For as many as are led by the Spirit of God, they are the sons of God.

For ye have not received the spirit of bondage again to fear; but ye have received the Spirit of adoption, whereby we cry, Abba, Father.

The Spirit itself beareth witness with our spirit, that we are the children of God:

And if children, then heirs: heirs of God, and joint-heirs with Christ; if so be that we suffer with him, that we may be also glorified together.

— Romans 8:14-17

As this person painfully realizes his many actual sins, the Holy Spirit deepens his awareness of his original sin — that his heart, motives, and desires are all sinful. The Spirit also reveals something of God's holiness, righteousness, and longsuffering goodness to him.

This two-fold revelation — who God is and who he is — causes the convicted person to diligently strive to improve his life. The more he tries to better himself, however, the more he experiences his failures, sins, and totally depraved heart. He sees God as a righteous Judge that cannot but justly condemn such a great sinner as he is.

When all hope of salvation through his own efforts to fulfill God's law is cut off, and his just condemnation is all that he can rightly expect; the Holy Spirit reveals a way of escape, a way of salvation through another — through a perfect substitute, the Lord Jesus Christ. How this convicted person, whose heart yearns for the God he has offended, longs for, needs, and pleads with the Savior! Jesus has such a richness, fullness, and righteousness for his poorness, emptiness, and sinfulness! As the Holy Spirit reveals more of Christ to him, his heart is won over in love and thankfulness to God for saving such a great sinner through such a great salvation! In this way, sinners are restored into God's favor and fellowship.

Through the saving work of Jesus Christ, the Holy Spirit leads the saved sinner back to God the Father, not seeing Him now as a punishing Judge, but as a reconciled and loving God — a Father whose love for His children knows no bounds.

Experiencing such an eternal and infinite love, his heart will desire to know, love, and serve God more and more. His deepest desire will be to obey and honor God in all things. To do this he will increasingly learn that he needs the continual, gracious, indwelling workings of the Holy Spirit, for in his old nature he remains a poor sinner.

This is the experiential knowledge of the saving work of the Triune God for which we should strive. The more we may experience of God, the more we will be able to love and rejoice in God the Father who thought, God the Son who bought, and God the Holy Spirit who wrought, a complete salvation for totally lost sinners as we are.

Do you know something experientially of yourself, and your sinfulness? Do you know something experientially of God: of Father, Son and Holy Spirit?

The following examples help to illustrate the experiential knowledge of self and God through a way of misery, deliverance, and thankfulness:

Barabbas was a criminal who had committed murder while participating in a rebellion (Mark 15:7,27). His crimes made him guilty under the Jewish, Roman, and divine laws. This triple criminal was caught and condemned. He was now only waiting for the execution of his sentence. Under the governing Romans, as a notable criminal, he would be put to death by crucifixion.

Both his being pronounced guilty by the judge and his upcoming punishment became true in his life's experience.

However, as Barabbas sat in prison, experiencing his misery, the Jews forced Pontius Pilate to crucify Jesus Christ. The sentencing of the innocent Jesus to crucifixion spoke the guilty Barabbas free. A message of deliverance was brought to Barabbas through the death of Jesus Christ. Can you imagine how Barabbas felt as he experienced this truth?

How does Barabbas picture us, as we are by nature? Before needing and experiencing deliverance, what must we learn? Why? How does this story relate to the experiential way in which a sinner comes to know the saving work of a Triune God?

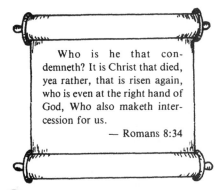

Who is he that condemneth? It is Christ that died, yea rather, that is risen again, who is even at the right hand of God, Who also maketh intercession for us.
— Romans 8:34

? How are misery, deliverance, and thankfulness pictured in the following scriptural references?

Psalm 40:2-3
He brought me up also out of an horrible pit, out of the miry clay, and set my feet upon a rock, and established my goings.

And He hath put a new song in my mouth, even praise unto our God: many shall see it, and fear, and shall trust in the LORD.

Psalm 50:15
And call upon Me in the day of trouble: I will deliver thee, and thou shalt glorify Me.

Mark 10:49-52
And Jesus stood still, and commanded him to be called. And they called the blind man, saying unto him, Be of good comfort, rise; He calleth thee.

And he, casting away his garment, rose, and came to Jesus.

And Jesus answered and said unto him, What wilt thou that I should do unto thee? The blind man said unto Him, Lord, that I might receive my sight.

And Jesus said unto him, Go thy way; thy faith hath made thee whole. And immediately he received his sight, and followed Jesus in the way.

? Can you mention other scriptural examples of the misery-deliverance-thankfulness cycle?

The *Form for the Administration of the Lord's Supper* states that true participants at the Lord's table need to know something experientially of the following three items:

? Some people believe that experiential knowledge of God is not necessary, but that only mental knowledge is sufficient. Why is this view both wrong and deceiving?

? Mental knowledge of God and His truth is good and necessary. Experiential knowledge does not contradict mental knowledge, but it is different from it. How is it different? Which is saving? Why?

? The Lord is free to deliver one sinner sooner than another. God knows what is best for each of his children. Do all persons who are saved experience misery, deliverance and thankfulness in the same depth or length of time? Can you name some scriptural examples of people experiencing salvation in Christ very rapidly or more gradually, and dramatically or more calmly?

Concerning true experiential knowledge of God, what must we carefully teach on one side, and not teach on the other?

First. That every one consider by himself, his sins and the curse due to him for them, to the end that he may abhor and humble himself before God: considering that the wrath of God against sin is so great, that (rather than it should go unpunished) He hath punished the same in His beloved Son Jesus Christ, with the bitter and shameful death of the cross.

Secondly. That every one examine his own heart, whether he doth believe this faithful promise of God, that all his sins are forgiven him only for the sake of the passion and death of Jesus Christ, and that the perfect righteousness of Christ is imputed and freely given him as his own, yea, so perfectly, as if he had satisfied in his own person for all his sins, and fulfilled all righteousness.

Thirdly. That every one examine his own conscience, whether he purposeth henceforth to show true thankfulness to God in his whole life, and to walk uprightly before Him; as also, whether he hath laid aside unfeignedly all enmity, hatred, and envy, and doth firmly resolve henceforward to walk in true love and peace with his neighbor.

How can the experiential knowledge of misery, deliverance, and thankfulness be related to experiential knowledge of God?

In his book, *Striving Together in the Divine Truths of Scripture*, Rev. Fraanje states:

"With all my heart I hope that the Holy Spirit will bring you to acknowledge the three divine Persons, while you are in your youth. This is sure: without having gotten knowledge of the First Person through the Third Person, there also shall be no genuine knowledge of the Second Person."

What does the last sentence of this quotation mean? Of what danger is Rev. Fraanje warning us of in this sentence?

? Why must a person be shown by the Holy Spirit that he is a lost sinner who is answerable to a righteous God, before he will truly need and beg for salvation in Jesus Christ?

GOD'S DECREE

God's decree is His eternal will, purpose, and plan, in which He has foreordained (determined from eternity) all things that come to pass. God's mind and will are revealed in His decree.

It is only fitting that God, who created and governs all things, should do so according to a definite plan.

A teacher once placed a chair on a table in the front of her classroom. She had arranged for a student to move the chair from one end of the table to precisely the same place on the other end, once every ten seconds, in a manner in which the student could not be seen by the class.

"As you can see," she told her class, "it's obvious that this chair moves itself."

"Of course not," her class responded. "Some force has to be moving the chair. Objects don't move themselves! Besides, the lifeless chair moves according to a pattern."

"Look at the sun, moon, and stars," she argued. "They are lifeless objects and they move themselves according to precise patterns, don't they?"

"They can't. Some force has to be moving them according to a plan."

"Who is generating the steady force required to keep our universe operating precisely according to His plan?" she asked.

How does God's universe testify of His decree, His plan?

● **God's decree** — God's eternal will, purpose, and plan for all things

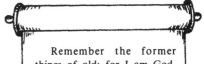

Remember the former things of old: for I am God, and there is none else; I am God, and there is none like Me, Declaring the end from the beginning, and from ancient times the things that are not yet done, saying, My counsel shall stand, and I will do all my pleasure.

— Isaiah 46:9-10

In whom also we have obtained an inheritance, being predestinated according to the purpose of Him who worketh all things after the counsel of His own will.

— Ephesians 1:11

? Today, some "Christian" people deny the doctrine of God's decree. Why is this denial actually a denying that God is God? What precious benefits are these people denying themselves when they deny the truth of God's decree?

? What type of ruler would God be if He ruled without a plan?

● **Particulars** — Details; items; individual parts

● **Comprehended** — Included; taken into account

Imagine visiting a large hospital construction site. As you observe, everything appears to be in a state of confusion. The electricians do not know where to string their wires, nor do the plumbers know where to install their pipes. A great deal of arguing is taking place over the size and location of various rooms and hallways.

In amazement, you ask the supervisor to see a set of plans for the building.

"We do not have any plans," he responds.

"What! Constructing a large building like this without any construction plans? How does everyone know what they are supposed to do? How do you know what the outcome will be?

"Oh, everyone decides for himself what he should do, and regarding the outcome — we don't really know what the end result will be like; the building keeps changing all the time."

What would you say in response to this supervisor? Have you ever heard of someone building or operating anything without a plan?

Why is it foolish to imagine God creating and operating His entire creation without a "plan"? What do we call God's "plan"? How is God's "plan" infinitely greater than any human plan?

God's decree includes so many **particulars** that it is often spoken of in a plural sense, as God's "decrees," but in reality there is only one divine decree in which all things are **comprehended**.

In the Bible, God's decree is named His:

1. Decree (Psalm 2:7)
2. Will (James 1:18)
3. Counsel (Psalm 33:11)
4. Pleasure (Ephesians 1:9)
5. Purpose (Romans 8:28)

The following chart reveals seven characteristics of God's decree that are revealed in Scripture:

- **All-inclusive** — Includes everything

- **Sovereign** — Having full rights, authority, and power; free from any outside influence or control

GOD'S DECREE IS:	
1. *Perfectly wise* — it is formed in the counsel of God's sinless will and infinite wisdom.	Great is our Lord, and of great power: His understanding is infinite. — Psalm 147:5
2. *Eternal* — it is from eternity to eternity.	The counsel of the LORD standeth forever, the thoughts of His heart to all generations. —Psalm 33:11
3. *All-powerful* — it will all certainly come to pass.	And all the inhabitants of the earth are reputed as nothing: and He doeth according to His will in the army of heaven, and among the inhabitants of the earth: and none can stay His hand, or say unto Him, What doest Thou? — Daniel 4:35
4. *Unchangeable* — it is faithful and true.	But He is in one mind, and who can turn Him? and what His soul desireth, even that He doeth. — Job 23:13
5. *All-inclusive* — it is the plan of the Creator of, and Ruler over, all things.	Oh house of Israel, cannot I do with you as this potter? saith the LORD. Behold, as the clay is in the potter's hand, so are ye in Mine hand, O house of Israel. —Jeremiah 18:6
6. *Unconditional* — it does not depend on anyone or anything outside of God.	Are not two sparrows sold for a farthing? and one of them shall not fall on the ground without your Father. But the very hairs of your head are all numbered. — Matthew 10:29-30
7. *Sovereign* — as Maker, God, does not have to answer to anyone outside of Himself.	Behold, He taketh away, who can hinder Him? who will say unto Him, What doest Thou? — Job 9:12

- **Internal** — Inside of; within

- **External** — Outside of; without

- **Providence** — God's caring for, upholding of, and ruling over all things

- **Redemption** — God's plan and purchase for the salvation of His children

? Is God's decree revealed to us? What is revealed to us? What is meant by God's secret and revealed wills?

For to do whatsoever Thy hand and Thy counsel determined before to be done.
— Acts 4:28

In whom also we have obtained an inheritance, being predestinated according to the purpose of Him who worketh all things after the counsel of His own will.
— Ephesians 1:11

But our God is in the heavens; He hath done whatsoever He hath pleased.
— Psalm 115:3

My counsel shall stand, and I will do all My pleasure.
— Isaiah 46:10b

God's decree is an **internal** work of God (His purpose and plan) regarding His **external** works (His creation, **providence**, and **redemption**).

God's works, both internal (within God) and external (outside of God) can be pictured as follows:

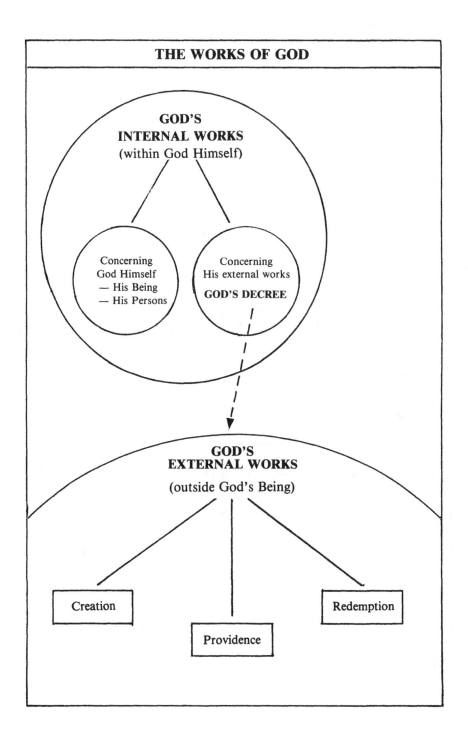

THE WORKS OF GOD

GOD'S INTERNAL WORKS
(within God Himself)

Concerning God Himself
— His Being
— His Persons

Concerning His external works
GOD'S DECREE

GOD'S EXTERNAL WORKS
(outside God's Being)

Creation

Providence

Redemption

PREDESTINATION

Predestination is God's decree in which He has determined the eternal state of all **rational** creatures to sovereign glory of His mercy and righteousness. "Pre" means "before," and "destination" refers to the "conclusion" or "final place" of all moral creatures — angels and human beings.

The **destination** of every **rational creature**, every angel and man, will be either heaven or hell. Predestination is God's decreeing, from eternity, the final place of each angel and human being. As moral creatures, predestination is a very important aspect of God's plan for all mankind.

Predestination includes the following two parts:

PREDESTINATION INCLUDES:	
1. Election	Having predestinated us unto the adoption of children by Jesus Christ to Himself, according to the good pleasure of His will, To the praise of the glory of His grace, wherein He hath made us accepted in the beloved. — Ephesians 1:4-5
2. Reprobation	Hath not the potter power over the clay, of the same lump to make one vessel unto honour, and another unto dishonour? What if God, willing to show His wrath, and to make His power known, endured with much longsuffering the vessels of wrath fitted to destruction. — Romans 9:21-22

Election is God's sovereign decree to graciously save certain sinners. As totally depraved sinners, these chosen people are not better than others. Their election is entirely based on the sovereign good pleasure of God. God freely chose to graciously save certain sinners through the merits of Jesus Christ.

Reprobation is God's sovereign decree to justly pass by other sinners with His grace and to punish them for their sins. As totally depraved sinners they have fully deserved eternal punishment. Reprobation reveals God's sovereign will to reveal His justice in fully punishing certain sinners for their sins.

The chart on the next page provides examples of predestination as it is found in Scripture and in our doctrinal standards.

- **Predestination** — God's decree in which He has determined the eternal state of all rational creatures

- **Rational** — Capable of reasoning, deeper thinking, and moral decision-making

- **Destination** — The end or final place

- **Rational creatures** — Angels and human beings

? Some people deny the doctrine of election, but if there were no divine, gracious election, why would no person ever be saved?

- **Election** — God's sovereign decree to graciously save certain sinners from their sins

- **Reprobation** — God's sovereign decree to justly punish certain sinners for their sins

? Why would God's reprobation of every sinner be perfectly just? How does His election reveal His great mercy?

137

PREDESTINATION IN SCRIPTURE

Ye have not chosen Me, but I have chosen you.

— John 15:16a

According as He hath chosen us in Him before the foundation of the world, that we should be holy and without blame before Him in love:

Having predestinated us unto the adoption of children by Jesus Christ to Himself, according to the good pleasure of His will.

— Ephesians 1:4-5

But we are bound to give thanks always to God for you, brethren beloved of the Lord, because God hath from the beginning chosen you to salvation through sanctification of the Spirit and belief of the truth.

— II Thessalonians 2:13

For the children being not yet born, neither having done any good or evil, that the purpose of God according to election might stand, not of works, but of Him that calleth;

It was said unto her, The elder shall serve the younger.

As it is written, Jacob have I loved, but Esau have I hated.

— Romans 9:11-13

I charge thee before God, and the Lord Jesus Christ, and the elect angels.

— I Timothy 5:21a

For we are His workmanship created in Christ Jesus unto good works, which God hath before ordained that we should walk in them.

— Ephesians 2:10

Elect according to the foreknowledge of God the Father, through sanctification of the Spirit, unto obedience and sprinkling of the blood of Jesus Christ.

— I Peter 1:2a

And we know that all things work together for good to them that love God, to them who are the called according to His purpose.

For whom He did foreknow, He also did predestinate to be conformed to the image of His Son, that He might be the firstborn among many brethren.

— Romans 8:28-29

For He saith to Moses, I will have mercy on whom I will have mercy, and I will have compassion on whom I will have compassion.

So then it is not of him that willeth, nor of him that runneth, but of God that showeth mercy.

— Romans 9:15-16

Who hath saved us, and called us with a holy calling, not according to our works, but according to His own purpose and grace, which was given us in Christ Jesus before the world began.

— II Timothy 1:9

Hath not the potter power over the clay, of the same lump to make one vessel unto honour, and another unto dishonour?

What if God, willing to shew His wrath, and to make His power known, endured with much longsuffering the vessels of wrath fitted to destruction:

And that He might make known the riches of His glory on the vessels of mercy, which He had afore prepared unto glory.

— Romans 9:21-23

PREDESTINATION IN OUR DOCTRINAL STANDARDS

Belgic Confession of Faith
Article 16 — Of Eternal Election

We believe that all the posterity of Adam being thus fallen into perdition and ruin, by the sin of our first parents, God then did manifest Himself such as He is; that is to say, merciful and just: Merciful, since He delivers and preserves from this perdition all, whom He, in His eternal and unchangeable counsel of mere goodness, hath elected in Christ Jesus our Lord, without any respect to their works: Just, in leaving others in the fall and perdition wherein they have involved themselves.

Canons of Dordt — First Head
Article 7

Election is the unchangeable purpose of God, whereby, before the foundation of the world, He hath out of mere grace, according to the sovereign good pleasure of His own will, chosen, from the whole human race, which had fallen through their own fault, from their primitive state of rectitude, into sin and destruction, a certain number of persons to redemption in Christ, whom He from eternity appointed the Mediator and Head of the elect, and the foundation of salvation.

Canons of Dordt — First Head
Article 15

What peculiarly tends to illustrate and recommend to us the eternal and unmerited grace of election, is the express testimony of sacred Scripture, that not all, but some only are elected, while others are passed by in the eternal decree; whom God out of His sovereign, most just, irreprehensible and unchangeable good pleasure, hath decreed to leave in the common misery into which they have willfully plunged themselves, and not to bestow upon them saving faith and the grace of conversion; but permitting them in His just judgment to follow their own ways, at last for the declaration of His justice, to condemn and perish them forever, not only on account of their unbelief, but also for all their other sins. And this is the decree of reprobation which by no means makes God the author of sin (the very thought of which is blasphemy), but declares Him to be an awful, irreprehensible, and righteous judge and avenger thereof.

Election, as the work of the Triune God, included God the Son (John 13:18) and God the Holy Spirit (I Corinthians 6:11). However, election is especially spoken of as the work of God the Father in Scripture.

The Bible speaks of the following six types of election:

SCRIPTURE SPEAKS OF AN ELECTION OF:	
1. Jesus Christ	Behold My servant, whom I uphold: Mine elect, in whom My soul delighteth; I have put My Spirit upon Him: He shall bring forth judgment to the Gentiles. — Isaiah 42:1
2. Angels	I charge thee before God, and the Lord Jesus Christ, and the elect angels, that thou observe these things without preferring one before another, doing nothing by partiality. — I Timothy 5:21
3. **Officebearers**	And Samuel said to all the people, See ye him whom the LORD hath chosen, that there is none like him among all the people? And all the people shouted, and said, God save the king. — I Samuel 10:24
4. Nations	For thou art an holy people unto the LORD thy God: the LORD thy God hath chosen thee to be a special people unto Himself, above all people that are upon the face of the earth. — Deuteronomy 7:6
5. Church	I will declare the decree: the LORD hath said unto Me, Thou art My Son; this day have I begotten Thee. Ask of Me, and I shall give Thee the heathen for Thine inheritance, and the uttermost parts of the earth for Thy possession. — Psalm 2:7-8
6. Individual persons	For whom He did foreknow, He also did predestinate to be conformed to the image of His Son, that He might be the firstborn among many brethren. — Romans 8:29

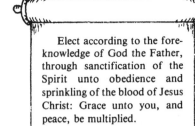

Elect according to the fore-knowledge of God the Father, through sanctification of the Spirit unto obedience and sprinkling of the blood of Jesus Christ: Grace unto you, and peace, be multiplied.
— I Peter 1:2

According as He hath chosen us in Him before the foundation of the world, that we should be holy and without blame before Him in love:
Having predestinated us unto the adoption of children by Jesus Christ to Himself, according to the good pleasure of His will.
— Ephesians 1:4-5

● **Officebearers** — Those chosen and placed by God in a church office (a minister, elder, deacon, professor of theology, evangelist or missionary)

God's election of individual persons contains the following five Scriptural characteristics:

GOD'S ELECTION OF INDIVIDUAL PERSONS IS:	
1. Personal	As it is written, Jacob have I loved, but Esau have I hated. — Romans 9:13
2. Particular	So the last shall be first, and the first last: for many be called, but few chosen. — Matthew 20:16
3. Eternal	According as He hath chosen us in Him before the foundation of the world, that we should be holy and without blame before Him in love. — Ephesians 1:4
4. Unchangeable	For the children being not yet born, neither having done any good or evil, that the purpose of God according to election might stand, not of works, but of Him that calleth. — Romans 9:11
5. Just	What shall we say then? Is there unrighteousness with God? God forbid. What if God, willing to show His wrath, and to make His power known, endured with much longsuffering the vessels of wrath fitted to destruction: And that He might make known the riches of His glory on the vessels of mercy, which He had afore prepared unto glory. — Romans 9:14, 22-23

● **Particular** — For certain ones; not including all

? Why is it true that God's nature, attributes, plan, predestination, promises, and threatenings are all unchangeable? How are all of these connected?

? How is the doctrine of election the hope and security of God's church?

? If a person trusted in his own works, feelings, or decisions, why would his foundation be far less secure than if he trusted in God's electing grace? Why would his foundation prove to be self-deceit and no security at all in the end?

Election is a wonderful and gracious doctrine. Election is the *hope* and *security* of the church. If there were no election, there would be no church — for no totally depraved sinner would ever turn to God on his own. God's gracious election is the foundational *hope* of the church. Election testifies that, despite our sinful and lost condition, God will bless His Word and sinners will be saved! Without election, there would be no hope for sinners.

God's gracious election is also the *security* of His people. If salvation depended upon them — upon their feelings, decisions, or works — then all would still be lost. Their security and comfort lies, instead, in God's wonderful election. Their salvation rests secure in God's eternal, unchanging, electing love.

The following chart reveals the names which refer to reprobation in the Bible:

SCRIPTURAL NAMES FOR REPROBATION	
1. Hated	As it is written, Jacob have I loved, but Esau have I hated. — Romans 9:13
2. Appointed to wrath	For God hath not appointed us to wrath, but to obtain salvation by our Lord Jesus Christ. — I Thessalonians 5:9
3. Appointed to disobedience	And a stone of stumbling, and a rock of offence, even to them which stumble at the word, being disobedient: whereunto also they were appointed. — I Peter 2:8
4. Fitted to destruction	What if God, willing to show His wrath, and to make His power known, endured with much longsuffering the vessels of wrath fitted to destruction. — Romans 9:22
5. Ordained to condemnation	For there are certain men crept in unawares, who were before of old ordained to this condemnation, ungodly men, turning the grace of our God into lasciviousness, and denying the only Lord God, and our Lord Jesus Christ. — Jude: 4

? Some people only believe and teach that "God is love." Is this the entire truth? Why is it deceiving and dangerous not to teach the whole truth regarding God and His dealings with sinful man?

God's predestination clearly teaches that:

1. God deserves all the credit and praise for each sinner who is saved. God sovereignly and graciously elected to save this totally lost and unworthy sinner.

2. Man deserves all the blame and guilt whenever a sinner remains lost. God sovereignly decreed to leave this person in the sin he chose, and to justly punish him for it.

? How are God's gracious election and just reprobation connected to man's total depravity?

How are these two truths clearly explained in the following two articles from the *Canons of Dordt* on the following page?

- **Confers** — Gives to; attributes to; places upon

- **Perplexing** — Confusing; complicating; hindering

- **Ascribed** — Credited; assigned; attributed

- **Heresy** — A false doctrine or teaching

- **Pelagius** — One who taught that natural man, of himself, could freely choose good or evil

- **Enmity** — Deep hatred; hostility; rebellion

ROMANS 9:13-21

As it is written, Jacob have I loved, but Esau have I hated.

What shall we say then? Is there unrighteousness with God? God forbid.

For He saith to Moses, I will have mercy on whom I will have mercy, and I will have compassion on whom I will have compassion.

So then it is not of him that willeth, nor of him that runneth, but of God that showeth mercy.

For the Scripture saith unto Pharaoh, Even for this same purpose have I raised thee up, that I might shew My power in thee, and that My name might be declared throughout all the earth.

Therefore hath He mercy on whom He will have mercy, and whom He will He hardeneth.

Thou wilt say then unto me, Why doth He yet find fault? For who hath resisted His will?

Nay but, O man, who art thou that repliest against God? Shall the thing formed say to Him that formed it, Why hast Thou made me thus?

over the clay, of the same lump to make one vessel unto honour, and another unto dishonour?

CANONS OF DORDT: *HEADS OF DOCTRINE III and IV*
ARTICLES 9 AND 10

Article 9. It is not the fault of the gospel, nor of Christ, offered therein, nor of God, who calls men by the gospel, and **confers** upon them various gifts, that those who are called by the ministry of the Word, refuse to come, and be converted: the fault lies in themselves; some of whom when called, regardless of their danger, reject the Word of life; others, though they receive it, suffer it not to make a lasting impression on their heart; therefore, their joy, arising only from a temporary faith, soon vanishes, and they fall away; while others choke the seed of the Word by **perplexing** cares, and the pleasures of this world, and produce no fruit.—This our Savior teaches in the parable of the sower (Matt.13).

Article 10. But that others who are called by the gospel, obey the call, and are converted, is not to be **ascribed** to the proper exercise of free will, whereby one distinguishes himself above others, equally furnished with grace sufficient for faith and conversions, as the proud **heresy** of **Pelagius** maintains; but it must be wholly ascribed to God, who as He has chosen His own from eternity in Christ, so He confers upon them faith and repentance, rescues them from the power of darkness, and translates them into the kingdom of His own Son, that they may show forth the praises of Him, who hath called them out of darkness into His marvelous light; and may glory not in themselves, but in the Lord according to the testimony of the apostles in various places.

According to this writing of our forefathers, based upon the Scriptures, who deserves all the blame when a sinner remains lost? Who deserves all the credit when a sinner is saved?

Predestination exalts God to the highest and humbles man to the lowest. By nature, our selfishly sinful hearts are at **enmity** with God. We want to be the deciding factor. We want to be most important. We selfishly want everyone and everything to serve, honor, and center upon, us and our wills. In short, we rebelliously fight to be God. Our sinful enmity often reveals itself when we think about doctrines, such as predestination, that clearly reveal God — as the One who is sovereign over all things — also over us.

In Romans 9 Paul writes clearly of God's sovereign predestination but also of natural man's enmity against this doctrine. Read Romans 9:13-21. How does Scripture show man's natural enmity against sovereign predestination in verses 14 and 19? How does it answer these outbreaks of enmity?

Man's natural enmity toward God's predestination often breaks forth into the following three objections:

1. ''Predestination is unjust; the people who are elected are no better than those who are not.''

2. ''Predestination takes away human freedom. I must do everything I do because it is in God's unchangeable decree. I have no choice.''

3. ''Predestination takes away all human responsibility and activity. If I'm elected, then I am; and if not, I'm not. Nothing that I do, or do not do, will change God's decree.''

Let us examine each of these three objections:

1. *''Predestination is unjust; the people who are elected are no better than those who are not.''*

It is true that those who are elected by God to salvation through Christ are not better than those whom God passed by with His grace. However, this does not mean that God's predestination is unjust. God cannot do anything that is unjust, for He is perfectly righteous.

It would be perfectly just for God to pass by and leave every person in his own sins. We have sinned away all rights or claims upon any blessing of God. ''The wages of sin is death.'' As sinners, we all deserve hell — anything above hell is grace. Therefore, God's condemnation of any sinner is just; His saving of a sinner is grace. Jesus Christ graciously paid the full price of sin for every saved sinner. No one can charge God with being unjust.

Read the Parable of the Laborers in Matthew 20:1-16:

> A Roman penny (approximately seventeen cents) was the wage for a full day's labor in New Testament times. The householder paid those who worked a full day that which they deserved. Because he chose to be gracious and to freely give of his own money to others who did not deserve it, he was spoken of as being unjust.
>
> God will justly give many sinners their full wages — ''the wages of sin is death.'' That He has chosen to be gracious to others and freely give to them of His wealth, is His perfect right. A rich man can freely give riches to whom he desires.
>
> In predestination, does God deal unjustly with anyone? Why do some complain about His gracious electing of some, as being unfair?

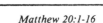

Matthew 20:1-16

For the kingdom of heaven is like unto a man that is an householder, which went out early in the morning to hire labourers into his vineyard.

And when he had agreed with the labourers for a penny a day, he sent them into his vineyard.

And he went out about the third hour, and saw others standing idle in the marketplace.

And said unto them: Go ye also into the vineyard, and whatsoever is right I will give you. And they went their way.

Again he went out about the sixth and ninth hour, and did likewise.

And about the eleventh hour he went out, and found others standing idle, and saith unto them, Why stand ye here all the day idle?

They say unto him, Because no man hath hired us. He saith unto them, Go ye also into the vineyard: and whatsoever is right, that shall ye receive.

So when even was come, the lord of the vineyard saith unto his steward, Call the labourers, and give them their hire, beginning from the last to the first.

And when they came that were hired about the eleventh hour, they received every man a penny.

But when the first came, they supposed that they should have received more; and they likewise received every man a penny.

And when they had received it, they murmured against the goodman of the house,

Saying, These last have wrought but one hour, and thou hast made them equal unto us, which have borne the burden and heat of the day.

But he answered one of them and said, Friend, I do thee no wrong: didst not thou agree with me for a penny?

Take that thine is, and go thy way: I will give unto this last, even as unto thee.

Is it not lawful for me to do what I will with mine own? Is thine eye evil, because I am good?

So the last shall be first, and the first last: for many be called, but few chosen.

God never condemns innocent people; He condemns sinners. The following story illustrates a common misunderstanding of this truth.

In 1985, thousands of people died in a terrible disaster in Columbia. An erupting volcano caused a huge mudslide which killed and buried alive thousands of people.

After reading of this awful catastrophe in the newspaper, a certain man said to a Christian person with whom he worked, "How can you believe in a loving and caring God? Read what happened in Columbia! Thousands of *innocent* people, buried alive — is that love and care?"

What was this man overlooking in his outburst against God's dealings? Since our fall, are there any "innocent" people? Were these people living innocently? If God would destroy all the cities in the world today by disasters like this one, would He be acting unjustly? God's sparing of thousands of cities from such disasters everyday speaks of God's wonderful love, care, and patience. In the light of these questions, how would you answer this man's remarks?

When we view the execution of God's sovereign predestination, what truth taught in this example must we keep in mind? Does God condemn "innocent" people?

2. *"Predestination takes away human freedom. I must do everything I do because it is in God's unchangeable decree. I have no choice."*

A person will perform all which God has decreed concerning his life. That this, however, removes a person's freedom of choice is not true.

Freedom means to be free from outside persuasion or force; free to do that which one desires. God never persuades or forces a person to sin. God is perfectly holy and cannot think or do anything sinful.

> *Let no man say when he is tempted, I am tempted of God: for God cannot be tempted with evil, neither tempteth He any man:*
> *But every man is tempted, when he is drawn away of his own lust, and enticed.*
> — *James 1:13-14.*

? When some people view God's punishment or condemnation of people as unjust, they are mistaking God's actions due to mistaken views of sin. Why is this true?

Therefore, while all things are in God's decree, yet God's decree is executed in such a way that no person is persuaded or forced to do evil.

Each person commits the sins he freely choses to do, but in so doing, he fulfills God's decree.

Imagine speaking to a young man in prison who had committed armed robbery when stealing money from a local gas station.

"It is not my fault," he states. "Everything is in God's unchangeable decree. My robbery of the gas station was in God's decree — nothing I could do, or not do, could change God's plan. So here I am, and it's God fault."

How would you answer this young man's argument and insult of God's honor? Did God force or persuade him to steal? Did he desire to rob in order to fulfill God's plan? What was his motive? If he freely chose and planned to commit this crime, who is fully guilty?

Why is it very important to understand that God's decree does not force or persuade a person to sin?

More than a thousand years before Judas Iscariot betrayed the Lord Jesus, God prophesied through David in Psalm 41:9, "Yea, Mine own familiar friend, in whom I trusted, which did eat of My bread, hath lifted up his heel against Me." Approximately five hundred years before Christ, Zechariah testified of the price for which Jesus would be sold in chapter 11:12, "So they weighed for My price thirty pieces of silver."

Yet, when Judas betrayed Christ, did he do this because he wanted to fulfill God's prophecy and decree? Did God force or persuade Judas to do this terrible act? Why did Judas betray Jesus? What was his motive? Why is Judas fully guilty for his deed?

How are both God's prophecy and Judas' guilt spoken of in Matthew 26:24, "The Son of man goeth as it is written of Him: but woe unto that man by whom the Son of man is betrayed! It had been good for that man if he had not been born"?

? Is the following statement true? Why or why not? When a person sins, this is the choice of his own free will.

? To state that a person has a free will to sin, and freely chooses to sin, is different from teaching that a person has a free will to choose and do good. Why?

? God judges our "hearts," the motives which underline all our thoughts, words, and actions. What was Judas' motive?

3. *"Predestination takes away all human responsibility and activity. If I'm elected, then I am; and if not, I'm not. Nothing that I do, or do not do, will change God's decree."*

This reasoning separates two truths which God has joined together in Scripture. God has not only decreed the end of all things, but also the means for arriving at the desired end.

> Imagine a person living carelessly and neglecting his health. This person does not take care to eat or dress properly. He never takes time for healthy exercise nor proper sleep. He smokes and drinks heavily, and ignores all good health practices. He never visits a doctor nor uses any medicine when ill.
>
> When you speak with him about his carelessness and lack of properly using the means which God has provided for his health, he answers, "I cannot add one year to my life. If God has decreed that I will be healthy, I will be. If He has decreed that I will be ill, I will be. Nothing I do, or do not do, will change God's decree. I cannot make, nor keep, myself healthy. Health is a gift from God."
>
> How would you answer this man? What he said is true, but is it the entire truth? How has this man separated God's means from His decree?

Study the following drawing which pictures both God's secret will (God's decree) and God's revealed will (God's means).

? Why is it deceiving and dangerous to separate God's secret and revealed wills?

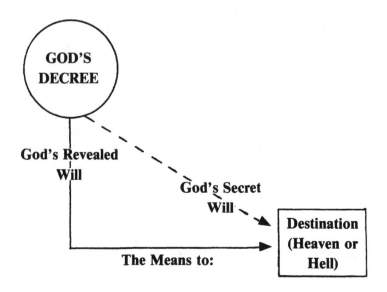

God's decree of predestination does not remove my responsibility and activity. To be spiritually healthy, I must actively use the means that God has provided. Although I cannot save myself and salvation is a gift from God, yet, I must actively seek it through the means God has given, the means which He has promised to bless for this purpose.

Imagine visiting your uncle who recently purchased an old corner grocery store. The store had been vacant for some time, but now he had re-opened it.

You are quite shocked, however, by that which you see. The shelves are very empty, the store is quite dirty, and the groceries are in disorder.

"You won't get many customers this way," you tell him. "Let's work hard to clean and straighten everything."

"No," he answers, "that doesn't matter. If God will bless my business then He will, and if not, then no matter what we do, it will not prosper."

What mistake is your uncle making regarding God's secret and revealed wills? His statement is true, but is it the full truth? Why not?

What similar mistake or excuse do some people make with God's decree of predestination and the means of grace that He has provided?

? Believing in God's predestination is not fatalistic. How does believing in God's decree differ from believing in fatalism, which teaches the following four points:

1. Everything that happens is a result of fate, an unintelligent, natural force.
2. Nothing is taking place according to any knowledgeable plan, nor leading to any planned end.
3. Human choices do not affect events which will take place regardless.
4. Man cannot be held responsible for his dealings for he is only a victim of fate.

When we eat a meal, we pray and acknowledge God's goodness in providing food for us. Bread is a gift from God.

God could sustain us without food as He did Moses, Elijah, and the Lord Jesus for forty days and nights. He could miraculously provide bread as He did for the four and five thousand men on different occasions. But God's normal way is to work through means.

Think of all the means God uses to provide us with bread: the farmer's plowing, disking, planting, fertilizing, and harvesting; the necessary rain, sunshine, and temperatures; the mill and its workers' processing of the wheat flour; the baker's preparing of the bread, etc.

We cannot make one seed grow, nor can we provide the proper weather. We could neither process the wheat nor bake the bread if God did not give the required health and strength.

Bread is a gift from God; yet He gives it to us through a way of means. What comparisons can you make between this example of natural bread and spiritual "bread"?

? Some "Christians" only emphasize the use of the means; little or nothing is spoken of God's election. What problems would this teaching promote?

Some emphasize only God's election; little or nothing is spoken about the person's responsibility to actively use the means. What problems would this instruction produce?

? What mistake in spiritual reasoning do these two examples illustrate?

147

? What opposite overemphasis is illustrated in this example?

Imagine a person telling you, "I will always be healthy because I eat the best foods, dress properly for the weather, exercise each day, obtain the recommended hours of sleep each night, and never smoke."

How would you respond to this person? Of what value would these means be if God did not bless them? How is this person's error the opposite from "the uncle's mistake" in the story on the previous page? Can you explain why both of these people's reasonings are in error?

The destination of all people is known by God in His *secret will*. By nature, no person knows whether or not he is elected. The *revealed will* of God, however, is known. God commands us to seek Him through the means of grace He has given: through serious Bible reading and study, careful church attendance, and sincere pleading with God in prayer for His blessing. God instructs and commands us in His Word to listen to His revealed will — not to attempt to pry into His secret will.

The truths of both God's sovereignty and man's responsibility must be properly taught and balanced. Study the chart on the following page very carefully which presents this important truth.

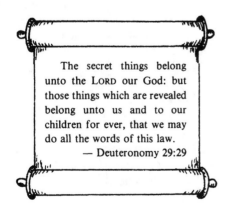

The secret things belong unto the LORD our God: but those things which are revealed belong unto us and to our children for ever, that we may do all the words of this law.
— Deuteronomy 29:29

PROPERLY BALANCING TWO TRUTHS

God's sovereign decree of predestination and man's responsibility to actively use God's means of grace are both truths that are emphasized in Scripture. Rev. Spurgeon spoke of these two truths as two parallel lines which come together in God in eternity. While we cannot fully understand with our limited minds at present how these two fit together, we must preach and teach both as biblical truths.

GOD'S SOVEREIGNTY
(Decree of Predestination)

No man can come to Me, except the Father which hath sent Me draw him; and I will raise him up at the last day.
— John 6:44

Ye have not chosen Me, but I have chosen you, and ordained you.
— John 15:16a

So then *it is not of him that willeth or of him that runneth, but of God that sheweth mercy.*
— Romans 9:16

For the children being not yet born, neither having done any good or evil, that the *purpose of God according to election might stand, not of works, but of Him that calleth.*
— Romans 9:11

According *as He hath chosen us in Him before the foundation of the world,* that we should be holy and without blame before Him in love:
Having predestinated us unto the adoption of children by Jesus Christ to Himself, according to the good pleasure of His will.
— Ephesians 1:4-5

MAN'S RESPONSIBILITY
(Active Use of God's Means of Grace)

Seek ye the LORD while He may be found, *call ye upon Him* while He is near.
Let the wicked forsake his way, and the unrighteous man his thoughts: and let him return unto the LORD, and He will have mercy upon him; and to our God, for He will abundantly pardon.
— Isaiah 55:6-7

And I say unto you, *Ask, and it shall be given you; seek, and ye shall find; knock, and it shall be opened unto you.*
For everyone that asketh receiveth; and he that seeketh findeth; and to him that knocketh it shall be opened.
— Luke 11:9-10

Behold, I stand at the door, and knock: *if any man hear My voice, and open the door, I will come in to him*, and will sup with him, and he with Me.
— Revelation 3:20

And the Spirit and the bride say, Come. And let him that heareth say, Come. And let him that is athirst come. *And whosoever will, let him take the water of life freely.*
— Revelation 22:17

Picture a railroad track with two parallel rails. If one rail is removed or misplaced, what will happen? Similarly, scriptural truths must also be placed in proper balance. If not, we err. If only the truths of God's sovereignty are emphasized, then we will fall into the error of fatalism (a "what will happen will happen" attitude), and we will neglect the active use of God's means of grace. If only man's responsibility is emphasized, we will fall into the error of Arminianism (a "free will" belief — a belief that we can decide, accept, and turn to Christ of ourselves), and we will miss the necessary, humble dependence upon God to bless His means of grace in our lives. We must strive to avoid falling into the ditch on either side.

God's election is not an excluding doctrine. Not repenting from sin exludes people from salvation, not election.

God's election holds an important place in Scripture and in the plan of salvation for the following four reasons:

1. Election *exalts God* to the highest as sovereign Ruler over all things, and *humbles man* to the lowest before Him.

This is the desire of all God's true children as illustrated by the following story:

When Dr. William Carey, the well-known missionary, was very ill, another missionary called to see him. This friend talked about Dr. Carey's great work for God. He spoke of Dr. Carey's great sacrifices for God. When the visitor prayed, he prayed about Dr. Carey's great achievements and wonderful life.

As the visitor was leaving the room, Dr. Carey called to him in a feeble voice and said, "Friend, you have been speaking much about 'Dr. Carey.' When I am gone speak *nothing* about 'Dr. Carey'. Speak *only* about Dr. Carey's Savior!"

How do Dr. Carey's words reveal his deep desire to humble himself and to exalt God? Those who know that their salvation is based on God's grace, and not on their own works or faith, love to glorify God. Do you?

Some people believe that they are saved because they "accepted" or "made a decision for" Christ of their own free will and power, while others did not make the right choice. Why does this "free-will belief" not humble man as does the doctrine of free grace?

2. Election is the *only hope* for spiritually dead sinners. Election reveals that God will not pass by all fallen sinners, but that He will, out of sovereign mercy, save many lost sinners. Election is a rich manifestation of God, who eternally has delighted Himself in His people, that He might save them and restore them unto Himself.

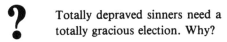 Totally depraved sinners need a totally gracious election. Why?

After preaching upon the doctrine of God's election, a minister was visited by a group of people. "We object to the teaching of God's electing of some people and not others," they stated. "Election denies the worth of each person and presents God as a harsh Ruler."

The minister answered, "My friends, you are not objecting to the doctrine of election, but to that of man's total depravity. Since our fall, all people are born with a totally sinful heart — loving and choosing self and sin rather than God and righteousness. Therefore, if God did not mercifully elect to save some, all would be eternally lost. It is man's sin which abases him, but God's wonderful electing grace that makes man's salvation possible and glorifies God's love and mercy."

How does this conversation testify of the truth that "election is the *only hope* for spiritually dead sinners"?

3. Election gives *rich encouragement to actively use God's means of grace.* In election, God has promised to richly bless His Word. Despite our sinfulness, God's election is sure. Sinners will be saved through God's blessing His means of grace.

 How does the experience of God's grace exalt God and humble man?

A servant once wanted to teach his master a needed lesson and sowed oat seed in an area where barley should have been planted.

When realizing this, his master called him and asked why he had sown oat seed there.

"I hoped to reap barley from it," he answered.

"That's ridiculous; how can you sow oats and expect to reap barley?"

"Master, you do that. You sow sin, neglect the Bible, and yet expect to reap heaven!"

How did this servant demonstrate his knowledge of the fact that God works through means? Which verse in Galatians 6 is clearly illustrated by this story?

If we say that we are "Christians," that we "believe in the Bible," but do not actively use God's Word nor live according to its teachings, how are we just as foolish as the master in this story?

151

4. Election is the only *true comfort for the saved*. As sinful people, they know their sinful hearts, tendencies, and failures. But their salvation is secure outside themselves in God's eternal electing decree.

An older woman, lying upon her deathbed, listened to one of her lady visitors, who said, "You have done much for the church, cared for many families, and I never remember you having serious quarrels with anyone. I wish I could live the type of life that you have."

"My friend," replied the woman, "my church work was filled with self-pride, my caring for others blotted with self-reputation, and inwardly I have fought with many. My hope for eternity is built upon a much firmer foundation — Jesus Christ and God's eternal, unchanging, electing love."

Why was God's decree of election a rich comfort to this woman? Why is it the only true comfort for saved sinners?

? What rich love, deep comfort, and eternal security, are missed by those who deny the truth of God's election?

Looking into our sinful hearts, or at our sinful world, the spiritual darkness and sinfulness would certainly discourage us. Salvation can appear to be very distant. It can seem so impossible!

But God's election shines forth as a beacon of light in the darkness. God will bless His Word to the salvation of many sinners. Despite all that we see around and within us, God's election shall stand. His Word shall not return unto Him void.

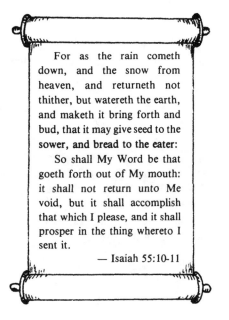

For as the rain cometh down, and the snow from heaven, and returneth not thither, but watereth the earth, and maketh it bring forth and bud, that it may give seed to the sower, and bread to the eater:

So shall My Word be that goeth forth out of My mouth: it shall not return unto Me void, but it shall accomplish that which I please, and it shall prosper in the thing whereto I sent it.

— Isaiah 55:10-11

Is God's gracious election through Jesus Christ your hope; your only hope? Have you experientially learned something of your sinfulness and God's gracious electing love? Are you actively using God's means of grace and praying for His blessing upon their use? Is your deepest desire to exalt God and to humble yourself before Him? Is it your longing to assuredly rest in God's electing love as Paul, when he confessed: "For I am persuaded, that neither death, nor life, nor angels, nor principalities, nor powers, nor things present, nor things to come, nor height, nor depth, nor any other creature, shall be able to separate us from the love of God, which is in Christ Jesus our Lord" (Romans 8:38-39)?

If so, then your God-given faith, hope, and love are fruits which evidence your eternal election by God through Jesus Christ.

CATECHISM MEMORIZATION
Questions from Rev. A. Hellenbroek's *Divine Truths* — Chapter IV

1. How many Persons are there in the Divine Being?
Three: the Father, the Son, and the Holy Ghost.

2. *How are the three Persons one?*
In divine essence.

3. How is the Trinity three?
In distinct Persons.

4. What is the personal attribute of the Father?
That He, as Father, is self-existent.

5. What is the personal attribute of the Son?
That He is begotten of the Father. "Thou art my Son, this day have I begotten Thee" (Ps. 2:7).

6. What is the personal attribute of the Holy Ghost?
That He proceeds from the Father and from the Son.

7. Is the Holy Ghost only a power or attribute of God?
No, He is a real Person, because He has (1) an understanding; (2) a will, for the Spirit searcheth all things, (I Cor. 2:10, 12:11) dividing to every man as He wills; and (3) He appeared at the baptism of Christ (Matt. 3:16,17).

8. Is the Holy Ghost a distinct Person?
Yes, He is specifically referred to as a separate Person. "I will pray the Father, and He shall give you another Comforter" (John 14:16).

9. How can we prove that the Son and Holy Ghost are God as well as the Father?
From (1) their divine names, (2) their divine attributes, (3) their divine work, and (4) their divine honor.

10. Is the doctrine of the Trinity necessary unto salvation?
Yes, because by this doctrine we receive a true knowledge of God and learn to seek atonement with the Father as Judge, in the satisfaction of the Son, through the work of the Holy Spirit (John 6:44).

11. Are God's decrees something separate from Himself?
No, these decrees are identical to the God who has decreed them. God's mind and will determine all matters that take place outside of the essence of His own Being.

12. When did God establish His decrees?
From eternity. "Known unto God are all His works from the beginning of the world" (Acts 15:18).

13. Did God establish His decrees freely?
Yes. "Even so, Father, for so it seemed good in Thy sight" (Matt. 11:26).

14. Are all God's decrees wise decrees?
Yes. "O the depth of the riches, both of the wisdom and knowledge of God! how unsearchable are His judgments, and His ways past finding out!" (Rom. 11:33).

15. Has God decreed who shall be saved and who not?
Yes, in His decree of predestination or fore-ordaining. "Whom He did predestinate, them He also called" (Rom. 8:30).

16. How many parts, or acts of God, are contained in predestination?
Two: election and reprobation. "God hath not appointed us to wrath, but to obtain salvation by our Lord Jesus Christ" (I Thess. 5:9).

17. When was the decree of election formed?
From eternity. "As He hath chosen us in Him before the foundation of the world" (Eph. 1:4).

18. Is election universal, that is, are all men elected?
No, the smaller portion of mankind are elected. "Many are called, but few chosen" (Matt. 20:16).

19. Does election apply to individual persons whom God knows by name?
Yes. "Jacob have I loved, but Esau have I hated" (Rom. 9:13).

20. Why has God elected one and not another?
This is only due to His free and sovereign good pleasure. "He hath mercy on whom He will have mercy, and whom He will He hardeneth" (Rom. 9:18).

21. Is election based on foreseen faith or the good works of man?
No. "It is not of him that willeth, nor of him that runneth, but of God that sheweth mercy" (Rom. 9:16).

22. Is God severe or unjust in sovereignly electing certain persons and rejecting others?
No, for God might justly have left all men to perish in their sins.

23. Is election changeable?
No, it is unchangeable. "That the purpose of God according to election might stand" (Rom. 9:11).

24. Since election is unchangeable, may we conclude that it does not make a difference how we live?
No, for God has also decreed the means which He will use in the conversion of a sinner (Rom. 8: 29-30).

25. If an elect person should refuse to use the means, will he still be saved?
God will give him a heart that desires to use the means (Phil. 2:13).

26. What are the marks of election?
Faith, hope, and love (I Thes. 1:3,4).

27. What does the doctrine of predestination promote?
(1) The glorification of God to the highest degree in His supreme power, independency, wisdom, grace righteousness, and truth, and (2) the humbling of man to the lowest degree before God (Rom. 9:20, 21; I Cor. 4:7).

CHAPTER 4

Part I. Chapter Review

1. The word "trinity" is formed from the words _____ and _____ ; it is only revealed in God's _____ revelation — the _____ .

2. Name the three types of Old Testament texts that reveal the Trinity:
   a. _____
   b. _____
   c. _____

3. Name the personal properties of:
   a. God the Father — _____
   b. God the Son — _____
   c. God the Holy Spirit — _____

4. State the name of the divine Person to whom each of the following works are primarily ascribed in Scripture:
   a. _____ Purchasing salvation.
   b. _____ Electing sinners to salvation.
   c. _____ Dwelling in the hearts of all true believers.
   d. _____ Applying salvation to the elect.
   e. _____ Providing for all things.
   f. _____ Giving both natural and spiritual life.

5. Three rhyming words which describe the primary work of each divine Person in the salvation of sinners are as follows: salvation is _____ by God the Father, _____ by God the Son, and _____ by God the Holy Spirit.

6. Four groups of texts which prove that both God the Son and God the Holy Spirit are actual divine Persons are those that give them:
   a. _____   c. _____
   b. _____   d. _____

7. Why is God's decree often referred to as God's "decrees"? _____
   _____
   _____

8. List five scriptural names for God's decree:

   a. _____   d. _____

   b. _____   e. _____

   c. _____

9. State seven characteristics of God's decree:

   a. _____   e. _____

   b. _____   f. _____

   c. _____   g. _____

   d. _____

10. God's decree is an _____ work of God regarding His external works which are His _____, _____, and _____.

11. Name and define the two parts of God's decree of predestination:

    a. _____ — _____

       _____

    b. _____ — _____

       _____

12. The Bible speaks of an election of:

    a. _____   d. _____

    b. _____   e. _____

    c. _____   f. _____

13. Personal election includes the following five characteristics:

    a. _____   d. _____

    b. _____   e. _____

    c. _____

14. Election is the _____ and _____ of God's church.

15. The doctrine of predestination _____ _____ to the highest and _____ _____ to the lowest.

16. Election holds an important place in Scripture for the following four reasons:

    a. _____

    b. _____

    c. _____

    d. _____

CHAPTER 4

Part II. Deepening Your Insight

1. List the expressions that the *Athanasian Creed* uses to clearly express that God is
   a. One Being — _____
      _____

   b. Three distinct Persons — _____
      _____

   c. Equal Persons — _____
      _____

2. How would you respond to a person who claimed that the Holy Spirit was not a divine Person, but only a divine power or influence flowing out from God? _____
   _____
   _____
   _____

3. What is the difference between mental and experiential knowledge, and why is experiential knowledge of God necessary? _____
   _____
   _____
   _____

4. How is God's decree related to His external works of creation, providence, and redemption? ____
   _____

5. Why is natural man at enmity with God's decree of predestination? _____
   _____
   _____

6. How would you answer a person who stated the following:
   a. "Predestination is unjust." — _____
      _____
      _____

   b. "Predestination erases human freedom." — _____
      _____
      _____

   c. "Predestination takes away human responsibility and activity." — _____
      _____
      _____

7. Why is a scriptural balance between God's sovereignty (God's decree of predestination) and man's responsibility (active use of God's means of grace) very important? _____
   _____
   _____
   _____

QUESTIONS

Part III. Biblical Applications

1. What reference to the Trinity can be found in the following chapters?
   a. Genesis 11 — _____
   b. Isaiah 6 — _____
   c. Luke 3 — _____
   d. Hebrews 9 — _____

2. How do the following verses reveal that the Holy Spirit is a divine Person, and not just a power flowing out from God?
   a. Acts 13:2 — _____
   b. Ephesians 4:30 — _____
   c. Matthew 28:19 — _____
   d. Romans 15:13 — _____
   e. John 14:26 — _____

3. What references to God's decree are found in the following chapters?
   a. Proverbs 16 — _____
   b. Malachi 1 — _____
   c. Isaiah 46 — _____

4. Which verses in James 1 clearly teach that God does not influence man toward any evil, even in the execution of His decree? _____

Part IV. From the Writings of our Church Forefathers

In your own words, explain the meaning of the following quotations:

1. "It is rashness to search, godliness to believe, safeness to preach, and eternal blessedness to know the Trinity" (Thomas Adams). _____
   _____
   _____
   _____

2. "Our spiritual estate standeth upon a sure bottom: the beginning is from God the Father, the dispensation from the Son, and the application from the Holy Ghost" (Thomas Manton). _____
   _____
   _____
   _____

3. "For no man is damned precisely because God hath not chosen him, because he is not elected; but because he is a sinner, and doth willfully refuse the means of grace offered" (Anthony Burgess). __
   _____
   _____
   _____

CHAPTER 4

Part V. From the Marginal Questions

1. Why is it more "understandable" to believe in a God we cannot fully understand, than to believe in a god that is completely understood by the human mind? _____

   _____

   _____

   _____

   _____

2. If God the Father, Son, or Holy Spirit were not God, why would the salvation of a sinner be impossible? _____

   _____

   _____

   _____

   _____

3. Concerning true, experiential knowledge of God, what must we carefully teach and not teach? ____

   _____

   _____

   _____

   _____

4. Some "Christians" today deny the doctrine of God's decree. Why is this denial actually denying that God is God? What type of ruler would God be if He ruled without a plan? _____

   _____

   _____

   _____

   _____

5. How is the doctrine of election the hope and security of God's church? _____

   _____

   _____

   _____

   _____

EXTRA CHALLENGE QUESTIONS

Part VI. Your Selection from the Marginal Questions

Write out and respond to two marginal questions that interest you which have not been previously asked in the chapter's question section.

1. Question: _____

_____

Response: _____

_____

_____

_____

_____

2. Question: _____

_____

Response: _____

_____

_____

_____

_____

Part VII. Project Ideas

1. Research and design a chart which shows the struggles with heresies regarding the Trinity that the church has had in its history.

2. Design a display which shows what the Jehovah's Witnesses, Mormons, and Christian Scientists believe about God's Person.

3. Construct a chart which shows how the divine Persons and their works are taught in the three universal creeds.

4. Draw a poster that displays how we can prove from Scripture that the Holy Spirit is a divine Person.

5. Make a large display that demonstrates the necessary balance between God's sovereignty (decree of predestination) and man's responsibility (active use of God's means of grace). Add as many texts as you can find to each side. State why a proper balance in this matter is very important.

5

God's Creation
Theory of Evolution
Angels

The heavens declare God's glory,
And His firmament displays
The handiwork and power of
The great Creator's ways.

Yet some, with vain imaginings,
Claim everything began
With simple forms,
And we evolved from animals to man.

But God has made each creature both
In heaven and on earth;
Let men and angels worship and
Extol His matchless worth.

FROM OUR REFORMED DOCTRINAL STANDARDS

Belgic Confession of Faith

Article 12 — Of Creation

We believe that the Father, by the Word, that is, by His Son, hath created of nothing, the heaven, the earth, and all creatures, as it seemed good unto Him, giving unto every creature its being, shape, form, and several offfices to serve its Creator. That He doth also still uphold and govern them by His eternal providence, and infinite power, for the service of mankind, to the end that man may serve his God. He also created the angels good, to be His messengers and to serve His elect; some of whom are fallen from that excellency, in which God created them, into everlasting perdition; and the others have, by the grace of God, remained steadfast and continued in their primitive state. The devils and evil spirits are so depraved, that they are enemies of God and every good thing, to the utmost of their power, as murderers, watching to ruin the Church and every member thereof, and by their wicked strategems to destroy all; and are, therefore, by their own wickedness, adjudged to eternal damnation, daily expecting their horrible torments. Therefore we reject and abhor the error of the Saducees, who deny the existence of spirits and angels: and also that of the Manichees, who assert that the devils have their origin of themselves, and that they are wicked of their own nature, without having been corrupted.

5

GOD'S CREATION

The first performing of God's decree outside of Himself began with His act of creating. "In the beginning God created the heaven and the earth" (Gen. 1:1).

The word "create" has both a human and a divine meaning. Human creative abilities are precious gifts from God. The following example illustrates various ways in which people can be creative:

> George is keenly interested in his Art classes, especially when working with water colors. Today, his paintbrush is in continuous motion as one idea after another flows from his mind onto paper. In fascination, George becomes more and more deeply involved in his work as his painting grows in design and color.
>
> Sally, however, does not enjoy Art class nearly as much as George, but has a deep feeling for music. She has already composed several of her own songs and loves playing the piano hour after hour.
>
> Robert, whose interests lie in the Industrial Arts area, has special skill for designing and constructing woodworking projects, especially furniture.
>
> Lisa has a special talent for writing poetry and loves composing verses about nature. Alice, however, is particularly fond of Home Economics, and cake decorating is her specialty.
>
> These young people are creative in various ways. However, do they create something from nothing, or from

? How is God's creation of the universe different from a person's creation of a beautiful nature scene in an oil painting?

? Our creative abilities reveal that we are created above the animals, but also, that we are not God. How are both of these statements true?

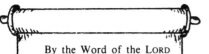

By the Word of the LORD were the heavens made; and all the host of them by the breath of His mouth.

For He spake, and it was done; He commanded, and it stood fast.

— Psalm 33:6,9

Thus saith God the LORD, He that created the heavens, and stretched them out; He that spread forth the earth, and that which cometh out of it; He that giveth breath unto the people upon it, and spirit to them that walk therein.

— Isaiah 42:5

● **Triune God** — The Trinity; God the Father, Son, and Holy Spirit

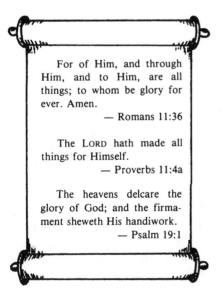

For of Him, and through Him, and to Him, are all things; to whom be glory for ever. Amen.

— Romans 11:36

The LORD hath made all things for Himself.

— Proverbs 11:4a

The heavens delcare the glory of God; and the firmament sheweth His handiwork.

— Psalm 19:1

● **Manifestation** — A revelation; a display

previously existing materials? Are their paintings, songs, and projects totally unrelated to any previously existing materials, objects, or ideas? Can a person create anything from nothing?

When man "creates," his creative ability is limited; he forms new ideas or projects from previous thoughts, words, shapes, colors, and materials. When God creates, however, His creative ability is unlimited. He created the entire universe and everything in it from nothing. Only an almighty God can do this; only He can speak and it will be done, command and it will stand firm. Only His Word is all-powerful.

Scripture teaches that creation is the work of a **Triune God.** The following chart reveals that God the Father, Son, and Holy Spirit all took part in God's creating work.

CREATION: THE WORK OF A TRIUNE GOD	
God the Father	But to us there is but one God, the Father, of whom are all things, and we in Him. — I Corinthians 8:6a Lord, Thou art God, which hast made heaven, and earth, and the sea, and all that in them is. — Acts 4:24b
God the Son	In the beginning was the Word, and the Word was with God, and the Word was God. All things were made by Him; and without Him was not any thing made that was made. — John 1:1,3 God, who created all things by Jesus Christ. — Ephesians 3:9b
God the Holy Spirit	And the earth was without form, and void; and darkness was upon the face of the deep. And the Spirit of God moved upon the face of the waters. — Genesis 1:2 Thou sendest forth Thy Spirit, they are created: and Thou renewest the face of the earth. — Psalm 104:30

God created all things to reveal His glory. God's creative work could not increase His excellence which is infinitely perfect, but it was an outward **manifestation** of the majesty of His Being.

Our happiness and welfare are connected to this truth. As human beings, we were created to know, love, and serve God. True happiness and **contentment** can only be found when God is the center of our lives and we live for His honor and glory rather than our own. What is the deepest desire, motivation, and purpose in your life?

David wrote the following truth concerning God's creation in Psalm 19:

PSALM 19:1-4a

The heavens declare the glory of God; and the firmament sheweth His handiwork.

Day unto day uttereth speech, and night unto night sheweth knowledge.

There is no speech nor language, where their voice is not heard.

Their line is gone out through all the earth, and their words to the end of the world.

? Can you list several ways in which creation reveals God's "handiwork"? How can God's "hand" be seen and His "voice" be heard day and night in His creation?

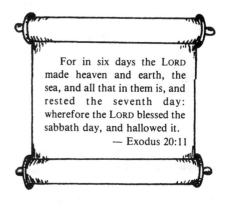

For in six days the LORD made heaven and earth, the sea, and all that in them is, and rested the seventh day: wherefore the LORD blessed the sabbath day, and hallowed it.
— Exodus 20:11

God created the entire universe and everything within it in six days. The following chart shows how the pattern of the first three days is repeated in the second three:

GOD'S CREATION WEEK			
FIRST DAY	God created *Light.*	FOURTH DAY	God created the sun, moon, and stars to be the *light bearers.*
SECOND DAY	God created the *firmament*, separating the *waters* above from the waters below.	FIFTH DAY	God created the *birds* which fly in the *firmament* and the *animals* which live in the *waters.*
THIRD DAY	God formed the *dry land* and created the *trees* and *plants.*	SIXTH DAY	God created the *animals* and *man* which live on *land* and feed upon *trees* and *plants.*
SEVENTH DAY — GOD RESTED: HIS CREATION WORK WAS COMPLETE It was perfect; without any sin			

- **Initial** — First; beginning

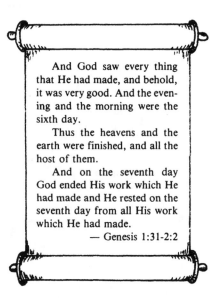

> And God saw every thing that He had made, and behold, it was very good. And the evening and the morning were the sixth day.
> Thus the heavens and the earth were finished, and all the host of them.
> And on the seventh day God ended His work which He had made and He rested on the seventh day from all His work which He had made.
> — Genesis 1:31-2:2

- **Theory** — A possible explanation; that which provides a framework for further experimentation and thought, but is not proven

- **Evolution** — A belief that all life developed from non-living and simpler forms to more complex on its own, without God

- **Origin** — Beginning; forming; creating

- **Solar system** — Our sun with the planets and other bodies that revolve around it

? Who is the evolutionist's "god"? What is his "bible"? What rich securities and purposes of life are missed by evolutionists?

- **Assumptions** — Things we suppose or take for granted to be true without careful examination or proof

In six days God completed His **initial** creating work. All things included in His perfect plan were created. God rested on the seventh day. Having completed His special creation work, God rested, viewing His complete creation with delight — for all was perfect and without sin.

THE THEORY OF EVOLUTION

Some people deny the truth of God's creation, and some even deny the existence of God altogether. These people believe that the universe, earth, and life gradually developed according to explanations given in the **theory** of **evolution**.

In our present society, there are two main beliefs regarding the **origin** of all things:

1. *Biblical Creationism* — Biblical creationists believe that God created the universe and everything in it through miraculous acts of His divine power as described in Genesis 1 and 2.

2. *Evolutionism* — Evolutionists believe that matter always existed or increased, and that either through a great explosion or some other process, our **solar system** was formed. Life on earth formed by chance from non-living substances and over billions of years, developed on its own from simpler to more complex forms. Evolutionists believe that this process is still taking place today.

Neither of these beliefs can be proven scientifically. Science is the observation and study of the physical universe and its properties. The origin of the universe was not witnessed by any human. No scientific experiment can create a universe for observation and testing to see how it may have originated. However, scientists can observe facts, properties, and laws of the present universe, and from these observations give suggestions, ideas, or theories, but not *proofs* of the beginning of all things. All scientific inquiries into the origins of things are greatly influenced by the person's own viewpoints, **assumptions**, and limited observations.

The following story illustrates how all human investigations are influenced by the persons' own assumptions and experiences.

Imagine three warriors from a secluded highland tribe deep in the mountainous highlands of Irian Jaya, suddenly stumbling upon an electric typewriter which had previously fallen from an airplane passing overhead. These natives have never seen a white person nor ever been exposed to any modern invention. The only tools they had were made of roughly-cut wood or stone.

They carry the strange object they found to their tribe and a special meeting of the village wisemen is called to examine this "new find." The entire tribe wants to know where this object came from and how it was formed.

After several days of meetings and hours of debate, the wisemen could not agree on all points of view, but they did adopt these principles of common explanation:

1.   This object originally came from stone, for its body was stone-like all over. It probably was hollowed out through rough water action — for what else could hollow out a rock is such a dramatic way?

2.   The equal size "pebbles" set in perfect rows within the hollow stone must have been washed and set into position by the stream in which it was originally sitting. How each pebble could be exactly the same size and be placed in perfect rows remains a remarkable mystery.

3.   The softer, round thing trapped inside the hollow stone above the pebbles was a section of vine which was stuck in the rock so tightly that it could not be pulled out.

Of greatest difficulty to explain, however, is how this hollowed rock with its stuck pebbles and vine could be found nearly a mile from, and hundreds of feet above, the nearest stream. This problem was finally resolved by the discovery of a cord-like vine sticking out of the side of the rock. From the pronged shape of the end, one could safely determine that it had been ripped. Since no one from the village had seen this stone before, it must have been dragged uphill by some animal that had stepped into the stream and snagged its foot in this vine. The animal had climbed as high as their village before the vine broke, leaving the rock where the natives found it.

The wisdom of the village wisemen to explain the origin and formation of this recent find was deeply admired by the villagers, who listened in awe and reverence to this explanation!

? If a person is truly sincere in that which he believes, does this necessarily mean that he is right? Can a person be sincere, but be sincerely wrong?

The native wisemen in the previous story made several careful observations. They then sincerely described what they believed to be the most logical explanation of the object's origin and formation. However, due to the limitations of their knowledge and experience, their assumption and explanations were wrong. They were sincere — but, sincerely mistaken.

This same principle applies to scientific theories regarding origins of the universe and life on earth. Due to the impossibility of actually observing their formation, the question of origins is not provable scientifically, but is believed by faith.

Through faith we understand that the worlds were framed by the Word of God, so that things which are seen were not made of things which do appear.

— Hebrews 11:3

And saying, Sirs, why do ye these things? We also are men of like passions with you, and preach unto you that ye should turn from these vanities unto the living God, which made heaven, and earth, and the sea, and all things that are therein.

— Acts 14:15

"The observable fact that many animals have similar bones, organs, and body systems shows that they evolved from one common type," Margaret argued.

"I don't agree," Lisa retorted. "These common characteristics reveal that they were made by the same Creator."

Which aspects of the two girls' arguments are scientific observations? Which are personal beliefs or theories?

"Where do you believe everything came from?" David asked.

"From God who created all things," responded Mark.

"Where did God come from?"

"I do not know," Mark answered hesitantly, "I believe...that He always existed."

"You see," laughed Dave. "You believe in things that you cannot prove."

However, Dave laughed too soon, for Mark decided to ask him the same questions. "Where do you believe everything came from?" he asked.

"Complex life gradually developed from simpler forms."

"From where did the simpler forms of life come?"

"From non-living matter."

"Where did the non-living matter come from?"

"Probably from an explosion of a huge substance of original matter and energy that blew apart billions of years ago."

"From where did that original substance come?"

This time David hesitated, "I don't know. I believe...that it always existed."

Thus saith the LORD thy redeemer, and He that formed thee from the womb, I am the LORD that maketh all things; that stretcheth forth the heavens alone; that spreadeth abroad the earth by Myself.
— Isaiah 44:24

Thou, even Thou, art LORD alone; Thou hast made heaven, the heaven of heavens, with all their host, the earth, and all things that are therein, the seas, and all that is therein, and Thou preservest them all; and the host of heaven worshippeth Thee.
— Nehemiah 9:6

Of old hast Thou laid the foundation of the earth: and the heavens are the work of Thy hands.
— Psalm 102:25

Answers concerning origins cannot be proven scientifically; they are believed by faith. Those believing in God's Word accept creation by faith; non-believers accept evolution by faith. The one group believes that life is the result of an eternal plan and purpose; the other that life is the result of a purposeless happening or accident.

It is important to observe that denying God's creation is not a small matter. The Bible begins with the important truth of God's creating work and refers back to it more than seventy-five times. The evolutionary theory attempts to replace God, teaching that life has come about by chance and that human beings are only higher forms of animals. Therefore, evolutionists believe that there is no Word or law of God, no such thing as sin, no eternal life or death, no need for salvation from sin, no divine miracles, and no divine Christ. Man is the highest creature; each person can determine right or wrong for himself; he is a "god" to himself. **Humanism** becomes the evolutionist's "religion" — his deepest belief. Science becomes his "bible" — his source of truth. This matter is very serious. The more evolution is believed by a person, school, or society, the more God will be replaced by "Mother Nature," God's laws by man's ideas, God's Word by scientific "truths," and living for God and eternal realities by living for self and **temporal** pleasures. Evolution rejects God, His Word, and the purpose for human life.

While one's belief in the beginning of all things is **ultimately** a matter of faith, scientific observation provides evidences which support biblical creation and contradict the evolutionary theory. Some evidences are:

? How would believing that one is a developing animal in an accidental chain of evolutionary development greatly change a person's outlook on life? How would this person's life differ from a true Christian's? Are there "Christians" who do not believe the evolutionary view, but actually live as if it is true? How?

● **Humanism** — A belief that man is the highest creature, that he is ultimately answerable only to himself, and that he may decide for himself what is true or false and right or wrong; a belief that man is god

? What results of the evolutionary way of thinking can you observe in our present-day society?

● **Temporal** — Existing only for a limited time; not eternal

● **Ultimately** — Finally; reaching the furthest point

Uniform — The same; identical

Rotating — Turning; spinning

Law (scientific) — That which has been tested and always proven to be true

Thermodynamics — The study of heat, work, and energy, and the changing of one into another

Complexity — The condition of being made of many different parts; complicated; the opposite of simplicity

1. *The lack of **uniform** materials and motion in our solar system.* Most evolutionists believe in some form of a "big bang" or explosion theory, in which a great body of matter and energy exploded forming different stars. Planets being thrown out from stars and moons from planets are the basic ideas of this theory.

If this theory of the origin of our solar system were true:

— Why is the sun **rotating** slower than all of its planets, while planets are rotating faster than their moons?
— Why are Venus and Uranus rotating in an opposite direction from all other planets in the solar system?
— Why do eleven moons rotate in the opposite direction from all the others in our solar system?
— Why are the proportions of the moon's elements different from the earth's, and the earth's different from the sun's?

Why are these observable facts illogical in, and contradictory to, the evolutionary theory? How can they be readily explained by creation?

2. *The Second Law of Thermodynamics.* This law teaches that all ordered systems left to themselves tend to become more disordered. A system left to itself tends to break down from its more complex forms to return to its simpler; it tends to move from order to disorder.

What happens to a running car engine when its power source is not continuously supplied? What would happen to an engine if it was left to itself for ten, fifty, or a thousand years? Would it tend to become more complex or to break down into simpler forms?

The theory of evolution is built upon the theory that matter and energy left to themselves developed from simpler to more complex forms.

How do the observable facts stated in the Second Law of Thermodynamics contradict the evolutionary theory? How do they agree with creation?

3. *The complexity of nature.* It is estimated that one human eye contains approximately 130 million rods and 7 million cones located in its retina. When light, which travels at 186,000 miles (or 300,000 kilometers) per second, strikes these cones or rods, chemical changes are produced which cause each cone or rod to transmit an electrical impulse through the nerve connected to it. These impulses

pass into the **optic nerve** which transmits them to the **visual cortex** of the brain. The brain continually and instantly reads the complex image of millions of electronic impulses with such precision that colors, and even shades of color — from red (434 trillion vibrations per second) to violet (740 trillion vibrations per second) — can be clearly distinguished. Can you imagine such an intricate system happening by chance?

Imagine a person trying to convince a group that his computer unit, with its thousands of wires all properly connected to produce a clear image on a screen, put itself together by chance — that no one constructed it, but that it evolved by itself. Would anyone in the group believe this explanation. Why not?

How does the observable fact of the complexity of nature contradict the theory of evolution? How does it agree with creation?

4. *The synchronization of nature.* Various parts of nature were made to fit other parts. If there were no Creator, no Master Planner, how would one part of creation know that it should develop in a certain way to fit another part? How would flowering plants have "known" that they should grow bright colored flowers and produce sweet smells, so that millions of years later these colors and smells would attract bees which are necessary for their cross-pollination?

? Do you see God's hand, and are you touched by God's wonderfulness when observing the tremendous complexity and synchronization of creation?

The human body is composed of 206 bones. Suppose that these 206 bones were all placed on the ground in an open area. If a person were to properly reconnect the entire skeleton by **randomly** placing bone ends together, the chance for doing this correctly would only be in 10^{357} attempts. 10^{357} is a number which would be written as a 1 with 357 zeroes behind it! The number "one million" is written with six zeroes, "one billion" with nine, and "one trillion" with twelve.

How does the observable fact of the synchronization of nature contradict the theory of evolution? How does it agree with creation?

5. *The beauty of nature.* The various shapes and colors, together with their coordination in nature, evidence beauty.

Margaret's teacher displayed a beautiful painting of a mountain lake scene in front of her class.

"This painting was formed without the work of an artist," she stated. "Over millions of years, various paints were blown by the wind onto this canvas. Rain, hail, and snow mixed with the paints to wash them into the various shades of color and shapes we see in this painting today."

No matter how Margaret's teacher attempted to convince her class that what she said was true, not one student believed that this beautiful painting was formed by chance. She used all types of similar explanations, speaking of leaves, sticks, pebbles, storms, and earthquakes as playing parts in forming this "painterless" painting. She especially emphasized that "almost anything could happen over millions of years."

Yet, everyone insisted that the beautiful painting had been produced by a painter. Why?

"Beauty" is "having the quality of being pleasing to the eye." This painting testified of its being produced by one who knew and appreciated beauty — otherwise he could not convey "beauty" to another. We were created with the ability to recognize and appreciate beauty, and were placed in a beautiful creation. What does this tell us about our Creator?

? Why would it be even more difficult to believe in a "creatorless" creation than in a "painterless" painting?

How does the observable fact of the beauty in nature contradict the theory of evolution? How does it agree with creation?

172

6. *The Law of Biogenesis*. The Law of Biogenesis states that only living things can produce living things. Thousands of experiments have been done in an attempt to show that life can be produced from non-living matter, but all have failed. These experiments have only shown confirmation of the law that life comes only from life.

How does this observable fact of nature contradict the theory of evolution? How does it agree with creation?

7. *The fossil record reveals distinct species*. Fossils are the remains of previously living plants or animals. Millions of fossils have been found and **classified** — many of which have become **petrified**. These millions of classified fossils reveal animals that can be grouped in distinct species. For instance, types of horses may differ from one another — some are smaller, others larger; some have heavier legs and feet, others lighter, etc. But in all known fossils a horse remains a horse. No known fossil reveals a half-dog and half-horse creature. This is true with all discovered fossils, including those of animals that have long become **extinct**.

> Evolutionists claim that birds developed from reptiles. The first feathers developed from frayed reptilian scales. If this gradual development from reptile to bird, and scale to feather, took place over millions of years, the fossil record should evidence this development. Creatures with quarter, half, and three-quarter wings; with quarter, half, and three-quarter feathers should be evident. But, this is not the case.
>
> Creationists believe that God created distinct "kinds" or species (Genesis 1:11-12;24-25). This is in agreement with the fossil record evidence which reveals distinct species of animals throughout its history.

How does the observable fact of distinct species in the fossil record contradict the theory of evolution? How does it agree with creation?

8. *Evolution from one species to another is not observable today*. **Adaptations** of animals within their own species are observable. For instance: insects will develop stronger resistances to chemical poisons, requiring the development of new insecticide sprays; moths will become lighter colored in drier, lighter climates and darker colored in wetter, darker climates. This type of adaptation within a species is often called "microevolution," with which we do not disagree. These changes are observable facts today.

- **Species** — Distinct kinds of plants and animals, each with its own distinct characteristics

- **Classified** — Named and placed in various classes or groups

- **Petrified** — Turned into stone

- **Extinct** — No longer in existence; having died out

And God said, Let the earth bring forth grass, the herb yielding seed, and the fruit tree yielding fruit after his kind, whose seed is in itself, upon the earth: and it was so.

And the earth brought forth grass, and herb yielding seed after his kind, and the tree yielding fruit, whose seed was in itself, after his kind: and God saw that it was good.

And God said, Let the earth bring forth the living creature after his kind, cattle, and creeping thing, and beast of the earth after his kind: and it was so.

And God made the beast of the earth after his kind, and cattle after their kind, and every thing that creepeth upon the earth after his kind: and God saw that it was good.
— Genesis 1:11-12; 24-25

- **Adaptations** — Changes to fit one's environment

? Why do biblical creationists believe in microevolution but not in macroevolution?

● **Instinct** — An inborn knowledge of necessary behaviors for the survival of each distinct animal species

● **Hybrid** — The offspring from two different types of plants or animals

● **Sterile** — Incapable of reproducing

However, the development of insects into amphibians, or of moths into other species of animals, has never been witnessed. One species developing into another is termed "macroevolution," with which we totally disagree. Generally, when speaking of evolution, macroevolution is meant.

Each species has its own **instincts**. A young duck "knows" how to swim soon after hatching. Try teaching this to a chicken! Try teaching a reptile that it should "think" about flying! You will never succeed, for each species of animal is born with its own instincts.

Distinct species of animals are observable today. Even the cross-breeding of animals is very limited. In the few cases where this is possible (only in cases of very similar species) the resulting **hybrid** is **sterile**. For instance, when a horse is cross-bred with a donkey a mule is formed. The mule, however, is sterile. It cannot reproduce itself as a new species.

? Why are the world and universe personal to the true Christian, but impersonal to the evolutionist? How would the two differ when viewing a "lake and forest" scene? Do you see the Creator in His creation?

A speaker, when once addressing an audience on the subject of origins, stated the following:

"When you tell an evolutionist that you cannot observe evolution from one species to another taking place today, he will tell you that evolution takes place 'too slowly' for a person to observe it in his lifetime. If this were true, then you would assume that the past history of our world would be full of examples. However, no evidence is found of gradual evolution in the fossil record. It seems to have occured 'too quickly' in the past to be recorded.

I tell you, this evolutionary process is a strange matter. If it is happening 'too slowly' today to see it, and has happened 'too quickly' in the past to find it, I think it is wiser to say that it has never happened at all!''

How does the fact that we cannot observe evolution from one species to another today contradict the theory of evolution? How does it agree with creation?

9. *Man's conscience and soul.* All human beings are born with a conscience — a sense of God and of right and wrong. All civilizations, even the most primitive cultures, have some form of god and religious worship. A sense of the importance of one's soul is felt in all people — all feel to some degree the moral responsibility and **accountability** attached to the exercise of their will.

- **Accountability** — Being held responsible; needing to give account for one's dealings

Human personhood, therefore, could not have developed from an impersonal, **morally-void**, material source. Man's personhood requires a personal, moral, and spiritual Creator.

- **Morally-void** — Without any morals or moral personhood

How does the observable fact of man's conscience contradict the theory of evolution? How does it agree with creation?

10. *The testimony of God's Word.* The most important and **irrefutable** evidence of creation is God's Word. The Bible clearly states that ''in six days the LORD made heaven and earth, the sea, and all that in them is'' (Exodus 20:11a). Evidences revealing that the Bible is the true Word of God were studied in Chapter Three.

- **Irrefutable** — Incapable of being proven wrong

God cannot contradict Himself. He cannot state that He has created the universe in a certain manner in His Word and testify of contrary realities in His creation. Therefore observable evidences of God's creative work are evident in His creation.

How does the observable fact of the testimony of God's Word contradict the theory of evolution? How does it agree with creation? Why is this the most important and irrefutable evidence of all?

Do you observe and rejoice in God's creation? Do you pause to quietly hear His voice and see His hand in nature? Is creation the personal work of a personal God to you, or is it impersonal matter from an impersonal source and power? How should our view of creation be reflected in how we think of, and use it? How can we undervalue and misuse creation? Has God opened your spiritual eyes, enabling you to see His majesty in creation?

? Why would a true Christian not only see, but also use, creation differently from an evolutionist?

? Why would a true child of God rejoice in God's creation, but even more in His Word? How does this question relate to God's general and special revelation?

Evolutionists claim the following evidences for the evolutionary theory:

1. *The similarities found in various plants and animals* — To the evolutionist, this is evidence that plants and animals evolved from common **ancestors.** To the creationists, however, this testifies of their common Creator.

2. *Vestigial organs* — Evolutionists believe that vestigial organs (parts of the body which do not seem to serve any necessary function) are evidences of organs that were needed in previous stages of development but are no longer necessary.

At one time 180 vestigial organs or structures were listed for the human body. Increased knowledge, however, has reduced this number to zero. Useful functions for all organs of the human body are known today. One that is still listed in some books as a vestigial organ is the appendix. However, it is now realized that this organ helps to provide protection against infection, especially in infants, and that it provides a storage place for vital intestinal organisms which might otherwise be lost in a severe case of diarrhea.

3. *The Embryonic recapitulation theory* — This once popular theory taught that a human embryo (a child developing in its mother's womb) went through its evolutionary ancestry as it formed. A human embryo first has one-celled animal characteristics, then it appears as a worm, fish, reptile, mammal, and finally as a human.

Today, increased study reveals that the most complex organs begin to develop first in the embryo, which gives it various exaggerated and strange appearances in the first months of its development. Matters such as a "tail formation" and "gill slits" which formerly were quoted as support for this theory have been proven to be incorrect. Presently, this theory has fallen from favor and has lost most of its supporters.

4. *A stratified fossil record* — This record shows simpler life forms located in the bottom layers of rock and more complex forms in the top layers. This simple to complex idea has been used to form the Evolutionary **Geological** Table as seen on the opposite page.

- **Ancestors** — Generations of parents; those from whom one has descended

- **Vestigial** — That which marks or evidences something no longer needed or present

- **Embryonic** — Pertaining to an embryo or the earliest stages of development in the womb before birth

- **Recapitulation** — A repeating of all previous steps or stages

- **Stratified** — Placed in strata or layers

- **Geological** — Dealing with the physical structure and history of the earth

EVOLUTIONARY GEOLOGICAL COLUMN				
Era	Period	Biological Features (First appearances of:)	Time (In years ago)	Age of:
CENOZOIC	Quaternary	Diversification of mammals and birds, man	70 million to the present	Mammals
	Tertiary			
MESOZOIC	Cretaceous	Larger mammals, insect-eating animals, multiplication of deciduous trees and grasses	135 to 70 million	Reptiles Flowering Plants
	Jurassic	Flying reptiles, birds, coniferous trees, small mammals	180 to 135 million	
	Triassic	Marine reptiles, dinosaurs, small mammals, flowering plants	225 to 180 million	
PALEOZOIC	Permian	Reptiles and large insects	270 to 225 million	Amphibians Seed plants
	Carboniferous	Insects, spiders, snails, large amphibians, seed plants	350 to 270 million	
	Devonian	Amphibians, sharks, small trees	410 to 350 million	Fishes Land plants
	Silurian	Small land plants	440 to 410 million	
	Ordovician	Fish, clams, corals	500 to 440 million	Invertebrates Seaweeds
	Cambrian	Trilobites, mollusks, seaweed	600 to 500 million	
PRE-CAMBRIAN		Algae, sponges, jellyfish, worms	Before 600 million	Algae

- **Ascending** — Climbing; advancing; rising

- **Trilobite** — An extinct, flat, oval arthropod that is believed by evolutionists to have lived and died in the ocean more than 500 million years ago

- **Protruding** — Extending; projecting

- **Sedimentary rock** — Rocks which have been formed by matter that settled and was deposited in water

- **Sediment** — Various materials which settle to the bottom in water

- **Mutations** — Sudden changes appearing in the offspring of plants or animals due to a change in their genetic structure

- **Genetic structure** — The pattern of genes (the units which carry the inherited characteristics to its offspring) in each species

Evidences of a simple to complex fossil arrangement in the earth's rock layers is not thoroughly convincing. For instance:

— No single rock layer structure in the world reveals fossils in the same total **ascending** order that the Evolutionary Geological Table suggests.

— Hundreds of reversals of the table's predicted order have been unearthed showing simpler life-form fossils in rock layers above more complex forms.

— Fossils are frequently found in vast numbers called "fossil graveyards." These graveyards contain mixed fossils of many different forms of animals in the same rock layers.

— Fossilized evidences of a **trilobite** in a human footprint, a human footprint in a dinosaur print, and other "impossibilities" according to the Evolutionary Geological Table have been documented.

— Cases of fossilized tree trunks **protruding** through several rock layers indicate that these layers were laid down in short succession and not over millions of years.

Creationists believe that the **sedimentary rock** layers, which are found in every continent of the world, testify of a worldwide flood, and not of an evolutionary process. As the flood waters rose, the simplest forms of life would generally die first and settle to the bottom; birds, larger mammals, and man would all fly or climb to the highest points available and die last. Animals would basically be buried in this order with numerous exceptions. The swirling waters would also bury thousands of creatures together in various places on earth, forming large "fossil graveyards" of mixed forms of life. As the flood subsided, layers of **sediment** settled and hardened, burying all forms of life in these various layers, at times settling around an upright tree trunk which penetrated through several rock layers. Trilobites, dinosaurs, and human beings all lived and perished together in a great worldwide flood; therefore their fossils can all be found together.

5. *Mutations* — Mutations are changes which occur in the **genetic structure** of a living creature. While mutations are rare, they do occur. Most present-day evolutionists believe in a "mutation and natural selection" model of evolution. They believe that one animal changed into another through a series of mutations.

For example, evolutionists believe that the bat evolved from mice or rats because the bodies of these animals are very similar. A teacher of evolution using the mutation and **natural selection** method would explain this process in a similar manner to the following example:

> "Over millions of years a mutation occurred in which a mouse was born with webbed front feet. As this mouse mated, other web-footed mice were born. In this manner, web-footed mice gradually became established. Over millions of years a second mutation took place which affected this same group of web-footed mice, doubling the size of their webbed feet. A similar series of mutations took place every several million years until eventually, present-day bats with large wings developed."

If we examine this explanation we need to note that mutations occur only once in an estimated ten million cell divisions. The odds of two mutations happening to one gene are one in a hundred trillion cell divisions.

To develop populations large enough before another mutation could reasonably be expected to occur would require millions of years. How would the first mice with their awkwardly webbed feet have survived for millions of years? How would the succeeding generations with half feet and half wings have been able to flee from their predators fast enough to survive for another period of millions of years until the next beneficial mutation would have occurred? How would natural selection actually work against species experiencing mutations of this drastic nature, if they ever would have occurred?

While minor mutations do occur, creationists believe this would never provide a reasonable explanation for the vast complexity of plant and animal species that we observe in the world today. They deny a reasonably possible "random mutation and natural selection theory" for these reasons:

a. A change from one species to another through mutations has never been observed, but only new **strains** of the same species.

b. A mutated form of a species is almost always weaker than its natural type.

● **Natural selection** — The theory that nature tends to keep and increase those species having characteristics best fitted for survival in their environments

? Believing in evolutionary theories requires tremendous faith in the unseen. Why?

● **Strains** — Varieties; stocks; races; variations within the same species

179

c. A mutation only changes species that already exists.

d. The structures of plants and animals are so complex and different from one another that imagining random mutations to have produced this vast variety would be reasonably impossible. This would be similar to imagining that a series of explosions in a print shop could drop all the necessary letters in **precise** order to form a complete dictionary.

- **Precise** — Exact

e. If one mutation occurs in ten million cell divisions and two in one hundred trillion, imagine what the odds are for three or four to randomly occur in the same species! Even if every mutation were positive (which the vast majority are not), the complexity of the living organisms we observe today would certainly have required thousands, possibly millions or billions of mutations to have occurred. Even millions or billions of years would not provide sufficient time for this number of random mutations to have taken place.

Julian Huxley, a famous evolutionist, said, "A one with three million zeroes after; this is the measure of the unlikeliness of the horse — the odds against it happening at all. No one would bet on anything so improbable happening; and yet it happened!"

If these are the odds against the development of the horse, one wonders what the odds would be for other animals, man, and all of creation!

It is evident that all evolutionary theories require great periods of time. Without this their theory would be ruled out immediately. Evolutionists claim the age of the earth and universe to be millions or billions of years. All attempts to date the age of the earth and universe are based on numerous **assumptions**. Two major assumptions of all evolutionary theories are:

- **Assumptions** — Things we suppose or take for granted to be true without careful examination or proof

1. Everything began "young"; it was not created with the appearance of age.

2. Everything has continued the same as we observe it today, at a constant rate of change; there was no worldwide flood or other great **catastrophe** that greatly altered present dating processes or calculations.

- **Catastrophe** — A sudden, violent disturbance; a widespread disaster

180

Mr. Wens addressed his eleventh grade Biology class, giving the following "proof" for the age of the universe: "Light travels at a speed of 186,000 miles or 300,000 kilometres per second. According to our best calculations, at this rate of speed it would take more than a million years for the light of some distant galaxies to reach the earth. Because their light has reached our earth, we know that the age of the universe is greater than a million years."

Mrs. Tyler also speaks to her eleventh grade Biology class about the age of the universe, and states: "God created all things in mature forms. Adam was not created as an infant, but as an adult. The trees were not brought into existence as seeds, but as mature plants bearing fruit. Birds were not formed as eggs, but as fully developed creatures. The stars were created completely fulfilling their purpose — their light was instantly directed by God to all parts of the universe. Through these examples and countless others, we can observe that God created a mature, fully-functioning universe—one which had the appearance of age."

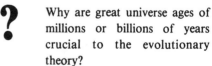 Why are great universe ages of millions or billions of years crucial to the evolutionary theory?

What assumptions were each of these Biology teachers making? Could either of these assumptions be scientifically proven to be true or false? Why or why not?

- **Meteor** — Small bodies of matter traveling through space which frequently collide with larger bodies such as moons, planets, etc.

- **Comet** — A celestial body which orbits the sun in large oval paths. It consists of a small dense nucleus (cone) and a "tail" of vapor

- **Orbits** — Circles around

- **Vaporized** — Converted from a solid or liquid into a vapor — a gaseous form

The following are ten observable evidences which testify of a young earth and universe — one which is thousands, rather than millions or billions of years old:

1. *Moondust* — The moon has no atmosphere. If it existed for millions or billions of years, then tens or hundreds of feet of **meteor** dust, particles and rocks would have collected upon its surface. However, Apollo astronauts found only one-eighth of an inch (two millimetres) of dust upon the moon's surface.

2. *Sun shrink* — It is estimated that the sun consumes some 4.2 million tons of matter per second to produce the energy and heat required for life as we know it to exist on earth. In order for the sun to have burned at this rate for billions of years, its original diameter would need to have been larger than the present distance between the earth and the sun. Mercury, Venus, and the Earth all would have been inside the sun!

3. *Comets* — Each time a **comet orbits** and passes close to the sun, it is heated. This results in some of its matter being **vaporized** and lost. This is seen as a hazy or misty tail. Calculations based upon the rate of material loss and maximum possible original size reveal a maximum lifespan of only thousands of years for the most frequently appearing comets.

4. *The earth's magnetic field* — The magnetic field of the earth is weakening at a measurable rate each year. Projecting this rate backward results in an earth which could not have existed more than several thousand years.

5. *The earth's atmosphere* — Decaying processes of radioactive elements (such as uranium and radium) form helium. The small amount of helium in the earth's atmosphere reveals a present decay rate on earth of several thousand years. Millions or billions of years of decay would have resulted in much higher levels of helium in our atmosphere today.

6. *The earth's surface* — Millions of tons of dust from meteors

and **meteorites** fall to the earth's surface each year. These particles contain large amounts of nickel, cobalt, and other heavy substances. The measurable amounts of these materials on the earth's land and in its oceans reveal an earth with an age of thousands, not millions or billions of years.

7. *Volcanism* — If the present rate of volcanic lava production had been constant for 4½ billion years, the amount of lava produced would equal the size of the earth! Furthermore, most evolutionists claim that the earth's volcanic activity is less today than in the past.

8. *The earth's oceans* — The average depth of sediment on the earth's ocean floors today is not even one-half mile. Approximately twenty-seven million tons of sediment are being removed from the earth's land and deposited on its ocean floors each year. If this rate had been maintained for one billion years, 18½ miles of sediment would have settled onto the ocean floors and each continent would have lost the top thirty-eight miles of its surface!

9. *The earth's human population* — The increase of the earth's human population from the time of the flood to the present day (including all wars, famines, etc.) reflects a slightly lower rate of increase than the two percent **annual** world population growth figures of the last centuries. The present earth's population, totalling approximately 4,000,000,000 (4 billion), agrees with a normal projection rate of growth in human population for a period of several thousand years.

- **Meteorites** — Meteors which reach the earth's surface without being consumed (burned up) in the earth's atmosphere

- **Volcanism** — Matters connected with volcanoes and volcanic acitivty

- **Annual** — Yearly

If humans had been on the earth for one million years, and even if they had lived in more difficult conditions so that the annual world population growth was only 1/200 of that which we have observed in past centuries, the present-day world population would be 10,000,000,000,000,000,000,000,000,000,000,000,000,000! This number of people would solidly fill 3,500 of our entire solar systems!

10. *The Word of God* — The Bible always speaks of an immediate creation — "God spake and it was done." It testifies of a world that is thousands, not millions or billions, of years in age.

- **Radioactivity** — The emission of various rays producing atomic breakdown from a radioactive to nonradioactive substance

- **Strata** — Layers

- **Glacier** — A vast accumulation of ice

- **Formation** — The making, producing, or developing of

- **Erosion** — The act of wearing away; the earth's surfaces being eaten away by water, wind, ice, etc.

Evolutionists use the following factors as evidence of an old universe and earth that are billions of years old:

1. **Radioactivity** matters (Uranium-lead, Potassium-argon, Carbon-14)
2. Pushed-up rock **strata**
3. **Glacier formation** or ice-ages
4. Coal and oil deposits
5. Large areas of **erosion**

These five evidences, when interpreted differently, however, can also be used to support a recent creation. Each of the five factors is heavily based on the previously-mentioned assumptions that the earth was formed without the appearance of age and that all rates of change have continued in the past as we observe them today. For instance, an evolutionary scientist, assuming that measurements of radioactivity indicate time, views a rock with a certain percentage of radioactive uranium and nonradioactive lead and dates the age of the rock to be 2½ billion years old, for it would take that long, he concludes, for a certain amount of radioactive uranium to change into a nonradioactive substance. The creation scientist would claim that this entire dating method is unreliable since God probably created rocks with both elements in them. That the rocks began with all uranium and no lead is a false assumption.

An evolutionary scientist's explanation of several fish fossils found near a mountain peak and pushed-up strata of rock in the mountains would be as follows: Knowing that rock layers are always laid down in water, that they always settle flat, and that fish only live in water, he assumes that the mountain was once under an ocean or lake and slowly pushed upward. Such an event, unnoticeable today, must have taken millions or billions of years. A creation scientist, believing in a worldwide flood, realizes that such a catastrophe could produce thousands of pounds (or kilograms) of pressure per square yard (or meter) upon the earth's surface, which in turn could cause large unsettlings and bucklings in the earth's hilly or mountainous surfaces. This would explain the pushed-up rock strata and fish fossils on the tops of mountains. The creationist understands that these factors could have been produced in days rather than in long periods of time.

Can you explain how a worldwide flood, with water covering the highest mountain peak could also produce glaciers, icecaps, coal and oil deposits (coal and oil are produced from buried plant and animal life) and large areas of erosion, (such as the Grand Canyon), in a very short period of time?

The evolutionist believes in an ancient universe and earth that are billions of years old, based upon his belief that everything was formed young, without the appearance of age, and that all things have continued in the past as we observe them today. The creationist believes in a young universe and earth that is thousands of years old, based upon his belief in the Bible as God's infallible Word. The Bible speaks of everything being created mature (with the appearance of age) and of a worldwide flood at the time of Noah. This is believed by faith in certain underlying truths.

It is very important to realize that true science does not contradict the Bible or Christian faith. Certain assumptions of evolutionary scientists and explanations of the evolutionary theory contradict the Word of God, but not scientific observation. God's general and special revelations, His creation and Word, can never contradict each other.

We know that the flood at the time of Noah was a worldwide, and not only a local, flood. The following two charts list the main reasons by which we know this.

? Do science and the Bible contradict each other? Can you think of some scientific assumptions and theories that contradict the Bible? What is the difference between these two?

TEN BIBLICAL PROOFS THAT THE FLOOD WAS WORLDWIDE

1. If the flood had only been of a local nature, an ark would not have been necessary.

2. The size of the ark was large enough to house two of all the unclean, and seven of all the clean, land animal species. (The total volume of the ark equaled that of 522 standard railroad boxcars!)

3. The purpose of the flood was to destroy *all* flesh (Genesis 6: 7,13,17; 7:4,21-23).

4. The flood's water covering the highest mountain on earth verifies its worldwide nature (Genesis 7:19-20).

5. The total duration of the flood was one year and ten days (Genesis 7:11; 8:14).

6. The raven and the dove would not have returned to the ark if the flood was only of a local nature.

7. God's promise speaks of never again sending this type of flood, one which would destroy all flesh (Genesis 8:21; 9:11,15).

8. All people have descended from Noah's three sons (Genesis 9:19).

9. Peter testified that the "world" was destroyed by the flood (II Peter 2:5; 3:6).

10. The Lord Jesus testified that "all" were destroyed in the flood, and compared this scene to the end of the world (Matthew 24:37-39; Luke 17:26-27).

SEVEN NON-BIBLICAL EVIDENCES OF A UNIVERSAL FLOOD

1. Sedimentary rock (rock laid down in water) is found in every continent throughout the world.

2. Mass graveyards of fossils can be found throughout the world.

3. Huge coal beds and oil fields have been discovered throughout the world.

4. Large numbers of ocean creature fossils have been found high in mountain ranges throughout the world.

5. Large areas of the world are still under ice.

6. Millions of animals, such as the Siberian mammoth elephants, have been found in ice in a condition which reveals their sudden death.

7. Nearly all tribes of the human race have traditions and legends concerning a universal flood.

Pre-flood World

Post-flood World

The Bible speaks of several differences between conditions on earth before, and after, the flood. The fossil record also reveals various changes. Several of these biblical truths and observable facts have been combined into an explanation known as the "Canopy Theory." While we may not speak of this theory as biblical fact, yet many consider this possible explanation of the **pre-flood** world to be worthwhile.

The "Canopy Theory" states that a large water-vapor canopy **encircled** the pre-flood earth above its **atmosphere**, producing a **universally** warm, mild climate by filtering and trapping the sun's rays in a "greenhouse-type" fashion. At God's command, the canopy **collapsed**, causing millions of tons of water to fall to the earth, which produced both a universal flood and new atmospheric conditions on the earth.

● **Canopy** — An overhanging, protecting covering

● **Pre-flood** — Before the worldwide flood at the time of Noah

● **Encircled** — Surrounded; enclosed; formed a circle around

● **Atmosphere** — The body of air surrounding the earth

● **Universally** — Wholly; entirely; worldwide

● **Collapsed** — Caved in; having given way

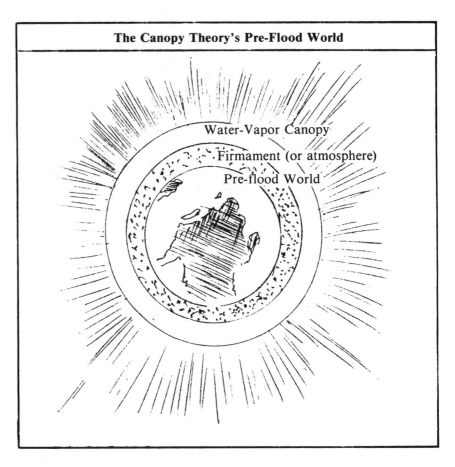

The Canopy Theory's Pre-Flood World

Water-Vapor Canopy
Firmament (or atmosphere)
Pre-flood World

● **Firmament** — The atmosphere of the earth

And God said, Let there be a firmament in the midst of the waters, and let it divide the waters from the waters.

And God made the firmament, and divided the waters which were under the firmament from the waters which were above the firmament: and it was so.

— Genesis 1:6-7

The same day were all the fountains of the great deep broken up, and the windows of heaven were opened.

— Genesis 7:11b

But there went up a mist from the earth, and watered the whole face of the ground.

— Genesis 2:6

I do set my bow in the cloud.

Genesis 9:13a

This theory is based upon the following biblical and scientific observations:

1. The pre-flood **firmament** separated "the waters which were under the firmament from the waters which were above the firmament" (Genesis 1:6-7). Today there are no waters *above* the atmosphere.

2. The passage of Scripture stating that "the windows of heaven were opened" (Genesis 7:11b), seems to picture an opening of the earth's atmosphere.

3. Rain is never mentioned in Scripture before the flood. "But there went up a mist from the earth, and watered the whole face of the ground" (Genesis 2:6). The post-flood atmosphere produced rain for watering the earth.

4. We do not read of a rainbow in the pre-flood world. *After* the flood, God testified, "I do set my bow in the cloud"

(Genesis 9:13a). This also points to a change in post-flood atmospheric conditions.

5. After the flood, God reduced the length of man's life. More direct exposure to the sun's **radiation** could be the means the Lord used to produce this change, as our aging process is influenced by radiation. A water-vapor canopy would have greatly reduced man's direct exposure to the sun's radiation. In the pre-flood world, people lived to be eight or nine hundred years of age.

6. The collapse of a water-vapor canopy surrounding the entire earth could be one of the means God used to provide for the tremendous amount of water which covered the entire earth during the flood. "And the windows of heaven were opened. And the rain was upon the earth forty days and forty nights" (Genesis 7:11b-12).

7. Larger forms of plant, animal, and human life existed before the flood: "There were giants in the earth in those days" (Genesis 6:4a). Excavations in snow-covered Siberia reveal large forms of tropical plant and animal life; fossils throughout the world reveal numerous gigantic plant and animal life forms that are extinct today. Knowing that the earth's climate would not be the mild, "greenhouse-type" after the flood, and that it would no longer support the rich, tropical vegetation it did previously; God may have allowed numerous larger forms of life, which require such a climate, to perish in the flood.

8. In II Peter 3:6-7 Peter writes: "Whereby the *world that then was,* being overflowed with water, perished: But the *heavens and the earth, which are now...*" Again, Scripture appears to point to differences between the pre- and post-flood worlds.

The "Canopy Theory" is a *theory*, a possible explanation. It is neither Scripture nor proven fact. However, because it does not contradict, but rather appears to be supported by Scripture and our knowledge of the pre-flood world, it certainly is a worthwhile explanation to consider.

● **Radiation** — Energy generated and transmitted (conveyed) by the sun and absorbed throughout our solar system — also by man on earth

The same day were all the fountains of the great deep broken up, and the windows of heaven were opened.

And the rain was upon the earth forty days and forty nights.
— Genesis 7:11b-12

There were giants in the earth in those days.
— Genesis 6:4a

Whereby the world that then was, being overflowed with water, perished:
But the heavens and the earth, which are now, by the same Word are kept in store, reserved unto fire against the day of judgment and peridition of ungodly men.
— II Peter 3:6-7

Theistic evolution — A belief that God created the universe, but through an evolutionary process

Compromise — An agreement between two disagreeing views in which something is surrendered from both sides

Encounter — Meet in opposition

Symbolic — Pertaining to that which pictures or represents something else; having a non-literal, deeper meaning

Due to the strong views of evolutionary scientists, teachings, publications and general acceptance, some Christians have proposed a compromising position between evolution and creation known as **theistic evolution**. Theistic evolutionists believe that God created all things, but that He did so through an evolutionary process. Quoting II Peter 3:8, that "one day is with the Lord as a thousand years," theistic evolutionists believe that the "days" of creation in Genesis 1 and 2 are long periods of time — each "day" being a time period of millions of years. During these millions or billions of years, God created, but in an evolutionary manner.

This attempted **compromise** position satisfies neither the evolutionary scientist nor the biblical creationist, however. The one does not want to acknowledge the presence and power of God in the universe, and the other desires to remain fully true to the creation account found in the infallible Word of God.

Theistic evolution or "long days of creation" theories **encounter** the following scriptural difficulties:

1. The Old Testament word "day" in Hebrew — "yom," when used with a numeral, always means a literal day of twenty-four hours. The only possible exceptions to this rule are found in the difficult, **symbolic** visions of Daniel (Daniel 8:14 and 12:11-12). These "days," being quoted in a *clearly symbolic* vision opens them to non-literal interpretation. The context *clearly* indicates that these chapters in Daniel are visions and not history. This is not true when reading Genesis 1.

2. Scripture always speaks of God's creative work as being instant in power. "By the Word of the LORD were the heavens made; and all the host of them by the breath of His mouth... For He spake and it was done; He commanded, and it stood fast" (Psalm 33:6-9). Read Genesis 1. How does the entire chapter testify of this truth? Which verses clearly portray God's instant creating power?

3. The fourth of God's ten commandments reads as follows:
   "Remember the sabbath day, to keep it holy. Six days shalt thou labour, and do all thy work: But the seventh day is the sabbath of the LORD thy God: in it thou shalt not do

190

any work, thou, nor thy son, nor thy daughter, thy manservant, nor thy maidservant, nor thy cattle, nor thy stranger that is within thy gates. For in six days the LORD made heaven and earth, the sea, and all that in them is, and rested the seventh day: wherefore the LORD blessed the sabbath day, and hallowed it'' (Exodus 20:8-11).

The same Hebrew words are consistently used for "day" and "days" in these verses. There is no hint in the **context** that some "days" are literal twenty-four hour periods and other "days" are not. Man is not to work for six periods of millions of years and rest for one such period. Man is instructed in this commandment to work for six twenty-four-hour days and to rest for one, as God did.

4. Genesis 2:7 informs us that "the LORD God formed man of the dust (literally, the 'powder' or 'dry crumbs') of the ground." The theistic evolutionist believes that "dust" must also be interpreted symbolically. Since man gradually developed from animals, "dust" must mean "lower life forms."

This interpretation encounters serious difficulties in the following chapter of Genesis, however, where God proclaims to Adam and all mankind: "In the sweat of thy face shalt thou eat bread, till thou return unto the *ground;* for out of it wast thou taken: for *dust* thou art, and unto *dust shalt thou return*" (Genesis 3:19).

The Hebrew word for "dust" and "ground" are identical in both verses. Neither verse is placed in a context requiring symbolic interpretations. If "dust" refers to "lower life forms," then Genesis 3:19 means that man will return to lower forms of animal life when he dies!

5. Each day representing long periods of time presents numerous contradictions to God's natural laws. For instance, plants were created on the third day and the sun on the fourth. Plants need sunlight to exist. If one day represented millions of years, how would plants have survived for millions of years without the sun? Insects were created on the fifth day. Plants need insects for cross-pollination. How would plants have reproduced for millions of years without insects?

● **Context** — The entire passage; the words and sentences which precede and follow a certain word or thought

> And God said, Let the waters under the heaven be gathered together unto one place, and let the dry land appear: and it was so.
> And God called the dry land Earth; and the gathering together of the waters called He Seas: and God saw that it was good.
> And God said, Let the earth bring forth grass, the herb yielding seed, and the fruit tree yielding fruit after his kind, whose seed is in itself, upon the earth: and it was so.
> And the earth brought forth grass, and herb yielding seed after his kind, and the tree yielding fruit whose seed was in itself, after its kind: and God saw that it was good.
> And the evening and the morning were the third day.
> And God said, Let there be lights in the firmament of the heaven to divide the day from the night; and let them be for signs, and for seasons, and for days, and years:
> And let them be for lights in the firmament of the heaven to give light upon the earth: and it was so.
> And God made two great lights: the greater light to rule the day, and the lesser light to rule the night: He made the stars also.
> And God set them in the firmament of the heaven to give light upon the earth,
> And to rule over the day and over the night, and to divide the light from the darkness: and God saw that it was good.
> And the evening and the morning were the fourth day.
> — Genesis 1:9-19

6. Combining the Genesis One creation account with the evolutionary theory is not possible; numerous differences in order confront those who attempt it. For instance, the biblical account speaks of the following sequences: the earth created before the sun, moon, and stars; plants one day before the sun; whales before land animals; birds before insects; fruit trees before fish; and birds before reptiles. All of these are presented in reverse order in evolutionary time tables, sometimes with millions or billions of years of reversed distance.

For these six reasons, Scripture rejects the idea of theistic evolution.

Another attempt to place millions or billions of years into biblical history is the "Gap Theory." This theory is based on the idea that a large gap of time can be found between Genesis 1:1 and 1:3.

The gap theorists interpret Genesis 1:1-3 in the following manner:

? What has promoted the recent attempts to locate large periods of time in the Bible? What danger can you see in the motives behind these attempts?

The Genesis 1:1-3 "Gap Theory"	
Genesis 1	"Gap Theory" Explanation
Verse 1: In the beginning God created the heaven and the earth.	This was God's first creation. The earth supported many forms of life that are extinct today.
Verse 2a: And the earth was without form, and void; and darkness was upon the face of the deep.	"Was" should be translated as "became." During this time Satan and his host fell and God destroyed His first creation. It "became" formless, void, and full of darkness.
Verses 2b-3 And the Spirit of God moved upon the face of the waters. And God said, Let there be light: and there was light.	God re-created a second creation on the earth which exists yet today. Millions or billions of years passed between the first and second creation.

The gap theory contradicts the following scriptural references:

Genesis 1:31

1. In Genesis 1:31 we read that at the close of the sixth and final day of creation, "God saw *everything* that He had made, and, behold, it was *very good.*" God could not have stated that *everything* He had made was very good if Satan had fallen, sin had marred creation, and a first creation had been destroyed by that time.

Romans 5:12

2. In Romans 5:12 Paul writes, "By one man sin entered into the world, and death by sin." Through Adam's sin death came into this world. Scripture does not support the idea of the previous death and destruction of an entire former creation on earth.

Genesis 2:2

3. In Genesis 2:2 the Hebrew text states "And the earth *was* without form," not *became*. *Was* links verse two to verse one, meaning this *was* the condition on the first day of creation before God created the light, order, and beauty which we observe in His finished creation.

Exodus 20:11

4. In Exodus 20:11 God declares, "For in six days the LORD made *heaven and earth,* the sea*, and all that in them is,* and rested the seventh day." Here Scripture states clearly that both the initial creation of heaven and earth, and all forms of matter and life in them, took place in the six days of creation specified in Genesis One.

The four verses of Scripture mentioned above reject the gap theorists' presentation.

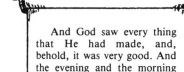

And God saw every thing that He had made, and, behold, it was very good. And the evening and the morning were the sixth day.
— Genesis 1:31

Wherefore, as by one man sin entered into the world, and death by sin; and so death passed upon all men, for that all have sinned.
— Romans 5:12

And on the seventh day God ended His work which He had made; and He rested on the seventh day from all His work which He had made.
— Genesis 2:2

For in six days the LORD made heaven and earth, the sea, and all that in them is, and rested the seventh day: wherefore the LORD blessed the sabbath day, and hallowed it.
— Exodus 20:11

Re-read the beginning paragraphs in this section entitled "The Theory of Evolution." Why is believing in creation a crucial matter for us personally, for our churches, and for our society? Who is the "god," and what is the "bible," of an evolutionist? Why would his religion need to be "humanism"? What dangers can you see when church people begin to believe in theistic evolution or gap theory ideas?

In II Peter 3:3-5, Peter writes the following:

> Knowing this first, that there shall come in the last days scoffers, walking after their own lusts.
>
> And saying, Where is the promise of His coming? for since the fathers fell asleep, all things continue as they were from the beginning of the creation.
>
> For this they willingly are ignorant of, that by the Word of God the heavens were of old, and the earth standing out of the water and in the water.

How are people, today, *willingly* ignorant of God's creating all things by the Word of His power? How do both God's general and special revelations testify of this truth?

? What results will be seen in daily living when evolution rather than creation is believed by:
— a person?
— a church?
— a society?

? True Christianity believes and trusts in a knowable, personal, almighty God who created all things and governs them for a purpose. Creation speaks of God — it is His work, the touch of His hand. In what does the evolutionist believe and trust?

? While God's revelation of Himself in creation is wonderful, it is not saving. What revelation and experience is necessary to truly love and serve God whole-heartedly?

Have you come to know, love, and serve God through His regenerating grace? If so, are you growing in dedication and service to Him?

ANGELS

God not only created the earth and its creatures, but He also created heaven with its inhabitants. The host of heavenly creatures are called "angels." The Greek word for "angel" (angelos) means "messenger" or " ambassador." Angels are also called by the following names in Scripture:

ANGELS	
Name	**Text**
1. Sons of God	Now there was a day when the sons of God came to present themselves before the LORD, and Satan came also among them. — Job 1:6
2. Morning stars	When the morning stars sang together, and all the sons of God shouted for joy? — Job 38:7
3. Watchers	I saw in the visions of my head upon my bed, and behold, a watcher and an holy one came down from heaven. — Daniel 4:13
4. Spirits	Who maketh His angels spirits; His ministers a flaming fire. — Psalm 104:4
5. Ministers	Bless ye the LORD, all ye His hosts; ye ministers of His, that do His pleasure. — Psalm 103:21

Angels are spiritual beings. The nature of angels differs from that of mankind, for man is both spiritual and physical, having both a soul and body. Angels are purely spiritual.

Scripture informs us that angels are holy, rational beings, with personal understandings and wills, possessing great intelligence and power.

While angels are very intelligent and powerful, they are not all-knowing nor all-powerful. Angels are creatures, created by God; they are not God. Therefore we may not worship, or pray to, angels.

Thus the heavens and earth were finished, and all the host of them.
— Genesis 2:1

For by Him were all things created, that are in heaven, and that are in earth, visible and invisible, whether they be thrones, or dominions, or principalities, or powers: all things were created by Him, and for Him.
— Colossians 1:16

Take heed that ye despise not one of these little ones; for I say unto you, That in heaven their angels do always behold the face of My Father which is in heaven.
— Matthew 18:10

To fetch about this form of speech hath thy servant Joab done this thing: and my lord is wise, according to the wisdom of an angel of God, to know all things that are in the earth.
— II Samuel 14:20

Bless the LORD, ye His angels, that excel in strength, that do His commandments, hearkening unto the voice of His word.
— Psalm 103:20

Are they not all ministering spirits, sent forth to minister for them who shall be heirs of salvation?
— Hebrews 1:14

Behold My hands and My feet, that it is I Myself: handle Me, and see; for a spirit hath not flesh and bones, as ye see Me have.
— Luke 24:39

But of that day and hour knoweth no man, no, not the angels of heaven, but My Father only.
— Matthew 24:36

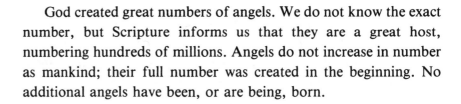

God created great numbers of angels. We do not know the exact number, but Scripture informs us that they are a great host, numbering hundreds of millions. Angels do not increase in number as mankind; their full number was created in the beginning. No additional angels have been, or are being, born.

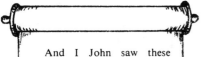

And I John saw these things, and heard them. And when I had heard and seen, I fell down to worship before the feet of the angel which showed me these things.

Then saith he unto me, See thou do it not: for I am thy fellowservant, and of thy brethren the prophets, and of them which keep the sayings of this book: worship God.
— Revelation 22:8-9

A fiery stream issued and came forth from before Him: thousand thousands ministered unto Him, and ten thousand times ten thousand stood before Him: the judgment was set, and the books were opened.
— Daniel 7:10

And I beheld, and I heard the voice of many angels round about the throne and the beasts and the elders: and the number of them was ten thousand times ten thousand, and thousands of thousands.
— Revelation 5:11

For in the resurrection they neither marry, nor are given in marriage, but are as the angels of God in heaven.
— Matthew 22:30

Where wast thou when I laid the foundations of the earth? declare, if thou hast understanding.

When the morning stars sang together, and all the sons of God shouted for joy?
— Job 38:4,7

"When were the angels created?" Angela asked her teacher.

"When do you think?" her teacher asked the class.

"During the six days of creation," was the answer, "because all things in heaven and earth were created in these six days." Together they found the following biblical support for their answer.

> Thus the heavens and earth were finished, and all the host of them.
> — Genesis 2:1

> For in six days the LORD made heaven and earth, the sea, and all that in them is.
> — Exodus 20:11a

> Thou, even Thou, art LORD alone; Thou hast made heaven, the heaven of heavens, with all their host, the earth, and all things that are therein, the seas, and all that is therein, and Thou preservest them all; and the host of heaven worshippeth Thee.
> — Nehemiah 9:6

> For by Him were all things created, that are in heaven, and that are in earth, visible and invisible, whether they be thrones, or dominions, or principalities, or powers: all things were created by Him, and for Him.
> Colossians 1:16

"But, I wanted to know, on which of the six days did God create the angels?" Angela replied.

"Probably on the first day," her teacher answered. "We know from Genesis 1:1 that God created the heavens and the earth on the first day. In Job 38:4-7, we read that the angels sang together and shouted for joy when God laid the foundations of (or created), the earth."

God's Word speaks of various angelic orders — different ranking or classes of angels. These are named in the chart on the opposite page.

ANGELIC ORDERS		
	ORDER	EXAMPLE TEXT
1.	Cherubims	So He drove out the man; and He placed at the east of the garden of Eden cherubims, and a flaming sword which turned every way, to keep the way of the tree of life. — Genesis 3:24
2.	Seraphims	Above it stood the seraphims: each one had six wings; with twain he covered his face, and with twain he covered his feet, and with twain he did fly. — Isaiah 6:2
3.	Principalities	To the intent that now unto the principalities and powers in heavenly places might be known by the church the manifold wisdom of God. — Ephesians 3:10
4.	Powers	And ye are complete in Him, which is the Head of all principality and power. — Colossians 2:10
5.	Thrones	For by Him were all things created, that are in heaven, and that are in earth, visible and invisible, whether they be thrones, or dominions, or principalities, or powers: all things were created by Him, and for Him. — Colossians 1:16
6.	Dominions	Far above all principality, and power and might, and dominion, and every name that is named, not only in this world, but also in that which is to come. — Ephesians 1:21
7.	Archangels	For the Lord Himself shall descend from heaven with a shout, with the voice of the archangel, and with the trump of God: and the dead in Christ shall rise first. — I Thessalonians 4:16
	a. Michael	Yet Michael the archangel, when contending with the devil he disputed about the body of Moses, durst not bring against him a railing accusation, but said, The Lord rebuke thee. — Jude: 9
	b. Gabriel	And the angel answering said unto him, I am Gabriel, that stand in the presence of God; and am sent to speak unto thee, and to show thee these glad tidings. — Luke 1:19

? How do the orders and vast numbers of angels testify of:
— God's power?
— God's glory?

? How are the scriptural teachings of various works of God's host of angels, a rich comfort to God's true children and a terror to the unbeliever?

The Bible does not speak in great detail about all the specific services that angels perform, but Scripture does inform us of the angelic functions described in the chart on the following page.

197

ANGELIC SERVICE	
WORK	**EXAMPLE TEXT**
I. In heaven	
A. Praising, worshipping, and serving God continually	Praise ye the LORD. Praise ye the LORD from the heavens: praise Him in the heights. Praise ye Him, all His angels: praise ye Him, all His hosts. — Psalm 148:1-2
B. Rejoicing over the conversion of sinners	Likewise I say unto you, there is joy in the presence of the angels of God over one sinner that repenteth. — Luke 15:10
C. Bringing the souls of true believers into heaven	And it came to pass, that the beggar died, and was carried by the angels into Abraham's bosom. — Luke 16:22a
II. On earth	
A. In God's Church	
1. Serving Jesus Christ	And there appeared an angel unto Him from heaven, strengthening Him. — Luke 22:43
2. Serving for the benefit of God's children	Are they not all ministering spirits, sent forth to minister for them who shall be heirs of salvation? — Hebrews 1:14
3. Being messengers of good tidings	And the angel said unto them, Fear not: for behold, I bring you good tidings of great joy, which shall be to all people. — Luke 2:10
4. Protecting God's elect	For He shall give His angels charge over thee, to keep thee in all thy ways. They shall bear thee up in their hands, lest thou dash thy foot against a stone. — Psalm 91:11-12
5. Assisting in the administration of God's law	Who have received the law by the disposition of angels. — Acts 7:53a
6. Assisting in the administration of God's gospel	But the angel of the Lord by night opened the prison doors, and brought them forth, and said, Go, stand and speak in the temple to the people all the words of this life. — Acts 5:19-20
B. In general	
1. Announcing and witnessing special happenings	And the angel which I saw stand upon the sea and upon the earth lifted up his hand to heaven, And sware by Him that liveth for ever and ever, who created heaven, and the things that therein are, and the earth, and the things that therein are, and the sea, and the things which are therein, that there should be time no longer. — Revelation 10:5-6
2. Carrying out God's punishments	And it came to pass that night, that the angel of the LORD went out, and smote in the camp of the Assyrians an hundred fourscore and five thousand: and when they arose early in the morning, behold, they were all dead corpses. — II Kings 19:35
3. Assisting on the final judgment day	So shall it be at the end of the world: the angels shall come forth, and sever the wicked from among the just, And shall cast them into the furnace of fire: there shall be wailing and gnashing of teeth. — Matthew 13:49-50

198

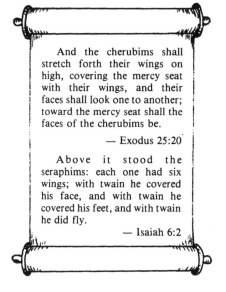

How are the scriptural teachings of various works of God's host of angels a rich comfort to God's true children and a terror to the unbeliever?

With keen interest, Vincent listened to a lively debate taking place among several friends.

"Angels do so have bodies," Becky argued. "Abraham and Lot *saw* the angels that came to them. They could not have seen them if they were invisible."

"Besides, angels have wings," Randy announced. "The angels on the mercy seat and veil in the tabernacle had wings; and God told Moses exactly how these angels should be pictured."

"The angels Isaiah saw each had six wings. Remember? They flew with two wings; with two they covered their faces and with two they covered their feet," Sue added.

"Well, I disagree," Mike replied firmly, "I still say that angels are spirits, and spirits do not have bodies — they are invisible."

Who is right?

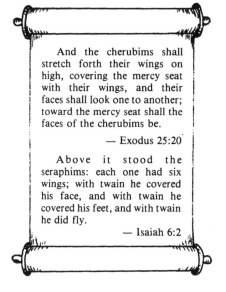

> And the cherubims shall stretch forth their wings on high, covering the mercy seat with their wings, and their faces shall look one to another; toward the mercy seat shall the faces of the cherubims be.
>
> — Exodus 25:20
>
> Above it stood the seraphims: each one had six wings; with twain he covered his face, and with twain he covered his feet, and with twain he did fly.
>
> — Isaiah 6:2

> Are they not all ministering spirits, sent forth to minister for them who shall be heirs of salvation?
>
> — Hebrews 1:14
>
> Behold My hands and My feet, that it is I Myself: handle Me, and see; for a spirit hath not flesh and bones, as ye see Me have.
>
> — Luke 24:39

Angels are ministering spirits, which means that they do not have physical bodies. However, in order to appear to people on earth — to be seen and heard by them, angels have often assumed a physical body and appeared to people in a human form. These human forms, however, were not the angels' actual bodies.

God pictures angels with wings in the tabernacle and temple, and in various visions or dreams, to represent them as heavenly messengers who can rapidly "fly" from heaven to all parts of the earth to perform God's will. These wings are symbolic; they picture the previous truth concerning angels, but these picturings do not mean that angels actually have physical bodies with wings. They are purely spiritual beings.

Not all of the angels remained in the holy and heavenly condition in which God created them. A large number of angels fell through the sin of pride. For their sinful rebellion, God cast them out of heaven and will punish them in hell. They will be sentenced and confined to hell forever on the final judgment day. These fallen angels are called devils, demons, or evil spirits.

The leader of the fallen angels is Satan. The Bible refers to Satan by the following names, which reveal his character and work:

For if God spared not the angels that sinned, but cast them down to hell, and delivered them into chains of darkness, to be reserved unto judgment.
— II Peter 2:4

And the angels which kept not their first estate, but left their own habitation, he hath reserved in everlasting chains under darkness unto the judgment of the great day.
— Jude: 6

And there was war in heaven. Michael and his angels fought against the dragon; and the dragon fought and his angels.
And prevailed not; neither was their place found any more in heaven.
And the great dragon was cast out, that old serpent, called the Devil, and Satan, which deceiveth the whole world: he was cast out into the earth, and his angels were cast out with him.
— Revelation 12:7-9

SCRIPTURAL NAMES OF SATAN	
1. Satan — "The adversary" or "the enemy" (Rev. 12:9)	8. The wicked one (Matt. 13:19)
2. Apollyon (Abaddon) — "The destroyer" (Rev. 9:11)	9. The father of lies (John 8:44)
3. Diabolos (The Devil) — "The accuser" or "the slanderer" (Rev. 12:9)	10. The god of this world (II Cor. 4:4)
4. Beelzebub — "Lord of the flies" or "dung god"; "prince of the demons" (Matt. 12:24)	11. The prince of the power of the air (Eph. 2:2)
5. Belial — "Worthlessness" (II Cor. 6:15)	12. A murderer (John 8:44)
6. The deceiver of the whole world (Rev. 12:9)	13. The old serpent (Rev. 12:9)
7. The great dragon (Rev. 12:9)	14. The tempter (Matt. 4:3)

? How does I Timothy 3:6 speak of the sin of Satan and his angels? "Not a novice, lest being lifted up with pride he fall into the condemnation of the devil."

What clear warning does this verse present to us?

Satan is very powerful and very active. He rules over a mighty kingdom of evil. While he is not **omnipresent**, yet by reigning over a vast number of evil spirits, he has worldwide influence. Scripture speaks of him as "the prince of the power of the air" and the "god of this world."

As a "roaring lion seeking whom he may devour," Satan restlessly goes "to and fro through the earth." Satan uses the weakness and sinfulness of men and the **allurements** of the sinful world to tempt men to evil.

Satan is a sworn enemy of God, and hates God with a bitter hatred. God has cast him out of heaven as a sinful rebel. Satan lost a position of great authority and will one day be confined to hell forever. No possibility of salvation exists for him nor for his followers.

From a spirit of bitter **enmity**, Satan hates and opposes God. He tries to hinder, mar, or destroy God's work, and hates to see God being honored and served. Man is the crown of God's creation. Therefore, Satan seeks to destroy him, to wreck God's work of creation, and to keep man from willingly loving and serving God.

While it appeared for a time that Satan had succeeded in doing this, God began to unfold a richer revelation of His grace, a deeper manifestation of His love, that He had planned from all eternity. Through the death of His own Son, God would find a way to yet love and restore fallen, sinful, and rebellious people. In the end, He would live with them forever in a restored and perfect creation.

God's plan of salvation amazed the angels. God's plan of salvation through Jesus Christ would enhance His glory. Instead of Satan's work and man's fall destroying God's work, God used them to promote His honor and glory in a deeper and richer manner! Jesus Christ would crush the head of Satan; he would be defeated for the second time. Therefore, with double fury, Satan hates God and His saved children, for all of God's attributes are especially glorified in the salvation of God's people.

- **Omnipresent** — Everywhere present at the same time

- **Allurements** — Attractions; temptations

- **Enmity** — Deep hatred; hostility

? The fallen angels have no possiblity of salvation. Fallen man does. How does this fact emphasize the wonderfulness of God's sovereign grace to man?

? What mistaken ideas will come from underestimating or overestimating Satan's power?

Although Satan is a mighty and determined enemy of God, of His work and people, Scripture informs us that Satan's power is limited. Satan is not almighty, all-knowing, or everywhere-present. God is. He may only act within the limits of God's permission. Through Jesus, Satan is also a defeated enemy. He knows what his final punishment will be — to suffer in hell forever.

By nature, we all serve self, sin, and world. By doing so, we all are slaves of Satan, for he is king of these things. He desires to keep us busy and trapped in them. Satan knows that the wages of sin is death. He is heading for eternal death in hell, and with hellish hatred, he wants as many as possible to suffer with him.

? Why is God's grace and power the only hope and expectation of the true Christian?

But God is almighty and wonderfully gracious. God can free us from our willful slavery to Satan. He can plant true faith, hope, and love in our hearts and turn us from death to life; from Satan to God; and from the love of self, sin, and world to the love of God and others.

Those who have been regenerated by God, experience, to a lesser or greater degree, the enmity of Satan. The true Christian is instructed to not remain ignorant of Satan's devices; to be watchful and diligent; to resist him; to put on the armor God has provided; and to fight against Satan.

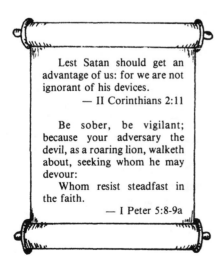

Lest Satan should get an advantage of us: for we are not ignorant of his devices.
— II Corinthians 2:11

Be sober, be vigilant; because your adversary the devil, as a roaring lion, walketh about, seeking whom he may devour:
Whom resist steadfast in the faith.
— I Peter 5:8-9a

While all God's children will experience that this is not possible in their own strength, they are to battle through faith in Jesus Christ. Their strength lies in their Savior alone. The apostle Paul testified, "I am persuaded, that neither death, nor life, nor angels, nor principalities, nor powers, nor things present, nor things to come, nor height, nor depth, nor any other creature shall be able to separate us from the love of God, which is in Christ Jesus our Lord" (Romans 8:38-39).

One day the complete victory shall be the people of God's. Then they shall rejoice in their King through whom they have obtained the victory. In heaven, there will be no more sin, sinful world, sinful self, or tempting Satan — but there they shall be conquerers through Him who eternally loved them.

In heaven, God's children will cast their crowns at the feet of their Savior, worshipping Him and saying, "Blessing, and honour, and glory, and power, be unto Him that sitteth upon the throne, and unto the Lamb for ever and ever" (Rev. 5:13b).

Which king are you serving — God or Satan? The king we serve now, will also be our king eternally!

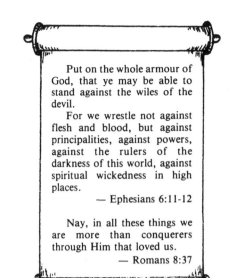

Put on the whole armour of God, that ye may be able to stand against the wiles of the devil.

For we wrestle not against flesh and blood, but against principalities, against powers, against the rulers of the darkness of this world, against spiritual wickedness in high places.
— Ephesians 6:11-12

Nay, in all these things we are more than conquerers through Him that loved us.
— Romans 8:37

CATECHISM MEMORIZATION
Questions from Rev. A. Hellenbroek's *Divine Truths* — Chapter VI

1. Does God also execute His decrees?
   Yes, in time by His works.

2. How does God work in time?
   In two ways (1) through nature and (2) through grace.

3. How does God work in nature?
   In two ways: (1) through creation and (2) through providence.

4. What does it mean to create something?
   To produce or give existence to something by an omnipotent act of a simple will. "For Thy pleasure they are and were created" (Rev. 4:11).

5. Who is the Creator of all things?
   The triune God. "In the beginning God created the heaven and the earth" (Gen. 1:1).

6. When did God create all things?
   In the beginning, as we read from the history of creation recorded in Genesis 1.

7. What means did God use to create all things?
   God created everything out of nothing. "He calleth those things which be not as though they were" (Rom. 4:17).

8. How long did God take to create all things?
   Respecting matter, only a moment, but respecting the further disposition of matter, six days.

9. Were the angels also created?
   Yes, "Who maketh His angels spirits, His ministers a flaming fire" (Ps. 104:4).

10. What are angels?
    Ministering spirits, sent forth to minister to the heirs of salvation (Heb. 1:14).

11. When were the angels created?
    Probably on the first day; for we read that when the earth was formed, the morning stars sang together, and all the sons of God shouted for joy (Job 38:6-7).

12. Did God create the angels in a perfect or imperfect condition?
    Perfect, for God saw everything that He had made, and behold it was very good (Gen 1:31).

13. Did all the angels continue in their upright state?
    No, some of them apostatized, and became devils in hell (Jude 5-6).

CHAPTER 5

Part I. Chapter Review

1. How is God's creating work different from man's?

   a. Human — _____

   _____

   b. Divine — _____

   _____

2. Define:

   a. Creationism — _____

   _____

   b. Theory — _____

   _____

   c. Theory of evolution — _____

   _____

   d. Humanism — _____

   _____

3. List ten evidences which support biblical creation and contradict the evolutionary theory:

   a. _____
   b. _____
   c. _____
   d. _____
   e. _____
   f. _____
   g. _____
   h. _____
   i. _____
   j. _____

4. What two major assumptions are made by all "age-of-the-earth" evolutionary theories?

   a. _____

   _____

   b. _____

   _____

5. Describe the Water-Vapor Canopy Theory: _____
_____
_____
_____

6. What is:
   a. Theistic evolution? _____
   _____

   b. The Gap Theory? _____
   _____

7. Describe how:
   a. Theistic evolution contradicts Genesis 3:19 — _____
   _____
   _____

   b. The Gap Theory contradicts Exodus 20:11 — _____
   _____
   _____

8. What does Scripture teach us about the following truths concerning angels?
   a. Their name — "angel" — _____
   _____

   b. Their being — _____
   _____

   c. Their number — _____
   _____

9. What is the work of angels on earth?
   a. _____
   b. _____
   c. _____
   d. _____
   e. _____
   f. _____

10. a. Who is Satan? _____
    _____

    b. Why does he hate God and God's children? _____
    _____

CHAPTER 5

Part II. Deepening Your Insight

1. How do the second three days repeat God's creation order found in the first three days?

    _____

    _____

    _____

2. What is the main lesson to be learned from the story about the men from Irian Jaya who discovered the typewriter?

    _____

    _____

    _____

3. Why is one's belief in the beginnings of creation ultimately a matter of *faith*?

    _____

    _____

    _____

4. Explain how the Second Law of Thermodynamics is a powerful evidence against the basic principle of the evolutionary theory: _____

    _____

    _____

    _____

5. How could a worldwide flood have produced the world's great coal and oil deposits in a very short time, rather than requiring millions of years? Why is the flood a more scientifically logical explanation? _____

    _____

    _____

    _____

6. Study the following references regarding cherubims (Genesis 3:24; Exodus 25:16-22; Exodus 26:31-35) and seraphims (Isaiah 6:1-7).

    a. Which group of angels especially maintains God's justice and law? _____

    b. Which group especially maintains God's holiness? _____

7. List four distinctions between the creation of people and angels:

    a. _____

    b. _____

    c. _____

    d. _____

QUESTIONS

Part III. Biblical Applications

1. How do Genesis 1:12, 28, and 29 reveal to us that God created a mature and fully-functioning creation, one which had the appearance of age? _____
   _____
   _____

2. Theistic evolutionists often quote one part of II Peter 3:8. Which part do they not quote?
   _____

   Read the surrounding verses. What is the meaning of the statement "One day is with the Lord as a thousand years," when read in its context? _____
   _____
   _____

3. What type of angelic service is spoken of in the following scriptural references?
   a. Matthew 24:31 — _____
   b. Matthew 4:11 — _____
   c. Acts 12:23 — _____
   d. Daniel 6:22 — _____

4. List the "armour" mentioned in Ephesians 6:11-18 that is used in the war against Satan, sin, and world:
   a. _____ e. _____
   b. _____ f. _____
   c. _____ g. _____
   d. _____

Part IV. From the Writings of our Church Forefathers

In your own words, explain the meaning of the following quotations:

1. "Thus does the world forget Thee, its Creator, and falls in love with what Thou hast created instead of with Thee" (Augustine). _____
   _____
   _____
   _____

2. "A 'dead God' is the creation of men; a living God is the Creator of men." _____
   _____
   _____
   _____

3. "God is the cause of all causes" (Christopher Nesse). _____
   _____
   _____
   _____

CHAPTER 5

Part V. From the Marginal Questions

1. How do man's creative abilities prove that he is neither animal nor God, that he is above one and under the other?

   _____
   _____
   _____
   _____
   _____

2. Who is the evolutionist's "god" ? What is his "bible"? What rich securities and purposes of life are missed by evolutionists?

   _____
   _____
   _____
   _____
   _____

3. Why is the world a personal one to the Christian, but impersonal to an evolutionist? What difference in outlook and practice would these two views produce?

   _____
   _____
   _____
   _____
   _____

4. What does God's revelation in creation reveal? What necessary truths does it not reveal?

   _____
   _____
   _____
   _____
   _____

5. The fallen angels have no possibility of salvation. Fallen man has. How does this fact emphasize the wonderfulness of God's sovereign grace to man?

   _____
   _____
   _____
   _____

EXTRA CHALLENGE QUESTIONS

Part VI. Your Selection from the Marginal Questions

Write out and respond to two marginal questions that interest you which have not been previously asked in this chapter's question section.

1. Question: _____
    _____

    Response: _____
    _____
    _____
    _____
    _____
    _____

2. Question: _____
    _____

    Response: _____
    _____
    _____
    _____
    _____

Part VII. Project Ideas

1. Draw a large chart that contrasts creationism and evolution. List and briefly describe supporting evidences and refutations for both.

2. Present a creation/evolution debate using pictures, overhead transparencies, examples, etc. Present this to your class, school assembly, adult meeting, etc.

3. Research for additional evidences of a young earth. Design a poster to display all the evidences you could find (including the ten in this chapter).

4. Design a poster, mural, or chart on:
    a. The Canopy Theory and its biblical support
    b. Theistic evolution and how it contradicts Scripture
    c. The Gap Theory and its biblical opposition

5. Locate numerous examples of angelic service in the Word of God; list these examples on a large chart under the heading it best exemplifies.

6

God's Providence

As not a bird falls to the ground
Without the Father's will,
So in His providence the Lord
Upholds creation still.

In Him we live and move and have
Our being; it is He
Who worketh both to will and do
His pleasure full and free.

The Lord directs all things to fit
A predetermined plan;
We may devise our way, but God
Directs the steps of man.

FROM OUR REFORMED DOCTRINAL STANDARDS

Belgic Confession of Faith

Article 13 — of Divine Providence

We believe that the same God, after He had created all things, did not forsake them, or give them up to fortune or chance, but that He rules and governs them according to His holy will, so that nothing happens in this world without His appointment: nevertheless, God neither is the author of, nor can be charged with, the sins which are committed. For His power and goodness are so great and incomprehensible, that He orders and executes His work in the most excellent and just manner, even then, when devils and wicked men act unjustly. And, as to what He doth surpassing human understanding, we will not curiously inquire into, farther than our capacity will admit of; but with the greatest humility and reverence adore the righteous judgments of God, which are hid from us, contenting ourselves that we are disciples of Christ, to learn only those things which He has revealed to us in His Word, without transgressing these limits. This doctrine affords us unspeakable consolations, since we are taught thereby that nothing can befall us by chance, but by the direction of our most gracious and heavenly Father; who watches over us with a paternal care, keeping all creatures so under His power, that not a hair of our head (for they are all numbered), nor a sparrow, can fall to the ground, without the will of our Father, in whom we do entirely trust; being persuaded, that He so restrains the devil and all our enemies, that without His will and permission, they cannot hurt us. And therefore we reject that damnable error of the Epicureans, who say that God regards nothing, but leaves all things to chance.

Heidelberg Catechism

Questions and Answers 26-28

Q. 26.   What believest thou when thou sayest, "I believe in God the Father, Almighty, Maker of heaven and earth"?

A.   That the eternal Father of our Lord Jesus Christ (who of nothing made heaven and earth, with all that is in them; who likewise upholds and governs the same by His eternal counsel and providence) is for the sake of Christ His Son, my God and my Father; on whom I rely so entirely, that I have no doubt, but He will provide me with all things necessary for soul and body: and further, that He will make whatever evils He sends upon me, in this valley of tears turn out to my advantage; for He is able to do it, being Almighty God, and willing, being a faithful Father.

27. Q.   What dost thou mean by the providence of God?

A.   The almighty and everywhere present power of God; whereby, as it were by His hand, He upholds and governs heaven, earth, and all creatures; so that herbs and grass, rain and drought, fruitful and barren years, meat and drink, health and sickness, riches and poverty, yea, and all things come, not by chance, but by His fatherly hand.

Q. 28.   What advantage is it to us to know that God has created, and by His providence doth still uphold all things?

A.   That we may be patient in adversity; thankful in prosperity; and that in all things, which may hereafter befall us, we place our firm trust in our faithful God and Father, that nothing shall separate us from His love; since all creatures are so in His hand, that without His will they cannot so much as move.

6

GOD'S PROVIDENCE

God is a God who **upholds** and governs His entire creation; One who performs that which He has **decreed.**

Imagine a person spending thousands of dollars and hundreds of hours on various plans for constructing a large sailboat, but never actually building it; or, after completing the construction of a beautiful, complex, detailed boat, never caring for, or using, it for any purpose.

Would you not find such actions very senseless and foolish? God is not like such a person. God performs His plan. He maintains and governs His creation for a purpose.

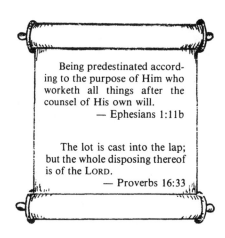

Being predestinated according to the purpose of Him who worketh all things after the counsel of His own will.
— Ephesians 1:11b

The lot is cast into the lap; but the whole disposing thereof is of the LORD.
— Proverbs 16:33

God's continual work in the caring for, and governing of, His creation according to His plan and purpose is called God's **divine providence**. The *Heidelberg Catechism* beautifully answers the

● **Divine Providence** — God's caring for, upholding of, and ruling over all things

- **Misconceptions** — Wrong or mistaken ideas

- **Deist** — One who believes that God created the universe and placed it under certain laws, but takes no part in its operations

- **Complex** — Made from numerous interconnecting parts

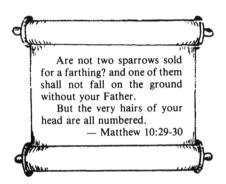

Are not two sparrows sold for a farthing? and one of them shall not fall on the ground without your Father.
But the very hairs of your head are all numbered.
— Matthew 10:29-30

- **Pantheist** — One who believes that creation is God and God is creation; no personal God lives above and reigns over creation. The universe is God.

? How would the deist and pantheist view life differently from the true Christian? Why would the Christian's world view be a personal one and the deist's and pantheist's not?

? Why is belief in, and talk about, "luck" or "good fortune" insulting to God?

? What rich comfort is missed in the lives of those who deny the truth of God's providence?

question, "What does God's providence mean?" in Answer 27: "The almighty and everywhere present power of God; whereby, as it were by His hand, He upholds and governs heaven, earth, and all creatures; so that herbs and grass, rain and drought, fruitful and barren years, meat and drink, health and sickness, riches and poverty, yea, and all things come, not by chance, but by His fatherly hand."

Regarding God's relationship with His creation, there are two major **misconceptions** to be avoided.

1. *The Deist Misconception* — The deist believes that God created the universe, set it in motion under various natural laws, and then withdrew from it. The deist believes that God views His creation from a distance, and never or only rarely interferes or involves Himself in its regular operation. To the deist, the world is like a **complex** watch which God created and started, and now runs by itself. The deist sees the world as a great ship that was made and set in motion by God, and then left to sail by itself.

2. *The Pantheist Misconception* — To the pantheist, God and the world are the same. All activities of nature and of people are direct actions of God. According to the pantheist, man is not a morally responsible being, for every action is a direct action of God.

Against the teachings of the deist, the scriptural truth that God cares for, upholds, and governs all things, needs to be maintained. Against the pantheist, the biblical truth that there is a personal God, One who is separate from, and reigns over, all things needs to be emphasized.

Belief in "good fortune," "luck," "good-luck charms," or "fate" is a confession of unbelief in God and in His providence. Nothing happens outside of God's care and government.

The scriptural doctrine of God's providence teaches us the comforting truth that all matters and events are in the hand of an almighty and all-knowing God — a personal God who cares for, upholds, and rules over all.

A young girl was sailing with her mother on a large ship over which her father was captain.

During the night, the ship encountered a severe storm, and was fiercely tossed about by great waves. All leaped from their beds. Fear was written upon each face.

Suddenly, over the fearful whisperings of the passengers, the voice of a young girl could be clearly heard, "Mother, is Father on deck?"

"Yes, he is, Dear," her mother replied.

"Then everything is fine; I'm going back to bed," the girl said decidedly.

How does this rich comfort of childike faith in one's father, even in times of storm, apply to the true Christian?

Why is God's child's faith in the Lord a more certain and secure trust, than this child's faith in her human father?

? Especially in stormy times, how can true faith in God and in His providence shine as a precious jewel?

? When experiencing times of severe trials and distressful events that are beyond man's control, to whom can the non-Christian turn?

215

● **Preservation** — God's keeping and upholding of all things by His power

God's providence includes three divine acts:

1. Preservation
2. Cooperation (or concurrence)
3. Government

Preservation is the almighty power of God by which He upholds all things in their existence until the time determined by Him. Without the continuous work of divine preservation, the entire creation would fall apart. God maintains all things in being and action. He sustains life in all living creatures.

Andrew lived near a steep mountain range. One day, as he hiked up the mountains, he sat on a rock next to a stream to rest for a few minutes from his strenuous climb. With increasing fascination, he watched the trickling stream as it splashed and fell around and over various rocks, logs, and pebbles in its cascade down the mountainside.

After watching this constant flow of water for some time, he wondered, "Why doesn't the water in this stream ever stop?"

The more he thought about this question and the complexities involved in producing the snow and rain necessary to supply the water for the stream, the more amazed he became.

"This stream is a miracle!" he suddenly stated aloud. He further noticed the abundance of ferns, mosses, shrubs, and trees which drew water from the stream. Then he thought of the birds and animals living in the trees. In this manner, his mind traveled from one object to another until he was moved to exclaim, "This whole mountainside is a miracle; the entire world and universe is one great miracle!"

God's work of preservation in maintaining one mountainside is tremendous. When we think of all the mountains, valleys, and fields in the world; all the living creatures needing daily food and shelter; the complexity of the universe in its constant operations — all requiring God's continued preserving work: this passes all human understanding.

Have you, like Andrew, experienced times when the greatness of God's work of preservation has overwhelmed you?

216

Cooperation or **concurrence** refers to the almighty power of God by which He cooperates in every action of His creatures by giving them the will and strength they need in order to act. As human beings, we cannot so much as lift our arms without God cooperating to give us the necessary will, energy, and strength to do so.

This is true, even when a person sins. God gives that person the ability to make a rational decision and perform an action. The person abuses the very abilities God is giving him, when he sins. The ability to act is from God, but the deviation, the sinfulness of the action, is from man. Yet, no action is outside of God's government and control.

● **Cooperation (concurrence)** — God's giving of will and strength to all living creatures which enables them to act

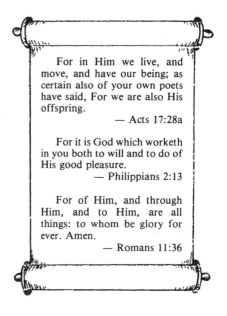

For in Him we live, and move, and have our being; as certain also of your own poets have said, For we are also His offspring.
— Acts 17:28a

For it is God which worketh in you both to will and to do of His good pleasure.
— Philippians 2:13

For of Him, and through Him, and to Him, are all things: to whom be glory for ever. Amen.
— Romans 11:36

? When speaking of divine cooperation, the deist disagrees with God's actions, and the pantheist with the creature's action. Why would this be, and how must we avoid both of these errors?

A teen-age boy was once walking to a theatre to see a film, which his conscience clearly told him was wrong. As he neared the place, the following questions entered his thoughts: "Who is giving you the power to walk right now? Who is giving you the ability to see?"

"God," he answered in his thoughts.

"Are you going to slap God in His face with the precious gifts of health and vision as He gives them to you?"

The young man stopped — he could not continue with his plans.

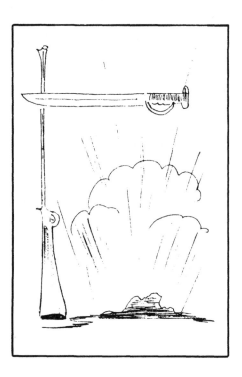

Imagine a person receiving thousand-dollar gifts on a regular basis from a kind, concerned friend. However, with the money he receives, this person purchases weapons to fight againt the giver of his gifts. What would you think of such a person?

How valuable are the gifts of mental and physical health, of eyesight and hearing, and of being able to walk? Who is continually giving us these priceless benefits?

When we sin, how are we using the precious gifts God is giving us to fight against Him, even while He is giving them to us?

Government is the almighty power of God by which He directs and controls all things so that they fulfill the purpose determined by Him. When creating the world, God had a definite purpose and end in view. He rules over all things to accomplish His plan — a plan in which all shall serve to promote God's honor and glory.

- **Government** — God's controlling and directing of all things according to His purpose

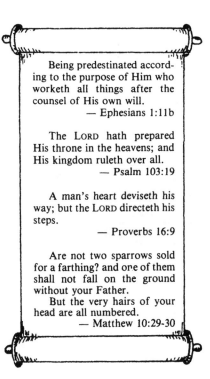

Being predestinated according to the purpose of Him who worketh all things after the counsel of His own will.
— Ephesians 1:11b

The LORD hath prepared His throne in the heavens; and His kingdom ruleth over all.
— Psalm 103:19

A man's heart deviseth his way; but the LORD directeth his steps.
— Proverbs 16:9

Are not two sparrows sold for a farthing? and one of them shall not fall on the ground without your Father.
But the very hairs of your head are all numbered.
— Matthew 10:29-30

Near the end of her reign, after having severely persecuted the Protestants in England, Queen Mary signed a commission to enforce similar action in Ireland. She appointed Dr. Cole to personally carry this commission to the proper authorities in Ireland.

On his way, Dr. Cole stopped in Chester and visited with the mayor of the city. While speaking together, Dr. Cole removed a leather box from his suitcase, and boastingly proclaimed, "Here is a commission that shall lash all the heretics in Ireland!" (As a Roman Catholic, he meant all "Protestants" when he used the term "heretics.")

The mayor's wife was alarmed when she heard these words. She had favorable impressions of the Protestants, and her brother, John Edmunds, was a well-respected Protestant leader in Dublin.

When the mayor took his visitor outside to see the gardens, his wife quickly opened the box, removed the royal commission, and replaced it with a deck of cards she had hastily wrapped in a sheet of paper, and again closed the box.

At the conclusion of his visit, Dr. Cole repacked the leather box in his suitcase, and continued his journey.

A few days later, he arrived in Ireland and obtained a hearing with all the chief authorities, including the Lord

Deputy, in the Castle at Dublin. After speaking about the purpose of his visit, he presented the leather box to the deputy, who commanded the box to be opened that the secretary might read the commission to all present.

To the shock of Dr. Cole, the Lord Deputy, and everyone in attendance, the box only contained a wrapped deck of cards!

After the initial confusion subsided, the Lord Deputy jokingly stated, "We will need another commission, and meanwhile, we will shuffle the cards!"

A much-embarrassed Dr. Cole returned to England to obtain a replacement commission at court. Due to adverse weather conditions, however, he had to wait a few days before a ship could sail to Ireland. While waiting, he received notice that the queen had died.

In this manner, the Protestants of Ireland were preserved from persecution and death. The new queen, Elizabeth, was so impressed by this story, that she had it published and rewarded the wife of the mayor, Elizabeth Edmunds, with a pension for the rest of her life.

God often uses small events, such as stopping to visit the mayor of Chester for an hour, to determine the outcome of major happpenings, such as the persecution of all Protestants in Ireland.

? A non-Christian reading this story would probably speak of this happening as a remarkable coincidence. How does faith in God's governing providence help a person to see beyond "coincidences" and to recognize God's hand in these events?

? Think of the biblical story of Esther. How many remarkable dealings of God's governing providence can you name which the non-Christian world would call "coincidences" or "luck"? Esther is the only scriptural book in which God's name is never directly mentioned — yet we consistently see His workings. What lesson regarding God's providence is the Book of Esther teaching? Why is God's name never mentioned directly?

Young Allan was traveling to a distant city by train to visit his grandmother. As he entered the train, fear swept through him. Did he dare to travel alone? Where was his seat? How would he know where to step off? Would he find his suitcases again?

As Allan stood there in a daze, the conductor kindly showed him to his seat, and the car attendant explained where the washrooms, diner, and sleeping compartments were. Frequently the attendants were stopping to talk, asking him if he had any questions, giving him snacks, books, etc., and helping him find whatever he needed.

As Allan neared his destination, the conductor came to see if he was ready, found and carried his suitcases and brought him to a waiting taxi that would bring him to his grandmother's home.

Allan was amazed that everything had gone so well. Everyone seemed to know about, and to care for, him. How could this be?

As Allan grew older, however, he began to understand. His father had made all the arrangements ahead of time. He had instructed and paid the conductor and car attendant to provide extra care for him. Due to his father's care, all his needs were provided for.

How is God's governing providence a rich comfort to God's children when traveling through life to their eternal destination? However, can they always see, experience, and rest in this truth to the same depth? Why not?

? What rich comfort is missed by all those who deny God's governing providence?

A young soldier, having returned from war, was continually being pressed to tell about his experiences. Each time, however, he tried to avoid the questions.

Finally, someone asked him directly, "Tell me, of all your war experiences, what impressed you the most?

"Well," the soldier replied, after some thought, "the thing which impressed me the most was the number of bullets that missed me."

Have you been impressed by God's governing providence in the number of dangers that have missed you? Have you seen and deeply appreciated God's hand in His daily protection of you?

On a Sunday night in 1914, the largest ship man had ever built, the "Titanic," sank in the Atlantic Ocean. Hundreds of people died in that terrible night.

One of the passengers on board was Colonel Gracie. His wife, who had remained behind, could not sleep that night. She felt a need to pray for her husband, and prayed earnestly for his safety.

Meanwhile, Colonel Gracie was helping to launch lifeboats from the sinking ship. He had given up hope of being saved. He knew that the ship would sink and that there were not nearly enough lifeboats for all the passengers.

After the last lifeboat was launched, the colonel felt the ship being drawn under and jumped into the ice-cold water. When he came to the surface, he found himself near an overturned lifeboat. He climbed on and clung to this boat until another lifeboat rescued him.

God's remarkable acts of governing providence are often witnessed in special times of distress and emergency. Can you and your family relate accounts of how God has helped in special ways in times of special need? Afterwards, were you more impressed with the directing God or the remarkable events? Did you end in the Giver or in His gifts?

? What rich security does the true Christian possess, that the world can never match? How is a life of trusting in God different from that of trusting in man, material goods, governments, or any other worldly trusting ground?

God's providence is referred to in Scripture by the following six terms:

GOD'S PROVIDENCE	
Term	**Example Text**
1. God's Reign	The LORD reigneth, He is clothed with majesty; the LORD is clothed with strength, wherewith He hath girded Himself: the world also is stablished, that it cannot be moved. — Psalm 93:1
2. God's Ordinances	They continue this day according to Thine ordinances: for all are Thy servants. — Psalm 119:91
3. God's Hand	For to do whatsoever Thy hand and Thy counsel determined before to be done. — Acts 4:28
4. God's Working	This also cometh forth from the LORD of hosts, which is wonderful in counsel, and excellent in working. — Isaiah 28:29
5. God's Care	Casting all your care upon Him; for He careth for you. — I Peter 5:7
6. God's Upholding	Who being the brightness of His glory, and the express image of His person, and upholding all things by the word of His power, when He had by Himself purged our sins, sat down on the right hand of the Majesty on high. — Hebrews 1:3

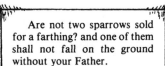

Are not two sparrows sold for a farthing? and one of them shall not fall on the ground without your Father.

But the very hairs of your head are all numbered.
— Matthew 10:29-30

He giveth to the beast his food, and to the young ravens which cry.
— Psalm 147:9

And the ravens brought him bread and flesh in the morning, and bread and flesh in the evening; and he drank of the brook.
— I Kings 17:6

According to the purpose of Him who worketh all things after the counsel of His own will.
— Ephesians 1:11b

A man's heart deviseth his way: but the LORD directeth his steps.
— Proverbs 16:9

God's providence extends over all things. He rules over all substances and powers, and over the wills, thoughts, words, and actions of all living creatures. God hears the ravens when they cry; He directed the ravens to bring food to Elijah; not a sparrow dies without God's will; even the hairs of our head are numbered by Him. Everything is included: there is nothing that is outside of God's providence.

David Brainerd, a famous godfearing eighteenth-century missionary to native Indians in the United States, was once traveling to visit a nearby tribe. On his way, he was overtaken by a severe storm.

Looking for a place of shelter, he found a large hollow tree with an opening at the base, and crawled into it. As he waited, he became increasingly hungry, but could not move on, due to the violence of the storm. This led him to pray — and ask God to graciously care for his needs.

After some time, he saw a squirrel enter the tree and deposit some nuts. After it left, he reached up, took, and ate the nuts. For three days the storm continued in its fury, and for three days the squirrel continued its trips to the hollow tree to deposit nuts.

Rev. Brainerd recorded this event in his diary. It was an encouragement to him in his work, for he saw that the God of Elijah was still living.

God often shows the greatness of His providence through His use of small things. What rich lessons did Elijah learn from the ravens, and Rev. Brainerd from the squirrel? What rich blessing is contained in knowing that God's providence extends over all things — even "little" things?

? When we see God's hand in all things, why is nothing actually a "little" thing? Why are even the smallest things important?

God's care over seemingly small or insignificant things is not a disgrace, but it promotes His glory. This is true because:

1. As it was not a disgrace, but to His glory, to create small things, so God is also glorified in providing for them.

2. By showing His constant care over smaller things, He reveals that He will not neglect caring for greater matters.

3. He often uses smaller things to effect greater matters.

A sparrow once built her nest in an unused freight car which was waiting in line for repair.

When the car was put back into service, a nest full of young birds was found. Although the car traveled several hundred miles, the mother bird never left her young.

The faithfulness of the mother sparrow touched the sympathy of the trainmen, and the division superintendent granted their request to have the car removed from service until the little birds had left the nest.

The care of the superintendent for the family of sparrows was no disgrace to him. So God's care for all small things is no disgrace, but serves to clearly reveal His glory and greatness.

If a great railroad system can be changed by the order of a superintendent to protect a few helpless sparrows, how much more are we called to believe in the care and power of the Superintendent of the entire universe, the King of kings, and in His providence!

God's providence can be distinguished as being of three types:

1. His *general providence* over creation

2. His *special providence* over rational creatures (angels and men)

3. His *very special providence* over His Church (His elect)

Each of these three types of providence reflects a greater degree of closeness to the central purpose, the deepest reason for God's creation and upholding of all things — the revelation and glorification of His being and attributes, which are especially glorified in the salvation of His church.

When we speak of all things being in God's providence and of God directing all things according to His purpose, we must also realize that God works His purpose through means. If it is in God's providence to grant us excellent health in the coming year, He generally works this through the means of good food, shelter, and clothing. If it is in God's providence to grant us a good harvest next year, He will probably produce this through granting proper amounts of rain and sunshine, and **appropriate** temperatures. God's normal way is to work through means.

Separating God's providence from the means that He uses to effect His purposes is a mistake. God is the **primary** cause, but it is His normal manner to work through means as **secondary** causes. This truth is of great practical importance in our daily lives. In all things we must realize the necessity of God's blessing and pray for this in the first place; but we must also actively use the means God has provided in the second place. We must *pray* and *work*. One without the other is not proper; we must actively do both, balancing these two scriptural truths in our daily lives. How do the following texts testify of this balance?

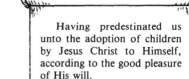

Having predestinated us unto the adoption of children by Jesus Christ to Himself, according to the good pleasure of His will.

To the praise of the glory of His grace, wherein He hath made us accepted in the beloved.

In whom also we have obtained an inheritance, being predestinated according to the purpose of Him who worketh all things after the counsel of His own will:

That we should be to the praise of His glory, who first trusted in Christ.

— Ephesians 1:5-6, 11-12

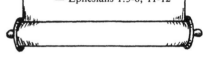

● **Appropriate** — Suitable; fitting; proper

● **Primary** — First, chief, principal

● **Secondary** — Second; subordinate; not of first or greatest importance

Except the LORD build the house, they labour in vain that build it: except the LORD keep the city, the watchman waketh but in vain. — Psalm 127:1	The soul of the sluggard desireth, and hath nothing: but the soul of the diligent shall be made fat. — Proverbs 13:4
I have planted, Apollos watered; but God gave the increase. So then neither is he that planteth any thing, neither he that watereth; but God that giveth the increase. — I Corinthians 3:6-7	Preach the Word; be instant in season, out of season; reprove, rebuke, exhort with all longsuffering and doctrine. — II Timothy 4:2
For He saith to Moses, I will have mercy on whom I will have mercy, and I will have compassion on whom I will have compassion. So then it is not of him that willeth, nor of him that runneth, but of God that showeth mercy. — Romans 9:15-16	Seek ye the LORD while He may be found, call ye upon Him while He is near: Let the wicked forsake his way, and the unrighteous man his thoughts: and let him return unto the LORD, and He will have mercy upon him; and to our God, for He will abundantly pardon. — Isaiah 55:6-7

What mistakes are made in the following persons' reasonings?

1. "I am not going to cultivate, fertilize, and irrigate my field as my neighbors do. If it is in God's providence that I will be blessed with a good harvest, I will be blessed; and if not, nothing that I can do will change that."

2. "I know that I will have a good crop this year. I've used the best fertilizer and irrigation system. I can't wait to see the volume of my harvest!"

3. "No, I do not really study the Bible or read any religious books, except a chapter from the Bible at mealtimes. I don't really care for reading. Besides, I don't believe in salvation by works. If I am one of God's elect and it is in His plan to save me, I will be saved. If not, nothing that I can do will change that."

4. "I know that I will be saved. I have been born and raised in a Christian home, attended a Christian school, and am a member of a Christian church. I regularly read religious material, pray, and have personal devotions."

Which of the four persons' reasonings overemphasize man's activity? Which wrongly underemphasize God's providence? Why?

The secret things belong unto the LORD our God: but those things which are revealed belong unto us and to our children for ever, that we may do all the words of this law.
— Deuteronomy 29:29

We must follow God's command — His revealed will — to actively use His means; realizing, however, that we are totally dependent upon His blessing. Without His blessing, we can accomplish nothing.

God can accomplish His purposes without means. He sustained Moses, Elijah, and the Lord Jesus for forty days without food, but His normal manner is to use means. God healed many people from disease instantly through a word or touch of the apostles, but His usual way is to work through means.

When God works in a special and extraordinary manner, we call this a "**miracle**." As the almighty Creator and Governor of heaven and earth, God can **intervene** by **suspending** or altering the normal

- **Miracle** — A very special or extraordinary happening

- **Intervene** — To come between; to interfere

- **Suspending** — Stopping for a time

laws and forces of nature — the ordinary means through which He upholds and governs the world. God can cause iron to float, daylight to be extended, the blind to see, and the dead to arise. We, however, may not make a rule from these exceptions. God's normal procedure is to work through means of the secondary causes He has established.

This is true, not only in the realm of nature, but also of grace. God could instantly convert, instruct, and bring into heaven all His children without the use of any means of grace, as He did with the thief on the cross. But God's normal manner of working is to convert and instruct His children through the use of His means of grace. Again, we may not make a rule from the exception. We must follow God's revealed will, His loving command to actively use His means of grace, asking Him to graciously bless their use in our hearts and lives.

? What dangers could possibly arise from the continual reading of unusual or exceptional conversion accounts? Which Book must be our source for determining the marks and fruits of true conversion?

As the doctrine of God's providence over all things does not render the use of means unnecessary, neither does it **diminish** the freedom nor responsibility of man. While God rules and governs all of us according to His will and decree, He does so in a manner in which we remain free **moral** beings. Whatever we do, we do willingly, from the free choice of our hearts. Due to our deep fall in Paradise we choose sin by nature. If God forced or compelled us to do things we did not want to do in order to fulfill His plan, then we could not be held responsible for our actions. However, sinful choices are freely and continually made by all people, as all are sinners.

- **Diminish** — To lessen; to reduce

- **Moral** — Conscious of right and wrong

This truth is very important when viewing man's sin. It was in God's plan that Joseph's brothers would sell him into Egypt; yet his brothers did not do this because God compelled them. They did so willingly, out of their heartfelt hatred for Joseph, hoping never to see him again. Joseph testifies of this later, when speaking to his brothers after their father's death, he says, "But as for you, *ye thought evil* against me; but *God meant it unto good*, to bring to pass, as it is this day, to save much people alive" (Genesis 50:20).

While we cannot fully comprehend how God's decree and governing providence extend over sin, yet each person remains fully responsible and guilty for his sins. We cannot fully understand how God can govern and yet not be the cause of sin. The following chart may help, however, in picturing and understanding some of these truths.

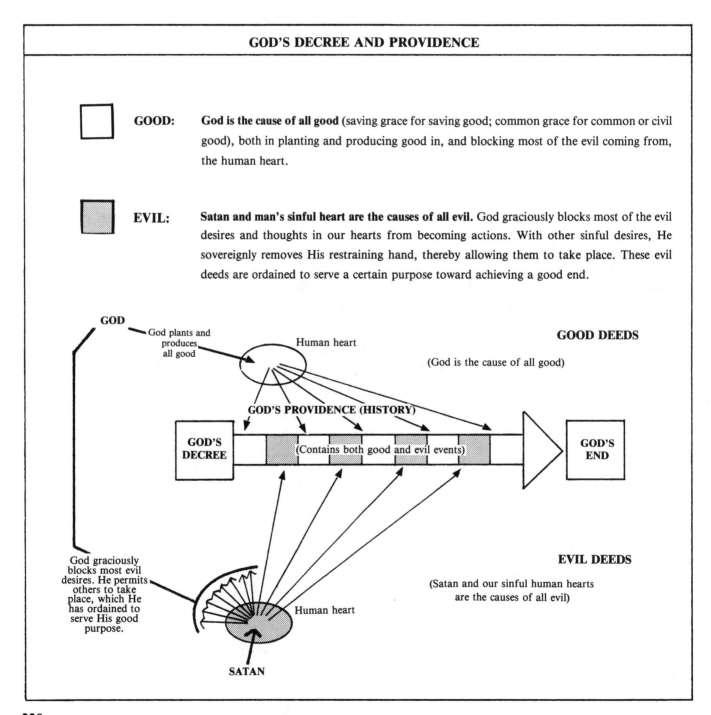

GOD'S DECREE AND PROVIDENCE

GOOD: **God is the cause of all good** (saving grace for saving good; common grace for common or civil good), both in planting and producing good in, and blocking most of the evil coming from, the human heart.

EVIL: **Satan and man's sinful heart are the causes of all evil.** God graciously blocks most of the evil desires and thoughts in our hearts from becoming actions. With other sinful desires, He sovereignly removes His restraining hand, thereby allowing them to take place. These evil deeds are ordained to serve a certain purpose toward achieving a good end.

GOD

God plants and produces all good

Human heart

GOOD DEEDS

(God is the cause of all good)

GOD'S PROVIDENCE (HISTORY)

GOD'S DECREE

(Contains both good and evil events)

GOD'S END

God graciously blocks most evil desires. He permits others to take place, which He has ordained to serve His good purpose.

Human heart

SATAN

EVIL DEEDS

(Satan and our sinful human hearts are the causes of all evil)

Freedom means "to be free from outside persuasion or force; to freely do that which one desires." When speaking of God's decree and governing providence, it is important to remember that every evil deed decreed and governed by God is done freely by the person committing the action. He performs his sinful deed because he desires to.

How would you respond to the following persons' viewpoints?

"Certainly, I stole several thousands of dollars from that millionaire. But my deed was in God's decree and providence. Probably my theft helped to teach the millionaire a much needed lesson. God had His purpose with my action. Besides, nothing I could or could not do can change His decree or providence."

"Sure, I missed certain days when I should have been working. Yes, I will admit I wasted several hours when I was trying to establish my business. But, God must have decreed that I would not be successful, because in His providence, He directed it so that my business has always done poorly. God must have decreed that I should always be poor."

"Of course, I have never prayed or read a lot, but religious books just don't interest me that much. It must be that God has decreed that I will be lost, because nothing has happened in His providence to change things in my life. This is not my fault. I can't convert myself! If God has decreed to save me, He will direct things to produce the necessary change in my life."

What is clearly wrong in these three viewpoints? Why?

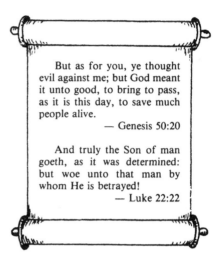

But as for you, ye thought evil against me; but God meant it unto good, to bring to pass, as it is this day, to save much people alive.
— Genesis 50:20

And truly the Son of man goeth, as it was determined: but woe unto that man by whom He is betrayed!
— Luke 22:22

? What is the difference between something being in God's providence or in His favor? Why is this difference important when considering the viewpoints expressed on this page?

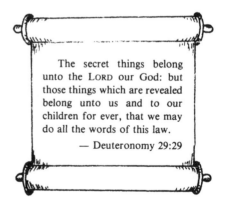

The secret things belong unto the LORD our God: but those things which are revealed belong unto us and to our children for ever, that we may do all the words of this law.
— Deuteronomy 29:29

? While very few may express themselves in the words of these three accounts, how can people testify of these beliefs in actions?

? How does the struggle between faith and unbelief, and trusting and doubting God's dealings, relate to the old and new natures within a true Christian?

Even for true Christians it is not always easy to understand why certain evil things, hardships, or problems take place in their lives; to see the "good ends" to which God is directing them; to realize God's purpose behind distressing circumstances, nor to always trust God's leading. This is especially true when His leading contradicts the way in which we think things should go. The following story illustrates this truth.

● **Suspended** — Hung

? What is pictured in our lives by "bright" and "dark" strings?

A minister was once very distressed over several difficult and confusing circumstances. No matter how he looked at these events, he could not see any reason or purpose for them in his life. He was filled with spiritual doubt and darkness.

While in this condition, he visited one of his members who worked in an oriental rug factory. Entering the weaving room, he paused to observe that which was taking place. A rug that was being woven was **suspended** above him. He could only see its underside, which showed various colored strands of yarn being strung here and there. There did not appear to be any reason, order, or pattern to the confusion of strings he saw.

He also observed that the workers did not question their director, who was stationed above the rug, but immediately obeyed him by handing up whatever colors he ordered at the various locations.

To meet the person he needed to see, he had to go to the second floor which was above the suspended carpet. When the minister climbed the stairs and reached the point where he could see the top of the suspended rug, he stopped in amazement. Now he could observe the beautiful pattern that was being woven from above.

There on the stairs, the Lord taught him a beautiful lesson. God was above, directing and weaving a perfect pattern in his life, using both bright and dark-colored strings. His duty was to trust his heavenly Director, to obediently hand up the strings, even when he, from underneath, could not see the pattern being woven.

How is this example a beautiful illustration of faith in God and His providence?

The Plan of the Master Weaver

My life is but a weaving between the Lord and me,
I may not choose the colors,
He knows what they should be;
For He can view the pattern upon the upperside,
While I can see it only on this, the underside...

Sometimes He weaveth sorrow, which seemeth strange to me,
But I will trust His judgment, and work on faithfully.
'Tis He who fills the shuttle, and He knows what is best.
So shall I weave in earnest, leaving to Him the rest...

Not till the loom is silent and the shuttles cease to fly
Shall God unroll the canvas and explain the reasons why—
The dark threads are as needed in the Weaver's skillful hand
As the threads of gold and silver in the pattern He has planned.

— Anonymous

? In the poem, "The Plan of the Master Weaver," what is meant by the following expressions?
— "Tis He who fills the shuttle"
— "Not till the loom is silent"
— "Shall God unroll the canvas and explain the reason why"

A woman, vacationing in Switzerland, visited a mountain shepherd's sheepfold. Off to one side, lying on a pile of straw, was one sheep that appeared to be suffering from pain.

"What is wrong with that sheep?" she asked the shepherd, pointing to the suffering animal.

"Its leg was broken," he answered.

"Poor thing. How did that happen?"

"I broke it," the shepherd replied.

"How could you be so cruel?" the lady responded in anger, feeling yet more sympathy for the suffering sheep.

"Madam, I will explain. Of all my sheep, this was the most stubborn. It continually went its own way instead of following the safe paths upon which I was leading the flock. Several times it came into perilous situations, upon cliffs where it could no longer turn around, and near dangerous canyons. Other sheep often followed it and ended in similar dangerous places. After calling and punishing it several times, it still would not listen. I knew then, that I had to break its leg."

"I still don't understand," replied the lady. "How does breaking its leg help? Doesn't it hate you for doing that?"

? How can we also make seriously wrong first judgments about matters in our lives, as this woman did about the shepherd breaking a sheep's leg?

232

"You see, Madam, I have been a shepherd for many years, and have had sheep like this one before. I will tell you what happens. The following day, after I break its leg, I go to it with food; but it tries to bite me — so I leave. I let it lie alone for another entire day. On the third day when I bring food, it is submissive; and a few days later it licks my hand. By the time the sheep is well again, it will set an excellent example for the entire flock. I can assure you that no sheep in my flock will hear my voice as quickly, nor seek to follow as closely at my side, as this one."

As the great, heavenly Shepherd, why does the Lord at times need to "break the legs" of His "sheep"? What practical lessons and cautions regarding God's governing providence over His children are illustrated by this story?

? How can this story be used to illustrate Psalm 119:67: "Before I was afflicted I went astray; but now have I kept Thy Word"?

Faith in God and trusting His providential dealings with a childlike confidence produce three wonderfully precious results in a person's life:

1. Patience in **adversity**

2. Thankfulness in **prosperity**

3. Trust for the future

● **Adversity** — Distress; affliction; hardship; disappointment

● **Prosperity** — Successfulness; advancement; pleasantness

The *Heidelberg Catechism* speaks of these three rich benefits in its Question and Answer 28.

HEIDELBERG CATECHISM: Question and Answer 28

Q. What advantage is it to us to know that God has created, and by His providence doth still uphold all things?

A. That we may be patient in adversity; thankful in prosperity; and that in all things, which may hereafter befall us, we place our firm trust in our faithful God and Father, that nothing shall separate us from His love; since all creatures are so in His hand, that without His will they cannot so much as move.

By nature, we are impatient and rebellious when things do not go as we want, proud and self-praising when things go well, and anxious and fearful when thinking of an unknown future. This is natural, because fallen man sees himself as the center of all things — as God. That which does not go according to my desires is most upsetting, what serves my honor and glory is most important, and that which will happen in the future is in my weak hands or it will be determined by unknowns — more powerful people or forces. Therefore, I am fearful.

Only God the Holy Spirit can produce the three precious jewels of patience, thankfulness, and trust. Only experiential religion can produce true humility, submission, and patience when experiencing adversities, hardships, and disappointments. Only seeing God's providential hand, trusting that He has His good purpose, and knowing that, as a sinner, I do not deserve anything but the results of sin, can truly give peace and submission in times of affliction and trial.

Only Spirit-worked grace in our hearts can produce true thankfulness in prosperity. This grace will show us that any abilities we have are God-given. The health, capabilities, and opportunities to exercise them are from God, and the blessing of our efforts is also graciously given by Him. Only this truth can produce a truly humble thankfulness in times of prosperity. Despite how we may compare to others, the seeing of God's expectation for us in His law, will keep us humble.

Finally, only true, experiential faith in God will produce a calm trust for the future. Trust in God is trusting in the Almighty. Everything lies in His providential hands. The future may be unknown, but if we know the God of the future, we have everything.

What a comfort is the Christian faith! What a joy is the Christian hope! What a life is Christian love! It is a peace which passes all understanding — both for our present and temporal, but also for our future and eternal, lives.

How was it possible for Paul and Silas to sing psalms in the inner prison with their feet in the stocks and their backs torn open by scourging? How was it possible for Daniel to calmly respond to King Darius from the lions' den? How was it possible for the Shunamite woman to say "All is well," when her son had just died? These were possible only through faith and trust in God and His fatherly providential hand.

We need God to implant faith in our hearts, and we need Him to exercise, enliven, and strengthen it in our lives. Do you know something of this in your life's experience, or are you yet a stranger of it?

The following stories help to illustrate some aspects of the blessedness of a lively faith in God and His fatherly providence.

? Paul writes in II Corinthians 12:8-10: "For this thing I besought the Lord thrice, that it might depart from me. And He said unto me, My grace is sufficient for thee: for My strength is made perfect in weakness. Most gladly therefore will I rather glory in my infirmities, that the power of Christ may rest upon me. Therefore I take pleasure in my infirmities, in reproaches, in necessities, in persecutions, in distresses for Christ's sake: for when I am weak, then am I strong."

How do these verses emphasize the same lesson illustrated by the story on this page?

Mr. Thomas, a godfearing father who was in very difficult and trying circumstances, entered his home carrying a heavy package for his wife. He saw his daughter, who was ill, lying on the living room couch.

Going up to her, he kissed her, and said, "Elsie, where is Mother? I have a surprise for her."

"She's upstairs, Dad. May I bring the surprise to her?"

"Why, my girl! You are not even strong enough to walk up the stairs yet, and could certainly never carry a heavy package like this!"

"I know," said his daughter, "but I can if you carry me."

With a smile, he gave his daughter the package and carried her upstairs to her mother.

The Lord used this event to teach him a profitable lesson. While God placed a burden upon him, as a greater Father, the Lord would also support and carry him with his burden.

Scott, a young pioneer boy, lived in a cabin which his father had built a few hundred yards (metres) into a deep forest. As a pioneering woodsman, he wanted his son to grow up without fear of the woods. Therefore, Scott's father told him that when school started, he would have to walk to school alone. Scott did not mind walking alone through the fields, but the section of trail which led through the woods scared him.

Everything went well the first few days, but on the fourth day, Scott stopped in his tracks. A black bear was crossing the path a short distance in front of him.

As he stood there — not knowing whether to scream, run, or continue — his father stood suddenly at his side. He explained that the bear would not bother him unless it was feeding on something in the path or if its young cubs were nearby.

Scott was so relieved to have his father at his side. "Where did you come from to help me so quickly, Dad?" he asked.

"Oh, I have been following you each day on a little path behind the first trees. I just wanted to make sure you were brave enough and knew what to do."

Knowing that an unseen heavenly Father is watching and caring for them is a great blessing for all God's children. Why? Who, however, are troubled by the knowledge of an all-seeing and all-knowing God? Why?

? How does Romans 8:28, "And we know that all things work together for good to them that love God, to them who are the called according to His purpose," relate to the truth illustrated in this story? Why can it be difficult at times for God's children to believe that all things are working for them, when it appears that all things are against them?

CATECHISM MEMORIZATION

Questions from Rev. A. Hellenbroek's *Divine Truths* — Chapter VII

1. Did God leave His creatures to themselves after He created them?
No, He continually oversees His creation through acts of Divine providence. "My Father worketh hitherto, and I work" (John 5:17).

2. How many acts of God are contained in His providence?
Three: God's preservation, cooperation, and government.

3. What is the preservation of God?
The almighty power of God through which He upholds the life of all things. "Who upholdeth all things by the word of His power" (Heb. 1:3).

4. What is the cooperation of God?
God's almighty power through which He cooperatively influences all the actions and functions of His creatures. "But it is the same God that worketh all in all" (I Cor. 12:6).

5. What is the government of God?
God's almighty power through which He directs all things to a certain determined end. "The Lord reigneth" (Ps. 93:1).

6. How far does the providence of God extend?
God's providence extends over all things. "He worketh all things after the counsel of His own will" (Eph. 1:11).

7. Does God's providence extend to small things?
Yes. "For even the hairs of your head are all numbered" (Matt. 10:30).

8. Is it a disgrace to God to extend His care over such trifling things?
No, because (1) it was no disgrace for Him to create them, (2) by this He shows that He does not neglect greater matters, and (3) He frequently uses these small things to effect great things.

9. Does the providence of God extend to things that appear to take place by chance?
Yes. "The lot is cast into the lap, but the whole disposing thereof is of the Lord" (Prov. 16:33).

10. Is there such a thing as an event happening by chance, that is, contingency?
Not with respect to God, but only as it appears to us.

11. Does the providence of God extend to one's life and death?
Yes, the time of one's life is determined by Him. "Seeing his days are determined, the number of his months is with Thee, Thou hast appointed his bounds that he cannot pass" (Job 14:5).

12. Can one prolong or shorten his life?
Not with respect to God, but only with respect to man.

13. Is it useless to use means for preserving life?
No, for God has decreed these means to preserve life and He gives man a willing mind to use them.

14. Does the providence of God also direct our most free actions?
Yes, even our very thoughts. "The king's heart is in the hand of the Lord, as the rivers of water: He turneth it whithersoever He will" (Prov. 21:1).

15. Does God's providence destroy man's freedom as a rational being?
No, for God's government is not one of compulsion, but He makes man willing to do His will (Ps. 110:3).

16. Does God's providence extend to sin also?
Yes, God permits sin, limits it, and directs it to a certain end. "Ye thought evil but God meant it unto good" (Gen. 50:20).

17. Does God then become the cause of sin?
No, a holy God cannot be the cause of anything that is sinful. He hates and punishes sin.

18. Is God the cause of all good?
Yes. "Not that we are sufficient of ourselves, to think any thing as of ourselves, but our sufficiency is of God" (II Cor. 3:5).

19. Does God give inherent power to do good or does He influence every good act?
God influences, motivates, and assists in every good act. "For it is God which worketh in you both to will and to do of His good pleasure" (Phil. 2:13).

20. What benefits are derived from the doctrine of God's providence?
That God's children may be patient in adversity, thankful in prosperity, and trust in God for all future things (Job 1:21,22; Gen. 32:10; Job 13:15).

CHAPTER 6

Part I. Chapter Review

1. Explain the errors of the following views concerning God's providence:

    a. Deists — _____

    b. Pantheists — _____

    c. Believers in "luck" or "fate" — _____

2. Define God's providence — _____

    _____

3. Name and define the three divine acts included in providence:

    a. _____

    _____

    b. _____

    _____

    c. _____

    _____

4. Name six scriptural terms for God's providence:

    a. _____   d. _____

    b. _____   e. _____

    c. _____   f. _____

5. God's care over seemingly insignificant things is not disgraceful but honoring to the Lord. Why?

    a. _____

    _____

    b. _____

    _____

    c. _____

    _____

6. Name and define three types of providence by which God's providential care can be distinguished:

   a. _____
   _____

   b. _____
   _____

   c. _____
   _____

7. When viewing all matter and events, what is meant by their:

   a. Primary cause? _____
   _____

   b. Secondary causes? _____
   _____

8. Explain the mistaken ideas and actions into which we fall if we:

   a. Overemphasize God's means — _____
   _____
   _____

   b. Underemphasize God's means — _____
   _____
   _____

9. What is a "miracle"? _____
   _____

10. Faith in God and His governing providences produces the following precious results:

    a. _____
    b. _____
    c. _____

11. How and why are views of natural man toward adversity, prosperity, and the future, directly opposite to a spiritual man's views when faith is in exercise? _____
    _____
    _____
    _____

CHAPTER 6

Part II. Deepening Your Insight

1. Why would it not be logical to believe in God's creation but not in His providence? _____
    _____
    _____
    _____

2. Does God command us to be concerned with the primary cause, or secondary causes of all things, or both? Explain. _____
    _____
    _____
    _____

3. Why is a person fully responsible and guilty when he sins, since his sin is in God's unchangeable decree, and happened under God's governing providence? _____
    _____
    _____
    _____

4. How is God the permitter of, and governor over sin, but not the "author" or cause of sin? _____
    _____
    _____

5. Explain why there often is a struggle in the heart of a regenerated person to believe in God and trust His providential dealings in time of adversity. _____
    _____
    _____
    _____

6. Explain why only Spirit-worked grace in our hearts can truly produce the precious fruits of:
    a. Patience in adversity — _____
        _____
    b. Humbleness in prosperity — _____
        _____
    c. Calm trust for the future — _____
        _____

QUESTIONS

Part III. Biblical Applications

1. How does Acts 17:28a teach us that when we sin, we do so by using the very gifts and powers that God is mercifully giving to us at that very moment? _____

_____

_____

2. How does Luke 22:22 testify that Judas Iscariot's betrayal of the Lord Jesus was in God's decree and providence, but also that Judas would be fully responsible and guilty when committing this act? _____

_____

_____

3. How can Genesis 32:24-31 be compared with the story of the shepherd who broke one of his sheep's legs? _____

_____

_____

_____

4. How is II Samuel 16:5-13 an example of true patience in adversity? _____

_____

_____

_____

Part IV. From the Writings of our Church Forefathers

In your own words, explain the meaning of the following quotations:

1. "Some providences, like Hebrew letters, must be read backwards" (John Flavel). _____

_____

_____

2. "Grace makes the promise, and providence the payment" (John Flavel). _____

_____

_____

3. "We may feel God's hand as a Father upon us when He *strikes* us as well as when He *strokes* us" (Abraham Wright). _____

_____

_____

_____

CHAPTER 6

Part V. From the Marginal Questions

1. Why is the Christian's world view a personal one; and the deist's, pantheist's, and humanist's not? _____
_____
_____
_____

2. What rich security does the true Christian possess that the world can never match? How is a life of trusting in God different from that of trusting in man or worldly items?
_____
_____
_____
_____

3. What is the difference between something being in God's providence or in His favor? Why is this distinction important?
_____
_____
_____
_____

4. In the poem, "The Plan of the Master Weaver," what is meant by each of the following expressions?
   a. "Tis He who fills the shuttle" _____
   _____

   b. "Not till the loom is silent" _____
   _____

   c. "Shall God unroll the canvas and explain the reasons why" _____
   _____

5. The less Christian and the more humanistic and materialistic our society becomes, the greater impatience, pride, and anxiety we will observe. Why?
_____
_____
_____
_____

EXTRA CHALLENGE QUESTIONS

Part VI. Your Selection from the Marginal Questions

Write out and respond to two marginal questions that interest you which have not been previously asked in the chapter's question section.

1. Question: _____
   _____

   Response: _____
   _____
   _____
   _____
   _____
   _____

2. Question: _____
   _____

   Response: _____
   _____
   _____
   _____
   _____
   _____

Part VII. Project Ideas

1. Describe a pond scene, with its plant and animal life interaction, from a deist's, a pantheist's, and a biblical (God's providential) view.

2. Design a chart which defines and provides examples of how God's preservation, cooperation, and government affect our daily lives.

3. Locate and print on a chart two lists of texts; one that speaks about all natural and spiritual gifts being freely given by God, and the second that commands us to actively use God's means.

4. Reproduce the chart provided that deals with God's decree and providence. Then using the stories of Joseph's brothers' selling him into Egypt, and Judas Iscariot's betrayal of Jesus; illustrate from the chart how these sins were in God's decree, governed by His providence, directed to a good end, and yet, were fully the desires and actions of the persons' own sinful hearts.

7

Creation of Man
Image of God
Man's Soul and Body
Covenant of Works

The Father, Son, and Holy Ghost
In special counsel stood
And said, as one, "Let Us make man,"
And it was very good.

God made man in His image,
And to further him extol,
God breathed into his nostrils and
Made man a living soul.

The crown of God's creation,
Man was placed to rule the herds
Of beasts and all within the sea,
As well as all the birds.

FROM OUR REFORMED DOCTRINAL STANDARDS

Belgic Confession of Faith

Article 14(a) — of the Creation and Fall of Man

We believe that God created man out of the dust of the earth, and made and formed him after His own image and likeness, good, righteous, and holy, capable in all things to will, agreeably to the will of God. But being in honor, he understood it not, neither knew his excellency, but willfully subjected himself to sin, and consequently to death, and the curse, giving ear to the words of the devil. For the commandment of life, which he had received, he transgressed; and by sin separated himself from God, who was his true life, having corrupted his whole nature; whereby he made himself liable to corporal and spiritual death.

Heidelberg Catechism

Question and Answer 6

Q. 6. Did God then create man so wicked and perverse?

A. By no means; but God created man good, and after His own image, in true righteousness and holiness, that he might rightly know God his Creator, heartily love Him and live with Him in eternal happiness to glorify and praise Him.

CREATION OF MAN

The final and highest creature God created on earth was man. As the crown of God's creation, man was placed by God as ruler over His earthly creation. Man was created to glorify His Maker in a special manner.

In Genesis 1 and 2, the specialness of man's creation is indicated in several ways. Only in the case of man do we read of:

1. *His creation proceeding from a special counsel of the Triune God.* Before creating man, God the Father, Son, and Holy Spirit took special counsel together. "And God said, Let Us make man" (Genesis 1:26a).

The story on the following page illustrates how this special meeting testifies of the importance of the coming event.

And God said, Let Us make man in Our image, after Our likeness: and let them have dominion over the fish of the sea, and over the fowl of the air, and over the cattle, and over all the earth, and over every creeping thing that creepeth upon the earth.

So God created man in His own image, in the image of God created He him; male and female created He them.

— Genesis 1:26-27

? In Genesis 1:26, how is God spoken of as being both singular and plural? How does this testify of God's Triune Being?

? How do the following scriptural references also testify of God's special, personal, direct, and immediate creation of man?

> Which was the son of Enos, which was the son of Seth, which was the son of Adam, which was the son of God.
>
> — Luke 3:38

> For in Him we live, and move, and have our being; as certain also of your own poets have said, For we are also His offspring.
>
> — Acts 17:28

> Woe unto him that striveth with his Maker! Let the potsherd strive with the potsherds of the earth. Shall the clay say to him that fashioneth it, What makest thou? or thy work, He hath no hands?
>
> — Isaiah 45:9

● **Solemn** — Serious; important

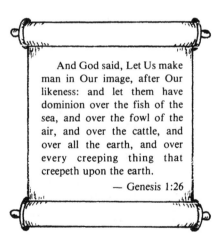

> And God said, Let Us make man in Our image, after Our likeness: and let them have dominion over the fish of the sea, and over the fowl of the air, and over the cattle, and over all the earth, and over every creeping thing that creepeth upon the earth.
>
> — Genesis 1:26

● **Image** — Reflection; likeness; resemblance

Roy is employed by a large department store. While working, Roy and the other employees hear the store manager make the following announcement over the store's public address system:

> "Would all administrators, department managers, and supervisors please report to the Board Room for a special directors' meeting. Our local and regional Boards of Directors have assembled and we wish to begin our meeting promptly. Thank you."

Roy is puzzled and anxious. Soon groups of employees can be seen whispering together. Everyone knows that something important is going to happen, but nobody knows what it is. Suspense can be felt throughout the store.

How did Roy and the other employees know that something of importance would soon take place?

When we read of a special, **solemn** counsel of God being held before creating man, how does this inform us that an event of great importance would be taking place?

While this story illustrates the importance attached to a special counsel being held, it cannot be compared to the solemn, holy counsel of the divine Trinity. Why not?

2. *His creation by a special, personal act of God.* When creating plants, we read, "And God said, Let the earth bring forth grass" (Genesis 1:11a). Of the creation of water animals and birds, Scripture states, "And God said, Let the waters bring forth" (Genesis 1:20a). When creating land animals, the Bible says, "And God said, Let the earth bring forth the living creature" (Genesis 1:24a). Of the creation of man, however, Scripture uses the most personal, direct, and immediate language possible. "And God said, Let Us make man" (Genesis 1:26a); "So God created man... in the image of God created He him" (Genesis 1:27). God speaks of personally forming man's body from the ground, and of personally breathing man's life into him. "And the LORD God formed man of the dust of the ground, and breathed into his nostrils the breath of life" (Genesis 2:7a).

3. *His being created in the **image** of God.* "And God said, Let Us make man in Our image, after Our likeness" (Genesis 1:26a); "So God created man in His own image, in the image of God created He him" (Genesis 1:27a).

4. *His being created with a soul.* No other creature was created with a living soul, only man; "And man became a living soul" (Genesis 2:7b).

5. *His being placed in* **dominion** *over the earthly creation.* "And God blessed them, and God said unto them, Be fruitful, and multiply, and replenish the earth, and subdue it: and have dominion over the fish of the sea, and over the fowl of the air, and over every living thing that moveth upon the earth" (Genesis 1:28).

> And the LORD God formed man of the dust of the ground, and breathed into his nostrils the breath of life; and man became a living soul.
> — Genesis 2:7

● **Dominion** — A position of rule, government, or power

IMAGE OF GOD

What is meant by the expression "the image of God"? What does it mean when we confess that "man was created in the *image* of God"? The word "image" in this sense refers to a reflection, resemblance, or likeness.

? What valuable lessons and truths about the meaning and importance of being created human are missed by those who deny the truth of man's creation as described in Genesis 1 and 2?

Ellen carefully studies her reflection in the mirror before leaving the house. She wants to see what she looks like. Would the reflection Ellen sees in the mirror reflect some of her characteristics? Would it reflect *all*? Would all of Ellen's joys, sorrows, feelings, thoughts, and desires be fully seen in this reflection?

John often looks at the painting of his **deceased** grandfather which hangs on the wall at the head of the stairway. This painting portrays such a clear resemblance of his grandfather to him, that John enjoys viewing it. However, would this painting reveal *every* aspect of his grandfather's character?

● **Deceased** — Departed from this life; one who has died

Mary's appearance, speech, and actions resemble her mother's to such an extent that people often say to her, "You are the 'picture' of your mother." Do you think Mary is a true "picture" of her mother in *every* sense?

? How do these examples of a mirror reflection, painting, and resembling appearance help to illustrate that which is meant by "image"?

These examples help us understand what is meant by the *image* of God. When God created man, He created him to reflect, to "mirror," some of His qualities on earth. Man bore a likeness to God, a resemblance of His righteous Being.

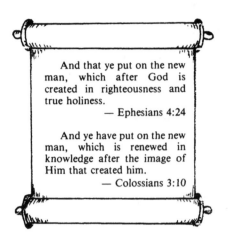

And that ye put on the new man, which after God is created in righteousness and true holiness.
— Ephesians 4:24

And ye have put on the new man, which is renewed in knowledge after the image of Him that created him.
— Colossians 3:10

● **Signifies** — Means; speaks of; refers to; indicates; represents

● **Traits** — Characteristics; qualities; features

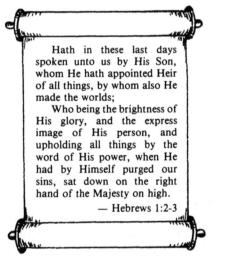

Hath in these last days spoken unto us by His Son, whom He hath appointed Heir of all things, by whom also He made the worlds;

Who being the brightness of His glory, and the express image of His person, and upholding all things by the word of His power, when He had by Himself purged our sins, sat down on the right hand of the Majesty on high.
— Hebrews 1:2-3

● **Resembling** — Bearing some likeness

● **Express** — Precise; exact

This image, reflection, resemblance, or likeness of God in man is centered in the following three qualities:

1. Knowledge
2. Righteousness
3. Holiness

Knowledge refers to man being created with a true knowledge of God, himself, others, and creation.

Righteousness speaks of man being created upright; in a right relationship with God; not guilty of breaking God's law; in a condition of total innocence; and living in complete love to God and others.

Holiness **signifies** man being created pure. In thoughts, words, and actions, he was entirely devoted to God and separated from evil. Man walked in total conformity to God's will.

This image of God — true knowledge, righteousness, and holiness, was reflected by man in Paradise. Before the fall, man beautifully resembled his Creator. **Traits** of God's loving knowledge, righteousness, and holiness could be seen in man. In Paradise, Adam walked with God as with a loving friend. With full devotion, he loved to serve his Creator, for his heart was one with God's. Without feeling fear or a need to hide, Adam enjoyed God's righteous and holy presence.

What an honor, what a glory, what a crown was placed upon man in his creation! In distinction from the rest of creation, man was chosen to reflect the image of God, his Creator!

This was a **resembling** image, not a *perfect* or **express** image. Man was not created to be divine. Adam was not God, nor did he possess the same infinite depth of knowledge, righteousness, and holiness as his infinite Creator. Only Jesus Christ was created in the *express* or *perfect* image of God. Only Jesus possessed infinite knowledge, righteousness and holiness. Adam's resembling image was perfect in *type*, but only Christ's was infinite in *degree*. The following example can help illustrate the difference between type and degree, and between resembling and express images.

After returning from a three-week trip to the Rocky Mountains, Sandy anxiously examined her newly-developed photographs.

She was very pleased with their clearness and color. They reminded her of the actual places and scenes she had visited.

Yet, the seemingly infinite depths and **immense** heights were not fully revealed in her photographs.

The pictures were perfect in *type* but not in *degree* when compared with the real scenes.

Bearing the image of God, Adam reflected God's being. When viewing Adam, one would be reminded of God. Yet, the infinite depth of **virtues** revealed were only to be found in the actual personhood of God Himself.

? How can this example of a nature scene and a photograph help illustrate the difference between the express and resembling images of God?

● **Immense** — Great; large; enormous

● **Bearing** — Carrying; holding up

● **Virtues** — Admirable qualities; characteristics; attributes

The beautiful state in which man was created and in which he lived in Paradise is described in the *Heidelberg Catechism*, Answer 6, in this manner:

> "God created man good and after His own image, in true righteousness and holiness, that he might rightly know God his Creator, heartily love Him and live with Him in eternal happiness to glorify and praise Him."

In Paradise, man fulfilled the purpose for which he was created: to know, love, serve, glorify and enjoy God, his Maker. Therefore, man lived in perfect happiness and contentment.

The image of God can be spoken of in a narrower sense and a wider sense. When this is done, the image of God in its *narrower* (or *restricted*) *sense* refers to the *image itself* — to the reflection of God's knowledge, righteousness, and holiness in man, as previously described.

The image of God in its *wider sense* refers to man as God's *image-bearer* — to the characteristics and qualities God has given man which place him above the animal creation and set him apart as God's image-bearer.

The image of God in its wider sense includes man's being created with:

1. *Rationality* — the ability to reason; think **abstractly**; deal with deeper meanings; and use language.

2. *Spirituality* — a soul which **enables** man to spiritually worship and communicate with God, who is a Spirit.

3. *Immortality* — a never-dying soul, and after the resurrection, a never-dying body.

4. *Conscience* — a deep awareness of God and a moral sense of right and wrong.

5. *Erect body posture* — standing and walking erectly on two legs instead of lowered to four; eating with our heads erect instead of lowered to the ground.

? If a person does not truly know, love, and serve God, why can he never be truly happy and content?

● **Abstractly** — Not physically; dealing with deeper thoughts and meanings

● **Enables** — Makes possible

● **Immortality** — Never-dying; unending existence

● **Erect** — Upright; straight

Some add a sixth distinction to this list — *dominion over God's earthly creation.* However, we do not include it, for this is not a created difference, but was assigned to man after his creation. It is, however, an additional difference which places man above the animal creation.

As Mike heard his teacher explaining the previous five characteristics, he felt that he disagreed on several points. When the explanation was finished, Mike voiced his disagreement.

"I have had a pet dog for several years," Mike stated, "and he is very smart. He's a pretty good thinker, too. Besides, everyone says he has a lot of spirit, and I know that he has a conscience. You can see it all over him when he's done something wrong. I don't agree with points 1, 2, and 4 which state that only man has these characteristics."

"Good thinking, Mike," his teacher responded, "but let me help you reason further. Your dog can be very intelligent in physical matters — things which he sees, hears, smells, tastes, or feels. But if you sit down with your dog to discuss the meaning of life, the purpose of creation, or some other abstract idea, will he understand you?

"When others speak of an animal having a great deal of 'spirit,' they mean that it is spirited or lively.

"Your dog may be lively, but it cannot worship nor communicate with God as man can — it does not have a soul. Your dog has a **consciousness** of certain behaviors being wrong because you have consistently punished him when he did them. But your dog does not have a consciousness of God, an inborn sense to live morally upright, or a sense of **accountability** to God, does he? Do you see, now, how only man was created with these characteristics?"

Why are these points of difference between man and animals especially important today when many promote the theory of evolution?

? How does the image of God in man contradict those who believe in the evolutionary theory — in its narrower sense? in its wider sense?

? What differences in the purpose and importance of human life would develop from believing that man is a developing animal rather than a special image-bearer of God?

? Which type of society would place more value upon human life: one believing in the evolution of man, or one believing in man as image-bearer of God?

- **Consciousness** — Inward knowledge and feelings

- **Accountability** — The state of being answerable and responsible

These five items set man above and in distinction from the animal creation as God's image-bearer. These characteristics are referred to as the image of God in its wider sense. Man's appearance, faculties, and abilities evidence his specialness as God's image-bearer.

THE IMAGE OF GOD IN MAN

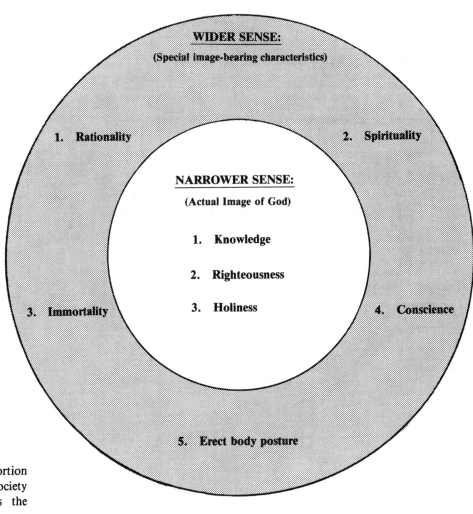

? Does the acceptance of abortion by choice speak of a society which believes or denies the truth of people being created in the image of God?

When man fell into sin in Paradise, he *lost* the *actual image* of God (in its narrower sense) *entirely*. All people are now born as fallen sinners. We no longer reflect God's image of true knowledge, righteousness, and holiness. Instead, we are born knowing and loving ourselves instead of God; guilty instead of righteous; and sinful instead of holy.

Since everyone is now born as a fallen sinner, can this lost image be restored in a person? From man's side — *no*. Each of us naturally desires to serve self, sin, world, and Satan. We are at enmity with the true God; we desire to be our own god. But, from God's side, the answer is — *yes*. Salvation is possible even for the chief of sinners. Through the Father's electing grace, the Son's meriting salvation, and the Holy Spirit's planting of new spiritual life in the sinner's heart, the lost image of God can be restored in man.

Is this your desire? We all need the Holy Spirit, not only to plant God's image in us by regeneration, but also to increase the reflecting of His image in our daily lives of sanctification. Then others will increasingly see a reflection of God's image in us. Are you a regenerated child of God? Are you increasingly reflecting the image of your Creator?

When Adam fell, the *image-bearing* characteristics (the image in its wider sense) were severely *damaged* — but not lost entirely. After the fall man's rationality, spirituality, immortality, conscience, and erect body posture are still retained, but not in their previously glorious state. We are still rational, but now are so often mistaken in our reasoning; we have a soul, but by nature, it now misses true communion with its Creator; we remain immortal, but eternity will be a state of eternal death for many; we have retained our conscience, but it so often misleads through improper training; we have kept our bodily characteristics, but our bodies now suffer from weaknesses, diseases, infirmities, aging, and death.

In our terrible fall in Paradise, we lost the restricted sense of the image of God entirely; but we yet retain, in a damaged state, its wider sense.

And have put on the new man, which is renewed in knowledge after the image of Him that created him.
— Colossians 3:10

And that ye put on the new man, which after God is created in righeousness and true holiness.
— Ephesians 4:24

But not as the offence, so also is the free gift. For if through the offence of one many be dead, much more the grace of God, and the gift by grace, which is by one Man, Jesus Christ, hath abounded unto many.
— Romans 5:15

For since by man came death, by Man came also the resurrection of the dead.
For as in Adam all die, even so in Christ shall all be made alive.
— I Corinthians 15:21-22

The first man is of the earth, earthy: the second Man is the Lord from heaven.
As is the earthy, such are they also that are earthy: and as is the heavenly, such are they also that are heavenly.
— I Corinthians 15:47-49

? When does the restoration of the narrower sense of the image of God begin in the lives of God's children? When will both senses of the image of God be perfectly restored in them?

During the reign of Theodosius the Great, a Roman emperor, a revolt took place in the city of Antioch. An angry mob in the city tore down and broke into pieces a statue of the emperor's wife.

When Emperor Theodosius heard of this, he became very angry. In revenge, he sent an army to the city to kill many of its citizens.

There was a wise monk living in this city, however, who sent a message to the emperor. He wrote, "You, oh Emperor, are angry, and that justly, because the image of your wife has been mistreated and broken; but shall not the King of kings be more angry to see people, who are created in His image, mistreated and killed? Of how much greater value is a never-dying soul than a brass statue!"

After reading this, the emperor drew back his forces.

? Why is the killing of an animal an altogether different matter from the killing of a person? What will happen to a society's values regarding human life as it departs further from God's truth and a belief of man as God's image-bearer?

Why is human life so valuable? Why may we never unjustly kill a human being? Why did God command that all murderers be put to death?

How does Genesis 9:6, "Whoso sheddeth man's blood, by man shall his blood be shed: for in the image of God made He man," assist in answering these questions?

Which of the following biblical references speak of all persons retaining God's image? Which testify of the unconverted being without the image of God?

Therewith bless we God, even the Father; and therewith curse we men, which are made after the similitude of God.
— James 1:9

And that ye put on the new man, which after God is created in righteousness and true holiness.
— Ephesians 4:24

And have put on the new man, which is renewed in knowledge after the image of Him that created him.
— Colossians 3:10

Whoso sheddeth man's blood, by man shall his blood be shed: for in the image of God made He man.
— Genesis 9:6

For a man indeed ought not to cover his head, forasmuch as he is the image and glory of God: but the woman is the glory of the man.
I Corinthians 11:7

I have said, Ye are gods; and all of you are children of the most High.
— Psalm 82:6

How would you explain the **apparent** contradiction of some verses which refer to men missing God's image and others which speak of all men retaining it?

? How do these biblical references establish the need to speak of the image of God in two different senses?

● **Apparent** — Seeming; according to appearances

● **Realm** — Region; sphere; domain

● **Unique** — Without like or equal; different

● **Spheres** — Aspects; regions; extents

MAN'S SOUL AND BODY

God created man with two distinct parts — soul and body. Man is created in a special manner — his body is physical, enabling him to relate with the physical creation; and his soul is spiritual, enabling him to relate with the spiritual **realm**. Man is **uniquely** created to interact in both the physical and spiritual **spheres** of life.

Both the highest and lowest of elements are found in man's creation. Nothing could grant higher nobility than to be created by the personal "breath" from the "mouth" of the Almighty God. Nothing could have a lower origin than to be made from the "dust" of the ground. Both of these factors teach us important lessons. The one testifies of the great importance of our being human, of our noble origin, and of our great calling. The other speaks of our necessary humbleness. Lest we become proud of our special creation and calling, God formed us from the dust of the ground. We are only "dust" — totally dependent upon our Creator for all things. To reflect this truth, the name "Adam," meaning "red earth," was given to the first man.

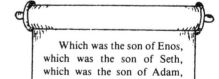

Which was the son of Enos, which was the son of Seth, which was the son of Adam, which was the son of God.
— Luke 3:38

For we are also His offspring.
— Acts 17:28b

And the LORD God formed man of the dust of the ground, and breathed into his nostrils the breath of life; and man became a living soul.
— Genesis 2:7

An evolutionist lecturer once spoke very scornfully and mockingly about God's being able to take "a piece of mud in His hand, and by breathing on it, to change it into a living man."

? How is the miracle of regeneration a divine act of re-creation?

A child of God in the audience received an opportunity to reply to the speaker. He said, "I will not argue with you about God's being able to create man from dust many years ago, but I will tell you this: God stooped down in this city and picked up the dirtiest, most worthless bit of mud in it. He breathed upon it with His Spirit and it received new life. God's breath changed a wicked wretch into a man who hates his former sins and loves the God who saved him. I was that piece of mud."

Why do both man's physical creation and spiritual re-creation require God's almighty power?

Our bodies are priceless gifts from God; they must be valued and cared for. Of how much value are your health, mind, eyesight, hearing, hands, legs, etc.? Is not a healthy body a priceless gift from God?

Sixteen-year-old Daniel lived with his seven brothers and sisters in a poor home and neighborhood. Several family difficulties had kept his family quite poor materially. Daniel did not have nice clothing or possessions as did the others in his class at school.

Daniel grew more and more discontent, and grumbled and complained more frequently. Finally, his father felt he had to do something to correct Daniel.

One Saturday noon, Father announced, "Daniel, you have been feeling quite sad and poor lately. This afternoon, I am going to take you to a place which I know will make you feel very happy and rich."

Daniel was full of questions and very anxious to know where his father would take him, but Father said no more. Even when driving through town together, Father was silent.

Finally, they stopped — at the city hospital!

"Why are you stopping here?" Daniel asked, completely bewildered.

"Follow me," Father responded.

They walked to the Extended Care Unit where his father had made arrangements for Daniel to spend the afternoon visiting, playing games, and going for walks with various patients.

That afternoon, Daniel helped with caring for people with severe handicaps and diseases, several of whom had been there for many years. A silent Daniel rode home later that afternoon. Finally, his father asked, "Do you still feel sorry for yourself, Daniel, that you are so poor and have so much to complain about?"

"Dad, I never realized that I am so rich. You're right! I have so much to be happy about."

How rich are you? For how much would you sell your health? How are we all "millionaires"?

? When viewing the value of the gifts of a healthy mind and body, how are we all "millionaires"?

? When we sin, how are we directly insulting and grieving the One who is giving us the precious gifts of life and health at that very moment?

Imagine a Christian school teacher, Mr. Adams, receiving a donation of a thousand dollars for the school where he is employed. Instead of using this gift for its given purpose, he decides to put it to personal use and uses the thousand dollars as a down payment for a car he had long been thinking of purchasing.

After he was proven guilty of this act, what would be your reaction to Mr. Adam's deed?

God has given you a "million-dollar" gift of a healthy mind and body to use for the purpose of loving, serving, and glorifying Him. If you decide to use this priceless gift for your own purposes instead of for its given purpose, what will God's reaction be to your deeds?

What would you think of a person who frequently received gifts worth thousands of dollars from a rich person, and yet, instead of being thankful, he repeatedly slapped or hit the giver with the gifts he had received?

How can we "slap" God in His face with the priceless gifts of eyesight or hearing that He has given?

Keep thy heart with all diligence; for out of it are the issues of life.
— Proverbs 4:23

For what man knoweth the things of a man, save the spirit of man which is in him?
— I Corinthians 2:11a

While our bodies are very precious gifts from God, our souls are yet more valuable; they are of infinite value.

What is a person's "soul" (or "heart" or "spirit")? One's soul is his inner being, will, core, and internal personhood. It is, in the deepest sense, who he is. It is the **essence** of his being from which his deepest motives, desires, affections, and thoughts arise. One's soul reasons, feels, and wills.

A person's soul is the most important element of his existence for the following three reasons:

1. One's soul is *the deepest element of his personhood.* It is who he really is — his deepest will, feelings, and thoughts. God perfectly knows and judges a person's heart.

2. A person's spirit is the faculty through which he can *worship and commune with God* who is a Spirit. Animals are not created with souls; therefore, they cannot spiritually worship and commune with God. Man is created with a soul for communing with and worshipping his Creator.

3. One's soul is *immortal.* When physical death takes place, a person's body dies and returns to the earth, but his soul returns to God and is sent to continue its life in heaven or hell, without its body, until the Resurrection Day.

● **Essence** — Nature; core; deepest aspect

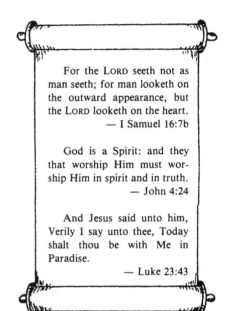

For the LORD seeth not as man seeth; for man looketh on the outward appearance, but the LORD looketh on the heart.
— I Samuel 16:7b

God is a Spirit: and they that worship Him must worship Him in spirit and in truth.
— John 4:24

And Jesus said unto him, Verily I say unto thee, Today shalt thou be with Me in Paradise.
— Luke 23:43

Because one's soul is the most valuable aspect of his being, he must care for it above all else. While one's body and physical health are valuable and important gifts from God and must be carefully treasured and cared for, his soul is yet more important and valuable. Therefore you must urgently seek your soul's welfare; you must be most concerned about your spiritual state; you must place heart matters first in your life.

To illustrate this truth, the Lord Jesus told the story found on the following page:

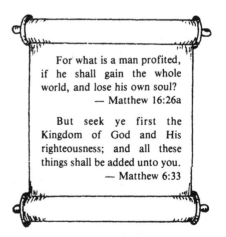

For what is a man profited, if he shall gain the whole world, and lose his own soul?
— Matthew 16:26a

But seek ye first the Kingdom of God and His righteousness; and all these things shall be added unto you.
— Matthew 6:33

? Who are truly "rich"? Who are really "poor"? How are the scriptural views of richness and poorness different from those of our society? Why are material views of richness deceiving?

And He spake a parable unto them, saying, The ground of a certain rich man brought forth plentifully;

And he thought within himself, saying, What shall I do, because I have no room where to bestow my fruits?

And he said, This will I do: I will pull down my barns, and build greater; and there will I bestow all my fruits and my goods.

And I will say to my soul, Soul, thou hast much goods laid up for many years; take thine ease, eat, drink, and be merry.

But God said unto him, Thou fool, this night thy soul shall be required of thee: then whose shall those things be, which thou hast provided?

So is he that layeth up treasure for himself, and is not rich toward God.

— Luke 12:16-21

Was this man rich materially or spiritually? Was he truly "rich"? Why was he a "poor" fool?

COVENANT OF WORKS

After creating him with soul and body, God placed man in Paradise — in the Garden of Eden. Paradise was not an abstract truth or imagined scene, as some claim. The Garden of Eden was an actual, historical place on earth. The Bible describes its location and names the rivers which watered it. The trees, animals, and people mentioned were actual, living realities. The first chapters of Genesis are not **allegorical**, but historical — not imagined stories in which the characters portray deeper meanings, but true accounts of history.

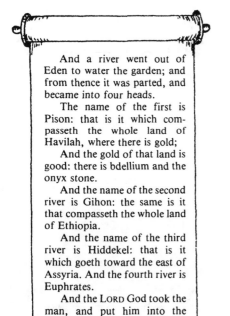

And a river went out of Eden to water the garden; and from thence it was parted, and became into four heads.

The name of the first is Pison: that is it which compasseth the whole land of Havilah, where there is gold;

And the gold of that land is good: there is bdellium and the onyx stone.

And the name of the second river is Gihon: the same is it that compasseth the whole land of Ethiopia.

And the name of the third river is Hiddekel: that is it which goeth toward the east of Assyria. And the fourth river is Euphrates.

And the LORD God took the man, and put him into the garden of Eden to dress it and to keep it.

— Genesis 2:10-15

● **Allegorical** — Symbolical; a fictional story in which the characters portray deeper ideas and truths (*Pilgrim's Progress* is allegorical)

God entered into a **covenant,** an intimate, personal relationship and binding agreement, with Adam in Paradise. This covenant is called the Covenant of *Works*, as the continuation of this relationship depended upon Adam's works of willful obedience or disobedience.

The Covenant of Works included a condition or test, a promise upon obedience, and a penalty for disobedience, as presented below:

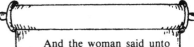 • **Covenant** — Binding agreement

---

COVENANT OF WORKS

CONDITION — WILLING OBEDIENCE
(Test or Probationary Command)

And the LORD God commanded the man, saying, Of every tree of the garden thou mayest freely eat,

But of the tree of the knowledge of good and evil thou shalt not eat of it.

— Genesis 2:16-17a

PROMISE — ETERNAL LIFE
(Upon obedience)

And now, lest he put forth his hand, and take also of the tree of life, and eat, and live for ever.

— Genesis 3:22b

PENALTY — DEATH
(Upon disobedience)

But of the tree of the knowledge of good and evil thou shalt not eat of it: for in the day that thou eatest thereof thou shalt surely die.

— Genesis 2:17

And the woman said unto the serpent, We may eat of the fruit of the trees of the garden:

But of the fruit of the tree which is in the midst of the garden, God hath said, Ye shall not eat of it, neither shall ye touch it, lest ye die.

— Genesis 3:2-3

But they like men have transgressed the covenant: there have they dealt treacherously against me.

— Hosea 6:7

Wherefore, as by one man sin entered into the world, and death by sin; and so death passed upon all men, for that all have sinned:

Therefore as by the offence of one judgment came upon all men to condemnation; even so by the righteousness of One the free gift came upon all men unto justification of life.

For as by one man's disobedience many were made sinners, so by the obedience of One shall many be made righteous.

— Romans 5:12,18-19

For since by man came death, by man came also the resurrection of the dead.

For as in Adam all die, even so in Christ shall all be made alive.

— I Corinthians 15:21-22

 In Paradise, how did the Tree of Life testify of God's promise, and the Tree of the Knowledge of Good and Evil, of God's test?

Robert loves his dog and his dog loves him. He has a bone which he has decided to give to his dog. This is Robert's decision and it reflects his love for his dog, for he is not bound to give this bone.

Robert wants to place a condition upon his dog's receiving this bone; he desires to test his dog's obedience. This is to his dog's liking, for it loves Robert's attention and wants to obey him.

Robert holds up the bone and says, "Beg!"

When his dog sits up and begs, Robert pats it, gives it the bone, and says, "Good dog."

If we look at this example and ask, "What is the real reason why the 'reward' bone was received?" we must answer, "Because Robert wanted to give him one." The obedience of his dog is its duty; it did not earn the right to require a bone from Robert by begging. Rather, Robert wanted to give his dog the bone and decided to make this act of obedience the condition upon which this gift would be given.

How does this example help picture that which took place in the Covenant of Works? God graciously promised man eternal life upon the condition of willing obedience, which was man's duty and desire. Man's obedience was his expected duty. It would not earn a right to require a special reward from God, but God graciously decided to make man's act of obedience the condition upon which the gift of eternal life would be given to him.

? How are both God's grace and justice seen in the Covenant of Works?

With man, however, God desired voluntary love and service. Man's freely choosing to love and obey God, not only because he was bound to, but because he wanted and freely chose to, was more honoring for both God and man.

In order that man might show whether he would freely choose to serve His Creator or not, God entered into a covenant with him. His will and desire would be tested through God's **probationary command** — not to eat from the Tree of the Knowledge of Good and Evil. The tree became the "Test Tree," the "Tree of God's Authority," in Paradise. This command actually tested whether Adam would obey God and His law entirely; whether he would love God and do His will or not.

● **Probationary command** — A testing or proving command

The Covenant of Works and its probationary command were most agreeable to Adam. He agreed wholeheartedly with this test for he loved God with his entire being — with soul, emotions, mind, and strength. To willingly obey God and to do His will was his deepest desire, the law of his heart.

What a wonderful covenant this was! As a true friend of God, Adam loved to do that which pleased the Lord. God also loved Adam, delighted in his willing obedience, and daily communed with him in Paradise.

Furthermore, God graciously attached a reward to Adam's obedience. God was not obliged to do this, for man was bound to love and serve his Creator. Willing obedience from man was to be expected, not necessarily rewarded. But, God chose to attach a gracious reward to the obedience which He had a right to require. Adam could never do that which would demand or make God owe him anything in return. Adam was created to love and serve God perfectly. His doing so, therefore, would only fulfill the purpose for which he was created — it would not deserve or earn additional payment from God. God's promised reward for obedience was a gracious reward.

The Lord Jesus illustrated this truth with the following example:

> But which of you, having a servant plowing or feeding cattle, will say unto him by and by, when he is come from the field, Go and sit down to meat?
> And will not rather say unto him, Make ready wherewith I may sup, and gird thyself, and serve me, till I have eaten and drunken; and afterward thou shalt eat and drink?

- **Confirmed** — Strengthened; proved; established

- **Pledge** — A sign which guarantees a promise

> But we are all as an unclean thing, and all our righteousnesses are as filthy rags; and we all do fade as a leaf; and our iniquities, like the wind, have taken us away.
> — Isaiah 64:6
>
> The LORD looked down from heaven upon the children of men, to see if there were any that did understand, and seek God.
> They are all gone aside, they are all together become filthy; there is none that doeth good, no, not one.
> — Psalm 14:2-3
>
> For if by one man's offence death reigned by one; much more they which receive abundance of grace and of the gift of righteousness shall reign in life by One, Jesus Christ.
> Therefore as by the offence of one judgment came upon all men to condemnation; even so by the righteousness of One the free gift came upon all men unto justification of life.
> For as by one man's disobedience many were made sinners, so by the obedience of One shall many be made righteous.
> — Romans 5:17-19
>
> For since by man came death, by Man came also the resurrection of the dead.
> For as in Adam all die, even so in Christ shall all be made alive.
> — I Corinthians 15:21-22

> Doth he thank that servant because he did the things that were commanded him? I trow not.
>
> So likewise ye, when ye shall have done all those things which are commanded you, say we are unprofitable servants: we have done that which was our duty to do.
> — Luke 17:7-10

Would this man pay his servant extra for doing his duty? Adam's obedience was simply the doing of his duty — that for which he was created. How does God's promise of a reward upon Adam's obedience reveal His grace?

God's promise of eternal life upon Adam's obedience included the perfectly joyful, holy, and never-dying existence of both soul and body. God's promise spoke of a higher state of good which man would receive. Upon his obedience, man would receive a yet richer, more glorious heavenly state in which he would be freed from temptation and have eternal life secured. This glorious and gracious promise was **confirmed** by the Tree of Life; it was a **pledge** of God's promise of eternal life.

God's penalty for willful disobedience was death; bodily, spiritual, and eternal death, as described in the following chapter.

After our terrible fall into sin in Paradise, we can no longer fulfill the condition of the Covenant of Works. Now, no person is born without sin; all are born with sinful hearts and commit actual sins daily. The penalty of death rests upon all of us — for all are sinners. The broken Covenant of Works condemns us all. It is a tragic testimony to the fact that we have willfully broken the wonderful relationship between God and us.

Have you experienced these sad truths in your life? Have you painfully experienced that, with all efforts and attempts to better your life by living in true love to God and others, you only discover sin, and more sin? Have your totally lost and hopeless condition and God's righteous judgment resting upon you for it, become real in your life? Has this become a heartfelt matter within you?

Blessed be God! When all was lost from our side, God opened a way for sinners to be saved from His side! God revealed a new covenant, the Covenant of Grace, with another covenant head, the Lord Jesus Christ. Jesus Christ perfectly fulfilled all the conditions of the broken Covenant of Works and fully paid the death penalty for all

His children. What Adam lost for his children, Jesus Christ gained for His. In Christ, His people are perfectly united to God again. God's grace in and through Jesus Christ is the hope, expectation, and salvation of all saved sinners. Is Jesus Christ your Savior? You need to know Him as your Savior for it to be well with you — both for time and eternity.

Adam stood in a two-fold relationship with God — as an individual human being, and as **covenant head**. As an individual, Adam was naturally obliged to love and obey God his Creator; for this, he was personally responsible. To this, however, was added his covenant relationship. As covenant head, or representative, he stood for the entire human race.

The agreeing parties in the Covenant of Works were God the Father, representing the Triune God; and Adam, representing the human race. This can be pictured as follows:

● **Covenant head** — Representative; decision maker; leader of a group

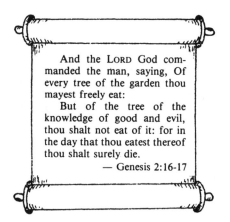

And the LORD God commanded the man, saying, Of every tree of the garden thou mayest freely eat:
But of the tree of the knowledge of good and evil, thou shalt not eat of it: for in the day that thou eatest thereof thou shalt surely die.
— Genesis 2:16-17

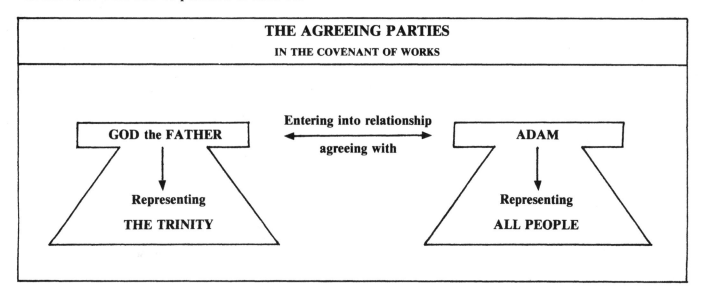

THE AGREEING PARTIES
IN THE COVENANT OF WORKS

GOD the FATHER   Entering into relationship / agreeing with   ADAM

Representing
THE TRINITY

Representing
ALL PEOPLE

One person's being placed in a position of representing others is fairly common. Think of the following examples:

· A large number of people vote for a representative (or member of parliament) to represent them in their federal government.

· A king's decision to go to war affects thousands of young men.

· A father's decision to move to another city involves everyone in his family.

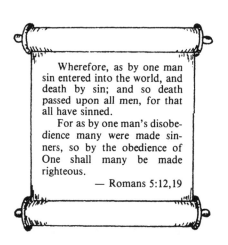

Wherefore, as by one man sin entered into the world, and death by sin; and so death passed upon all men, for that all have sinned.
For as by one man's disobedience many were made sinners, so by the obedience of One shall many be made righteous.
— Romans 5:12,19

In the well-known story of David and Goliath, how is the principle of one person's standing or falling for his entire nation shown in the challenge of Goliath?

> And he stood and cried unto the armies of Israel, and said unto them, Why are ye come out to set your battle in array? am not I a Philistine, and ye servants to Saul? choose you a man for you, and let him come down to me.
> If he be able to fight with me, and to kill me, then will we be your servants: but if I prevail against him, and kill him, then shall ye be our servants, and serve us.
> — I Samuel 17:8-9

How does this example of Goliath's representing the Philistines, and David's standing for the nation of Israel, compare to Adam's position as covenant head?

? In the Covenant of Works, who stood as head of all his children?
In the Covenant of Grace, who stands as Head of all His children? What did each earn for their people?

God chose to place man in a covenant relationship with Himself. This covenant was honoring to both God and man. Man was placed in a higher position than all other earthly creatures. All animals served God **involuntarily**; they did so by created **instincts**. They were not created with a rational mind and free will to choose whether they desired to serve God or not.

Through God's regenerating grace, is your deepest desire to love God with all your soul, mind, and strength?

- **Involuntarily** — Without choice

- **Instincts** — Inborn, automatic impulses in animals which cause them to act in their various manners

268

CATECHISM MEMORIZATION

Questions from Rev. A. Hellenbroek's *Divine Truths* — Chapters VIII and IX

1. Was man capable of fulfilling the covenant of works?
   Yes, God had created man capable of keeping it.

2. How did God create man?
   God created man good and upright.

3. Was man created merely in a state of nature between good and evil?
   No, for man was created in a moral, upright state. "Lo, this only have I found, that God hath made man upright; but they have sought out many inventions" (Eccles. 7:29).

4. How did God create man?
   After His own image (Gen. 1:27).

5. What constitutes the image of God?
   Knowledge, righteousness, and holiness.

6. Does the image of God refer to man's body?
   No, because God does not have a body.

7. Does the image of God refer to man's dominion over the animals?
   No, this dominion is only a result of God's image and will not exist in heaven where the image of God will be completely perfect in man.

8. How can we prove that the image of God consisted of knowledge?
   From Colossians 3:10, "And have put on the new man, which is renewed in knowledge, after the image of Him that created him."

9. How can we prove that the image of God consisted of righteousness and true holiness?
   From Ephesians 4:24, "And that ye put on the new man which after God is created in righteousness and true holiness."

10. Was Adam immortal, having God's image?
    Yes, for death was first threatened as the punishment of sin. "In the day thou eatest thereof thou shalt surely die" (Gen. 2:17).

11. Does God use any other special means to direct man?
    Yes, God governs man in a covenantal manner.

12. How many covenants are there?
    Two: the covenant of works and the covenant of grace.

13. When was the covenant of works in effect?
    Before man's fall.

14. With whom did God make this covenant?
    With Adam, and through his being the representative head of the covenant, with all his posterity.

15. What did God require of man in the covenant of works?
    Perfect obedience to the law.

16. What law did God require man to obey?
    The law of love, to love God with all his heart and his neighbor as himself.

17. How did Adam receive knowledge of this law?
    God implanted it in Adam's heart when He created him.

18. What did God promise to man in the covenant of works?
    God promised eternal life upon Adam's continued obedience.

19. Was this promise confirmed by any sacrament?
    Yes, the tree of life confirmed God's promise.

20. What did God threaten in this covenant?
    Death upon disobedience.

21. Did God add a probationary command to test Adam's obedience?
    Yes, God commanded Adam not to eat of the tree of the knowledge of good and evil (Gen. 2:17).

CHAPTER 7

Part I. Chapter Review

1. Name five ways in which the specialness of man's creation is emphasized in Genesis 1 and 2:
   a. _____
   b. _____
   c. _____
   d. _____
   e. _____

2. Name and define the three qualities of the image of God in man in its restricted sense:
   a. _____
      _____
   b. _____
      _____
   c. _____
      _____

3. a. Explain the difference between the *resembling* and the *express* images of God: _____
      _____
      _____
      _____
   b. Which did Adam have? _____
   c. Which does Christ possess? _____

4. Name and define the five qualities included in the image of God in man in its wider sense:
   a. _____
      _____
   b. _____
      _____
   c. _____
      _____
   d. _____
      _____
   e. _____

QUESTIONS

5. Answer "wider" for the wider sense, or "narrower" for the narrower sense of the image of God according to which sense is being referred to in the following statements:

   a. _____ Damaged, but not lost entirely in man's fall in Paradise

   b. _____ Restored in type through regeneration and in degree in heaven.

   c. _____ Lost entirely when man fell into sin

6. Explain how both the highest and lowest of substances were used in man's creation: _____

   _____

   _____

   _____

7. While our bodies are valuable and precious gifts from God, our souls are yet more valuable and important. List three reasons why:

   a. _____

   b. _____

   c. _____

8. In the Covenant of Works, what was:

   a. The condition? _____

   b. The promise? _____

   c. The penalty? _____

9. The agreeing parties in the Covenant of Works were _____ representing the Trinity, and _____ representing all _____.

10. In Paradise, which tree served as:

    a. The symbol of God's authority? _____

    b. The pledge of God's promise? _____

11. Fallen man can only be delivered from the penalty of sin in one way, and that is: _____

    _____

    _____

    _____

CHAPTER 7

Part II. Deepening Your Insight

1. What reasons can you list for including, and not including, "dominion over God's earthly creation" as a sixth characteristic of the image of God in its wider sense?

   _____
   _____
   _____
   _____

2. In what ways does a person's conscience differ from an animal's so-called "conscience"?

   _____
   _____
   _____
   _____

3. Why was man created with both a body and a soul? _____
   _____
   _____
   _____

4. What great danger is involved when people believe that Genesis 1 and 2 are allegorical instead of historical? _____
   _____
   _____
   _____

5. Describe two reasons why God chose to place man in a covenant relationship with Himself and why this was a great honor for man:
   a. _____
   _____
   _____

   b. _____
   _____
   _____

6. Explain why God's promise of eternal life as a reward upon Adam's obedience was a *gracious* reward, and not one which God would have been *obliged* to give: _____
   _____
   _____
   _____

QUESTIONS

Part III. Biblical Applications

1. What can be learned from contrasting Genesis 5:1b, "In the likeness of God made He him," with verse 3, "And Adam...begat a son in *his own* likeness, after *his* image"? _____
   _____
   _____

2. Do the following verses refer to the wider or narrower sense of the image of God?
   a. I Corinthians 11:7 _____   d. Ephesians 4:24 _____
   b. Colossians 3:10   _____   e. Genesis 9:6   _____
   c. James 3:10   _____   f. Psalm 82:6   _____

3. Pelagius taught three great errors early in church history. Write out a text from the listed chapters which contradicts his false teachings.
   a. Man was created neither good nor bad. Ecclesiastes 7: _____
      _____
   b. The image of God in man only referred to its wider sense. Colossians 3: _____
      _____
      Ephesians 4: _____
      _____
   c. Death was natural; Adam was created mortal. Romans 6: _____
      _____

Part IV. From the Writings of our Church Forefathers

In your own words, explain the meaning of the following quotations:

1. "True obedience hath no lead at its heels" (Thomas Adams). _____
   _____
   _____
   _____

2. "If the soul be lost, then man is lost" (John Flavel). _____
   _____
   _____
   _____

3. "Man lost not his faculties but the rectitude of them" (Thomas Goodwin). _____
   _____
   _____
   _____

CHAPTER 7

Part V. From the Marginal Questions

1. What valuable lessons and truths about the meaning and importance of being created human are missed by those who deny the truth of Genesis One and Two?

   _____

   _____

   _____

   _____

2. How do both the wider and narrower senses of the image of God in man contradict the evolutionary theory?

   _____

   _____

   _____

   _____

3. When does the restoration of God's image in its narrower sense begin in the life of a child of God? When will both senses of God's image be perfectly restored in him?

   _____

   _____

   _____

   _____

4. When viewing the value of the gifts of a healthy mind and body, how are we all "millionaires"?

   _____

   _____

   _____

   _____

5. When we sin, how are we directly insulting and grieving the One who is giving us the precious gifts of life and health at that very moment?

   _____

   _____

   _____

   _____

EXTRA CHALLENGE QUESTIONS

Part VI. Your Selection from the Marginal Questions

Write out and respond to two marginal questions that interest you which have not been previously asked in this chapter's question section.

1. Question: _____

   _____

   Response: _____

   _____

   _____

   _____

2. Question: _____

   _____

   Response: _____

   _____

   _____

   _____

Part VII. Project Ideas

1. Plan and hold a debate with a friend, on "The Value of Human Life." Have one person do so from a scriptural perspective and the other from an evolutionary point of view.

2. Design a poster which clearly displays and defines the various elements contained in both the wider and narrower senses of the image of God.

3. Sketch a "You Are A Millionaire" poster, using a human body shape with arrows to various parts. Attach to the arrows such questions as, "Would you sell both eyes for $500,000? Would you sell both legs for $300,000?" Apply lessons regarding our need to appreciate and care for our bodies. Also, include reasons why our soul is even more valuable and needs the most care of all.

4. Construct a chart which displays the promise, condition, penalty, and agreeing parties of the Covenant of Works.

8

Fall of Man
Sin
Death

How silent is the graveyard that
So loudly testifies
That man who fell in sin is like
The lowly beast that dies.

Created with the will to choose
To love God and obey,
Man rather chose to sin, but he
Sin's price can never pay.

But God, from all eternity,
Prepared salvation's plan,
Whereby He gave His Son to live
And die for sinful man.

FROM OUR REFORMED DOCTRINAL STANDARDS

Belgic Confession of Faith

Article 14(b) — of the Fall of man, and his Incapacity to perform what is truly good

But being in honor, he understood it not, neither knew his excellency, but willfully subjected himself to sin, and consequently to death, and the curse, giving ear to the words of the devil. For the commandment of life, which he had received, he transgressed; and by sin separated himself from God, who was his true life, having corrupted his whole nature; whereby he made himself liable to corporal and spiritual death. And being thus become wicked, perverse, and corrupt in all his ways, he hath lost all his excellent gifts, which he had received from God, and only retained a few remains thereof, which, however, are sufficient to leave man without excuse; for all the light which is in us is changed into darkness, as the Scriptures teach us, saying: The Light shineth in darkness, and the darkness comprehendeth it not: where St. John calleth men darkness. Therefore we reject all that is taught repugnant to this, concerning the free will of man, since man is but a slave to sin; and has nothing of himself, unless it is given from heaven. For who may presume to boast, that he of himself can do any good, since Christ saith, No man can come to Me, except the Father, which hath sent Me, draw him? Who will glory in his own will, who understands, that to be carnally minded is enmity against God? Who can speak of his knowledge, since the natural man receiveth not the things of the Spirit of God? In short, who dare suggest any thought, since he knows that we are not sufficient of ourselves to think anything as of ourselves, but that our sufficiency is of God? And therefore what the apostle saith ought justly to be held sure and firm, that God worketh in us both to will and to do of His good pleasure. For there is no will nor understanding, conformable to the divine will and understanding, but what Christ hath wrought in man; which He teaches us, when He saith, Without Me ye can do nothing.

Article 15 — Of Original Sin

We believe that, through the disobedience of Adam, original sin is extended to all mankind; which is a corruption of the whole nature, and an hereditary disease, wherewith infants themselves are infected even in their mother's womb, and which produceth in man all sorts of sin, being in him as a root thereof; and therefore is so vile and abominable in the sight of God, that it is sufficient to condemn all mankind. Nor is it by any means abolished or done away by baptism; since sin always issues forth from this woeful source, as water from a fountain; notwithstanding it is not imputed to the children of God unto condemnation, but by His grace and mercy is forgiven them. Not that they should rest securely in sin, but that a sense of this corruption should make believers often to sigh, desiring to be delivered from this body of death. Wherefore we reject the error of the Pelagians, who assert that sin proceeds only from imitation.

Heidelberg Catechism

Questions and Answers 7-11,42

Q. 7. Whence then proceeds this depravity of human nature?

A. From the fall and disobedience of our first parents, Adam and Eve, in Paradise; hence our nature is become so corrupt, that we are all conceived and born in sin.

Q. 8. Are we then so corrupt that we are wholly incapable of doing any good, and inclined to all wickedness?

A. Indeed we are; except we are regenerated by the Spirit of God.

Q. 9. Doth not God then do injustice to man, by requiring from him in His law, that which he cannot perform?

A. Not at all; for God made man capable of performing it; but man, by the instigation of the devil, and his own wilful disobedience, deprived himself and all his posterity of those divine gifts.

Q. 10. Will God suffer such disobedience and rebellion to go unpunished?

A. By no means; but is terribly displeased with our original as well as actual sins; and will punish them in His just judgment temporally and eternally, as He hath declared, "Cursed is every one that continueth not in all things, which are written in the book of the law, to do them."

Q. 11. Is not God then also merciful?

A. God is indeed merciful, but also just; therefore His justice requires that sin which is committed against the most high majesty of God, be also punished with extreme, that is, with everlasting punishment of body and soul.

Q. 42. Since then Christ died for us, why must we also die?

A. Our death is not a satisfaction for our sins, but only an abolishing of sin, and a passage into eternal life.

Canons of Dordt

SECOND HEAD OF DOCTRINE
OF THE DEATH OF CHRIST, AND THE REDEMPTION OF MEN THEREBY

Article 1. God is not only supremely merciful, but also supremely just. And His justice requires (as He hath revealed Himself in His Word), that our sins committed against His infinite majesty should be punished, not only with temporal, but with eternal punishment, both in body and soul; which we cannot escape, unless satisfaction be made to the justice of God.

THIRD AND FOURTH HEADS OF DOCTRINE
OF THE CORRUPTION OF MAN, HIS CONVERSION TO GOD, AND THE MANNER THEREOF

Article 1

Man was originally formed after the image of God, His understanding was adorned with a true and saving knowledge of his Creator, and of spiritual things; his heart and will were upright; all his affections pure; and the whole man was holy; but revolting from God by the instigation of the devil, and abusing the freedom of his own will, he forfeited these excellent gifts; and on the contrary entailed on himself blindness of mind, horrible darkness, vanity and perverseness of judgment, became wicked, rebellious, and obdurate in heart and will, and impure in his affections.

Article 2

Man after the fall begat children in his own likeness. A corrupt stock produced a corrupt offspring. Hence all the posterity of Adam, Christ only excepted, have derived corruption from their original parent, not by imitation, as the Pelagians of old asserted, but by the propagation of a vicious nature.

Article 3

Therefore all men are conceived in sin, and by nature children of wrath, incapable of saving good, prone to evil, dead in sin, and in bondage thereto, and without the regenerating grace of the Holy Spirit, they are neither able nor willing to return to God, to reform the depravity of their nature, nor to dispose themselves to reformation.

Article 4

There remain, however, in man since the fall, the glimmerings of natural light, whereby he retains some knowledge of God, of natural things, and of the differences between good and evil, and discovers some regard for virtue, good order in society, and for maintaining an orderly external deportment. But so far is this light of nature from being sufficient to bring him to a saving knowledge of God, and to true conversion, that he is incapable of using it aright even in things natural and civil. Nay further, this light, such as it is, man in various ways renders wholly polluted, and holds it in unrighteousness, by doing which he becomes inexcusable before God.

Article 5

In the same light are we to consider the law of the decalogue, delivered by God to His peculiar people the Jews, by the hands of Moses. For though it discovers the greatness of sin, and more and more convinces man thereof, yet as it neither points out a remedy, nor imparts strength to extricate him from misery, and thus being weak through the flesh, leaves the transgressor under the curse, man cannot by this law obtain saving grace.

8

FALL OF MAN

Adam did not remain in the sinless state in which God had created him, nor did he uphold the Covenant of Works which God had made with him. Sadly, Adam chose to disobey, to sin against God. He did this by freely choosing to eat from the forbidden tree, the Tree of the Knowledge of Good and Evil.

Satan, using a serpent as a means, approached Eve in the following manner:

1. *Satan placed God's command in a negative light.* He asked Eve, "Yea, hath God said, Ye shall not eat of *every* tree of the garden?" (Genesis 3:1b). God had actually stated that Adam and Eve could eat from *all* the trees, from the thousands of trees in the Garden of Eden, *except one*. Eve corrected Satan and told him, "We may eat of the fruit of the trees of the garden: But of the fruit of the tree which is in the midst of the garden, God hath said, Ye shall not eat of it, neither shall ye touch it, lest ye die" (Genesis 3:2-3).

Now the serpent was more subtle than any beast of the field which the Lord God had made. And he said unto the woman, Yea, hath God said, Ye shall not eat of every tree of the garden?

And the woman said unto the serpent, We may eat of the fruit of the trees of the garden:

But of the fruit of the tree which is in the midst of the garden, God hath said, Ye shall not eat of it, neither shall ye touch it, lest ye die.

And the serpent said unto the woman, Ye shall not surely die:

For God doth know that in the day ye eat thereof, then your eyes shall be opened, and ye shall be as gods, knowing good and evil.

— Genesis 3:1-5

- **Slanderously** — In a lying manner, attempting to injure the reputation of another

- **Motive** — Deepest purpose, will, cause, and desire

- **Enticed** — Attracted; allured; excited desire for

? These four methods of temptation used by Satan can also be named: deception, perversion, pride, and lust. How would you link these four terms with the four described temptation methods?

- **Techniques** — Methods of performance; ways used to accomplish a goal

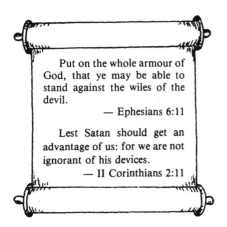

Put on the whole armour of God, that ye may be able to stand against the wiles of the devil.
— Ephesians 6:11

Lest Satan should get an advantage of us: for we are not ignorant of his devices.
— II Corinthians 2:11

2. *Satan **slanderously** questioned God's nature and **motive***. He lied and told Eve, "Ye shall not surely die: for God doth know that in the day ye eat thereof, then your eyes shall be opened, and ye shall be as gods" (Genesis 3:4-5).

3. *Satan **enticed** man with the proud thought of being his own god*. "And ye shall be as gods, knowing good and evil" (Genesis 3:5b). In other words, "You can decide for yourself what is right and wrong; you can determine that which you want to do — you do not need to listen to others, not even God. Be your own god. Decide for yourself." This is rebellion against the one, true God.

4. *Satan made sin appear pleasurable and attractive*. "And when the woman saw that the tree was good for food, and that it was pleasant to the eye, and a tree to be desired to make one wise, she took of the fruit thereof, and did eat, and gave also unto her husband with her; and he did eat" (Genesis 3:6).

How does the following story illustrate the truth that Satan still uses the same **techniques** today when approaching, tempting, and stirring up people to sin and rebel?

"Mark, you go ask the boss," Mark's co-workers urge him.

Upon entering the office of his employer, Mark asks him, "Sir, would it be possible for us to have the Monday and Tuesday off before Christmas Day? This would give us a nice break from Saturday through Wednesday."

After pausing in deep reflection and studying his calendar, his employer replies, "Mark, I would love to say yes, but this year I can't. You know that we promised the ABC Company to ship their large order by the end of the year. Looking at the calendar, I'm afraid that we're going to have to use every hour to make it by January 1. I'd love to look at your request again next year, though!"

"What did he say?" the other employees ask eagerly, crowding around Mark upon his return.

"He said, 'Nope! We have to work good and hard right through January 1'," Mark angrily reported.

"I knew it," said another. "He wants to rake in more profits from us yet before the year ends. That's why he won't even consider giving us a day off!"

"Maybe we should just take an extra day or two off anyway," suggested a third. "I'm tired of his treating us

like little kids. I think we have a right to make some decisions around here! If we all phone in sick — what can he do about it? He won't fire us, I promise you!"

"I can picture it already," added another dreamily. "Peacefully sleeping in, a nice day with the family, going out for a leisurely dinner in the evening — it sounds good to me!"

Can you identify the same four steps of temptation being used by Satan to entice Mark and his co-workers to sinfully rebel?

When Satan tempts people in this manner and they sin, they must blame themselves as well as Satan. Their own hearts agree with the temptation. The following story illustrates this truth.

"I can't help it; others told me to," Sam stated, trying to defend himself.

"I'm sorry, but that doesn't matter," his teacher replied. "You agreed to do it. Do you think a judge would excuse you from guilt after robbing a gas station if you told him that others told you to do it?"

Satan wanted Adam to sin for he was man's covenant head — the one whom God had appointed as the representative of all mankind. Why then did Satan approach Eve instead of Adam? Satan knew that Adam would be less suspicious and more easily persuaded if his temptation was presented by a trusted friend. Does Satan still use this same technique today?

? This type of slanderous twisting of another's words or evil judging of his motives is devilish. Why?

? What types of division and damage has this type of evil reporting and exaggeration caused between persons, families, churches, and countries?

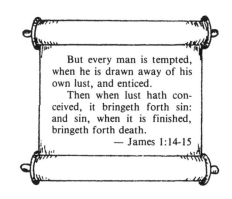

But every man is tempted, when he is drawn away of his own lust, and enticed.
Then when lust hath conceived, it bringeth forth sin: and sin, when it is finished, bringeth forth death.
— James 1:14-15

? How does Satan's use of the influence of others emphasize the truth that whom we have as friends is very important?

And the great dragon was cast out, that old serpent, called the Devil, and Satan, which deceiveth the whole world: he was cast out into the earth, and his angels were cast out with him.

Therefore rejoice, ye heavens, and ye that dwell in them. Woe to the inhabiters of the earth and of the sea! for the devil is come down unto you, having great wrath, because he knoweth that he hath but a short time.

— Revelation 12:9,12

But our God is in the heavens: He hath done whatsoever He hath pleased.

— Psalm 115:3

The LORD hath made all things for Himself: yea, even the wicked for the day of evil.

— Proverbs 16:4

What if God, willing to show His wrath, and to make His power known, endured with much longsuffering the vessels of wrath fitted to destruction.

— Romans 9:22

What shall we say then? Is there unrighteousness with God? God forbid.

— Romans 9:14

- ● **Irrational** — Not able to reason or think abstractly

- ● **Instincts** — Any inborn, automatic impulse necessary for a creature's health and survival

After being defeated and punished by God for his rebellious actions, Satan is full of hatred and enmity against God. As man was the crown of God's creation, Satan saw a possibility of attacking God, damaging God's work of creation, and increasing the number of his followers by tempting Adam and Eve to sin.

Adam's tragic sin — which brought with it the terrible consequences of fear, pain, sorrow, separation, and death — is called *the fall*. The term speaks of mankind's deep fall into sin.

Neither the devils' nor mankind's fall surprised God, however. God permitted sin and the fall of both Satan and Adam to take place. These events were included in His eternal decree. Why God decreed to permit sin to enter into His creation is a mystery which no person can fully answer. God had His own reasons for doing so, for God makes no mistakes. We must submit to this truth even when we cannot fully understand it, knowing that God does no wrong. We may not pry beyond that which God has revealed to us in Scripture. Neither may we, as creatures, rebelliously set ourselves up as judge, as if we will try God, our Creator!

While God has not fully shown us all the reasons why He created Adam with the possibility to fall, He has revealed the following reasons in Scripture. While we are forbidden to pry beyond Scripture, we are commanded to search and study the reasons that are taught in Scripture. Scripture reveals that God created man perfectly upright, loving to obey his Creator, but with the possibility to choose sin and disobedience because:

1. *Man's free and voluntary love and obedience to God was more honoring to both God and man.* Mountains, trees, fish, birds, planets, and stars glorify God — all creation sings His praise. But each of the objects, plants, and animals God created honored Him without personal choice. God placed all lifeless objects and **irrational** creatures under various laws and **instincts** which control their actions — they are bound to serve God because He has placed them under certain laws of operation that they cannot break.

Man, however, as a rational being, was created at a higher level. He served God, not because he was *bound* to, but because he *chose* to. Man's higher position of freely choosing obedience to God was

284

not only more honoring for man, but it also exalted God. God's highest creature, the crown of His earthly creation, loved and served his Creator; not from **compulsion**, but by free choice. How man's free choice was more honoring to both God and man is illustrated by the following story.

Tom and Mark met at the school playground as both were walking their dogs.

"Come!" Tom commanded as he gave a sharp tug on the chain leash firmly attached to the neck of his dog. On account of the frequent tugs and pulls on the leash, the dog reluctantly followed his master.

"Come, Rex," Mark called, and instantly his unleashed dog jumped up and walked in step at his side. Rex could be observed perfectly stopping, sitting, and running according to his master's commands.

Which combination was more honoring to both dog and owner? Why?

2. *Man's freely choosing to love and obey God would lead to a higher state.* Through obedience, man would receive the reward of eternal life. By giving man both the freedom of choice and the ability to serve Him, God gave him the possibility of earning a wonderfully joyful, holy, and **immortal** existence for both soul and body.

● **Compulsion** — The act of being strongly pressured or forced to act in a certain manner

? How did man's higher state of blessing bring with it greater responsibility? What truth and lesson does this emphasize?

? How can we observe that God always dealt at a higher level with man than with animals? Those teaching that man is an evolving animal will always promote lower views of human life. Why?

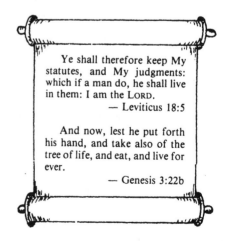

Ye shall therefore keep My statutes, and My judgments: which if a man do, he shall live in them: I am the LORD.
— Leviticus 18:5

And now, lest he put forth his hand, and take also of the tree of life, and eat, and live for ever.
— Genesis 3:22b

● **Immortal** — Never-dying

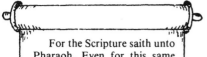

For the Scripture saith unto Pharaoh, Even for this same purpose have I raised thee up, that I might show My power in thee, and that My name might be declared throughout all the earth.

Therefore hath He mercy on whom He will have mercy, and whom He will He hardeneth.

Thou wilt say then unto me, Why doth He yet find fault? For who hath resisted His will?

Nay but, O man, who art thou that repliest against God? Shall the thing formed say to him that formed it, Why hast thou made me thus?

— Romans 9:17-20

● **Remedy** — That which corrects, removes, or heals an evil; a corrective

? The heavenly song of praise that saved sinners will sing eternally is named "The Song of Moses and of the Lamb" (Rev. 15:3). Why is this song of deliverance called the song of:

— Moses?

— the Lamb?

Who only will be able to sing this song? Why?

● **Mutual** — Pertaining alike to both sides; shared alike; common to two or more

But, did God not know ahead of time that Adam would choose disobedience rather than obedience — death instead of life? Was the fall not in God's decree? Yes, God did know. This event, as all events, was in His decree. If God knew ahead of time that Adam would make the wrong choice, why then did He create man and give him the ability of choosing?

Again, we must be very cautious with these types of questions. Man's sinful, rebellious heart strongly desires to blame anyone else for its own sins — even God! There is, however, no unrighteousness in God. He is the perfection of righteousness and holiness. Even when we cannot fully understand why God has acted as He has, we may rest assured that His dealings are perfect and upright. Again, while not prying beyond Scripture into God's secret will, God's Word does reveal the following reasons for His creating and testing of man, and the permitting of his fall:

1. *In His decree, God saw not only the fall but also the* **remedy** *for the fall — Jesus Christ.* He saw not only the deadly disease of sin, but also the medicine and physician to cure this deadly disease. In Jesus Christ and the Covenant of Grace, God would give more to man than he lost in Adam and the Covenant of Works. This is presented in greater detail in the following chapter which deals with the Covenant of Grace.

2. *Through man's fall, God's glorious Being would be more richly revealed and glorified.* God's profound love and perfect righteousness — all of God's attributes are proclaimed through the salvation and punishment of sinners. God's justice is clearly revealed through His hatred of sin and punishment of unrepentant sinners. God's grace is richly shown through the suffering and death of Jesus Christ to save undeserving, hell-worthy sinners.

Before their fall in Paradise, Adam and Eve knew God's love, a **mutual** love. God loved His creature, man, who loved Him in return. But after the fall, saved sinners experience God's grace — a rich, one-sided, forgiving love to sinners who do not deserve it. Since their fall, saved sinners will experience and rejoice in a deeper knowledge of God's love than the angels which never fell.

As studied in Chapter Six regarding God's providence, God has decreed to permit sin, to use it for His own good purpose and end. In so doing, however, sin remains a crime and the sinner a criminal. Scripture forbids us to ever view sin as a good thing.

God decreed from eternity and prophesied hundreds of years before that Judas Iscariot would betray the Lord Jesus Christ. God would use this sinful action for His own good and wonderful purpose — the salvation of an innumerable multitude of elect sinners. But Judas' sin remains a crime and he a traitor, for God did not persuade nor force Judas to commit this sin. From his own sinful motives of hatred and revenge, Judas freely chose to betray Christ. When committing this sin, Judas' motives were different from God's reasons for permitting it. Therefore Judas is fully judged for his crime, while God's prophecy is fulfilled and His eternal purpose stands, as Jesus states, "The Son of man goeth as it is written of Him: but woe unto that man by whom the Son of man is betrayed! it had been good for that man if he had not been born" (Matthew 26:24).

This same truth applies to our view of the fall. While God used the fall of man to fulfill His own purpose, we may never speak of the fall as a "good thing" or Adam's sin as a "wonderful happening." Adam's sin was and remains a rebellious crime. He willfully chose to plunge himself and all his posterity into sin with its terrible **consequences**. The truth of a person's remaining fully guilty for his own actions, despite God's using it for good purposes which he never intended, is clearly illustrated in the following remarkable story.

> After traveling for two hours on an interstate freeway, a family with two small children stopped for a ten-minute break at a rest area. In their haste, they left their keys in the car, and it was stolen.
>
> As upset as they were at the moment, so thankful they were later; for a few miles from the rest area, at exactly the time they would have been there, a terrible accident involving seventeen vehicles took place.
>
> The car thief was **apprehended** and his lawyer, at his trial, told the jury the previous remarkable story, of how this theft preserved the lives of a family. The judge **intervened**, however, and asked the thief, "Did you know that this accident would be taking place? Did you steal this

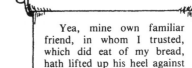

Yea, mine own familiar friend, in whom I trusted, which did eat of my bread, hath lifted up his heel against me.
— Psalm 41:9

Then one of the twelve, called Judas Iscariot, went unto the chief priests,
And said unto them, What will ye give me, and I will deliver Him unto you? And they covenanted with him for thirty pieces of silver.
And from that time he sought opportunity to betray Him.
— Matthew 26:14-16

The Son of man goeth as it is written of Him: but woe unto that man by whom the Son of man is betrayed! it had been good for that man if he had not been born.
— Matthew 26:24

? Why is it very important to keep both of the following truths in balance? All things are included in God's decree and providence and yet, God does not persuade or force sinners to sin; a sinner freely chooses to commit each of his sins.

How are both of these truths taught in Joseph's words to his brothers in Genesis 50:20: "But as for you, ye thought evil against me; but God meant it unto good, to bring to pass, as it is this day to save much people alive"?

● **Consequences** — Results; effects; outcomes

● **Apprehended** — Caught; seized; arrested

● **Intervened** — Came between; interfered; stepped into a matter to clarify factors that are involved

? When speaking of God's decree and providence, why is it important to clearly distinguish these truths from God's judgment? Will God judge a person by his motives and intended actions or by His use of their actions for other outcomes? Why?

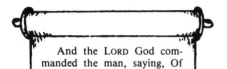

And the LORD God commanded the man, saying, Of every tree of the garden thou mayest freely eat:

But of the tree of the knowledge of good and evil, thou shalt not eat of it: for in the day that thou eatest thereof thou shalt surely die.
— Genesis 2:16-17

For God doth know that in the day ye eat thereof, then your eyes shall be opened, and ye shall be as gods, knowing good and evil.
— Genesis 3:5

God hath said, Ye shall not eat of it, neither shall ye touch it, lest ye die.

And the serpent said unto the woman, Ye shall not surely die.
— Genesis 3:3b-4

Wherefore, as by one man sin entered into the world, and death by sin; and so death passed upon all men, for that all have sinned.

Therefore as by the offence of one judgment came upon all men to condemnation; even so by the righteousness of One the free gift came upon all men unto justfication of life.
— Romans 5:12,18

● **Posterity** — All future and succeeding descendants and generations

family's automobile for the purpose of sparing them from a serious accident?''

The thief had to meekly answer "no" to both questions.

"Then this fact can be dismissed," the judge instructed the jury. "It has nothing to do with the guilt or innocence of the person being tried."

The judge was clearly separating the person's present motive and action from their unintended and unknown outcomes. Why is this distinction important when viewing all sinful actions, also Adam's sin in Paradise?

Adam's sin was a very terrible and grievous sin for the following four reasons:

1. *Adam's sin was premeditated.* He sinned with full knowledge of that which he was doing; his sin was not a sin of ignorance.

2. *Adam's sin declared rebellion against God.* In choosing to disobey God, Adam chose to rebel against God and to establish himself as god. He desired to determine right or wrong, good or evil for himself. In doing so, Adam despised God's rich love and communion. His sinful rebellion stepped upon the very "heart" of God his Creator.

3. *Adam's sin proclaimed his belief that God was a liar.* Either God or Satan must be lying. God had declared that man would die by eating from the Tree of the Knowledge of Good and Evil. Satan had said that man would not die. In choosing to believe Satan, Adam proclaimed his belief that God was a liar.

4. *Adam's sin separated himself and all his **posterity** from God.* As representative of all mankind in the Covenant of Works, Adam's sin brought separation from God and death upon the entire human race.

The chart on the following page explains how Adam broke all ten commandments of God's moral law with his one, terrible act of sinful disobedience in Paradise.

ADAM'S SIN TRANSGRESSED GOD'S TEN COMMANDMENTS

God's Commandment	Adam's Transgression
1. We may not worship idols or other gods.	Adam chose new gods — self and Satan. Anything placed above, or equal to God, is an idol.
2. We may not worship God in ways He has not ordained.	Adam set up his own way of worship when he rejected God's clear ordinance.
3. We may not misuse God's name.	Adam misused God's name by proclaiming Him to be a liar and despising His attributes and Word.
4. We may not misuse the Sabbath for unholy or self-centered purposes.	Adam broke the Sabbath state of rest and communion in which God had placed him.
5. We may not disobey or dishonor those placed in authority over us.	Adam refused to honor and obey his Father in heaven and chose to rebelliously do his own will.
6. We may not hate, harm, or kill others.	Adam murdered himself and all mankind by bringing death upon the entire human race.
7. We may not have nor use adulterous or unclean thoughts, words, or actions.	Adam committed spiritual adultery by joining himself with Satan and his lies and forsaking God and His truth.
8. We may not cheat nor steal from others.	Adam stole by taking fruit from the Tree of the Knowledge of Good and Evil, for this fruit was not his and its taking was forbidden by its Owner.
9. We may not lie, bear false witness, nor slander others.	Adam bore false witness against God and His Word by testifying that God's truth was a lie and Satan's lie the truth.
10. We may not covet or envy others or their possessions.	Adam coveted God's position; he was sinfully discontented with the state in which God had placed him and desired to be in God's position.

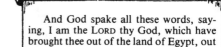

And God spake all these words, saying, I am the LORD thy God, which have brought thee out of the land of Egypt, out of the house of bondage.

I

Thou shalt have no other gods before Me.

II

Thou shalt not make unto thee any graven image, or any likeness of any thing that is in heaven above, or that is in the earth beneath, or that is in the water under the earth:

Thou shalt not bow down thyself to them, nor serve them: For I the LORD thy God am a jealous God, visiting the iniquity of the fathers upon the children unto the third and fourth generation of them that hate Me;

And showing mercy unto thousands of them that love Me and keep My commandments.

III

Thou shalt not take the name of the LORD thy God in vain; for the LORD will not hold him guiltless that taketh His name in vain.

IV

Remember the sabbath day, to keep it holy.

Six days shalt thou labour and do all thy work:

But the seventh day is the sabbath of the LORD thy God: in it thou shalt not do any work, thou, nor thy son, nor thy daughter, thy manservant, nor thy maidservant, nor thy cattle, nor thy stranger that is within thy gates:

For in six days the LORD made heaven and earth, the sea, and all that in them is, and rested the seventh day: wherefore the LORD blessed the sabbath day, and hallowed it.

V

Honour thy father and thy mother: that thy days may be long in the land which the LORD thy God giveth thee.

VI

Thou shalt not kill.

VII

Thou shalt not commit adultery.

VIII

Thou shalt not steal.

IX

Thou shalt not bear false witness against thy neighbour.

X

Thou shalt not covet thy neighbour's house, thou shalt not covet thy neighbour's wife, nor his manservant, nor his maidservant, nor his ox, nor his ass, nor any thing that is thy neighbour's.

— Exodus 20:1-17

Adam's tragic sin has plunged the entire human race into a fallen state of misery. Mankind's state of misery includes its:

1. *Origin* — our deep fall in Paradise
2. *Cause* — our sin
3. *Reality* — our total depravity (our incapability of curing or delivering ourselves from our sinful state)
4. *Consequence* — the loss of God's presence, favor, and fellowship resulting in the punishment of death (the separations caused by sin in corporal, spiritual, and eternal death)

We all need to experience the truths of the origin, cause, reality, and consequence of our misery. Are these truths real in your life? Have you experienced the truth of them?

Those convinced and convicted of their sinful misery are in a condition similar to that of one who is both convinced that he has an incurable disease and convicted of a crime requiring a death penalty. His misery is unspeakable.

Except for Satan and his fallen angels, there is no one in a more grievous and miserable condition than fallen man. In our fall, we broke our covenant relationship with God and formed an agreement with sin, self, world, and Satan. We left God, intending never to return to Him again.

If it were not for Jesus Christ's payment for sin, life-giving grace, and almighty converting power, there would be no hope for fallen man. His case would be hopeless. But, thanks be to God for His wonderful grace and salvation in Jesus Christ! In Him, there is help for the helpless, hope for the hopeless, and spiritual life for the spiritually dead.

Have you experienced the great weight and burden of your misery due to sin? Has all hope and expectation to save or help yourself been cut off? Has deliverance through Jesus Christ become your only hope and expectation?

Jesus Christ is God's answer to man's fall, the only Savior of lost sinners, the one name by which we can be saved.

For if by one man's offence death reigned by one; much more they which receive abundance of grace and of the gift of righteousness shall reign in life by One, Jesus Christ.

Therefore as by the offence of one judgment came upon all men to condemnation; even so by the righteousness of One the free gift came upon all men unto justification of life.

For as by one man's disobedience many were made sinners, so by the obedience of One shall many be made righteous.

— Romans 5:17-19

For since by man came death, by Man came also the resurrection of the dead.

For as in Adam all die, even so in Christ shall all be made alive.

— I Corinthians 15:21-22

The first man is of the earth, earthy: the second Man is the Lord from heaven.

As is the earthy, such are they also that are earthy: and as is the heavenly, such are they also that are heavenly.

And as we have borne the image of the earthy, we shall also bear the image of the heavenly.

— I Corinthians 15:47-49

But now hath He obtained a more excellent ministry, by how much also He is the Mediator of a better covenant, which was established upon better promises.

— Hebrews 8:6

And she shall bring forth a son, and thou shalt call His name JESUS: for He shall save His people from their sins.

— Matthew 1:21

Neither is there salvation in any other: for there is none other name under heaven given among men, whereby we must be saved.

— Acts 4:12

SIN

Sin is the **transgression** of, or lack of **conformity** to, God's law. Sin refers to anything that breaks, or is wrong in, our relationship with God.

Scripture teaches the following six characteristics of sin:

1. *Sin is moral evil.* Sicknesses, pains, plagues, famines, destructive storms, etc., are evils, but they are not sin. These **calamities** are the results of sin but they are not acts of sin. The modern tendency is to speak of evil in a more general sense, **implying** that evil is something which man cannot help and therefore, something for which he cannot be held fully responsible. But Scripture speaks of sin as a specific type of evil — a *moral* evil, for which man is directly responsible and condemnable as a moral being.

2. *Sin is absolutely wrong.* Scripture teaches us that all motives, thoughts, words, and actions of moral beings are right or wrong. They are good or evil; there is no morally neutral position between the two. We must love and serve God from our hearts in all we do, or we are sinning. Modern ideas of neutral intentions and actions are not biblical. Man is either right or wrong in all his dealings.

3. *Sin is a lack of conformity to God's law.* Modern definitions of sin as only human weakness, physical influence, selfishness, unkindness to others, **sensuality**, etc., are not complete. Sin may include some or all of these elements, but most importantly, sin is a transgression of God's law. Sin is not only social; it is not only an action which harms others. Sin can also be inward thoughts or personal ideas and motives known only to God and the individual. All lack of conformity to God's law is sin.

4. *Sin includes both guilt and pollution.* Sin is a transgression of God's law which results in guilt, a deserving of punishment from a righteous God. Modern ideas of denying that sin includes guilt are not scriptural. Sin also pollutes the person, spotting his personhood and character with the stains of its uncleanness and impurity.

- **Transgression** — The breaking or violation of a law

- **Conformity** — Agreement; harmony; accordance

- **Moral** — Concerned with the principles of right and wrong according to God's law

- **Calamities** — Disasters; afflictions; adversities

- **Implying** — Hinting at; pointing to; signifying

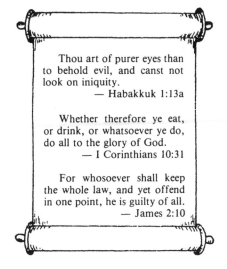

Thou art of purer eyes than to behold evil, and canst not look on iniquity.
— Habakkuk 1:13a

Whether therefore ye eat, or drink, or whatsoever ye do, do all to the glory of God.
— I Corinthians 10:31

For whosoever shall keep the whole law, and yet offend in one point, he is guilty of all.
— James 2:10

- **Sensuality** — Excessive indulgence in physical lusts, attractions, appetites, gratifications, etc.

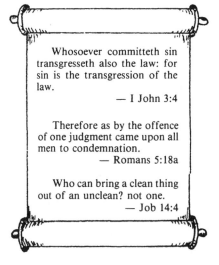

Whosoever committeth sin transgresseth also the law: for sin is the transgression of the law.
— I John 3:4

Therefore as by the offence of one judgment came upon all men to condemnation.
— Romans 5:18a

Who can bring a clean thing out of an unclean? not one.
— Job 14:4

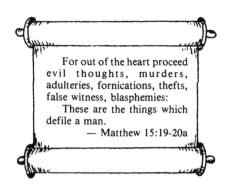

For out of the heart proceed evil thoughts, murders, adulteries, fornications, thefts, false witness, blasphemies:
These are the things which defile a man.
— Matthew 15:19-20a

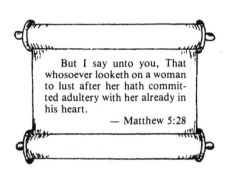

But I say unto you, That whosoever looketh on a woman to lust after her hath committed adultery with her already in his heart.
— Matthew 5:28

5. *Sin arises from the heart*. Sin involves the total person. It arises from the heart, the core of a person's being. Modern teachings that sin is just reflecting the thoughts or imitating the actions of others are not scriptural. God speaks of sin as arising from the deepest element of one's existence, from his heart, out of which are the issues of life.

6. *Sin includes motives and thoughts*. Modern explanations that only expressed words or performed actions can be sinful are not biblical. God judges the heart. Hidden from others, all our secret intentions and thoughts are perfectly known to the Lord — these, too, can be sinful.

? What wrong "advice" and "comfort" is being given to Jack in this story? Why?

After Jack had angrily yelled at his employer in the presence of his fellow employees, and was suspended from work for three days, one of his friends and co-workers attempted to comfort him. "Jack, don't worry about it. You could not help it. After the way he mistreated you, how could you help it? Maybe you were a little too strong, but you weren't really wrong. A bit of unkindness has to be expected. No one can say that you're really guilty of doing something wrong. It was just a quick, mental reaction to that which he said. Besides, nobody can hold you responsible for the things you didn't say, but may have been thinking! If that were true, I would not only be suspended, I'd be fired! Cheer up and forget it. When you return it'll all be forgiven and forgotten.''

How does the reasoning of Jack's friend contradict six of the previous scriptural characteristics of sin? What seriously wrong ''advice'' and ''comfort'' is implied in this friend's conversation with Jack?

Scripture speaks of two types of sin which affect our relationship with God — one is *original* and the other is *actual sin.*

Original sin refers to Adam's first sin, his eating from the forbidden tree in Paradise, the *original* sin of mankind.

Due to our two-fold relationship with Adam, since the fall, every person is born in sin — in both a sinfully guilty state and polluted condition. Original sin includes both original:

1. Guilt
2. Pollution

Original *guilt* refers to the guilt from Adam's original sin. This *guilt* is **imputed** to every person because Adam was their covenant father in the Covenant of Works. He was appointed by God as the covenant head or representative of the entire human race. Through obedience, Adam would have earned eternal life for all mankind, but through disobedience he brought guilt and the sentence of death upon all people.

Mr. Martin protested the high costs of federal taxes he was required to pay. ''Why do I have to pay this amount?'' he asked angrily.

''Your present government and several previous ones have spent this much money,'' answered his accountant.

''But I didn't do that! How can they charge me?'' he demanded.

''The present and previous governments are the official representatives of our country,'' was the reply. ''As a citizen, we share in the benefits and consequences of our citizenship.''

As citizens of the human race, who was our representative in the Covenant of Works? Why is the debt of his sin imputed to each of us?

● **Original** — First; the beginning of

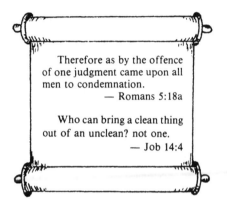

Therefore as by the offence of one judgment came upon all men to condemnation.
— Romans 5:18a

Who can bring a clean thing out of an unclean? not one.
— Job 14:4

● **Imputed** — Placed on one's account; charged; credited

Wherefore, as by one man sin entered into the world, and death by sin; and so death passed upon all men, for that all have sinned.

But not as the offence, so also is the free gift. For if through the offence of one many be dead, much more the grace of God, and the gift by grace, which is by one Man, Jesus Christ, hath abounded unto many.

For if by one man's offence death reigned by one; much more they which receive abundance of grace and of the gift of righteousness shall reign in life by One, Jesus Christ.

Therefore as by the offence of one judgment came upon all men to condemnation; even so by the righteousness of One the free gift came upon all men unto justification of life.
— Romans 5:12,15,17-18

For as in Adam all die, even so in Christ shall all be made alive.
— I Corinthians 15:22

? What two covenants are being compared in this example? How is the same principle of covenant head representation displayed in both covenants?

"I still don't think it's fair," Sandy answered. "I can't help it that Adam sinned."

Sandy's teacher thought for a moment and then wrote the following on the chalkboard:

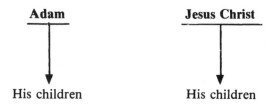

Adam	Jesus Christ
↓	↓
His children	His children

Sandy's teacher then asked, "Sandy, why are all God's children saved?"

"Because Jesus paid the price for their sins," she answered.

"Didn't each one of God's children earn his own righteousness?"

"Of course not," Sandy answered, wondering why her teacher would suggest that. "Jesus earned their righteousness and it's given to each of them."

"How can it be given to each of them?"

"Jesus is their Head; their representative. What He earned is applied to His children."

"Is that fair?"

Sandy paused. "I understand," she replied. "It's just the same, isn't it?"

What did Sandy mean with her last comment, "It's just the same"? What did she understand?

Original *pollution* refers to the pollution of sin which all people **inherit** from Adam as their *natural father*. As descendants of Adam, sinful parents bring forth sinful children.

Original pollution is also called "total depravity." This means that man is born totally without spiritual good, and full of evil. Fallen man is born with a polluted heart which loves self, sin, world, and Satan. He is totally without, and is totally incapable and unwilling of producing, spiritual good. Due to God's common grace, however, fallen man is not a devil. God restrains man's sinful, devilish heart and gives him a common sense of authority, decency, concern for others, and outward good. Without God's common grace, life on earth would not be possible. In hell, God's common grace will be removed, and sinners' devilish hearts will be unrestrained, and fully given over to themselves.

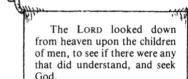

● **Inherit** — To receive from an ancestor; to have through heredity

The LORD looked down from heaven upon the children of men, to see if there were any that did understand, and seek God.
They are all gone aside, they are all together become filthy: there is none that doeth good, no, not one.
— Psalm 14:2-3

But we are all as an unclean thing, and all our righteousnesses are as filthy rags; and we all do fade as a leaf; and our iniquities, like the wind, have taken us away.
— Isaiah 64:6

The LORD is gracious, and full of compassion; slow to anger, and of great mercy.
The LORD is good to all: and His tender mercies are over all His works.
— Psalm 145:8-9

"I'm tired of gardening," Tim complained.

"What's wrong?" his mother asked.

"I keep trying to get my watermelon plants to grow. I do everything I can, but it's so hard to make them grow. The weeds grow by themselves. Even when I keep pulling them out, they grow back."

"Do you know of what this is a picture?" asked his mother. "Last Sunday our minister preached on the subject of which I'm thinking."

"Oh, I know," Tim responded, "our sinful hearts. The good things are so hard to grow, but the sinful things spring up without any help all the time."

How can our sin-filled hearts be compared to weed-filled gardens?

"How cute!"

"He's the picture of his father."

"There's no problem seeing whose baby he is!"

"If he's not a perfect image of his father!"

This natural scene is a picture of that which takes place spiritually when a child is born.

Read Genesis 5:1-5:

1. This is the book of the generations of Adam. In the day that God created man, in the likeness of God made He him;

2. Male and female created He them; and blessed them, and called their name Adam, in the day when they were created.

3. And Adam lived an hundred and thirty years, and begat a son in his own likeness, after his image; and called his name Seth:

4. And the days of Adam after he had begotten Seth were eight hundred years: and he begat sons and daughters:

5. And all the days that Adam lived were nine hundred and thirty years: and he died.

What great contrast can be observed between verse 1 and 3? What sad result from this change is noted in verse 5?

Since man's fall, all infants that are born resemble their fallen father. All are born with the guilt and pollution of original sin.

The Lord Jesus Christ was the only exception. Why? Who was His Father? Of whom was He the express image, the "perfect picture"?

? Why is a clear understanding of the Covenant of Works required for a proper comprehension of the Covenant of Grace? Why is the experience of my sin and misery necessary in order to appreciate Christ and His salvation?

? Why is Jesus Christ the only person ever born into the human race without original sin?

296

To review, our two-fold relationship with Adam and original sin can be pictured as follows:

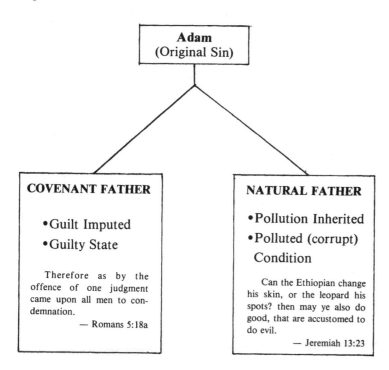

Adam
(Original Sin)

COVENANT FATHER

- Guilt Imputed
- Guilty State

Therefore as by the offence of one judgment came upon all men to condemnation.
— Romans 5:18a

NATURAL FATHER

- Pollution Inherited
- Polluted (corrupt) Condition

Can the Ethiopian change his skin, or the leopard his spots? then may ye also do good, that are accustomed to do evil.
— Jeremiah 13:23

? Are all of Adam's sins imputed to each of us, or only one sin? Why?

The guilty state and polluted condition in which man is born does not take away his responsibility, however. God created man good and upright, and God will not lower His expectations to suit sinful man. He expects perfect love to God and others. The **standards** for mankind are set by God, the Creator; not by man, the creature. God is unchangeable and therefore His standards are unchangeable.

● **Standards** — Set levels of expectation and requirement for behavior

Phil, a new employee at a clothing store, is asked by his employer to locate several boxes of new winter coats in the supply room, and to unpack and display them on coatracks in the store.

However, Phil chose to visit a tavern for several hours before coming to work this particular afternoon, and arrived in a drunken condition. Therefore, when he tried to find the boxes of coats in the storage room, he could not. Even if he would have, his coordination would not have been steady enough to unpack and display the coats.

His employer sends Phil home with a stiff warning and refuses to pay him for the afternoon.

Phil becomes very upset with his employer, and grumbles, "I am being treated unfairly. My employer

? How does a willful inability differ from unwillful inability? Is fallen man's inability to love and serve God a willful or unwillful inability? Why?

● **Abolished** — Ended; destroyed; put out of existence

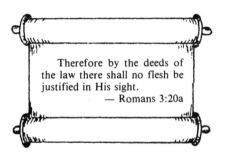

Therefore by the deeds of the law there shall no flesh be justified in His sight.
— Romans 3:20a

required me to do things which he knew I could never perform. I was not able to find or unpack those coats. I'm being punished for not doing something I could not do!''

When the employer heard this, he approached Phil and asked him, ''My friend, is it my fault that you came to work drunk? If you had not made yourself incapable of performing that which I asked, you would have been able to do it, isn't that right? Which is wrong and unreasonable — my request or your behavior?''

How can this story help illustrate the truth of God's justice in requiring from us that which we cannot perform?

Man's breaking of the Covenant of Works with God has **abolished** the possibility of his earning eternal life through his works. Fallen man is guilty of, and polluted with, sin. Man's fall has not ended God's requirements, however. God still justly demands perfect righteousness and holiness from each person.

Actual sin flows out from original sin. Our sinfully-polluted heart is the fountainhead which spews forth a host of actual sins in our lives. Actual sins are the sins in *thoughts, words, and actions* that each of us actually commit.

''When you see a wormhole on the outside of an apple, has the worm eaten its way into or out of the apple?'' Linda's teacher asked.

Several students had different responses. Linda did not know.

Finally her teacher responded, ''From the inside to the outside. The egg was laid already in the blossom and the worm was hatched in the core of the apple. As soon as it hatched, it began eating its way to the outside.''

How does this illustration picture the ''worm of original sin'' in people's lives? When is it planted? Where does it "hatch"? After "hatching," how does it continually "eat its way" to the outside?

A minister once answered a group of people who were arguing against the truth of original sin in this manner:

"You believe in actual sin, do you not?"

"Yes, certainly."

"Tell me, then, have you ever seen a tree growing without a root?"

Actual sins are of two types:

1. Sins of **omission**
2. Sins of **commission**

Sins of omission are sins of not doing, of omitting, that which God commands us to do — not thinking, saying, and doing that which God requires of us in His law. Sins of omission testify of our *failure* to live up to the standard of God's law, to live the life we should.

Sins of commission are sins of doing, of committing, that which God forbids us to do — thinking, saying, and doing that which God forbids in His law. Sins of commission testify of our *rebellion* against God, our transgressions of His commandments.

> "Tonight when you retire to bed," a minister once explained to his catechism class, "if you do not read a portion of Scripture, asking God's blessing upon it, you commit a sin of omission. If you read an evil book instead, you perform a sin of commission."
>
> A child not obeying her mother's request to first clean her room before playing, commits a sin of omission. A boy doing that which his mother told him not to do, commits a sin of commission.
>
> Not speaking a comforting, supporting, or rebuking word when necessary is a sin of omission. Saying a cruel, degrading, or unnecessary word is a sin of commission.
>
> On his deathbed, an old, faithful servant of God prayed aloud, "O God, forgive my sin — especially my sins of omission!"
>
> Why did this minister emphasize his sins of omission?

The chart on the following page illustrates the various kinds of sin:

- **Omission** — Neglect or failure to do that which should have been done

- **Commission** — Acting or doing that which was decided upon

TYPES OF SIN

SIN — A LACK OF CONFORMITY TO GOD'S LAW

ORIGINAL SIN

My sinful guilt and pollution
from the fall of mankind in Paradise

My sinfully-polluted heart (source
or fountain) from which my actual
sins flow forth

ACTUAL SIN

The foul
stream of my daily
sins

SINS OF OMISSION

Not doing that which
God commands of me

THOUGHTS

Not thinking that which I should

WORDS

Not saying that which I should

ACTIONS

Not doing that which I should

SINS OF COMMISSION

Doing that which God
forbids me

THOUGHTS

Thinking that which I should not

WORDS

Saying that which I should not

ACTIONS

Doing that which I should not

Sins vary not only in kind but also in degree. While any sin committed is terrible in its unrighteousness, rebellion, pollution, and punishment, (for only one transgression makes us guilty law-breakers in God's sight), there are degrees of sin. Sin and its punishment increase in degree according to the knowledge, opportunities, and blessings given to a person.

> When preaching on earth, Jesus clearly warned the cities of Chorazin, Bethsaida, and Capernaum, where He frequently spoke, with the following powerful message:

> > Then began He to upbraid the cities wherein most of His mighty works were done, because they repented not: Woe unto thee, Chorazin! woe unto thee, Bethsaida! for if the mighty works, which were done in you, had been done in Tyre and Sidon, they would have repented long ago in sackcloth and ashes. But I say unto you, It shall be more tolerable for Tyre and Sidon at the day of judgment, than for you. And thou Capernaum, which art exalted unto heaven, shalt be brought down to hell: for if the mighty works, which have been done in thee, had been done in Sodom, it would have remained until this day. But I say unto you, That it shall be more tolerable for the land of Sodom, in the day of judgment, than for thee (Matthew 11:20-24).

> Why should the punishment ascribed to the citizens of Tyre, Sidon, and Sodom be more **tolerable** than that pronounced upon those of Chorazin, Bethsaida, and Capernaum? How does this relate to the degree of knowledge, opportunity, and blessing received?

The worst degree of sin mentioned in Scripture is *the unpardonable* (or *unforgivable*) *sin*. This sin is also called *the sin against the Holy Ghost*. When using the term "the sin against the Holy Ghost," distinction must be made between *pardonable* sins, and the *unpardonable* sin against the Holy Spirit. Scripture speaks of **vexing** the Spirit (Isaiah 63:10), lying to the Spirit (Acts 5:3), grieving the Spirit (Ephesians 4:30), **quenching** the Spirit (I Thessalonians 5:19), and resisting the Spirit (Acts 7:51). All of these are sins against the Holy Ghost, but they are not the unpardonable sin.

The unpardonable sin is a sin which Scripture teaches is unforgivable, after which a change of heart is impossible, and for

> And that servant, which knew his lord's will, and prepared not himself, neither did according to his will, shall be beaten with many stripes.
> But he that knew not, and did commit things worthy of stripes, shall be beaten with few stripes. For unto whomsoever much is given, of him shall be much required: and to whom men have committed much, of him they will ask the more.
> — Luke 12:47-48

● **Tolerable** — Capable of being endured or suffered

● **Vexing** — Provoking

● **Quenching** — Extinguishing; suppressing; stifling

301

> Wherefore I say unto you, All manner of sin and blasphemy shall be forgiven unto men: but the blasphemy against the Holy Ghost shall not be forgiven unto men.
>
> And whosoever speaketh a word against the Son of man, it shall be forgiven him: but whosoever speaketh against the Holy Ghost, it shall not be forgiven him, neither in this world, neither in the world to come.
>
> — Matthew 12:31-32
>
> But he that shall blaspheme against the Holy Ghost hath never forgiveness, but is in danger of eternal damnation.
>
> — Mark 3:29

- **Maliciously** — With deep hatred, evil intent, and desire to inflict injury upon another

- **Blasphemes** — Speaks irreverently and evilly of God and sacred matters in order to mock with true religion

- **Transcends** — Goes above or beyond

> And whosoever shall speak a word against the Son of man, it shall be forgiven him: but unto him that blasphemeth against the Holy Ghost it shall not be forgiven.
>
> — Luke 12:10
>
> For it is impossible for those who were once enlightened, and have tasted of the heavenly gift, and were made partakers of the Holy Ghost.
> And have tasted the good word of God, and the powers of the world to come.
> If they shall fall away, to renew them again unto repentance; seeing they crucify to themselves the Son of God afresh, and put Him to an open shame.
>
> — Hebrews 6:4-6

which it is not necessary to pray. It is a sin of degrees, of deepening steps taken over time. It is the ultimate rejection of God. To commit this sin one must have received a clear knowledge of the truth and have "tasted" an impression of the truth in his conscience and emotions. He must be convinced of God's truth to a degree to make an honest denial of it impossible. In his mind and conscience, he must be convinced of the truth.

The unpardonable sin is committed when, against this background of mental knowledge and conviction, a person consciously, willfully, and **maliciously** rejects, slanders, and **blasphemes** the evidence and testimony of the Holy Spirit regarding the grace of God in the Lord Jesus Christ. In the end, from his deep hatred and enmity, he speaks of the truth as the lie, Christ as Satan, and the Holy Spirit as the spirit of hell.

This sin is unpardonable, not because its guilt **transcends** the merits or abilities of Christ to save or because the person who committed it is beyond the power of the Holy Spirit to save; but because, in this sin of degrees, the sinner refuses to repent, hardens his heart, sears his conscience, and God finally gives him over to himself.

The result of this sin is a person who displays a pronounced hatred of God, a defiant attitude toward true religion, and a devilish delight in mocking and slandering that which is holy without any remorse, sorrow, or concern for his soul or eternity.

This terrible sin and frightful condition was displayed in Scripture by some of the Pharisees and members of the Sanhedrin, who — after hearing Christ's words and seeing His miracles, being convicted mentally of His truth, having emotionally "tasted" impressions of His power, and knowing in their consciences that He was from heaven — increasingly fought against these convictions.

Because Jesus' teachings testified against them, the more powerfully they were convicted of the truth, the more they hated Him; until with hellish fury they denied, argued, mocked, ridiculed and blasphemed Christ. Finally, God gave them over to themselves — to the full hardening of heart and searing of conscience — to say and try to convince others that Christ was a devil; and that His spirit of power was from Beelzebub, the chief of the devils; to publicly state that Christ's testimony was blasphemy, and finally with devilish delight, to persecute, capture, try, scourge, mock, and crucify the Savior. Finally, in the end, this was done with a pronounced hatred and defiance of Christ, a devilish pleasure in mocking and slandering Him, and without any remorse, sorrow or concern for their souls or for eternity.

"Can a person commit the unpardonable sin today? If so, how would this take place?" Marie asked.

"Let me give an example," her teacher replied. "Randy was born and raised in a Christian home and always attended a Christian school and church. He was convinced of the truth in both mind and conscience. At special times in his life, he even 'tasted,' or emotionally felt something of the power of God and His truth.

"However, in his teen-age years, Randy found other friends who influenced him to attend places, engage in behaviors, and lead a lifestyle which contradicted that which he was being taught in home, school, and church. The first time he attended a wrong place, his conscience warned him loudly. But, he overstepped his conscience repeatedly. After some time, his conscience hardly sounded when he went there. God the Holy Spirit had lit the candle of conscience several times, but each time he had chosen to blow it out. Finally, God did not light it anymore.

"Worse yet, because home, school, and church testified against his new lifestyle, Randy began to hate what was good and to call the truth a lie and good as evil in his life. Statements like the following were heard from him increasingly: 'I hate my parents — they're so strict. They just don't want me to have any fun,' or 'This rotten school — you can't do a thing here. All there is here is a bunch of preaching and I'm sick of it!'; or 'Church is such a bore. If I didn't have to go, for sure I wouldn't be there!'

"Deep down, Randy knew better. He knew the truth. But instead of changing his lifestyle and seeing sin and Satan as enemies, he hardened his heart against the truth to hold on to his sins. Religion and Christ began to become his enemies. He began to hate, mock, and ridicule his home, school, and church — especially because they were Christian, because they taught God's truth. Feelings of remorse or sorrow over his attitude or evil comments regarding parents, teachers, or church officebearers became less and less. Concern for his soul and eternity grew colder and colder. Satan, sin, world, and doing his own desires became the good things to speak well of; and God, religion, and Christian teachings increasingly became

For if we sin wilfully after that we have received the knowledge of the truth, there remaineth no more sacrifice for sins,

But a certain fearful looking for of judgment and fiery indignation, which shall devour the adversaries.

He' that despised Moses' law died without mercy under two or three witnesses:

Of how much sorer punishment suppose ye, shall he be thought worthy, who hath trodden under foot the Son of God, and hath counted the blood of the covenant, wherewith he was sanctified, an unholy thing, and hath done despite unto the Spirit of grace?

— Hebrews 10:26-29

If any man see his brother sin a sin which is not unto death, he shall ask, and he shall give him life for them that sin not unto death. There is a sin unto death: I do not say that he shall pray for it.

— I John 5:16

? Why is sinning against the testimony of a speaking consience a very serious type of sin?

? Why could a heathen, one who has never heard the gospel, not commit the unpardonable sin?

> Come now, and let us reason together, saith the LORD: though your sins be as scarlet, they shall be as white as snow; though they be red like crimson, they shall be as wool.
> — Isaiah 1:18

? In actuality, why is there no such thing as a "little sin"?

'the enemies' to attack, mock, and slander."

"Did Randy commit the unpardonable sin?" Marie asked seriously.

"I would not dare to say that he did, yet," her teacher responded. "When the unpardonable sin is committed there is no fear for, nor repentance from, sin anymore. But Randy is dangerously heading in that direction. He is fighting to call evil good and good evil.

When the Holy Spirit impresses and convicts a person of his sin, Satan often tries to convince him that there is no hope for him, that he has sinned too greatly, or that he has committed the unpardonable sin. However, those who receive warnings of conscience concerning sin — impressions regarding their soul's condition, or convictions of the truth of eternity — receive evidence that they have not committed the unpardonable sin. Those who have committed this sin never experience any remorse, sorrow, or concern over these matters. The Word of God encourages all those who feel the weight of their sin, not to despair, but to plead for salvation in Jesus Christ, for "He is able also to save them to *the uttermost* that come unto God by Him" (Hebrews 7:25a). No sinner can place himself beyond *the uttermost*.

In Hampton Court Gardens there were many large, stately oak trees. However, several of these trees were killed by ivy vines.

Had the ivy been uprooted or killed when it was a young plant, the oaks would not have become the victims of the ivy. But for many years, the ivy was allowed to grow unchecked and its coils grew and entwined themselves around the trunks and branches of the trees. Serpent-like, the ivy surrounded and gradually killed the trees on which it was allowed to grow.

What lesson regarding sin can be learned from this illustration?

DEATH

Sin is always a very serious matter, and it is always taken seriously by God. Sin is not only a transgression of God's law but it also is rebellion against the Lawgiver. It is an **affront** to God's righteousness and holiness. Therefore God will always righteously punish sin. Throughout the Bible God continually warns us of the terrible consequences of sin — for sin results in death, and death means separation — separation of man's soul from its body and from God. Already in Paradise, God warned man, "For in the day that thou eatest thereof thou shalt surely die" (Genesis 2:17b).

- **Affront** — Insult; disgrace

The death God spoke of is a three-fold death.

1. **Corporal** (physical, bodily, or temporal) death
2. Spiritual death
3. Eternal death

? Why is corporal death also named "*temporary*" death"?

Corporal death is the death of a person's body. When corporal death occurs, a person's soul and body separate. The body is buried and returns to the ground, but his soul returns to God who judges and sends it to heaven or hell.

- **Corporal** — Pertaining to the human body; physical

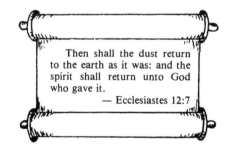

Then shall the dust return to the earth as it was: and the spirit shall return unto God who gave it.
— Ecclesiastes 12:7

Man was not created to die; it is unnatural. Corporal death is the result of our sin.

Jesus Christ has passed through and conquered death and the grave for His people. Therefore death has become a passageway to eternal life for the souls of all true believers. While some of God's children receive more faith than others to clearly see this when dying, all shall be safely brought through death into eternal life. This truth caused Paul to testify, "O death, where is thy sting? O grave, where is thy victory? The sting of death is sin; and the strength of sin is the law. But thanks be to God, which giveth us the victory through our Lord Jesus Christ" (I Corinthians 15:55-57).

? Why is the knowledge that Jesus has already passed through death and the grave a rich comfort for all true believers?

? What hope does the non-Christian have when facing death?

A wealthy Paris gentleman went to visit his slowly-dying friend and promised to hire the best nurse in the city to care for him.

After gathering information from various sources, he approached a highly-respected nurse in order to hire her to care for his dying friend. After being approached, the nurse asked, "Is your friend a Christian?"

The man was surprised by her question. "Why, yes he is," he replied. "But if you don't mind my asking, why do you ask me that?"

"Sir," the nurse answered. "I took care of the atheist, **Voltaire**, on his deathbed, and for all the money in Europe, I would not be willing to see another unbeliever die!"

Why is facing death a very different matter for believers than for unbelievers?

● **Voltaire** — The pen name of a famous French author and philosopher who lived from 1694-1778. A strong and public promoter of atheism, he experienced powerful judgments of God upon his deathbed and died a terrible death.

? How is the fact that God sends His Word to fallen man a proof of man's rationality?

● **Perverse** — Wicked; stubborn; contrary to that which is right

? How do those who teach that natural man can freely choose good or evil of himself, or earn part or all of his salvation through good works, deny the scriptural teachings of man's fall, original sin, and total depravity?

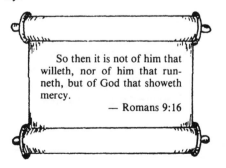

So then it is not of him that willeth, nor of him that runneth, but of God that showeth mercy.
— Romans 9:16

Spiritual death is the condition of separation from God's saving grace, favor, and communion, the sad condition in which all fallen men are born. Man is born with original sin — in a sinfully guilty state and polluted condition. Spiritual death is total depravity, man's being born spiritually dead in sin. Man's sin has spiritually separated him from God, his only source of spiritual life and growth. God's Spirit no longer dwells in man in his natural state.

Spiritual death does not mean, however, that man's will is dead or that his freedom to act is lost. Fallen man is still a rational being, and through God's common grace, he still retains characteristics of the wider sense of God's image as taught in the previous chapter. Fallen man still freely chooses and acts for himself according to his own will. Since the fall, however, natural man's will is **perverse**. It is reversed and desires to serve self, sin, world, and Satan instead of God. It is inclined to all evil and is totally depraved of any spiritual good — of love to God and others. Natural man's will is active; he freely makes choices continually; but being a spiritually dead sinner, he chooses for sin instead of righteousness — for self instead of God.

Some people base their hope for salvation upon spiritually dead sinners, upon their making a decision for Christ, or choosing to live for God. These, and any other hopes based upon totally-depraved sinners making right choices of themselves, are false hopes. Believing that fallen man will exercise his free will to choose for God, denies the truths of Scripture regarding man's fall, total depravity, and spiritual death.

To illustrate the hopelessness of spiritually dead sinners ever being able to bring forth spiritual fruits of themselves, a father cut off some flowers from their roots, laid them in the grass, and told his son that he believed that the flowers would continue to live and bloom.

When his son replied that this was impossible, he responded, "You are right, son. This is the same truth with spiritually dead sinners. Those who are separated from God, their only source of spiritual life and growth, can never bring forth spiritual fruits apart from Him."

Hope for man's salvation must be based upon God, not upon fallen man. God is almighty and gracious. He has sovereignly declared His desire to save lost sinners through the merits of Jesus Christ. God's willingness, grace, and work — not fallen man's willingness, decision, and works — is the scriptural foundation of hope.

The results of spiritual death were experienced immediately after man's first sin in Paradise. Spiritual death, being separated from God's favor and communion, included the following:

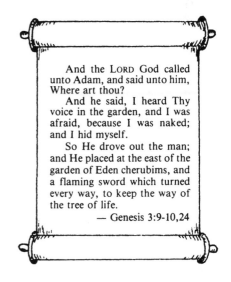

And the LORD God called unto Adam, and said unto him, Where art thou?

And he said, I heard Thy voice in the garden, and I was afraid, because I was naked; and I hid myself.

So He drove out the man; and He placed at the east of the garden of Eden cherubims, and a flaming sword which turned every way, to keep the way of the tree of life.

— Genesis 3:9-10,24

1. *The loss of God's image* — In its restricted sense; the reflection in man of godly knowledge, righteousness, and holiness.

2. *The awareness of nakedness* — A feeling of shame; the loss of openness and comfortableness in God's presence.

3. *Horror of conscience* — A sense of guilt and fear of God; the loss of innocency.

4. ***Expulsion from Paradise*** — The casting out of all unrighteousness from God's presence; the loss of God's blessed communion in the intimate relationship man had with the Lord.

● **Expulsion** — The state of being expelled or driven out

The manchineel tree, which grows in the West Indies, bears a very attractive apple. The fruit looks delicious and smells very fragrant. But to eat, is death. The natives dip their arrows into the sap of this tree in order to poison their enemies. A few drops of its sap or juice is very dangerous.

How does this tree in its appearance and consequence, illustrate the fall of man and the truth of sin?

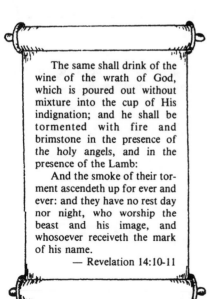

? Why is natural man's reaction to God's call, spiritually, the same as Adam's, as we read it in Genesis 3:9-10? "And the LORD God called unto Adam, and said unto him, Where art thou? And he said, I heard Thy voice in the garden, and I was afraid, because I was naked; and I hid myself."

? Does sin only produce separation between people and God, or does it also separate people? What evidences of both can you observe in our society today?

> The same shall drink of the wine of the wrath of God, which is poured out without mixture into the cup of His indignation; and he shall be tormented with fire and brimstone in the presence of the holy angels, and in the presence of the Lamb:
>
> And the smoke of their torment ascendeth up for ever and ever: and they have no rest day nor night, who worship the beast and his image, and whosoever receiveth the mark of his name.
>
> — Revelation 14:10-11

Cindy always enjoyed talking with her mother. Usually the day after an evening's activity, Cindy enjoyed sharing and talking about everything which took place.

Last evening, however, Cindy had lied to her parents. She told them she was going to a school event with her usual friends, but she actually went to another place with others.

The following morning, Cindy felt very uncomfortable. She delayed going to the breakfast table and stayed in her room. She felt afraid to be in her mother's presence. She started to think of lies, like fig leaves, to cover the naked truth. She couldn't describe her feelings in words, but she felt naked and afraid of being in her mother's presence, and yet guilty for wanting to avoid her.

How are the results from sin the same today as they have been from the beginning? How are Cindy's feelings in the presence of her mother similar to Adam and Eve's in God's presence?

Eternal death is the eternal punishment of sinners in both soul and body in hell. This is the fullest extent of God's punishment of sin. It is the ultimate consequence of man's fall. In hell, sinners are fully given over to themselves and God's wrath against sin is fully poured out. Here they are completely separated from a gracious God, being not only separated from God's saving grace, but also from any blessings of common grace. Eternal death in hell is spoken of in Scripture as being without intermission, mixture, or end. Here unrepenting sinners will eternally experience what it means to willfully sin against an eternal, infinite, holy, and righteous God.

Man's three-fold death can be defined in the following terms:

THREE-FOLD DEATH	
Type of Death:	**Separation of:**
1. Corporal	Soul from body
2. Spiritual	Soul from God's saving grace, favor, and communion
3. Eternal	Person (soul and body) from God's saving and common grace eternally

Fallen man is in a most miserable condition. His misery includes:

1. *His sin* (or *sinful state*) which separates him from God, his only source of spiritual life and growth.

2. *His impotency* (or *sinful condition*) of being unable to deliver himself from his state of spiritual death.

3. *His punishment* (or *the result of sin*) for the wages of sin is death, resulting in total separation from God's grace and eternal punishment under the full wrath of God.

Sadly, fallen man is blind for his own blindness. He does not feel his misery. He is unconcerned over his sinful state. The sadness of this condition is illustrated in the following story.

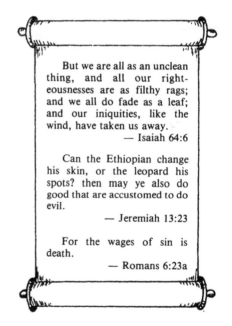

But we are all as an unclean thing, and all our right-eousnesses are as filthy rags; and we all do fade as a leaf; and our iniquities, like the wind, have taken us away.
— Isaiah 64:6

Can the Ethiopian change his skin, or the leopard his spots? then may ye also do good that are accustomed to do evil.
— Jeremiah 13:23

For the wages of sin is death.
— Romans 6:23a

● **Impotency** — Powerlessness; incapability; total lack of strength or ability

At one time, convicts were employed in building the high, thick walls around the prison grounds in Portland. Every block that was laid made their escape more impossible. Yet the imprisoning walls were being built by the very people imprisoned by them.

How does this picture an unrepentant sinner? The prisoners in this story were *forced* to build their own walls, but sinners build their own imprisoning walls *willingly*. How does this increase the sadness of sinful man's condition?

309

Imagine a soldier breaking through the outside wall, cutting through metres (or yards) of barbed wire, and finally, one night, quietly knocking on the window of an old barracks where several of his soldier friends are being held captive as prisoners of war. Excitedly, he tells them of the way of escape that has been opened for them.

To his dismay, however, he finds that his friends have been so brainwashed that they believe they are living in quite decent surroundings and do not want to leave. He tries every approach possible — showing them the extreme poverty of their food rations, clothing, and living quarters; pointing out to them their slavery; and describing to them the terrible final result of death by remaining where they are. But they are not concerned. "Things could be worse," they respond.

In desperation he describes to them the excellent way of escape that is available, the beauty of the freedom which awaits them, and the honor that would be theirs in their home country; but they are not interested.

Finally, they tell him that they will think about that which he has told them, but for now to leave them alone, as they want to sleep yet for a few hours.

How can this illustration be compared to fallen man's condition and his response to the way of deliverance opened up by Jesus Christ through which sinners may escape from the bondage of sin? Certainly the condition of prisoners of war is pitiful; but that they do not see their misery is even more sorrowful. Why?

? How is Revelation 3:17 and 18 applicable to the spiritual lesson illustrated by this story? "Because thou sayest, I am rich, and increased with goods, and have need of nothing; and knowest not that thou art wretched, and miserable, and poor, and blind, and naked: I counsel thee to buy of Me gold tried in the fire, that thou mayest be rich; and white raiment, that thou mayest be clothed, and that the shame of thy nakedness do not appear; and anoint thine eyes with eyesalve, that thou mayest see."

Rev. Ledeboer wrote this question and answer in his booklet, *Simple Catechism Questions for Children:*

Q. What is the greatest misery?

A. Not to feel our misery.

Why is this true?

? Why is man's natural condition of not feeling his misery, his greatest misery?

After **Chrysostom**'s arrest, the emperor asked his advisors what they should do with him. "What will make him most fearful — so afraid, that he will **recant**"?

After various ideas were mentioned, one of the advisors answered, "Your Honor, I know him. Prison, **banishment**, nor even death will cause him to fear. There is only one thing that he is afraid of — and that is sin."

Is sin your greatest fear?

- **Chrysostom** — Archbishop of Constantinople who died in banishment in A.D. 438

- **Recant** — To publically retract or deny that which was previously confessed to be true

- **Banishment** — Exile; the condition of being condemned to leave a country

When viewing man's deep misery, his sin, impotency and punishment, we are inclined to despairingly ask, "Is man's case hopeless?" From man's side it is; but man's sin is not the total picture. The following story provides us with an instructive illustration.

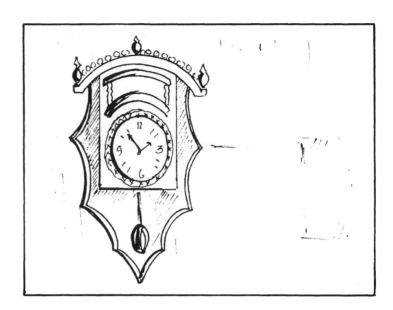

A man once owned a beautiful clock which would not run. "Leave it alone for a while," suggested one. "Oil it," advised another. "Shake it!" "Put it in a new location," or "Bring it to this or that shop," said others. But nothing helped — its case appeared hopeless.

When all else had failed, the man brought the clock back to its maker who thoroughly renewed it so that it ran well.

Man's heart is spiritually dead. His only hope is returning to his Maker to have it thoroughly renewed.

Genesis 3, which relates man's sin, fall, and punishment, is often referred to as "the black chapter" of Scripture. But the first gospel promise, the promise of the Savior, is also found in this chapter. Blessed be God! He did not leave all men in the miserable state into which they had brought themselves, but He graciously opened a wonderfully complete, rich, and glorious way of salvation for lost sinners through the death payment of His Son — the Lord Jesus Christ. After man broke the Covenant of Works and plunged himself into hopeless misery, God revealed a second covenant, the Covenant of Grace, through which man can again be brought into relationship and communion with God, and be restored into God's favor and fellowship eternally. This Covenant of Grace is examined in our next chapter.

Have you been brought to know, feel, and own your actual and original sin? If so, all hope and expectation in your own efforts, works, and righteousness have been cut off. Have you been led to see, hope, and trust in Jesus Christ for deliverance? If so, your heart has been won over to most deeply desire to increasingly love and serve Him in all things.

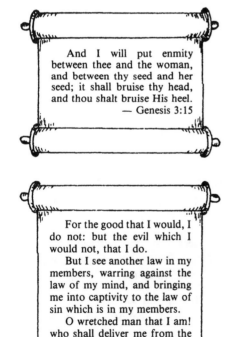

And I will put enmity between thee and the woman, and between thy seed and her seed; it shall bruise thy head, and thou shalt bruise His heel.
— Genesis 3:15

For the good that I would, I do not: but the evil which I would not, that I do.

But I see another law in my members, warring against the law of my mind, and bringing me into captivity to the law of sin which is in my members.

O wretched man that I am! who shall deliver me from the body of this death?

I thank God through Jesus Christ our Lord.
— Romans 7:19, 23-25a

CATECHISM MEMORIZATION
Questions from Rev. A. Hellenbroek's *Divine Truths* — Chapter X

1. Does man still possess God's image?
   No, he lost it by sin.
2. What was the first sin of man?
   Eating from the tree of the knowledge of good and evil.
3. Where was the tree of the knowledge of good and evil?
   In Paradise, in the garden of Eden.
4. What fruit did this tree bear?
   We do not know, for the Bible does not tell us.
5. Who ate from the tree first, Adam or Eve?
   Eve.
6. Who deceived her?
   The devil, by assuming the form of a serpent (Gen. 3:1-7).
7. What did he convince her to believe?
   That if she ate the forbidden fruit she would not die, but be like God, knowing good and evil.
8. Who enticed Adam to eat?
   His wife; she gave the forbidden fruit to him, and he did eat.
9. Where can we read the history of the fall of man?
   Genesis 3.
10. What consequences did this sin have on Adam and Eve?
    (1) The loss of God's image, (2) Sensibility of nakedness, (3) Horror of conscience, (4) Expulsion out of Paradise, and (5) Death itself.
11. Does Adam's sin affect us?
    Yes, it is imputed to each of us.
12. Why is Adam's sin imputed to us?
    Because Adam was the representative of all his posterity as the head of the Covenant of Works. "Wherefore, as by one man sin entered into the world, and death by sin; and so death passed upon all men, for that all have sinned" (Rom. 5:12).
13. What kind of sin do we possess as a result of Adam's fall?
    Original sin. "Behold, I was shapen in iniquity, and in sin did my mother conceive me" (Ps. 51:5).
14. How many kinds of sin are there?
    Two kinds: original and actual sin.
15. How does original sin become ours?
    By imputation and heredity.
16. Who imputes Adam's sin to us?
    God.
17. What does God impute to us?
    The guilt of sin. "For as by one man's disobedience many were made sinners, so by the obedience of One shall many be made righteous" (Rom. 5:19).
18. What do we inherit?
    The pollution of sin. "Who can bring a clean thing out of an unclean? Not one" (Job 14:4).
19. From whom do we inherit original sin?
    From our parents.
20. What is included in the guilt of our original sin?
    Our being subject to punishment for Adam's sin (Rom. 5:18).
21. What is the pollution of original sin?
    Inherent corruption which comprehends the entire man.
22. Do all men have original sin?
    Yes, all except Christ. "For that which is born of flesh is flesh" (John 3:5).
23. Why did Christ not have original sin?
    Because He was conceived by the Holy Ghost.
24. Do all men have actual sin?
    Yes. We all offend in many things (James 3:2).
25. How are actual sins committed?
    In thoughts, words, and actions.
26. Are all men by nature in a state of misery?
    Yes, for all men are born in a fallen state.
27. What three things represent the essence of misery?
    (1) Our sins, (2) our inability to overcome our sins, and (3) the punishment we deserve for our sins.
28. Are all men by nature incapable of doing spiritual good?
    Yes. "The carnal mind is enmity against God; for it is not subject to the law of God, neither indeed can be" (Rom. 8:7).
29. Does man have a free will or an internal ability to choose to do spiritual good?
    No. "And you hath He quickened who were dead in trespasses and sins" (Eph. 2:1).
30. Are then all God's commands, threatenings, and promises in vain?
    No, for these are means that God uses to operate upon man as a rational creature to the discharge of his duty.
31. What is the punishment of sin?
    Death. "The wages of sin is death" (Rom. 6:23).
32. How many kinds of death are there?
    Three: corporal, spiritual and eternal.
33. What is corporal death?
    The separation of soul and body.
34. What is spiritual death?
    Separation from God's favor and an inability to do, say, or think anything that is not sinful.
35. What is eternal death?
    Suffering eternal punishment for sin in hell.
36. Do all sins deserve punishment in hell?
    Yes, even the smallest sin. "Cursed is every one that continueth not in all things which are written in the book of the law to do them" (Gal. 3:10).
37. Are there then no pardonable sins?
    Yes, all sins may be forgiven in Christ, except the sin against the Holy Ghost, but none can be forgiven in themselves (James 2:10).
38. Was the Covenant of Works abolished by sin?
    Yes, with respect to its power to justify a man through his works.
39. What conclusion must we draw from the misery of man?
    That (excepting Satan) there is not a more miserable creature than natural man after the fall.

CHAPTER 8

Part I. Chapter Review

1. Name four techniques that Satan used with Eve, and still often uses today, when tempting a person to sin:

    a. _____

    b. _____

    c. _____

    d. _____

2. What is meant by "the fall"? _____

    _____

    _____

3. List four scriptural reasons why God created Adam with the possibility to fall, even when knowing that he would fall:

    a. _____

    b. _____

    c. _____

    d. _____

4. Describe two dangers with asking questions regarding God's reasons for creating Adam and permitting the fall in His eternal decree:

    a. _____

    _____

    b. _____

    _____

5. State four reasons why Adam's original sin was a very grievous action:

    a. _____

    b. _____

    c. _____

    d. _____

6. What does mankind's state of misery include? Name and define four characteristics:

    a. _____ — _____

    b. _____ — _____

    c. _____ — _____

    d. _____ — _____

7. Define the word "sin": _____
   _____

8. Scriptural teaching, in contrast with modern definitions, includes the following six characteristics regarding sin:
   a. _____
   b. _____
   c. _____
   d. _____
   e. _____
   f. _____

9. Original sin includes both original _____ and _____ . Original _____ is *imputed* to each person because Adam was our _____ father. Original _____ is *inherited* by each person because Adam was our _____ father.

10. Name and define the two types of actual sins:
    a. _____ — _____
       _____
    b. _____ — _____
       _____

11. All people commit both sins of omission and commission in their _____, _____, and _____ .

12. Name and define each type of death included in a three-fold death:
    a. _____ — _____
    b. _____ — _____
    c. _____ — _____

13. List four results of spiritual death which were experienced immediately after man's fall:
    a. _____
    b. _____
    c. _____
    d. _____

14. Name three elements included in man's condition of misery which makes it very terrible:
    a. _____
    b. _____
    c. _____

CHAPTER 8

Part II. Deepening Your Insight

1. What lessons can we learn regarding how not to speak about others, from the manner in which Satan questioned and spoke about God? _____
_____
_____
_____

2. When a person performs that which is in God's unchangeable decree, why is he held personally responsible and accountable? _____
_____
_____

3. a. Did Adam have a free will to choose either good or evil in Paradise? Explain your answer.
_____
_____

   b. Fallen man continually makes free choices. Why will he never choose for God, of himself?
_____
_____

   c. Why must fallen man's hope of salvation be God's free grace instead of man's free will?
_____
_____

4. Study the six scriptural characteristics of sin mentioned. How do the fifth and sixth qualities clearly distinguish God's law and definition of sin from man's? _____
_____
_____
_____

5. a. Describe several characteristics of the unpardonable sin: _____
_____
_____
_____

   b. Why is this sin unpardonable? _____
_____
_____

   c. Why is the name, "the unpardonable sin" one which more clearly distinguishes this particular sin than the term "the sin against the Holy Ghost"? _____
_____
_____
_____

6. How do the following add to the terribleness of his fallen condition?
   a. Fallen man's impotency — _____

   b. Fallen man's lack of realization of, or feeling for, his misery — _____
_____

QUESTIONS

Part III. Biblical Applications

1. a. How does Romans 5:19-21 speak of the glorification of God's grace taking place through man's fall and sin? _____
    _____
    _____

    b. How does Romans 6:1-2 sharply warn us against ever speaking of man's fall or sin as a good thing? _____
    _____
    _____

2. Write out a verse from each of the following chapters which clearly teaches the sad truth of fallen man's total depravity:
    a. Romans 3: _____ — _____
    _____

    b. Ephesians 2: _____ — _____
    _____

    c. Ecclesiastes 3: _____ — _____
    _____

3. Study the following verses. How does each speak about individuals fulfilling God's will, but being fully responsible for their own sins?
    a. Genesis 25:23 and 29-34 — _____
    _____

    b. Romans 9:17 and Exodus 8:15, 32 — _____
    _____

4. What clear and powerful lesson is repeatedly taught in Genesis 5 concerning the consequences of man's sinful fall? _____
    _____

Part IV. From the Writings of our Church Forefathers

In your own words, explain the meaning of the following quotations:

1. "Sin hath the devil for its father, shame for its companion, and death for its wages" (Thomas Watson). _____
    _____

2. "Sin is the strength of death and the death of strength"(Thomas Adams). _____
    _____

3. "God would never permit evil, if He could not bring good out of evil" (Augustine). _____
    _____
    _____

CHAPTER 8

Part V. From the Marginal Questions

1. The heavenly song of praise that saved sinners will sing eternally is named "The Song of Moses and of the Lamb" (Rev. 15:13). Why is this song of deliverance called the song of "Moses," and of the "Lamb"? Who only will be able to sing this song? Why?

_____

_____

_____

_____

2. Why is a clear understanding of the Covenant of Works required for a proper comprehension of the Covenant of Grace? Why is the experience of my sin and misery necessary in order to appreciate Christ and His salvation?

_____

_____

_____

_____

3. Why is Jesus Christ the only Person ever born into the human race without original sin?

_____

_____

_____

_____

4. Are all Adam's sins imputed to each of us, or only one sin? Why?

_____

_____

_____

_____

5. How do those who teach that natural man can freely choose good of himself, or earn part or all of his salvation through good works, deny the scriptural teachings of man's fall, original sin, and total depravity?

_____

_____

_____

_____

EXTRA CHALLENGE QUESTIONS

Part VI. Your Selection from the Marginal Questions

Write out and respond to two marginal questions that interest you which have not been previously asked in this chapter's question section.

1. Question: _____

    _____

    Response: _____

    _____

    _____

    _____

2. Question: _____

    _____

    Response: _____

    _____

    _____

Part VII. Project Ideas

1. Design a chart which displays the techniques Satan used to tempt man to sin in Paradise and why Adam's sin was a very grievous sin. You may wish to include some examples of how Satan still uses the same age-old techniques today when tempting people to sin.

2. Plan and hold a debate in which one person tries to define the characteristics of sin in a modern manner, and the other, using Scripture.

3. Draw a poster which clearly teaches fallen man's relationship to Adam as his covenant father and natural father, and the results from both relationships.

4. Construct a chart which portrays the various types of sin.

5. Write a report on the unpardonable sin, clearly specifying its various characteristics. Research different biblical references which point to some of the Pharisees and members of the Sanhedrin as having committed this sin during the ministry of Christ on earth.

6. Make an instructive poster which clearly shows and defines the three types of death. Research and include several verses of Scripture which speak of each on your poster.

9

Covenant of Grace

As dying stumps give nourishment
To each new plant and flower,
So Christ, through death, grants life by His
Regenerating power.

God's covenant of grace is from
Eternity in span;
It carries out in time the act
Of saving sinful man.

'Twas thought by God the Father;
'Twas bought by God the Son;
And wrought by God the Holy Ghost;
And yet Their work is one.

FROM OUR REFORMED DOCTRINAL STANDARDS

The Belgic Confession of Faith

Article 17 — of the Recovery of Fallen Man

We believe that our most gracious God, in His admirable wisdom and goodness, seeing that man had thus thrown himself into temporal and eternal death, and made himself wholly miserable, was pleased to seek and comfort him, when he trembling fled from His presence, promising him that He would give His Son, who should be made of a woman, to bruise the head of the serpent, and would make him happy.

The Canons of Dordt

SECOND HEAD OF DOCTRINE
OF THE DEATH OF CHRIST, AND
THE REDEMPTION OF MEN THEREBY

Article 8

For this was the sovereign counsel, and most gracious will and purpose of God the Father, that the quickening and saving efficacy of the most precious death of His Son should extend to all the elect, for bestowing upon them alone the gift of justifying faith, thereby to bring them infallibly to salvation: that is, it was the will of God, that Christ by the blood of the cross, whereby He confirmed the new covenant, should effectually redeem out of every people, tribe, nation, and language, all those, and those only, who were from eternity chosen to salvation, and given to Him by the Father; that He should confer upon them faith, which together with all the other saving gifts of the Holy Spirit, He purchased for them by His death; should purge them from all sin, both original and actual, whether committed before or after believing; and having faithfully preserved them even to the end, should at last bring them free from every spot and blemish to the enjoyment of glory in His own presence forever.

Article 9

This purpose proceeding from everlasting love towards the elect, has from the beginning of the world to this day been powerfully accomplished, and will henceforward still continue to be accomplished, notwithstanding all the ineffectual opposition of the gates of hell, so that the elect in due time may be gathered together into one, and that there never may be wanting a church composed of believers, the foundation of which is laid in the blood of Christ, which may steadfastly love, and faithfully serve Him as their Savior, who as a Bridegroom for his bride, laid down His life for them upon the cross, and which may celebrate His praises here and through all eternity.

THIRD AND FOURTH HEADS OF DOCTRINE
OF THE CORRUPTION OF MAN, HIS CONVERSION
TO GOD, AND THE MANNER THEREOF

Article 15

God is under no obligation to confer this grace upon any; for how can He be indebted to man, who had no previous gifts to bestow, as a foundation for such recompense? Nay, who has nothing of his own but sin and falsehood? He therefore who becomes the subject of this grace, owes eternal gratitude to God, and gives Him thanks forever. Whoever is not made partaker thereof, is either altogether regardless of these spiritual gifts, and satisfied with his own condition; or is in no apprehension of danger, and vainly boasts the possession of that which he has not. With respect to those who make an external profession of faith, and live regular lives, we are bound, after the example of the apostle, to judge and speak of them in the most favorable manner. For the secret recesses of the heart are unknown to us. And as to others, who have not yet been called, it is our duty to pray for them to God, who calls the things that are not, as if they were. But we are in no wise to conduct ourselves towards them with haughtiness, as if we had made ourselves to differ.

9

THE COVENANT OF GRACE

God is a covenant-making and covenant-keeping God. The Lord delights in revealing Himself to, and forming a relationship with, His creatures.

The word "**covenant**" means "agreement," an agreement between two or more parties. This is true when we speak of human agreements or covenants. Human agreements benefit both agreeing parties. However, when we speak of the covenant-making and covenant-keeping God, we are referring to gracious covenant-making.

God is an infinite, perfect, complete, and self-sufficient Being. Nothing can be added to His greatness or perfections. He has no need for anything outside of His own Being. Therefore, His desiring to enter into a covenant relationship with His creatures is a freely-given, one-sided revelation of God's grace — His rich, overflowing love.

The Lord is not bound to enter into any relationship or agreement with mankind. If God would choose never to reveal Himself to man, man could not claim injustice. As creatures, we cannot lay any claims upon our Creator. Therefore, God's covenanting, His willingness to enter into relationship with man, reflects His grace — His rich, deep, one-sided love and care.

● **Covenant** — An agreement; a contract between two or more parties

The following chart indicates the covenants of God which stem from His common grace, pertaining to nature and applying to man's **temporal** state; and those which arise from His saving grace, pertaining to salvation and applying to man's eternal state.

Temporal — Pertaining to this life; only having limited existence

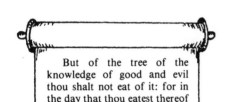 How do God's temporary covenants reveal *grace* to man? Why are they important? How do God's eternal covenants reveal a deeper grace? Why are they most important?

Noachian — Referring to Noah

But of the tree of the knowledge of good and evil thou shalt not eat of it: for in the day that thou eatest thereof thou shalt surely die.
— Genesis 2:17

But we are all as an unclean thing, and all our righteousnesses are as filthy rags; and we all do fade as a leaf; and our iniquities, like the wind, have taken us away.
— Isaiah 64:6

For if God spared not the angels that sinned, but cast them down to hell, and delivered them into chains of darkness, to be reserved unto judgment.
— II Peter 2:4

THE COVENANTS GOD HAS ESTABLISHED WITH MAN		
I. TEMPORARY (COMMON GRACE) COVENANTS **(Concerning nature and man's relationship with his temporal state)**		
A. *The Covenant of Nature* (or the Covenant of Common Grace or the **Noachian** Covenant)	And God spake unto Noah, and to his sons with him, saying, And I, behold, I will establish My covenant with you, and your seed after you; And with every living creature that is with you, of the fowl, of the cattle, and of every beast of the earth with you; from all that go out of the ark, to every beast of the earth. And I will establish My covenant with you; neither shall	all flesh be cut off anymore by the waters of a flood; neither shall there anymore be a flood to destroy the earth. And God said, This is the token of the covenant which I make between Me and you and every living creature that is with you, for perpetual generations; I do set My bow in the cloud, and it shall be for a token of a covenant between Me and the earth. — Genesis 9:8-13
B. *The Covenant of Day and Night*	Thus saith the LORD; if ye break My covenant of the day, and My covenant of the night, and that there should not be day and night in their season;	Thus saith the LORD; If My covenant be not with day and night, and if I have not appointed the ordinances of heaven and earth. — Jeremiah 33:20,25
II. ETERNAL (SAVING GRACE) COVENANTS **(Concerning salvation and man's relationship with God and his eternal state)**		
A. *The Covenant of Works*	And the LORD God commanded the man, saying, Of every tree of the garden thou mayest freely eat: But of the tree of the knowledge of good and evil, thou shalt not eat of it. — Genesis 1:16-17a	For since by man came death, by Man came also the resurrection of the dead. For as in Adam all die, even so in Christ shall all be made alive. — I Corinthians 15:21-22
B. *The Covenant of Grace*	But now hath He obtained a more excellent ministry, by how much also He is the Mediator of a better covenant, which was established upon better promises. — Hebrews 8:6 For if by one man's offence death reigned by one; much	more they which receive abundance of grace and of the gift of righteousness shall reign in life by one, Jesus Christ. Therefore as by the offence of one judgment came upon all men to condemnation; even so by the righteousness of One the free gift came upon all men unto justification of life. — Romans 5:17-18

As studied previously, God entered into a saving, covenant relationship with Adam and his descendants in Paradise called the "Covenant of Works." With heart, feeling, mind, and body, Adam was fully capable of keeping the covenant; indeed his deepest desire

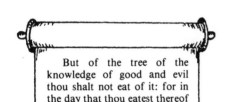

was to love and serve his Creator. Through yielding to the temptation of sinful pride, however, Adam and all his posterity broke the Covenant of Works. Sin totally altered man's condition and plunged him from glory into misery. Through his fall, mankind separated himself from God, brought upon himself the just sentence of a three-fold death, and made himself incapable of changing his condition.

God would have been perfectly righteous and just, to have left the entire human race in the sin and misery into which they had brought themselves. God has justly and eternally condemned all the angels that fell into sin. Knowing the painful results of this condemnation and that God cannot lie nor pass by His righteousness, Satan thought that he had won an irreversible victory when Adam fell. That God had planned and now revealed a second covenant of salvation, one of redemption through Christ for fallen sinners, took Satan by surprise.

This new covenant, the Covenant of Grace, revealed the grace and mercy of God in a yet richer manner than the Covenant of Works. It is named the "Covenant of Grace" because it most clearly proclaims God's grace. The sovereign, gracious love of God toward rebellious, undeserving sinners is the only origin, source of merit, and cause of blessing in this covenant. In contrast with the Covenant of Works, in which man had to earn eternal life through his own obedience, the Covenant of Grace freely gives eternal life upon the basis of Christ's perfect obedience. The two covenants pertaining to man's eternal state are named according to how the benefits of the covenant, communion with God and eternal life, were to be received; the first by the *works* of Adam, the second by *grace* as a gift from God upon the merits of Christ.

To **redeem** and save sinners through a new covenant, all God's attributes, including His truth, righteousness, and justice, must be fully satisfied. Therefore, the Covenant of Grace had to perfectly replace the Covenant of Works. A sinless covenant head must replace sinful Adam and the same test of obedience must be passed, the same penalty paid, and the same promise earned.

In the Covenant of Grace, the Lord Jesus Christ was willing from eternity and came in time to perfectly pass the test of obedience as Covenant Head of His children, pay the penalty for their

For God so loved the world, that He gave His only begotten Son, that whosoever believeth in Him, should not perish, but have everlasting life.
— John 3:16

For the wages of sin is death; but the gift of God is eternal life through Jesus Christ our Lord.
— Romans 6:23

But where sin abounded, grace did much more abound.
— Romans 5:20b

But God commendeth His love toward us, in that, while we were yet sinners, Christ died for us.
— Romans 5:8

But not as the offence, so also is the free gift. For if through the offence of one many be dead, much more the grace of God, and the gift by grace, which is by one Man, Jesus Christ, hath abounded unto many.
— Romans 5:15

● **Redeem** — To buy back; to pay the full price for; to purchase

The blood of Jesus Christ His Son cleanseth us from all sin.
— I John 1:7b

Forasmuch as ye know that ye were not redeemed with corruptible things, as silver and gold, from your vain conversation received by tradition from your fathers;
But with the precious blood of Christ, as of a lamb without blemish and without spot.
— I Peter 1:18-19

sin, and earn their right to the promise of eternal life. How the same principles of representation by covenant head, testing, penalty, and promise apply to both covenants is shown more clearly in the charts on the following page.

? To be saved, why is it necessary to experience my misery, death in Adam, and being cut off from the Covenant of Works; as well as experiencing my deliverance, life in Christ, and being implanted in the Covenant of Grace? Why are both necessary?

Rev. John Newton, a well-known minister in England, when his memory was nearly gone before death, used to tell others, "I forget much, but two things I have never forgotten. First, that I am a great sinner, but secondly, that Jesus Christ is a great Savior."

When Rev. M'Laren was on his deathbed, one of his fellow ministers in Scotland visited him and asked, "What are you doing, brother?"
He answered, "I will tell you. I am gathering together all my prayers, all my sermons, all my good and ill deeds; and I am going to throw them all overboard, to swim to glory on the plank of free grace."

What personal, saving knowledge regarding both the Covenant of Works and the Covenant of Grace did these men reveal on their deathbeds? How does the statement "Death in Adam and life in Christ" refer to these two covenants?

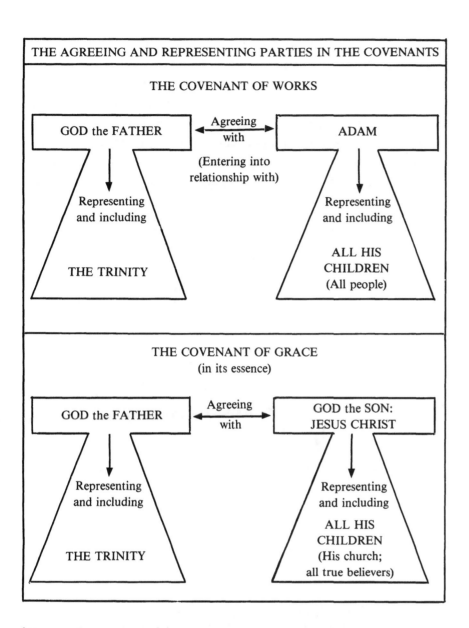

THE AGREEING AND REPRESENTING PARTIES IN THE COVENANTS

THE COVENANT OF WORKS

GOD the FATHER ←Agreeing with→ ADAM

(Entering into relationship with)

Representing and including

THE TRINITY

Representing and including

ALL HIS CHILDREN (All people)

THE COVENANT OF GRACE
(in its essence)

GOD the FATHER ←Agreeing with→ GOD the SON: JESUS CHRIST

Representing and including

THE TRINITY

Representing and including

ALL HIS CHILDREN (His church; all true believers)

THE RESULTS UPON THOSE INCLUDED WITH EACH COVENANT HEAD

COVENANT	COVENANT OF WORKS	COVENANT OF GRACE
Representative head	Adam	Jesus Christ
Work accomplished	Fell into sin	Perfectly fulfilled God's law
Result	Death	Eternal life
Those included with representative head	All his children; all people	All His children; His church; all true believers
Principle upon which result is applied to others	Covenant head representation	Covenant Head representation

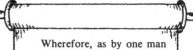

Wherefore, as by one man sin entered into the world, and death by sin; and so death passed upon all men, for that all have sinned.

(For until the law sin was in the world: but sin is not imputed when there is no law. Nevertheless death reigned from Adam to Moses even over them that had not sinned after the similitude of Adam's transgression, who is the figure of Him that was to come.

But not as the offence, so also is the free gift. For if through the offence of one many be dead, much more the grace of God, and the gift by grace, which is by one Man, Jesus Christ, hath abounded unto many.

And not as it was by one that sinned, so is the gift: for the judgment was by one to condemnation, but the free gift is of many offences unto justification.

For if by one man's offence death reigned by one; much more they which receive abundance of grace and of the gift of righteousness shall reign in life by one, Jesus Christ.)

Therefore as by the offence of one judgment came upon all men to condemnation; even so by the righteousness of One the free gift came upon all men unto justification of life.

For as by one man's disobedience many were made sinners, so by the obedience of One shall many be made righteous.

Moreover the law entered, that the offence might abound. But where sin abounded, grace did much more abound:

That as sin hath reigned unto death, even so might grace reign through righteousness unto eternal life by Jesus Christ our Lord.

— Romans 5:12-21

When referring to God's salvation of a sinner, what is meant by the expressions that salvation is:
— Thought by God the Father?
— Bought by God the Son?
— Wrought by God the Holy Spirit?
How would these three truths relate to the Covenant of Grace?

Have you seriously thought about the wonderful love and grace that God shows when He saves a sinner? God the Father was willing to plan a way of salvation for elected sinners; Jesus was willing to die to earn eternal life for His church; and God the Holy Spirit was willing to work salvation in the hearts of His chosen! God provided complete deliverance for sinners who did not love Him, but were His enemies! Have you experienced something of the richness and wonderfulness of God's grace? Do you need God and His free grace in your life?

A young boy, one from a very poor family of seven children, met with an accident and was taken to the hospital. After he was made as comfortable as possible, a nurse brought him a large glass of milk. At home, half a glass of milk had to be shared between three or four children. Glancing at the others in his hospital room, the hungry and thirsty boy asked the nurse, "How deep may I drink?"

The nurse, with tears filling her eyes, and a lump gathering in her throat, kindly replied, "You may drink it all, dear!"

To poor sinners, hungering and thirsting after God's favor and communion, why are the truths of God's Covenant of Grace overwhelming? To "drink deeply" of these truths seems too good to be true. Why?

Why is the wonder of received grace more amazing to a convinced sinner than the rich care was to this poor boy? Why are the truths of the Covenant of Grace overwhelming to needy sinners?

330

Speaking of salvation by grace, a minister has been heard to say: "It is good that man cannot save himself; for if a man could only work his own way to heaven, you would never hear the last of it. Why, if a man happens to get a little ahead of his fellows and scrapes a few thousand dollars together, you'll hear him boast of his accomplishments. I've heard so much of this sort of talk that I am tired of the whole business. I am glad that through all eternity in heaven we will never hear anyone bragging of how he worked his way to get there."

How does salvation through the Covenant of Grace do away with all boasting on the part of man? How is God exalted to the highest and man abased to the lowest in the Covenant of *Grace*?

? How does the Covenant of *Grace* exalt God to the highest and abase man to the lowest?

The Covenant of Grace includes the following two aspects:

1. The Covenant of Grace *from eternity* (also referred to as the "Counsel of Peace" or the "Covenant of Redemption")

2. The Covenant of Grace *in time*.

? Read Ephesians 2:8-9: "For by grace are ye saved through faith; and that not of yourselves: it is the gift of God: Not of works, lest any man should boast."

How do these verses teach a practical truth of, and outcome from, the doctrine of the Covenant of *Grace*?

The Covenant of Grace from eternity (or the Counsel of Peace or Covenant of Redemption) refers to the agreement from eternity within God Himself to save His elect church through Christ its Covenant Head. In this agreement, God the Father represented and included the entire Trinity and God the Son represented and included His entire church (all His elect children or true believers).

The Covenant of Grace in time refers to the performance or execution of this agreement in time; the actual saving of the church through Christ its Covenant Head.

Being born as children of wrath, God's elect are ingrafted into the Covenant of Grace in time by regeneration through which they are adopted to be children of God and actually receive the rich benefits this covenant relationship includes.

> Elect according to the foreknowledge of God the Father, through sanctification of the Spirit, unto obedience and sprinkling of the blood of Jesus Christ: Grace unto you, and peace, be multiplied.
>
> Blessed be the God and Father of our Lord Jesus Christ, which according to His abundant mercy hath begotten us again unto a lively hope by the resurrection of Jesus Christ from the dead.
> — I Peter 1:2-3
>
> And you hath He quickened, who were dead in trespasses and sins.
> — Ephesians 2:1

For we are His workmanship, created in Christ Jesus unto good works, which God hath before ordained that we should walk in them.
— Ephesians 2:10

Having made known unto us the mystery of His will, according to His good pleasure which He hath purposed in Himself:
That in the dispensation of the fulness of times He might gather together in one all things in Christ, both which are in heaven, and which are on earth; even in Him;
In whom also we have obtained an inheritance, being predestinated according to the purpose of Him who worketh all things after the counsel of His own will.
— Ephesians 1:9-11

According to the eternal purpose which He purposed in Christ Jesus our Lord.
— Ephesians 3:11

In hope of eternal life, which God, that cannot lie, promised before the world began.
— Titus 1:2

But with the precious blood of Christ, as of a lamb without blemish and without spot;
Who verily was foreordained before the foundation of the world, but was manifest in these last times for you.
— I Peter 1:19-20

Therefore as by the offence of one, judgment came upon all men to condemnation; even so by the righteousness of One the free gift came upon all men unto justification of life.
For as by one man's disobedience many were made sinners; so by the obedience of One shall many be made righteous.
— Romans 5:18-19

The basis for the Covenant of Grace being established from eternity rests upon the scriptural teachings displayed in the following chart:

THE BIBLICAL BASIS FOR THE COVENANT OF GRACE *FROM ETERNITY*	
Scriptural Teachings	**Example References**
1. Scripture speaks of God's plan of redemption being included in the *eternal decree* or counsel of God.	According as He hath chosen us in Him before the foundation of the world, that we should be holy and without blame before Him in love; Having predestinated us unto the adoption of children by Jesus Christ to Himself, according to the good pleasure of His will. — Ephesians 1:4-5 Who hath saved us, and called us with an holy calling, not according to our works, but according to His own purpose and grace, which was given us in Christ Jesus before the world began. — II Timothy 1:9
2. *From eternity, the elements of a covenant were present,* such as agreeing parties, conditions to be met, and a promise.	*Agreeing Parties* I will declare the decree: the LORD hath said unto Me, Thou art My Son; this day have I begotten Thee. — Psalm 2:7 *Conditions* Then said I, Lo, I come: in the volume of the book it is written of Me, I delight to do Thy will, O My God: yea, Thy law is within My heart. — Psalm 40:7-8 *Promise* Ask of Me, and I shall give Thee the heathen for Thy inheritance, and the uttermost parts of the earth for Thy possession. — Psalm 2:8
3. *Christ's* speaking repeatedly of a *commission* which He previously received from His Father, and had come upon this earth to fulfill.	For I came down from heaven, not to do Mine own will, but the will of Him that sent Me. And this is the Father's will which hath sent Me, that of all which He hath given Me I should lose nothing, but should raise it up again at the last day. — John 6:38-39
4. *Christ* is clearly spoken of *as the second Covenant Head,* salvation through Him was promised from Paradise.	For as in Adam all die, even so in Christ shall all be made alive. — I Corinthians 15:22 And I will put enmity between thee and the woman, and between thy seed and her seed; it shall bruise thy head, and thou shalt bruise His heel. — Genesis 3:15
5. References which speak of the *Savior being appointed to work through God's covenant.*	I the LORD have called Thee in righteousness, and will hold Thine hand, and will keep Thee, and give Thee for a covenant of the people, for a light of the Gentiles. — Isaiah 42:6 I have made a covenant with My chosen, I have sworn unto David My servant. — Psalm 89:3

332

The Covenant of Grace from eternity is closely connected to God's decree of election, but the two are not identical and should be distinguished. The decree of election determined *who* are to be saved — their *number*; the Covenant of Grace from eternity (the Counsel of Peace), determined *how* the elect were to be saved — the *way*.

The Covenant of Grace in time is revealed throughout the Bible. In the following examples, Scripture speaks of the performance of God's plan of salvation in time, through Christ, in the hearts of His children, as a gracious covenant relationship:

? Not to believe in God's Covenant of Grace *from eternity* would be an insult to God, to both His attributes and decree. Why?

THE BIBLICAL BASIS FOR THE COVENANT OF GRACE *IN TIME*

And I will establish My covenant between Me and thee and thy seed after thee in their generations for an everlasting covenant, to be a God unto thee, and to thy seed after thee.
— Genesis 17:7

And God said, Sarah thy wife shall bear thee a son indeed; and thou shalt call his name Isaac: and I will establish My covenant with him for an everlasting covenant, and with his seed after him.
— Genesis 17:19

For this is as the waters of Noah unto Me: for as I have sworn that the waters of Noah should no more go over the earth; so have I sworn that I would not be wroth with thee, nor rebuke thee. For the mountains shall depart, and the hills be removed; but My kindness shall not depart from thee, neither shall the covenant of My peace be removed, saith the LORD that hath mercy on thee.
— Isaiah 54:9-10

Moreover I will make a covenant of peace with them; it shall be an everlasting covenant with them; and I will place them, and multiply them, and will set My sanctuary in the midst of them for evermore.
— Ezekiel 37:26

For this is the covenant that I will make with the house of Israel after those days, saith the Lord; I will put My laws into their mind, and write them in their hearts: and I will be to them a God, and they shall be to Me a people.
— Hebrews 8:10

And for this cause He is the Mediator of the New Testament, that by means of death, for the redemption of the transgressions that were under the first testament, they which are called might receive the promise of eternal inheritance.
— Hebrews 9:15

From eternity, the Lord Jesus Christ agreed to serve, and in time He perfectly fulfilled all requirements as second Covenant Head and Representative Head of His church. In this position, He is named the Head, Mediator, Surety, Minister, and Testator of the Covenant of Grace, as the chart on the following page demonstrates:

? What rich security is lost by those who deny the truth that nothing depends upon man but all depends upon Christ, as Head of the Covenant of Grace?

The Titles of Christ's Official Position in the Covenant of Grace		
Title	**Meaning**	**Example Text**
1. Head	The representative of His children in the Covenant of Grace as Adam was representative of his children in the Covenant of Works	For as by one man's disobedience many were made sinners, so by the obedience of One shall many be made righteous. — Romans 5:19
2. Mediator	The One standing between a holy God and the guilty sinners who are included in Him, in the Covenant of Grace	And to Jesus the Mediator of the new covenant, and to the blood of sprinkling, that speaketh better things than that of Abel. — Hebrews 12:24
3. Surety	The One who obligated Himself and guaranteed to pay the full price for the debts of His elect church	By so much was Jesus made a surety of a better testament. — Hebrews 7:22
4. Minister	The servant of God serving in God's presence and performing all that is needed for the benefit of His people	Now of the things which we have spoken this is the sum: We have such an high priest, who is set on the right hand of the throne of the Majesty in the heavens; A minister of the sanctuary, and of the true tabernacle, which the Lord pitched, and not man. — Hebrews 8:1-2
5. Testator	The life-giving Savior, who grants rich benefits through His death to all that are included in Him in the Covenant of Grace.	For where a testament is, there must also of necessity be the death of the testator. For a testament is of force after men are dead: otherwise it is of no strength at all while the testator liveth. — Hebrews 9:16-17

The second covenant is a covenant *of grace* for all those represented by, and included with, Christ. But for Jesus Christ it was a covenant of *works*. He had to earn the right to eternal life for His church through perfectly obeying God's law. Christ received eternal life for His people, not as a free gift of grace, but as a reward for His faithful obedience, for His perfect *work*. Upon the basis of His fully-earned salvation, Christ freely gives the gift of eternal life to His church, as a gift of *grace*.

Jesus not only had to earn eternal life for His church through perfectly fulfilling God's law (Christ's active obedience), but He had to also willingly suffer and die a three-fold death to pay the full price for man's sin and his breaking of the Covenant of Works (Christ's passive obedience). The *work* of bearing the full punishment of sin had to be accomplished by Jesus Christ in order for the *grace* of the forgiveness of sins to be freely given to sinners.

On Dr. Adam Clarke's tomb in London, the figure of a candle completely consumed in its socket is engraved with the words, "In giving light to others, he has been consumed." A beautiful confession — why? While this statement can be partially true when referring to various persons, it is totally and infinitely true only when speaking of Christ.

When Jesus Christ was consumed by God's wrath against sin and was dying on the cross, we read that the people, the chief priests, scribes, and elders mocked Him, saying, "He saved others; Himself He cannot save" (Matthew 27:42a).

In a manner in which these mockers never realized, their statement expressed a **profound** truth. In order to save others, he could not save Himself — why not? How are the two parts of this statement directly related? If He had chosen to save Himself, what would have happened to "the others," to His church?

As Covenant Head of His children, He *could not* save Himself. How is this meaning different from that which the mockers of Jesus had in view?

? Why does a sinner need both Christ's active and passive obedience? Which delivers from hell? Which opens heaven? How is Jesus Christ a perfect Substitute and complete Savior for His church as the Head in the Covenant of Grace?

● **Profound** — Significant; intense; deep

Trinitarian— Referring to the Trinity; three divine Persons in one Godhead

Each of the three divine Persons in the Trinity is active in the Covenant of Grace. The Covenant's three-fold **Trinitarian** and gracious nature is revealed in the following breakdown:

The Three-Fold Trinitarian and Gracious Nature of the Covenant of Grace		
Divine Person	**Gracious Work**	**Example Verse**
1. God the Father	*Thought* of the *gracious* plan of salvation for His church by means of a perfectly righteous Substitute; one who was both God and man.	But when the fulness of the time was come, God sent forth His Son made of a woman, made under the law, To redeem them that were under the law, that we might receive the adoption of sons. — Galatians 4:4-5
2. God the Son	*Bought* salvation for His Church through *graciously* offering Himself as the perfect human sacrifice for sin and fulfiller of God's law.	Neither by the blood of goats and calves, but by His own blood He entered in once into the holy place, having obtained eternal redemption for us. — Hebrews 9:12
3. God the Holy Spirit	*Wrought*, or works, salvation *graciously* in the hearts of His church, personally applying the rich benefits they have in Christ.	Not by works of righteousness which we have done, but according to His mercy He saved us, by the washing of regeneration, and renewing of the Holy Ghost. — Titus 3:5

God's plan of salvation and Christ's **redemption** are both perfect and eternal works; therefore, His Covenant of Grace is eternal and unbreakable. Scripture testifies of this in numerous places.

? Read I Peter 1:2: "Elect according to the foreknowledge of God the Father, through sanctification of the Spirit, unto obedience and sprinkling of the blood of Jesus Christ: Grace unto you, and peace, be multiplied."

How can the three-fold gracious work of the Trinity, as specified in the chart on this page, be clearly seen in this verse?

● **Redemption** — The act of Christ's purchasing, of paying the full price for, the sins of His church

---

THE COVENANT OF GRACE IS ETERNAL AND UNBREAKABLE

And God said, Sarah thy wife shall bear thee a son indeed; and thou shalt call his name Isaac: and I will establish My covenant with him for *an everlasting covenant,* and with his seed after him.
— Genesis 17:19

Although my house be not so with God; yet He hath made with me *an everlasting covenant,* ordered in all things, and sure: for this is all my salvation, and all my desire, although He make it not to grow.
— II Samuel 23:5

Now the God of peace, that brought again from the dead our Lord Jesus, that great Shepherd of the sheep, through the blood of *the everlasting covenant.*
— Hebrews 13:20

Nevertheless My lovingkindness will I not utterly take from him, nor suffer My faithfulness to fail.

My covenant will I not break, nor alter the thing that is gone out of My lips.
— Psalm 89:33-34

Moreover I will make a covenant of peace with them; it shall be *an everlasting covenant* with them: and I will place them, and multiply them, and will set My sanctuary in the midst of them forevermore.
— Ezekiel 37:26

For this is as the waters of Noah unto Me: for as I have sworn that the waters of Noah should no more go over the earth; so have I sworn that I would not be wroth with thee, nor rebuke thee.
For the mountains shall depart, and the hills be removed; but My kindness shall not depart from thee, *neither shall the covenant of My peace be removed,* saith the LORD that hath mercy on thee.
— Isaiah 54:9-10

As in all covenants, the Covenant of Grace not only includes agreeing parties, God the Father and God the Son (and in Christ, all His church), but it also contains *requirements* or conditions to be met, and *promises* or rewards upon its fulfillment.

The *promises*, or rewards, of the Covenant of Grace center upon Christ and in Him are graciously given to all His church. The saved are included in the promises of the Covenant of Grace through Christ Jesus their Covenant Head. In Christ, God gives Himself and all the promises of salvation — the forgiveness of sin, the right to eternal life, and eternal communion with Him — to His church.

> For the Son of God, Jesus Christ, who was preached among you by us, even by me and Silvanus and Timotheus, was not yea and nay, but in Him was yea.
>
> For all the promises of God in Him are yea, and in Him Amen, unto the glory of God by us.
>
> Now He which stablisheth us with you in Christ, and hath anointed us, is God.
>
> — II Corinthians 1:19-21

The *requirements*, or conditions, of the Covenant of Grace also center in Jesus Christ. To meet the requirements of the Covenant, Jesus had to take upon Himself the human nature, perfectly fulfill and obey God's law, and apply His merits to the salvation of His church.

Scripture also speaks of related "requirements" or "conditions" of repentance, faith, and obedience to be met by those that will be saved. When speaking of these "requirements," however, we must emphasize that there is not one requirement that sinners, including regenerated sinners, can fulfill of themselves. All the "requirements" of the saved are actually benefits that Christ earned and freely gives to them. Christ not only merited, but also applies all the benefits of the Covenant of Grace to His people. These benefits include all their "requirements" — also repentance, faith, and obedience.

> But as many as received Him, to them gave He power to become the sons of God, even to them that believe on His name:
>
> Which were born, not of blood, nor of the will of the flesh, nor of the will of man, but of God.
>
> — John 1:12-13
>
> Now then we are ambassadors for Christ, as though God did beseech you by us: we pray you in Christ's stead, be ye reconciled to God.
>
> For He hath made Him to be sin for us, who knew no sin; that we might be made the righteousness of God in Him.
>
> — II Corinthians 5:20-21

To deny that all conditions in the Covenant of Grace are earned and given by Christ would make the Covenant of Grace a second Covenant of Works. Man's salvation would then again become dependent upon man and his works of fulfilling the covenant's requirements. As fallen sinners, from where would the elect obtain faith and obedience if these were not freely given to them by Christ as benefits of the covenant?

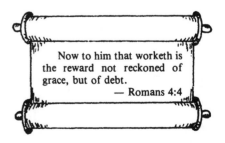

> Now to him that worketh is the reward not reckoned of grace, but of debt.
>
> — Romans 4:4

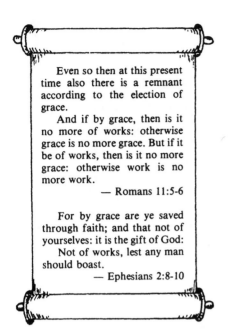

Even so then at this present time also there is a remnant according to the election of grace.

And if by grace, then is it no more of works: otherwise grace is no more grace. But if it be of works, then is it no more grace: otherwise work is no more work.

— Romans 11:5-6

For by grace are ye saved through faith; and that not of yourselves: it is the gift of God:

Not of works, lest any man should boast.

— Ephesians 2:8-10

Scripture speaks of conditions to be met to teach us that repentance, faith, and obedience are necessary in the lives of those who will be saved. But these conditions are not such that they must first be fulfilled by a person's own efforts before they can be included in the covenant. This teaching would return the second covenant to the works of man. No; repentance, faith, and obedience are earned and graciously given to the elect by Christ. By means of His Spirit, He freely plants and exercises these inward-working graces in the hearts of the saved, converting their wills, that the corresponding outward-working fruits are evidenced in their lives.

In this manner, Scripture teaches that there are "requirements" or "conditions" which must be found in the lives of the saved, and yet, these "requirements" are actually "benefits" that are graciously earned by, and applied to, the hearts of the elect by Jesus Christ their Covenant Head.

? Why is the truth of, and the security from, trusting in God's grace undermined by the teaching that man must *produce* instead of *receive* the grace to bring forth repentance, faith, and obedience?

Augustine once wrote the following prayer, "Lord, give what Thou commandest, and then command what Thou wilt."

How does this statement express the truth of the Covenant of Grace, that the "conditions" required from those included in the covenant are actually benefits graciously given to them by God through their Covenant Head, Jesus Christ?

Rev. Brakel wrote the following, "How desirable, how firm is this covenant in which *all the heavy conditions* are laid upon the Surety, and *all the blessings* come to the members of the covenant by the Mediator Jesus Christ, in whom all the promises are yea and amen."

What serious error will be the result from teaching that man, from himself, needing to meet the requirements of a "conditional covenant" or "conditional gospel"?

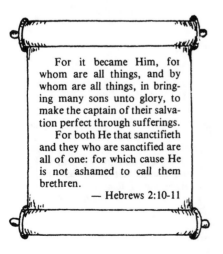

For it became Him, for whom are all things, and by whom are all things, in bringing many sons unto glory, to make the captain of their salvation perfect through sufferings.

For both He that sanctifieth and they who are sanctified are all of one: for which cause He is not ashamed to call them brethren.

— Hebrews 2:10-11

The requirements and promises of the Covenant of Grace between God the Father and the Son (and in Him His elect) are specified in the following charts. Note how that the corresponding "requirements" of God's church are actually gracious, God-given benefits, freely granted to them through Christ their Covenant Head:

THE REQUIREMENTS OF THE COVENANT OF GRACE

The Earning of the Covenant's Benefits by Christ	The Applying of the Covenant's Benefits by the Spirit of Christ
REQUIREMENTS OF GOD THE FATHER FROM THE SON AS HEAD OF THE COVENANT	CORRESPONDING "REQUIREMENTS" FROM THOSE INCLUDED IN THE COVENANT (Gracious benefits given to them through their Covenant Head)

Of Grace for Faith

1. That Christ would take upon Himself the human nature by being born of a woman into this sinful world, to represent His church.

   > But when the fulness of the time was come, God sent forth His Son, made of a woman, made under the law, To redeem them that were under the law, that we might receive the adoption of sons.
   > — Galatians 4:4-5

Through Christ, graciously given the benefit...

1. To believe in Christ as the true Immanuel (the God-man); as God who took upon Himself the human nature to represent them.

   > He that believeth on the Son hath everlasting life: and he that believeth not the Son shall not see life; but the wrath of God abideth on him.
   > — John 3:36

2. That Christ would place Himself under God's law in order to fully pay the penalty for sin (through His passive obedience) and to completely merit eternal life (through His active obedience) for His church.

   > Think not that I am come to destroy the law, or the prophets: I am not come to destroy, but to fulfill.
   > — Matthew 5:17

Through Christ, graciously given the benefit...

2. To believe and trust, by faith, in the finished work of Christ, both in the payment for their sins and in the earning of their right to eternal life through His perfect work (their justification through Christ).

   > For what saith the Scripture? Abraham believed God, and it was counted unto him for righteousness. Now to him that worketh is the reward not reckoned of grace, but of debt. But to him that worketh not, but believeth on Him that justifieth the ungodly, his faith is counted for righteousness.
   > — Romans 4:3-5

Of Grace for Repentance and Obedience

3. That Christ would apply His merits to His church; that through the applying power of the Holy Spirit, He would regenerate; convert; grant faith to, and work holiness in them; and preserve them in the dedication of their lives to God forever.

   > Howbeit when He, the Spirit of truth, is come, He will guide you into all truth: for He shall not speak of Himself; but whatsoever He shall hear, that shall He speak: and He will show you things to come. He shall glorify Me: for He shall receive of Mine, and shall show it unto you.
   > — John 16:13-14

Through Christ, graciously given the benefit...

3. To repent from sin and consecrate themselves to God, by the power of the Holy Spirit working within them, to wholeheartedly serve God in loving obedience (their sanctification through Christ).

   > Follow peace with all men, and holiness, without which no man shall see the Lord.
   > — Hebrews 12:14

THE PROMISES OF THE COVENANT OF GRACE

THE PROMISES OF GOD THE FATHER TO THE SON AS HEAD OF THE COVENANT		THE CORRESPONDING PROMISES TO THOSE INCLUDED IN THE COVENANT THROUGH THEIR COVENANT HEAD
1. That the Father would prepare a sinless body for Christ, and grant Him the anointing and supporting strength of His Spirit to conquer Satan (Genesis 3:15).	Through Christ...	1. Grace and faith are promised to His church enabling them to believe and trust in Christ (the God-man Savior) and be delivered from Satan's power (Ephesians 1:5-7).
2. That the Father would deliver Christ from the power of death and grant Him eternal life (Psalm 16:10-11).	Through Christ...	2. The forgiveness of sins, resurrection from death, and the right to eternal life are promised to the elect (Hebrews 8:12).
3. That the Father would provide Christ with a seed, a church, which no man could number for multitude from all nations on earth (Psalm 22:27).	Through Christ...	3. The communion of saints with Christ, as their Head, and with each other, as His body, are promised to true believers (II Corinthians 6:16b).
4. That the Father would enable Christ to send forth the Holy Spirit to regenerate, instruct, sanctify, and preserve His church that all will be saved and none be lost (John 6:37,39).	Through Christ...	4. The Holy Spirit is promised to God's children to regenerate, work repentance in, instruct, sanctify, and preserve them forever (Ezekiel 36:26-27).
5. That the Father would grant Christ the rule over all things, both natural and spiritual, to the glory of God (Psalm 110:1).	Through Christ...	5. All things present and future, for both natural and spiritual life, are promised to God's people (I Corinthians 3:21b-23).
6. That the Father would exalt Christ to His own right hand and grant His church to eternally be with Him, to witness the glory of God (John 17:24).	Through Christ...	6. The saved receive the blessings of heaven: to enjoy perfect communion with God, to live without sin, and glorify Him forever (Revelation 21:3).

340

In summary, the Covenant of Grace stands unbreakably and eternally sure in God. All its requirements are fully satisfied in Christ. His people receive all the benefits they stand in need of, both for time and eternity, grace here and eternal life with God hereafter, through their eternal Covenant Head, the Lord Jesus Christ. Everything pertaining to man's entire salvation is contained in the wonderful Covenant of Grace!

> Nevertheless the foundation of God standeth sure, having this seal, The Lord knoweth them that are His.
> — II Timothy 2:19a
>
> For I am persuaded, that neither death, nor life, nor angels, nor principalities, nor powers, nor things present, nor things to come,
> Nor height, nor depth, nor any other creature, shall be able to separate us from the love of God, which is in Christ Jesus our Lord.
> — Romans 8:38-39

A certain man, walking by a large cage of imprisoned birds at an open market, asked the surprised owner the price for purchasing the entire cage of birds. To everyone's astonishment, he bought all the birds.

The people were even more amazed when he then threw open the cage door and let them all fly away!

How did these birds become this man's property? Once the full price for them had been paid and they were his possession, why did he have every right to graciously free them?

In the Covenant of Grace, Jesus Christ agreed to pay the full price for the sins of His people. After payment, to whom do they belong? What similar comparisons can you draw between this story and the Covenant of Grace? How are they different?

As we have seen, the Bible speaks of God's Covenant of Grace as eternal and unbreakable and established only with His elect church, His spiritual seed. However, Scripture also speaks in several places of a relationship to the covenant as being breakable and of the natural seed of the church (all the circumcised or baptized), as being included in a covenant relationship with God. The following charts provide several example texts of both of these scriptural teachings.

? To redeem His guilty, sinful children, what price was Jesus required to pay? Why?

THE COVENANT OF GRACE: BREAKABLE OR UNBREAKABLE?

UNBREAKABLE RELATIONSHIP		BREAKABLE RELATIONSHIP	
And God said, Sarah thy wife shall bear thee a son indeed; and thou shalt call his name Isaac: and I will establish My covenant with him for an everlasting covenant, and with his seed after him. — Genesis 17:19	Moreover I will make a covenant of peace with them; it shall be an everlasting covenant with them: and I will place them, and multiply them, and will set My sanctuary in the midst of them forevermore. — Ezekiel 37:26	And the uncircumcised man child whose flesh of his foreskin is not circumcised, that soul shall be cut off from his people; he hath broken My covenant. — Genesis 17:14	Set the trumpet to thy mouth. He shall come as an eagle against the house of the LORD, because they have transgressed My covenant, and trespassed against My law. — Hosea 8:1
Brethren, I speak after the manner of men; Though it be but a man's covenant, yet if it be confirmed, no man disannulleth, or addeth thereto. — Galatians 3:15 If his children forsake My law, and walk not in My judgments; Nevertheless My lovingkindness will I not utterly take from him, nor suffer My faithfulness to fail. My covenant will I not break, nor alter the thing that is gone out of My lips. — Psalm 89: 30,33-34	For the mountains shall depart, and the hills be removed; but My kindness shall not depart from thee, neither shall the covenant of My peace be removed, saith the LORD that hath mercy on thee. — Isaiah 54:10 Now the God of peace, that brought again from the dead our Lord Jesus, that great Shepherd of the sheep, through the blood of the everlasting covenant. — Hebrews 13:20	But they like men have transgressed the covenant: there have they dealt treacherously against Me. — Hosea 6:7 Not according to the covenant that I made with their fathers in the day that I took them by the hand to bring them out of the land of Egypt; which My covenant they brake, although I was an husband unto them, saith the LORD. — Jeremiah 31:32	But the children of the kingdom shall be cast out into outer darkness: there shall be weeping and gnashing of teeth. — Matthew 8:12 I am the vine, ye are the branches: He that abideth in Me, and I in him, the same bringeth forth much fruit: for without Me ye can do nothing. If a man abide not in Me, he is cast forth as a branch, and is withered; and men gather them, and cast them into the fire, and they are burned. — John 15:5-6

THE COVENANT OF GRACE: INCLUDES ONLY THE SPIRITUAL SEED OR ALSO ALL THE NATURAL (BAPTIZED) SEED?

ONLY THE SPIRITUAL (ELECT) SEED		ALL THE BAPTIZED (CIRCUMCISED) SEED	
They answered and said unto him, Abraham is our father. Jesus said unto them, If ye were Abraham's children, ye would do the works of Abraham. — John 8:39 For this is the covenant that I will make with the house of Israel after those days, saith the Lord; I will put My laws into their mind, and write them in their hearts: and I will be to them a God, and they shall be to me a people. — Hebrews 8:10 For they are not all Israel, which are of Israel: Neither, because they are the seed of Abraham, are they all children: but, In Isaac shall thy seed be called. That is, They which are the children of the flesh, these are not the children of God: but the children of the promise are counted for the seed. — Romans 9:6b-8	For in Isaac shall thy seed be called. — Genesis 21:12b For he is not a Jew, which is one outwardly: neither is that circumcision, which is outward in the flesh: But he is a Jew, which is one inwardly; and circumcision is that of the heart, in the spirit, and not in the letter; whose praise is not of men, but of God. — Romans 2:28-29 And think not to say within yourselves, We have Abraham to our father: for I say unto you, that God is able of these stones to raise up children unto Abraham. And now also the axe is laid unto the root of the trees: therefore every tree which bringeth not forth good fruit is hewn down, and cast into the fire. — Matthew 3:9-10	And I will establish My covenant between Me and thee and thy seed after thee in their generations for an everlasting covenant, to be a God unto thee, and to thy seed after thee. And God said unto Abraham, Thou shalt keep My covenant therefore, thou, and thy seed after thee in their generations. This is My covenant, which ye shall keep, between Me and you and thy seed after thee; Every man child among you shall be circumcised. — Genesis 17:7,9-10 And thou shalt say unto Pharoah, Thus saith the LORD, Israel is My son, even My firstborn: And I say unto thee, Let My son go, that he may serve Me: and if thou refuse to let him go, behold I will slay thy son, even thy firstborn. — Exodus 4:22-23	Ye are the children of the LORD your God: ye shall not cut yourselves, nor make any baldness between your eyes for the dead. For thou art an holy people unto the LORD thy God, and the LORD hath chosen thee to be a peculiar people unto Himself, above all the nations that are upon the earth. — Deuteronomy 14:1-2 Which My covenant they brake, although I was an husband unto them, saith the LORD. — Jeremiah 31:32b And the woman which hath an husband that believeth not, and if he be pleased to dwell with her, let her not leave him. For the unbelieving husband is sanctified by the wife, and the unbelieving wife is sanctified by the husband: else were your children unclean; but now are they holy. — I Corinthians 7:13-14

342

What is meant by these seemingly contradictory verses of Scripture? Is the Covenant of Grace unbreakable or breakable? Does the covenant include only the elect church or all the baptized church? The difficulties in trying to **reconcile** these apparently contradictory questions have led some to divide the Covenant of Grace into two different covenants with differing covenant heads. They believe that Scripture speaks of three distinct covenants pertaining to man's salvation instead of two. This has added a third complicated question to this matter — are there two or three covenants pertaining to man's salvation spoken of in Scripture?

These three questions have led to different views and explanations of the Covenant of Grace in various church denominations. For instance, the Baptist church denominations speak only of an unbreakable Covenant of Grace which includes only the saved church. Therefore, only saved persons may be baptized and join the church after making a personal confession of true saving faith. While clearly emphasizing the "unbreakable" and "elect church" groups of text, this view does not explain the "breakable" and "circumcised" or "baptized" listings of scriptural verses.

Each of the Reformed church denominations have included both groups of apparently contradicting texts in their explanations of the Covenant of Grace, but each denomination has explained them in a different manner. These differing explanations of the Covenant and the resulting differences regarding how to properly view those who are related to the Covenant (the baptized and the elect), have produced the major doctrinal differences to be found among the Reformed denominations.

The following three questions, with the fourth related one, become four important questions regarding the possible relationships of church members to the Covenant of Grace:

1. Are there two or three covenants pertaining to man's salvation?

2. Is the Covenant of Grace breakable or unbreakable, or both?

3. Are all the natural (baptized) seed or only the spiritual (elect) seed of the church included in a Covenant of Grace relationship with God, or both?

4. How are the natural (baptized) seed to be distinguished from the spiritual (elect) seed of the church?

● **Reconcile** — To remove apparent differences and formulate a consistent, harmonious, and agreeable solution

? Are the scriptural verses on the preceding page contradictory? How can you know that they are not? What needs to be done in all cases where initial apparent contradictions appear in the Word of God?

Arminius — Jacobus Arminius (1560-1609) was a professor of theology in the University of Leiden in the Netherlands. Arminius taught that natural man had both the freedom and ability to believe in, and choose for, God from himself. He disagreed with the doctrines contained in the five points of Calvinism.

? Why is it incorrect to teach that Christ died for all people in the same manner?

Question 1: Are there two or three covenants pertaining to man's salvation? **Arminius** was the first to teach a three-covenant view in church history. He presented the Covenant of Works with the same agreeing parties and representation as do all Reformed Churches:

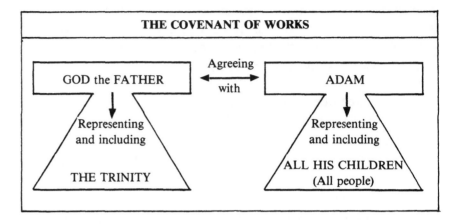

To Arminius, however, the Covenant of Redemption (made in eternity) and the Covenant of Grace (formed in time) were two different covenants, both having different agreeing parties and representations. His covenant teaching can be pictured as follows:

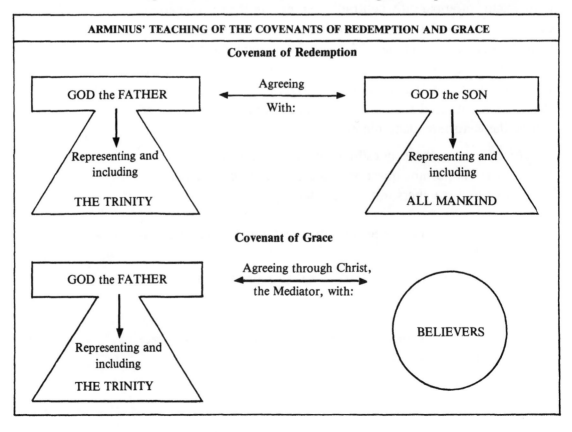

Arminius introduced "free will" or "decisional regeneration" in place of "free grace" or "Spirit-worked regeneration" as the manner of salvation. The term "free will" refers to the will of natural man having both the freedom and ability to choose the good or bad, God or self, love or sin. Salvation depends upon natural man's decision for God, his acceptance of Christ, his turning to God.

"Free will" denies the scriptural truth, however, that due to man's fallen condition and his totally sinful and depraved heart, he will only choose for self, sin, world, and Satan. If salvation depended upon natural man's "choices," "decisions," "repentance," or "faith," no sinner would ever be saved, for his will is perverse — against God and for self. God needs to first plant new spiritual life in a spiritually dead sinner, to give him a new heart. Upon receiving spiritual gifts of God's free grace, sinners will be made willing to repent from sin, believe in God, and choose for Christ.

Arminius' covenant teaching is directly related to his view of man and the plan of salvation. Notice, from the previous sketch, that Arminius believed that Jesus Christ died for all mankind in the same manner in the Covenant of Redemption. He taught that Christ removed everyone's original sin — not just the elect's. On this basis, salvation is offered to mankind and all have the ability of themselves, to repent, believe, and make a decision for Christ. Those that accept Christ's offer enter into a Covenant of Grace with God. This covenant is made directly with them. Man is again his own agreeing party with God in Arminius' covenant presentation. God did His part by giving Christ, removing man's original sin, and offering salvation. Man now must do his part by accepting this teaching, turning from sin, and believing on God. Those that make this "decision" enter into a Covenant of Grace with God. Those that faithfully continue to "choose for God" and remain in the covenant will be saved.

Arminius' teaching was and remains very popular. Many present-day churches follow his covenant and salvation view. Many large, modern evangelistic crusades use approaches which are based upon this covenant and decisional regeneration view.

As it is written, There is none righteous, no, not one: There is none that understandeth, there is none that seeketh after God.
— Romans 3:10-11

Ye have not chosen Me, but I have chosen you, and ordained you that ye should go and bring forth fruit, and that your fruit should remain: that whatsoever ye shall ask of the Father in My name, He may give it you.
— John 15:16

And she shall bring forth a son, and thou shalt call His name JESUS: for He shall save His people from their sins.
— Matthew 1:21

For it is God which worketh in you both to will and do of His good pleasure.
— Philippians 2:13

No man can come to Me, except the Father which hath sent Me draw him.
— John 6:44a

For by grace are ye saved through faith; and that not of yourselves: it is the gift of God.
— Ephesians 2:8

Being confident of this very thing, that He which hath begun a good work in you will perform it until the day of Jesus Christ.
— Philippians 1:6

? How does the teaching of Arminius contradict the marginal scriptural references on this page and the following five points of Calvinism:

— Total depravity?
— Unconditional election?
— Limited atonement?
— Irresistible grace?
— Perseverance of the saints?

No Reformed church denomination directly teaches Arminius' three-covenant view today. No Reformed church believes that Jesus Christ died for *all men* in the same manner in the Covenant of Redemption. No Reformed denomination preaches "free will" as the way in which lost sinners can be saved. However, several Reformed church denominations do hold three-covenant, in distinction from two-covenant, views pertaining to man's salvation. A three-covenant view means believing in three distinct convenants pertaining to man's salvation, each with different agreeing parties.

The two principal reasons for their adopting of a three-covenant view are as follows:

Reason 1 — *Scriptural references to God's establishing His covenant with His elect*; for example: "And I will make My covenant between Me and thee" (Genesis 17:2); "And I will make an everlasting covenant with you" (Isaiah 55:3); or "I sware unto thee, and entered into a covenant with thee" (Ezekiel 16:8).

Reason 2 — Scriptural verses which speak of *conditions to be met by all those that are included in the covenant*; for example: faith — "He that believeth on the Son hath everlasting life: and he that believeth not on the Son shall not see life" (John 3:36); repentance — "Repent ye therefore, and be converted" (Acts 3:19); and obedience — "He that doeth the will of God abideth for ever" (I John 2:17).

Others, however, *do not believe,* that these types of scriptural references **necessitate** *a third, different covenant,* for the following reasons:

In Reply to Reason 1 —

1. The personal **inclusion** of the elect in the Covenant of Grace is *identical to the manner of personally including all people in the Covenant of Works under Adam its covenant head.* As each person is spoken of as having personally sinned, broken the covenant, and earned death in Adam's transgression; so each of the elect is spoken of as personally entering into a new, gracious covenant relationship with God through Jesus Christ, his second Covenant Head. For example: "Wherefore, as by one man sin entered into

- **Necessitate** — Require; make necessary

- **Inclusion** — The act of including; placement within

346

the world, and death by sin; and so death passed upon all men, for that all have sinned. For as by one man's disobedience many were made sinners, so by the obedience of One shall many be made righteous'' (Romans 5:12,19).

2. The scriptural references to God's establishing His covenant with the elect speak of *God's personal application of His covenant truths to their hearts.* This is only possible through Christ their second Covenant Head, for outside of Christ God is a consuming fire. ''For this is the covenant that I will make with the house of Israel after those days, saith the Lord; I will put My laws into their mind, and write them in their hearts: and I will be to them a God, and they shall be to Me a people'' (Hebrews 8:10). ''Now the God of peace, that brought again from the dead our Lord Jesus, that great Shepherd of the sheep, through the blood of the everlasting covenant'' (Hebrews 13:20).

3. References to the personal inclusion of the elect in the covenant always *speak of God's gracious, one-sided work which is based upon Christ's merits as Covenant Head.* Notice that each of the texts quoted in the previous sections under *Reason 1* testifies of God's one-sided work, speaking of ''I will make,'' or ''I sware,'' or ''I entered'' when referring to the Covenant of Grace.

In Reply to Reason 2 —

The scriptural reasons for not using the verses which speak of ''conditions'' or ''requirements'' to be met by the saved as a basis for establishing a new covenant were explained previously in this chapter, in the section which deals with the ''requirements or conditions of the Covenant of Grace.'' In summary, all the ''conditions'' to be met by God's children are gracious benefits freely given to them through Christ their Covenant Head. No sinner could ever produce any acts of faith, repentance, or obedience from himself.

For the previous reasons, Scripture does not testify of three covenants when speaking of man's salvation. On the contrary, we believe that God's Word teaches a two-covenant view, for the following reasons:

> For by grace are ye saved through faith; and that not of yourselves: it is the gift of God:
> Not of works, lest any man should boast.
> For we are His workmanship, created in Christ Jesus unto good works, which God hath before ordained that we should walk in them.
> — Ephesians 2:8-10

> Even so then at this present time also there is a remnant according to the election of grace.
> And if by grace, then is it no more of works: otherwise grace is no more grace. But if it be of works, then is it no more grace: otherwise work is no more work.
> — Romans 11:5-6

> A new heart also will I give you, and a new spirit will I put within you: and I will take away the stony heart out of your flesh, and I will give you an heart of flesh.
> — Ezekiel 36:26

> Not by works of righteousness which we have done, but according to His mercy He saved us, by the washing of regeneration, and renewing of the Holy Ghost.
> — Titus 3:5

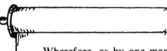

Wherefore, as by one man sin entered into the world, and death by sin; and so death passed upon all men, for that all have sinned.

(For until the law sin was in the world: but sin is not imputed when there is no law.

Nevertheless death reigned from Adam to Moses even over them that had not sinned after the similitude of Adam's transgression, who is the figure of Him that was to come.

But not as the offence, so also is the free gift. For if through the offence of one many be dead, much more the grace of God, and the gift by grace, which is by one Man, Jesus Christ, hath abounded unto many.

And not as it was by one that sinned, so is the gift: for the judgment was by one to condemnation, but the free gift is of many offences unto justification.

For if by one man's offence death reigned by one; much more they which receive abundance of grace and of the gift of righteousness shall reign in life by One, Jesus Christ.)

Therefore as by the offence of one judgment came upon all men to condemnation; even so by the righteousness of One the free gift came upon all men unto justification of life.

For as by one man's disobedience many were made sinners, so by the obedience of One shall many be made righteous.

Moreover the law entered, that the offence might abound. But where sin abounded, grace did much more abound:

That as sin hath reigned unto death, even so might grace reign through righteousness unto eternal life by Jesus Christ our Lord.
— Romans 5:12-21

SCRIPTURAL REASONS FOR A TWO-COVENANT VIEW REGARDING MAN'S SALVATION
(The Covenant of Works and the Covenant of Grace)

Reason	Example Text
A two-covenant presentation: 1. Most clearly maintains the direct comparisons of *two covenants* pertaining to man's salvation found in Scripture (the Covenant of Works compared to the Covenant of Grace).	Therefore as by the offence of one judgment came upon all men to condemnation; even so by the righteousness of One the free gift came upon all men unto justification of life. For as by one man's disobedience many were made sinners, so by the obedience of One shall many be made righteous. — Romans 5:18-19 For as in Adam all die, even so in Christ shall all be made alive. And so it is written, the first man Adam was made a living soul; the last Adam was made a quickening spirit. The first man is of the earth, earthy: the second man is the Lord from heaven. — I Corinthians 15:22,45,47
2. Most clearly presents the inseparable connection between God's thoughts of salvation from eternity with His performance of salvation in time according to the plan and agreement of His Covenant of Grace.	Who hath saved us, and called us with an holy calling, not according to our works, but according to His own purpose and grace, which was given us in Christ Jesus before the world began. — II Timothy 1:9 According as He hath chosen us in Him before the foundation of the world, that we should be holy and without blame before Him in love: Having predestinated us unto the adoption of children by Jesus Christ to Himself, according to the good pleasure of His will, To the praise of the glory of His grace, wherein He hath made us accepted in the beloved. In whom we have redemption through His blood, the forgiveness of sins, according to the riches of His grace. — Ephesians 1:4-7
3. Most clearly pictures the inseparable connection between Christ as Head of His church and covenant, and His elect church as body and recipients of His covenant blessings.	For the husband is the head of the wife, even as Christ is the head of the church: and He is the Saviour of the body. Therefore as the church is subject unto Christ, so let the wives be to their own husbands in every thing. — Ephesians 5:23-24 And He is the head of the body, the church: who is the beginning, the firstborn from the dead; that in all things He might have the preeminence. — Colossians 1:18
4. Most clearly proclaims Christ as the only meriting cause and foundation of salvation, and eliminates the dangerous tendencies of again making man a directly-agreeing party with God through his conditional obedience.	That in the ages to come He might show the exceeding riches of His grace in His kindness toward us through Christ Jesus. For by grace are ye saved through faith; and that not of yourselves: it is the gift of God: Not of works, lest any man should boast. For we are His workmanship, created in Christ Jesus unto good works, which God hath before ordained that we should walk in them. — Ephesians 2:7-10

*Questions Two and Three: Is the Covenant of Grace breakable, unbreakable, or both? Are all the **natural** (baptized) **seed** or only the **spiritual** (elect) **seed** of the church or both included in a Covenant of Grace relationship with God?*

In the example texts previously listed in the charts relating to these questions, Scripture testifies to us that both of these are true — the Covenant of Grace is breakable, yet unbreakable. It includes only the spiritual (elect) seed and yet all the natural (baptized) seed. How can both parts of these apparent contradictions be true?

The answer lies in the manner in which God has chosen to reveal His covenant and church in the world. God has chosen to do so in both an inward and outward form, or manner. Therefore a person can be related to God's Covenant of Grace or church in only an outward and breakable way or in an inward and unbreakable manner. These two different relationships to the same covenant make it possible for both groups of texts to be true and yet not contradictory.

An inward covenant and church relationship refers to the essence, the heart of God's covenant and church in which the full spiritual blessings are received — forgiveness of sin and the right to eternal life and fellowship with God. This relationship includes all God's elect children, the spiritual, born-again seed of the church. In them, the eternal, unbreakable benefits of the covenant are realized. Through regeneration all true believers are inseparably connected to Jesus Christ, the Head of the covenant and church.

An outward covenant and church relationship refers to the visible revelation of God's covenant and church that He has chosen to reveal in the world. God has made an outward distinction and separation among people. The gathering together to worship and call upon God's name draws a visible line of separation among people on earth — those who publicly gather to worship God and those who do not. All those related to God's covenant or church bore in the Old Testament, and bear in the New Testament, a special mark of separation from the world — circumcision in the Old, and baptism in the New.

- **Natural seed** — Those who are born and baptized into the church, but not regenerated by the Holy Spirit

- **Spiritual seed** — God's elect children; those who are spiritually born again; the saved

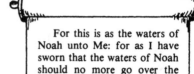

For this is as the waters of Noah unto Me: for as I have sworn that the waters of Noah should no more go over the earth; so have I sworn that I would not be wroth with thee, nor rebuke thee.
For the mountains shall depart, and the hills be removed; but My kindness shall not depart from thee, neither shall the covenant of My peace be removed, saith the LORD that hath mercy on thee.
— Isaiah 54:9-10

For this is the covenant that I will make with the house of Israel after those days, saith the Lord; I will put My laws into their mind, and write them in their hearts: and I will be to them a God, and they shall be to Me a people.
— Hebrews 8:10

But they like men have transgressed the covenant: there have they dealt treacherously against Me.
— Hosea 6:7

This is My covenant, which ye shall keep, between Me and you and thy seed after thee; Every man child among you shall be circumcised.
— Genesis 17:10

An outward relationship to God's covenant and church includes many rich blessings, of which the following are the principal four:

FOUR BENEFITS OF AN OUTWARD RELATIONSHIP TO THE COVENANT	
Benefit	Example Text
1. It includes a person as *a member in God's church outwardly* (the Church Visible).	This is My covenant, which ye shall keep, between Me and you and thy seed after thee; Every man child among you shall be circumcised. — Genesis 17:10 For the unbelieving husband is sanctified by the wife, and the unbelieving wife is sanctified by the husband: else were your children unclean; but now are they holy. — I Corinthians 7:14
2. It places a person under *God's Word — His law and gospel,* which He has promised to bless to the salvation of many. Therefore, to be placed under God's means of grace, under His sincere warnings and invitations, is a priceless blessing.	What advantage then hath the Jew? or what profit is there of circumcision? Much every way: chiefly, because that unto them were committed the oracles of God. — Romans 3:1-2 So then faith cometh by hearing, and hearing by the Word of God. — Romans 10:17
3. It personally places *God's name and mark of outward separation* from the world and dedication to Him, upon a person. This personally confirms His truth and promise that He will forever be a gracious covenant-keeping God, who will be found by all those that need and ask for Him. The baptized may plead upon the truth of this promise sealed in their baptism.	This is My covenant, which ye shall keep, between Me and you and thy seed after thee; Every man child among you shall be circumcised. — Genesis 17:10 And when she was baptized, and her household. — Acts 16:15a
4. It continually includes a person in *the teachings, warnings, and prayers of the church.*	And all Judah stood before the LORD, with their little ones, their wives, and their children. — II Chronicles 20:13 These all continued with one accord in prayer and supplication, with the women, and Mary the mother of Jesus, and with His brethren. — Acts 1:14

? In what ways are external church members separated from the world? In what additional ways are internal church members separated from the world? How are both of these distinctions important?

Being placed in an outward relationship to God's covenant and church is a great blessing. God has made a gracious distinction in placing us there. By nature, we are not better than many others to whom God has not granted the precious benefits of an outward covenant relationship with Him.

As with all God's blessings — greater privileges result in greater responsibilities. The more benefits God graciously gives, the more He justly requires.

How do the following scriptural references teach that our responsibilities increase with our privileges, and that we will be judged accordingly?

> And into whatsoever city or town ye shall enter, inquire who in it is worthy; and there abide till ye go thence. And when ye come into an house, salute it. And if the house be worthy, let your peace come upon it: but if it be not worthy, let your peace return to you. And whosoever shall not receive you, nor hear your words, when ye depart out of that house or city, shake off the dust of your feet. Verily I say unto you, It shall be more tolerable for the land of Sodom and Gomorrha in the day of judgment, than for that city.
>
> — Matthew 10:11-15

> Then began He to upbraid the cities wherein most of His mighty works were done, because they repented not: Woe unto thee, Chorazin! woe unto thee, Bethsaida! for if the mighty works, which were done in you, had been done in Tyre and Sidon, they would have repented long ago in sackcloth and ashes. But I say unto you, It shall be more tolerable for Tyre and Sidon at the day of judgment, than for you. And thou, Capernaum, which art exalted unto heaven, shalt be brought down to hell: for if the mighty works, which have been done in thee, had been done in Sodom, it would have remained unto this day. But I say unto you, That it shall be more tolerable for the land of Sodom in the day of judgment, than for thee.
>
> — Matthew 11:20-24

> The men of Nineveh shall rise in judgment with this generation, and shall condemn it: because they repented at the preaching of Jonas; and, behold, a greater than Jonas is here. The queen of the south shall rise up in the judgment with this generation, and shall condemn it: for she came from the uttermost parts of the earth to hear the wisdom of Solomon; and, behold, a greater than Solomon is here.
>
> — Matthew 12:41-42

> He that rejecteth Me, and receiveth not My words, hath one that judgeth him: the word that I have spoken, the same shall judge him in the last day.
>
> — John 12:48

? What do these examples teach us about God's judgments?

How do these verses testify of the great responsibilities and judgments attached to the great privileges and blessings of outward church and covenant relationship?

And Esau said to Jacob, Feed me, I pray thee, with that same red pottage; for I am faint: therefore was his name called Edom.

And Jacob said, Sell me this day thy birthright.

And Esau said, Behold, I am at the point to die: and what profit shall this birthright do to me?

And Jacob said, Swear to me this day; and he sware unto him: and he sold his birthright unto Jacob.

Then Jacob gave Esau bread and pottage of lentiles; and he did eat and drink, and rose up, and went his way: thus Esau despised his birthright.

— Genesis 25:30-34

Lest there be any fornicator, or profane person, as Esau, who for one morsel of meat sold his birthright.

— Hebrews 12:16

? Can you relate other ways in which modern "Esaus" sell spiritual "birthrights" for material "morsels of meat"?

Esau was born and circumcized into an outward covenant relationship with God and His promises. However, he despised his birthright, and valued earthly matters more than spiritual promises. He sold his birthright for a mess of pottage. We think of Esau as very foolish and wicked, do we not?

Martin was born and baptized into an outward covenant and church relationship with God, but, in his teen-age years, he began to despise his birthright. He saw less and less value in the blessings and promises of his relationship with God's covenant and church. He saw more and more value in earthly possessions. Finally, he valued his car more than church, his automobile magazines more than his Bible, and his Saturdays more than his Sundays. He "needed" time to work on his car, but not to pray. His car "had" to be spotlessly clean, but not his soul. He carefully studied his car repair manual because it was so "important" to know how to properly fix his engine, but religious books were boring. Two hundred dollars for new wheels were "necessary," but two dollars for church was too much. A scratch on his car door was "terrible," but a sinful blot on his soul was nothing to get upset about.

In this manner, Martin sold his wonderful "birthright" for a "mess of pottage." Is the selling of spiritual "birthrights" for worldly "messes of pottage" today, just as serious as Esau's? Why? What terrible consequences will result from the selling of spiritual "birthrights" if persons harden themselves in their condition as Esau, and do not sincerely repent?

While an outward covenant relationship is a great privilege and includes significant benefits and responsibilities, it is not sufficient for salvation.

A person can be related to God's covenant and church in an outward manner and still be lost. How does the following chart provide scriptural proof of this truth?

? How is the blessing of opportunity different from the blessing of fulfillment? How does this distinction apply to outward and inward covenant relationships?

SCRIPTURAL EXAMPLES OF LOST OUTWARDLY-RELATED COVENANT MEMBERS	
Person	Reference
1. Ishmael	Nevertheless what saith the Scripture? Cast out the bondwoman and her son: for the son of the bondwoman shall not be heir with the son of the freewoman. — Galatians 4:30
2. Esau	As it is written, Jacob have I loved, but Esau have I hated. — Romans 9:13
3. The children of Israel during their wilderness wanderings	And did all drink the same spiritual drink: for they drank of that spiritual Rock that followed them: and that Rock was Christ. But with many of them God was not well pleased: for they were overthrown in the wilderness. — I Corinthians 10:4-5
4. Judas Iscariot	The Son of man goeth as it is written of Him: but woe unto that man by whom the Son of man is betrayed! it had been good for that man if he had not been born. — Matthew 26:24
5. Simon the Sorcerer	Thou hast neither part nor lot in this matter: for thy heart is not right in the sight of God. For I perceive that thou art in the gall of bitterness, and in the bond of iniquity. — Acts 8:21,23

We may not overvalue nor undervalue the outward covenant relationship God has graciously granted to us.

How do the following examples illustrate these two errors?

Example 1

"I am a Christian person. I have been brought up in a Christian home, enrolled in a Christian school, and faithfully attended a Christian church. I read the Bible and live a Christian lifestyle. No one can point a finger at me for any public sin. I have purchased several Christian books and received Christian baptism. As a Christian person, I am confident for the future."

Example 2

"Baptism and church membership do not really make a difference. Regardless of whether or not a person has an outward relationship to the covenant or church, God must savingly regenerate him. God can save and convert someone from the midst of the world who never has attended church, or someone who has attended church his entire life. If God has elected you to be saved, you will be; and if not, you won't be. An outward church and covenant relationship makes no difference."

What is frightfully wrong with the views expressed in these examples? How would you correct each viewpoint?

? How can the following scriptural references assist you in correcting the mistaken views expressed in Example One and Two?

For he is not a Jew, which is one outwardly; neither is that circumcision, which is outward in the flesh:
But he is a Jew, which is one inwardly; and circumcision is that of the heart, in the spirit, and not in the letter; whose praise is not of men, but of God.
What advantage then hath the Jew? or what profit is there of circumcision?
Much every way: chiefly, because that unto them were committed the oracles of God.
— Romans 2:28-3:2

Jesus answered and said unto him, Verily, verily, I say unto thee, Except a man be born again, he cannot see the kingdom of God.
— John 3:3

So then faith cometh by hearing, and hearing by the Word of God.
— Romans 10:17

The two-fold manner in which a person may be related to the Covenant of Grace must be clearly understood with the corresponding benefits and responsibilities of each.

To be saved we must be regenerated by God the Holy Spirit, we must be born again spiritually. Only then will we be brought into the essence, unbreakableness, and eternal benefits, of the Covenant of Grace.

The two possible relationships to God's covenant and church are shown in the following chart:

THE COVENANT OF GRACE

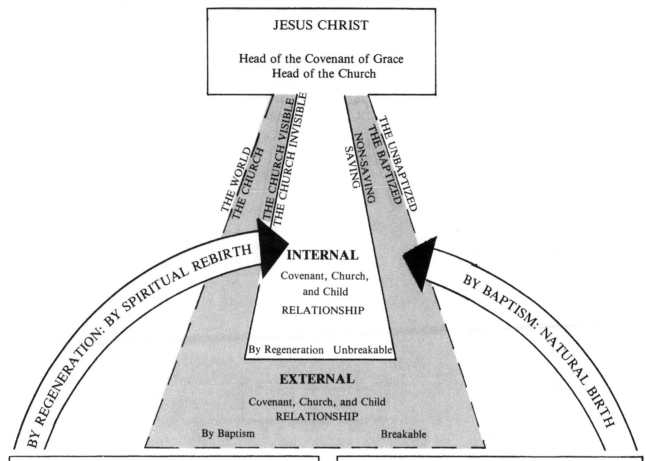

JESUS CHRIST

Head of the Covenant of Grace
Head of the Church

THE WORLD
THE CHURCH
THE CHURCH VISIBLE
THE CHURCH INVISIBLE

THE UNBAPTIZED
THE BAPTIZED
NON-SAVING
SAVING

BY REGENERATION: BY SPIRITUAL REBIRTH

BY BAPTISM: NATURAL BIRTH

INTERNAL

Covenant, Church,
and Child
RELATIONSHIP

By Regeneration   Unbreakable

EXTERNAL

Covenant, Church, and Child
RELATIONSHIP

By Baptism   Breakable

INWARD COVENANT RELATIONSHIP	OUTWARD COVENANT RELATIONSHIP
(Baptism applied *Inwardly*)	(Baptism applied *Outwardly*)
*An **inward** relationship to the essence of the Covenant of Grace by regeneration includes:*	*An **outward** relationship to the Covenant of Grace by baptism includes:*
Membership in the **Church Invisible**	Membership in the **Church Visible**
Being placed in an **inward**, spiritual, and saving separation from the world internally, blessings of being spiritually born again as God's child.	**Outward** blessings of separation from the world, bearing God's mark of separation
Unbreakable, eternal relationship to the essence of the Covenant of Grace	Being placed in a **breakable**, temporal relationship to the Covenant of Grace
Coming under God's **inward call**: the regenerating and converting work of the Holy Spirit	Coming under God's **outward call**: His Word, the invitation of the gospel, and the teachings, prayers, and warnings of the church, which God blesses to work salvation in the lives of many.
These are the **greatest** blessings: securing salvation and restoration into eternal fellowship with God	These are **great** blessings, but not sufficient for salvation

A person becomes a citizen of a country by his oath of allegiance as an adult, or by birth as a child.

In Acts 22:27-28, we read the following conversation between Paul and the chief captain:

> Then the chief captain came, and said unto him, Tell me, art thou a Roman? He said, yea.
> And the chief captain answered, With a great sum obtained I this freedom. And Paul said, But I was free born.

How are these men an example of the two different ways in which citizenship can be obtained?

Today, in our country, a person can become a citizen by birth, or by oath of allegiance as an adult, after living for some years in our country. What privileges and responsibilities are connected with national citizenship?

How can these examples be compared with covenant and church membership?

This two-fold manner of attaining citizenship is also true for *outward* covenant or church membership. Through natural birth onto "church soil" as a child, or through confession as an adult, (after living on "church soil" for sometime), a person may be baptized into outward church membership. However, spiritual and internal membership is different. Only through spiritual rebirth, being born again, may a person be brought into the essence of the Covenant — into an inward, saving, and eternal relationship with God through Christ as Covenant Head.

To represent both possible relationships to the Covenant of Grace and answer the previously-stated three difficult covenant questions, the following two and three covenant presentations are used within the circle of Reformed denominations. As mentioned previously, these various views of the Covenant of Grace, with the fourth related difference (how the natural seed should be distinguished from the spiritual seed of the church), have produced the major difference in doctrine between Reformed denominations.

View 1 on the corresponding page visualizes the presentation of God's covenants according to the two-covenant view. Views 2, 3, and 4 on the following pages present the various three-covenant presentations within Reformed circles.

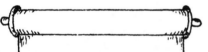

Jesus answered and said unto him, Verily, verily, I say unto thee, Except a man be born again, he cannot see the kingdom of God.
— John 3:3

Which were born, not of blood, nor of the will of the flesh, nor of the will of man, but of God.
— John 1:13

Therefore if any man be in Christ, he is a new creature: old things are passed away; behold, all things are become new.
— II Corinthians 5:17

Being born again, not of corruptible seed, but of incorruptible, by the Word of God, which liveth and abideth for ever.
— I Peter 1:23

Not by works of righteousness, which we have done, but according to His mercy He saved us, by the washing of regeneration, and renewing of the Holy Ghost.
— Titus 3:5

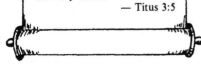

VIEW 1: TWO COVENANT VIEW

1. *Covenant of Works*
    (same in each of the
    following views)

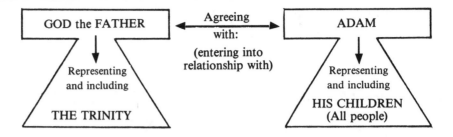

2. *Covenant of Grace*
    A. From eternity
    (also named the
    "Counsel of Peace"
    or the "Covenant of
    Redemption")

    B. *In time*

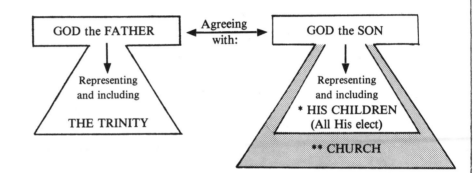

* INWARD COVENANT RELATIONSHIP only with the spiritual seed, the elect, and the Church Invisible; an unbreakable, eternal relationship with God through Christ as Covenant Head; the essence of the Covenant in which the full benefits of regeneration, conversion, forgiveness of sin, and a right to eternal life and fellowship with God are realized in true believers, for Christ's sake.

** OUTWARD COVENANT RELATIONSHIP with the natural, baptized, seed; the Church Visible; a temporary relationship which is breakable through man's sin and rejection; special benefits are received but they are not sufficient for salvation; if broken, the benefits of this relationship will testify against its recipients.

This presentation of the covenants retains the following advantages:

1. It clearly maintains the scriptural comparison of two covenants pertaining to man's salvation — the first being broken by Adam, and the second being secured by Christ.
2. It clearly presents the inseparable connection between God's plan from eternity and His performance in time concerning His election, plan of salvation, and Covenant of Grace.
3. It clearly pictures Christ as the Head of His church and covenant and yet directly connected with His church as body and the recipients of covenant blessings through His headship.
4. It clearly proclaims Christ as the only meriting cause of salvation and shows how "conditions" to be met by the elect are actually *benefits* given to them by Christ their Covenant Head. It eliminates the dangerous tendency of again attempting to make man an agreeing party with God through his conditional obedience.
5. It clearly reveals how the essence of the covenant is unbreakable and only includes God's elect church (the spiritual seed), and yet, how a breakable and outward relationship with the covenant is granted to all baptized members of the church (the natural seed).

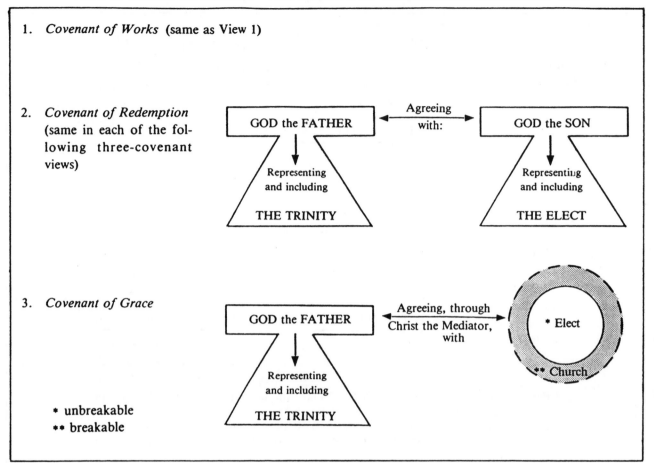

VIEW 2: THREE COVENANT — COVENANT OF GRACE WITH THE ELECT VIEW

1. *Covenant of Works* (same as View 1)

2. *Covenant of Redemption (same in each of the following three-covenant views)*

GOD the FATHER

Agreeing with:

GOD the SON

Representing and including

THE TRINITY

Representing and including

THE ELECT

3. *Covenant of Grace*

GOD the FATHER

Agreeing, through Christ the Mediator, with

Representing and including

THE TRINITY

* Elect

** Church

* unbreakable
** breakable

This three-covenant presentation retains the following advantages:

1. It clearly maintains the inseparable connection between God's Covenant of Redemption from eternity and His Covenant of Grace in time concerning His elect.

2. It clearly reveals both an unbreakable aspect of the Covenant of Grace which includes the elect only and a breakable relationship with all the baptized members.

This view also presents the following disadvantages:

1. It introduces the dangerous tendency of again making man a direct agreeing party with God in the Covenant of Grace.

2. It obscures the scriptural contrast of two covenants — the first being broken by Adam and the second being secured by Christ.

3. In the Covenant of Grace, it separates the scriptural connection of Christ as Head of His church and covenant with His people as body and recipients of covenant blessings through His headship.

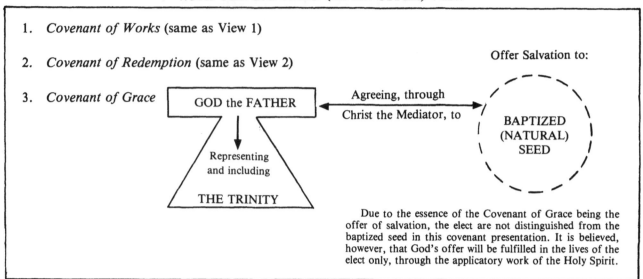

**VIEW 3: THREE COVENANT — COVENANT OF GRACE
WITH THE BAPTIZED (AS AN OFFER) VIEW**

1. *Covenant of Works* (same as View 1)

2. *Covenant of Redemption* (same as View 2)

3. *Covenant of Grace*

GOD the FATHER

Representing
and including

THE TRINITY

Offer Salvation to:

Agreeing, through
Christ the Mediator, to

BAPTIZED
(NATURAL)
SEED

Due to the essence of the Covenant of Grace being the offer of salvation, the elect are not distinguished from the baptized seed in this covenant presentation. It is believed, however, that God's offer will be fulfilled in the lives of the elect only, through the applicatory work of the Holy Spirit.

This presentation of the covenants retains the following advantages:

1. It includes the natural (baptized) seed of the church in a breakable covenant relationship, called the "Covenant of Grace," and only the elect (spiritual) seed in an unbreakable, eternal covenant relationship with God through Christ as their Head, called the "Covenant of Redemption."

2. In preaching and practice, this three-covenant presentation is very similar to the two-covenant presentation, found in View 1. Because the Covenant of Grace in View 3 is not necessarily saving, but is God's *offering* through Christ of salvation to the baptized seed, this view is very similar to the outward relationship to the Covenant of Grace presented in View 1. The Covenant of Redemption in this view (the saving covenant made through Christ, the Head of the elect), is very similar to the unbreakable relationship to the Covenant of Grace in View 1.

   In summary, that which is taught as a two-fold relationship to one Covenant of Grace in View 1 is taught as two separate covenants in this view.

This division of the covenants, however, produces the following, primarily theological rather than practical, disadvantages:

1. This covenant division denies the eternalness and unbreakableness of the Covenant of Grace, for God's offer of salvation is neither eternal nor unbreakable. The Covenant of Grace is reduced to only a breakable offer and conditional promise.

2. In its covenant theology, this presentation obscures God's line of election from eternity into time. The Covenant of Redemption (or Counsel of Peace) refers to God's plan of *salvation* for His *elect* from eternity, but the Covenant of Grace is an *offer* to the *natural seed*, in time. (If the Covenant of Redemption would be given both an eternal and time aspect to correct this difficulty, then the church in time would be given two different, separate covenants, while Scripture only speaks of one.) This difficulty is primarily a theological one, however, as in practice, this view believes that God's offer and promise will be fulfilled in the elect only. The problem is that the elect, in time, are not clearly shown in its covenant theology.

3. It obscures the scriptural comparison of two covenants — the first being broken by Adam and the second being secured by Christ.

**VIEW 4: THREE COVENANT — COVENANT OF GRACE
WITH THE BAPTIZED (AS RECEIVING ALL THE PROMISES) VIEW**

1. *Covenant of Works* (same as View 1)

2. *Covenant of Redemption* (same as View 2)

3. *Covenant of Grace*

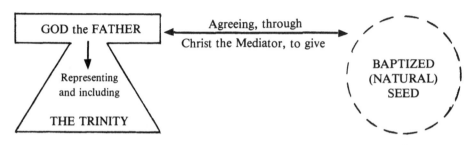

This presentation of the covenants grants all the promises of the Covenant of Grace, all its saving blessings — forgiveness of sins and right to eternal life and communion with God — to all the baptized seed of the church. Each baptized person is called upon to receive, believe, and rest in this covenant gift by faith. The essence of the Covenant promises can be confirmed by faith, or broken by rejection, in the lives of the baptized seed.

This presentation of the covenants produces the following disadvantages:

1. It denies the unbreakableness of the Covenant of Grace. God's line of election from eternity, (in the Counsel of Peace), being fulfilled in time, (in the Covenant of Grace), is broken. Man can break all the promises of the Covenant through his unbelief.

2. It places all baptized members within the Covenant of Grace in the same manner, which denies the distinction of only the elect, the spiritual seed, being in the essence of the covenant with God.

3. It introduces the dangerous tendency of again making man an agreeing party with God in the Covenant, through his conditional faith and obedience.

4. It obscures the scriptural contrast of two covenants — the first being broken by Adam and the second secured by Christ.

5. It separates the scriptural connection of Christ as Head of His church and covenant, with His people as body and recipients of covenant blessings through His headship. Each person stands or falls according to his own faith.

Question 4: How are the natural (baptized) seed to be distinguished from the spiritual (elect) seed of the church?

From the differing presentations of God's Covenant of Grace arises differing beliefs regarding how to properly view the baptized (natural) seed of the church. How are they to be distinguished from the saved (spiritual) seed of the church?

As previously mentioned, Scripture requires us to treasure the blessings and opportunities given to, and to stress the responsibilities which rest upon, all those who are outwardly related to God's covenant and church. Yet, Scripture also forbids us from speaking of any person as being saved that has not experienced God's inward-working graces and evidenced God's outward-working fruits or good works (except for the possibility of a person who is incapable of producing visible good works, due to physical or mental incapabilities, such as children dying in infancy, the severely mentally-handicapped, persons living in paralyzed or coma conditions, etc.)

The *inward-working graces* of the Holy Spirit required in Scripture before viewing ourselves or others as saved are as follows:

1. A heartfelt experiencing of *misery* (or *repentance*) — This speaks of a person being convinced of his sin. He is convicted by the Holy Spirit of his actual sins but also of their source, his original sin — his totally depraved and sinful heart. A sincere sorrow for, and desire to turn from, all sin is experienced. However, all attempts at self-reformation fail as conviction deepens. His totally lost state and condition become real — without God in the world and unable, because of his own sinful heart, to save himself. His need to be saved and the impossibility of saving himself is worked by the Holy Spirit in his heart, to direct him outside of himself, to God's appointed Savior.

2. A heartfelt experiencing of *deliverance* (or *faith*) — When experiencing that his sin has cut off all hope for self-salvation, has separated him from God and made him ripe for God's judgments, the Holy Spirit directs the soul's eyes outside of self to Jesus Christ. He begins to see the wonderful way of salvation by grace opened for lost sinners in Jesus Christ. As these truths are applied to his heart, he learns to hope, believe, and trust in Jesus Christ as his way of escape. As faith deepens, Jesus Christ increasingly becomes his hope, righteousness, holiness; in short — his everything for salvation. Jesus Christ becomes his personal Savior. He has, and is graciously willing to give, everything which the sinner lacks and needs for salvation.

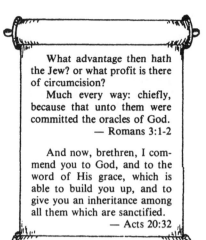

What advantage then hath the Jew? or what profit is there of circumcision?

Much every way: chiefly, because that unto them were committed the oracles of God.
— Romans 3:1-2

And now, brethren, I commend you to God, and to the word of His grace, which is able to build you up, and to give you an inheritance among all them which are sanctified.
— Acts 20:32

How was the infant child of David who died shortly after his birth an example of this type of exception?

And he said, While the child was yet alive, I fasted and wept: for I said, Who can tell whether GOD will be gracious to me, that the child may live?

But now he is dead, wherefore should I fast? can I bring him back again? I shall go to him, but he shall not return to me.
— II Samuel 12:22-23

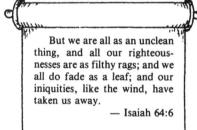

But we are all as an unclean thing, and all our righteousnesses are as filthy rags; and we all do fade as a leaf; and our iniquities, like the wind, have taken us away.
— Isaiah 64:6

O wretched man that I am! who shall deliver me from the body of this death?
— Romans 7:24

Then Simon Peter answered Him, Lord, to whom shall we go? Thou hast the words of eternal life.

And we believe and are sure that Thou art that Christ, the Son of the living God.
— John 6:68-69

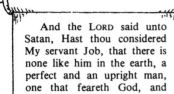

And the LORD said unto Satan, Hast thou considered My servant Job, that there is none like him in the earth, a perfect and an upright man, one that feareth God, and escheweth evil?

— Job 1:8

I will mention the loving-kindnesses of the LORD, and the praises of the LORD, according to all that the LORD hath bestowed on us.

— Isaiah 63:7a

I will praise Thee with uprightness of heart, when I shall have learned Thy righteous judgments.
I will keep Thy statutes: O forsake me not utterly.

— Psalm 119:7-8

3. A heartfelt experiencing of *thankfulness* (or *obedience*) — Experiencing something of the deep, gracious, saving love of God through Jesus Christ for sinners, will produce an overflowing love toward God in return. With true thankfulness of heart, he desires to love, serve, and honor God — to do that which is pleasing in God's sight. He wants to obey God wholeheartedly and perfectly. God's law is not a burden or something which he is forced to do, but it is a delight and that which he wants to do more than all else. His remaining sin deeply grieves him for his deepest motives, desires, and affections are to love and serve God perfectly in all things with his entire being.

Can you find the three inward-working graces of misery, deliverance, and thankfulness described in the examples located on this and the following page?

? Can you relate the heartfelt experience of misery, deliverance, and thankfulness in the following persons' conversions to God?

— The Philippian jailor
— Saul (Paul)
— The thief on the cross
— The Ethiopian eunuch
— The Syrophoenecian woman
— Bartimeus
— The paralyzed man that was lowered through the roof to Christ
— The man cured at the Pool of Bethesda

Can you add others to this list?

SCRIPTURAL EXAMPLES OF MISERY, DELIVERANCE, AND THANKFULNESS

He brought me up also out of an horrible pit, out of the miry clay, and set my feet upon a rock, and established my goings.
And He hath put a new song in my mouth, even praise unto our God: many shall see it, and fear, and shall trust in the LORD.

— Psalm 40:2-3

For ye were sometimes darkness but now are ye light in the Lord: walk as children of light.

— Ephesians 5:8

For He hath not despised nor abhorred the affliction of the afflicted; neither hath He hid His face from him; but when he cried unto Him, He heard.
My praise shall be of Thee in the great congregation: I will pay my vows before them that fear Him.

— Psalm 22:24-25

I will freely sacrifice unto Thee: I will praise Thy name, O LORD; for it is good.
For He hath delivered me out of all trouble: and mine eye hath seen His desire upon mine enemies.

— Psalm 54:6-7

O wretched man that I am! Who shall deliver me from the body of this death?
I thank God through Jesus Christ our Lord.

— Romans 7:24-25a

And call upon Me in the day of trouble: I will deliver thee, and thou shalt glorify Me.

— Psalm 50:15

Thou hast turned for me my mourning into dancing: Thou hast put off my sackcloth, and girded me with gladness:
To the end that my glory may sing praise to Thee, and not be silent, O LORD, my God, I will give thanks unto Thee for ever.

— Psalm 30:11-12

Thy vows are upon me, O God: I will render praises unto Thee.
For Thou hast delivered my soul from death: wilt not thou deliver my feet from falling, that I may walk before God in the light of the living?

— Psalm 56:12-13

CHURCH DOCTRINAL STANDARD AND *LITURGY*

EXAMPLES OF MISERY, DELIVERANCE, AND THANKFULNESS

● **Liturgy** — The official church forms that are used for special occasions

? How can we observe that the entire *Heidelberg Catechism* is based upon the theme of misery, deliverance, and thankfulness?

Heidelberg Catechism

Q. 2. How many things are necessary for thee to know, that thou, enjoying this comfort, mayest live and die happily?

A. Three; the first, how great my sins and miseries are; the second, how I may be delivered from all my sins and miseries; the third, how I shall express my gratitude to God for such deliverance.

Form for the Administration of the Lord's Supper

The true examination of ourselves consists of these three parts:

First. That every one consider by himself, his sins and the curse due to him for them, to the end that he may abhor and humble himself before God: considering that the wrath of God against sin is so great, that (rather than it should go unpunished) He hath punished the same in His beloved Son Jesus Christ, with the bitter and shameful death of the cross.

Secondly. That every one examine his own heart, whether he doth believe this faithful promise of God, that all his sins are forgiven him only for the sake of the passion and death of Jesus Christ, and that the perfect righteousness of Christ is imputed and freely given him as his own, yea, so perfectly, as if he had satisfied in his own person for all his sins, and fulfilled all righteousness.

Thirdly. That every one examine his own conscience, whether he purposeth henceforth to show true thankfulness to God in his whole life and to walk uprightly before Him; as also whether he hath laid aside unfeignedly all enmity, hatred, and envy, and doth firmly resolve henceforward to walk in true love and peace with his neighbor.

Form for the Consolation of the Sick

Since then the law of God requires this perfection of us, as it is written, Cursed is every one who doth not keep the whole law; as James also saith, Whosoever offendeth in one point, he is guilty of all. Again whosoever doth the law, shall live by it: But we do not keep the least commandment perfectly. As the wise man saith, When we imagine to have done we only begin (and in case we did do it, we only do our duty), wherefore we are by the law condemned in God's righteous judgment; for this we have a sure remedy and cure, namely Christ who hath redeemed us (as Paul saith) from the curse of the law, and hath satisfied the righteousness of God for us, making reconciliation; and who hath broken down the wall which was between us, namely the law, contained in ordinances, and forgiven us our sins, and torn the hand-writing of them, and nailed it to the cross: For this great love of Christ, we ought also to love Him, and to be thankful to Him, with good works, and verily to believe in Him, for the gift of these excellent benefits: For he that cometh to God, must believe that He is a rewarder of them that seek Him; for the just shall live by his faith. Therefore we conclude that a man is justified by faith, without the deeds of the law; and although we suffer a little with Christ, we must not despair, for we see that Christ Himself when He was smitten for our sins, did not smite again, but suffered patiently.

The inward-working graces of misery, deliverance, and thankfulness (or repentance, faith, and obedience) produce outward-working fruits. They produce good works of love toward God and others. While conversion on earth is not perfect, due to a remaining sinful nature, yet, good works will and must evidence themselves in the lives of true believers. In certain cases of physical or mental inability, *expression* of the inward graces in outward actions is not possible. This, however, is not a hindrance to God who knows and judges the hearts of all. God's normal manner of working, however, is that the inward-working graces reveal themselves in outward-working fruits, in good works of love toward God and others.

How do the following references testify of the need for good works of love toward God and others to reveal themselves in the lives of all who claim to be saved?

THE NECESSITY OF GOOD WORKS

Then said he to the multitude that came forth to be baptized of him, O generation of vipers, who hath warned you to flee from the wrath to come?

Bring forth therefore fruits worthy of repentance, and begin not to say within yourselves, We have Abraham to our father: for I say unto you, That God is able of these stones to raise up children unto Abraham.

And now also the axe is laid unto the root of the trees: every tree therefore which bringeth not forth good fruit is hewn down, and cast into the fire.

— Luke 3:7-9

Though I speak with the tongues of men and of angels, and have not charity, I am become as sounding brass, or a tinkling cymbal.

— I Corinthians 13:1

But be ye doers of the word, and not hearers only, deceiving your own selves.

— James 1:22

They answered and said unto Him, Abraham is our father. Jesus saith unto them, If ye were Abraham's children, ye would do the works of Abraham.

— John 8:39

For not the hearers of the law are just before God, but the doers of the law shall be justified.

— Romans 2:13

For we are His workmanship, created in Christ Jesus unto good works, which God hath before ordained that we should walk in them.

— Ephesians 2:10

Who gave Himself for us, that He might redeem us from all iniquity, and purify unto Himself a peculiar people, zealous of good works.

— Titus 2:14

Therefore whosoever heareth these sayings of Mine, and doeth them, I will liken him unto a wise man, which built his house upon a rock.

— Matthew 7:24

Based upon the previous references, Scripture forbids us from viewing or speaking of anyone as being saved, one of the elect, or in the essence of the Covenant until he has personally experienced something of the inward-working graces and evidenced something of the outward-working fruits. Therefore, a clear distinction, a line

---

Beware of false prophets, which come to you in sheep's clothing, but inwardly they are ravening wolves.

Ye shall know them by their fruits. Do men gather grapes of thorns, or figs of thistles?

Even so every good tree bringeth forth good fruit; but a corrupt tree bringeth forth evil fruit.

A good tree cannot bring forth evil fruit, neither can a corrupt tree bring forth good fruit.

Every tree that bringeth not forth good fruit is hewn down, and cast into the fire.

Wherefore by their fruits ye shall know them.

— Matthew 7:15-20

Even so faith, if it hath not works, is dead, being alone.

Yea, a man may say, Thou hast faith, and I have works: show me thy faith without thy works, and I will show thee my faith by my works.

Thou believest that there is one God; thou doest well: the devils also believe, and tremble.

But wilt thou know, O vain man, that faith without works is dead?

Was not Abraham our father justified by works, when he had offered Isaac his son upon the altar?

Seest thou how faith wrought with his works, and by works was faith made perfect?

And the Scripture was fulfilled which saith, Abraham believed God, and it was imputed unto him for righteousness: and he was called the Friend of God.

— James 2:17-23

And think not to say within yourselves, We have Abraham to our father: for I say unto you, that God is able of these stones to raise up children unto Abraham.

And now also the axe is laid unto the root of the trees: therefore every tree which bringeth not forth good fruit is hewn down, and cast into the fire.

— Matthew 3:9-10

of separation must be drawn in church between those who are only outwardly related to the covenant through baptism and those who are placed in the covenant in an inward manner through personal regeneration and conversion to God.

Personal, experiential regeneration and conversion can be pictured as follows, by following steps 1-3:

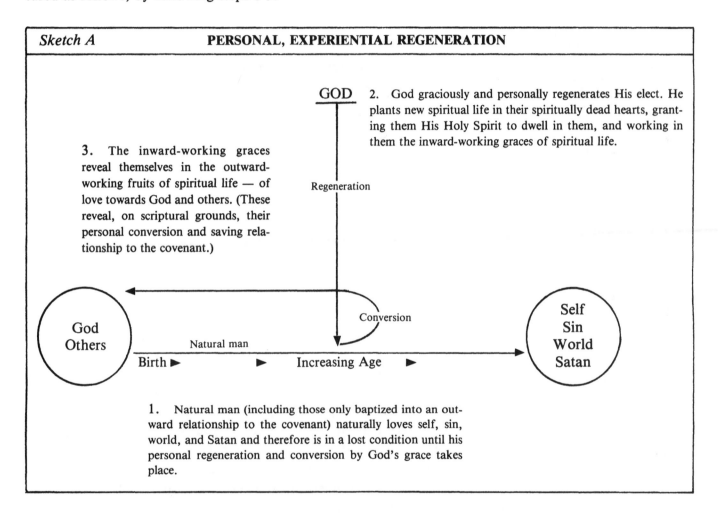

Sketch A   **PERSONAL, EXPERIENTIAL REGENERATION**

GOD

2. God graciously and personally regenerates His elect. He plants new spiritual life in their spiritually dead hearts, granting them His Holy Spirit to dwell in them, and working in them the inward-working graces of spiritual life.

3. The inward-working graces reveal themselves in the outward-working fruits of spiritual life — of love towards God and others. (These reveal, on scriptural grounds, their personal conversion and saving relationship to the covenant.)

Regeneration

God
Others

Self
Sin
World
Satan

Conversion

Natural man

Birth ▶   ▶   Increasing Age   ▶

1. Natural man (including those only baptized into an outward relationship to the covenant) naturally loves self, sin, world, and Satan and therefore is in a lost condition until his personal regeneration and conversion by God's grace takes place.

This line of distinction and judgment of whether one is outwardly or inwardly related to the covenant, saved or yet unsaved, is to be made personally between God and one's own soul based solely upon Scripture. Church officebearers or members are not to judge others, but themselves. The church's duty, in this respect, is to preach and teach the scriptural marks and fruits of God's regenerating grace. We may not subtract from, nor add to, the God-given scriptural marks, but we are to teach, learn, and examine ourselves by them.

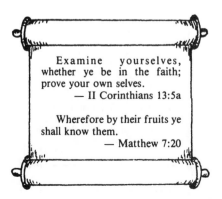

Examine yourselves, whether ye be in the faith; prove your own selves.
— II Corinthians 13:5a

Wherefore by their fruits ye shall know them.
— Matthew 7:20

Have mercy upon me, O God, according to Thy lovingkindness: according unto the multitude of Thy tender mercies blot out my transgressions.

Wash me thoroughly from mine iniquity, and cleanse me from my sin.

For I acknowledge my transgressions: and my sin is ever before me.

Against Thee, Thee only, have I sinned, and done this evil in Thy sight: that Thou mightest be justified when Thou speakest, and be clear when Thou judgest.

Behold, I was shapen in iniquity; and in sin did my mother conceive me.

Behold, Thou desirest truth in the inward parts: and in the hidden part Thou shalt make me to know wisdom.

Purge me with hyssop, and I shall be clean: wash me, and I shall be whiter than snow.

Make me to hear joy and gladness; that the bones which Thou hast broken may rejoice.

Hide Thy face from my sins, and blot out all mine iniquities.

Create in me a clean heart, O God; and renew a right spirit within me.

Cast me not away from Thy presence; and take not Thy Holy Spirit from me.

Restore unto me the joy of Thy salvation; and uphold me with Thy free Spirit.

Then will I teach transgressors Thy ways; and sinners shall be converted unto Thee.

Deliver me from bloodguiltiness, O God, Thou God of my salvation: and my tongue shall sing aloud of Thy righteousness.

O Lord, open Thou my lips; and my mouth shall show forth Thy praise.

For Thou desirest not sacrifice: else would I give it: Thou delightest not in burnt offering.

The sacrifices of God are a broken spirit: a broken and a contrite heart, O God, Thou wilt not despise.

Do good in Thy good pleasure unto Zion: build Thou the walls of Jerusalem.

Then shalt Thou be pleased with the sacrifices of righteousness, with burnt offering and whole burnt offering: then shall they offer bullocks upon Thine altar.

— Psalm 51

The scriptural marks by which I am to examine myself to determine my present spiritual state and relationship with God's covenant are as follows:

A. *Inward-working graces* — Do I know something in my heart's experience of:

1. *Misery* (or repentance)?
2. *Deliverance* (or faith)?
3. *Thankfulness* (or obedience)?

B. *Outward-working graces* — Do I know something in my life's experience of the fruits of:

1. *Love toward God?*
2. *Love towards others?*

When you examine your own heart and life, do you experientially know something of these graces? If so, then your desire is to grow spiritually, to grow in the experience and exercise of these inward and outward working graces. If not, then you are yet missing that which is most necessary in your life — personal conversion to God and a saving, eternal, unbreakable covenant relationship with Him. Then prayerfully seek God through the use of the means of grace that He has given you in your outward relationship with Him. Plead with Him and do not let Him go until He has confirmed the saving truths of His Word in the experience and fruits of your life. He is a wonderfully gracious God! He delights to save needy and lost sinners.

In contrast with the previously described belief (of not viewing any baptized child or adult as regenerated or included in a saving relationship to the Covenant of Grace until the inward-working graces of the Holy Spirit are experienced and the outward-working fruits are evidenced), three other views have developed within the Reformed circles. These differing views are as follows:

1. *Dormant regeneration* — Dormant regeneration is a belief that most of the children that are born and baptized into the church are regenerated by God in their infancy. However, this "seed" of regeneration may lie dormant within the soul for a longer or shorter time before conversion to God takes place and evidences of spiritual life appear. According to this view, regeneration and conversion, receiving spiritual life and bringing forth the fruits of spiritual life, may be separated by several years.

Dormant regeneration can be pictured as follows:

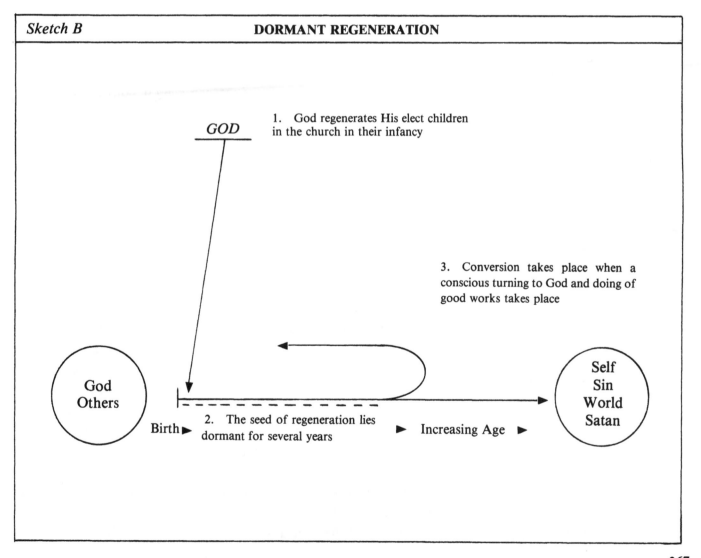

? Does Scripture permit us to speak of a tree as being good, as having a good root, before it brings forth good fruit? Does Scripture permit us to speak of persons as being regenerated before they bring forth the fruits of spiritual life? Why not?

> A good tree cannot bring forth evil fruit, neither can a corrupt tree bring forth good fruit.
>
> Every tree that bringeth not forth good fruit is hewn down, and cast into the fire.
>
> Wherefore by their fruits ye shall know them.
> — Matthew 7:18-20

> Bring forth therefore fruits worthy of repentance, and begin not to say within yourselves, We have Abraham to our father: for I say unto you, That God is able of these stones to raise up children unto Abraham.
>
> And now also the axe is laid unto the root of the trees: every tree therefore which bringeth not forth good fruit is hewn down, and cast into the fire.
> — Luke 3:8-9

? Does Scripture give us the right to presume that individuals will be saved, and to view them in that manner, before the evidences of saving grace are evidenced in their lives? Why not?

> Therefore whosoever heareth these sayings of Mine, and doeth them, I will liken him unto a wise man, which built his house upon a rock.
> — Matthew 7:24

> For not the hearers of the law are just before God, but the doers of the law shall be justified.
> — Romans 2:13

> But be ye doers of the Word, and not hearers only, deceiving your own selves.
> — James 1:22

AN EXAMPLE OF DORMANT REGENERATIONAL TEACHING

In the second place, we must bear in mind that our covenant seed, exactly because they are covenant seed, are also born again, even as children. The Bible gives every indication that within the sphere of the covenant our elect children are regenerated in infancy, perhaps even before birth. It's true of course that in infancy and early childhood our children are not conscious of this new life they have in Jesus Christ. Nor does that new life immediately bear fruit in their lives, at least not fruit that is discernible to us as parents. Nevertheless, the power of the new life is present, implanted into their hearts by the Holy Spirit.

We may view this new life in our covenant children in much the same way that we view other natural gifts with which our children are endowed even at birth. At birth our children are endowed with the potential of speaking, singing, walking, reading, writing, and a host of other essential things. However, in early childhood our children are neither conscious of these gifts nor are they able to use them. Our children become conscious of these powers and are able to use them only through proper development and training. In much the same way do our covenant children receive the power of the new life in Jesus Christ at birth.

— Rev. J. Slopsema, *The Standard Bearer*

---

2. *Presumptive (or Presupposed) Regeneration* — Presumptive regeneration is a belief that, based upon God's covenant promises, we should presume or presuppose baptized children and young people to be saved until it would be clearly shown by the fruits of their lives that they are not. Such falling away would be shown by breaking with religion, living unrepentantly in public sins, promoting God-dishonoring doctrines, or in other similarly public ways. Public confession of faith, on the other hand, would testify of a desire to remain with God and His church. Presumptive regeneration does not teach that all children are actually in a saving relationship in the Covenant of Grace, but that we must presume they are until the contrary would clearly manifest itself.

Presumptive regeneration can be pictured as follows:

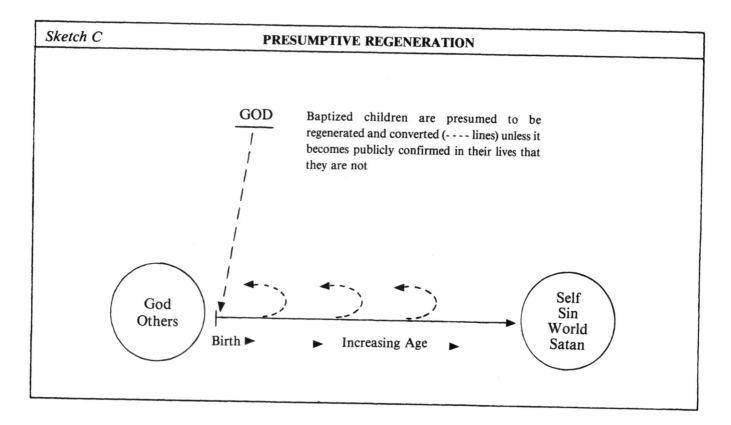

It may be well to quote in this connection the first half of the fourth point of the *Conclusions of Utrecht*, which were adopted by our Church in 1908. We translate this as follows: "And, finally, as far as the fourth point, that of *presumptive regeneration*, is concerned, Synod declares that, according to the confession of our Churches, the seed of the covenant must, in virtue of the promise of God, be presumed to be regenerated and sanctified in Christ, until, as they grow up, the contrary appears from their life or doctrine.

— Rev. L. Berkhof, *Systematic Theology*

3. *Covenantal regeneration* — Covenantal regeneration refers to the belief that *all* the gifts of the Covenant of Grace, including the forgiveness of sins and right to eternal life, are promised to the children of the church in their baptism. There is no inward or outward relationship to the covenant — all are included in the covenant

in the same manner through baptism. Each baptized person is called upon to believe God's promise and receive His gift. Faith in God's promise and obedience to His will are required conditions for remaining in the covenant. God's covenant "vengeance" falls upon those who reject His covenant through unbelief.

Covenantal regeneration can be pictured as follows:

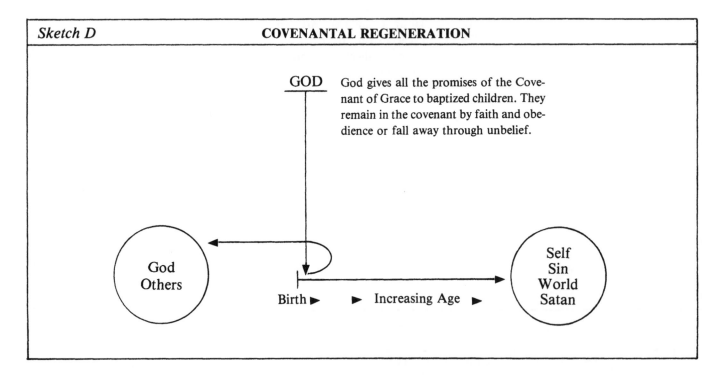

Sketch D — COVENANTAL REGENERATION

GOD — God gives all the promises of the Covenant of Grace to baptized children. They remain in the covenant by faith and obedience or fall away through unbelief.

God Others

Self Sin World Satan

Birth ▶ ▶ Increasing Age ▶

AN EXAMPLE OF COVENANTAL REGENERATIONAL TEACHING

God's promises were given to *all* those that were baptized — your baptism was full. The more urging becomes the demand to keep God's covenant, holding fast to God's promises and directing yourself to His commands. Children of the Kingdom will be cast out and cut off the true vine, when they are disobedient and bear no fruit.

So the children of the covenant must keep their covenant. God wants to be acknowledged and adhered to as covenantal God. They must love and serve Him by faith. Thereby trusting in Him who worked their salvation. Both sides (parties) must keep the covenant.

Baptism is serious business — in the name of God the Father, Son, and Holy Spirit. A covenant cannot be broken — but by self-chosen death.

— Rev. J. Van Bruggen, *The Belgic Confession of Faith*

Using the previously quoted biblical references, how does Scripture contradict the teachings of dormant, presumptive, and covenantal regeneration? Only upon what grounds does Scripture permit us to view ourselves or others as saved, elect, or included in an eternal covenant relationship with God? Why does the Word of God forbid the separation of regeneration from conversion, the presuming of regeneration and conversion, and the believing of God's promise for salvation without the personal experiencing of the inward-working graces of the Holy Spirit?

How do the following articles of the *Canons of Dordt* define the personal experience of the Holy Spirit's work of regeneration in the hearts of those that are saved? How does this description contradict the teachings of dormant, presumptive, and covenantal regeneration?

But when God accomplishes His good pleasure in the elect, or works in them true conversion, He not only causes the gospel to be eternally preached to them, and powerfully illuminates their minds by His Holy Spirit, that they may rightly understand and discern the things of the Spirit of God; but by the efficacy of the same regenerating Spirit, pervades the inmost recesses of the man; He opens the closed, and softens the hardened heart, and circumcises that which was uncircumcised, infuses new qualities into the will, which though heretofore dead, He quickens; from being evil, disobedient, and refractory, He renders it good, obedient, and pliable; actuates and strengthens it, that like a good tree, it may bring forth the fruits of good actions.

And this is the regeneration so highly celebrated in Scripture, and denominated a new creation: a resurrection from the dead, a making alive, which God works in us without our aid. But this is in no wise effected merely by the external preaching of the gospel, by moral suasion, or such a mode of operation, that after God has performed His part, it still remains in the power of man to be regenerated or not, to be converted, or to continue unconverted; but it is evidently a supernatural work, most powerful, and at the same time most delightful, astonishing, mysterious, and ineffable; not inferior in efficacy to creation, or the resurrection from the dead, as the Scripture inspired by the author of this work declares; so that all in whose heart God works in this marvelous manner, are certainly, infallibly, and effectually regenerated, and do actually believe. — Whereupon the will thus renewed, is not only actuated and influenced by God, but in consequence of this influence, becomes itself active. Wherefore also, man is himself rightly said to believe and repent, by virtue of that grace received.

— Articles 11 and 12 of the III and IV Heads of Doctrine

The different denominational beliefs regarding: the number of covenants, covenant presentations, persons that are included in covenant relationships, and regenerational views, are shown in the chart on the following pages.

? How and why does Scripture emphasize a clear distinction between the natural/baptized seed and the spiritual/saved seed in the church?

Bring forth therefore fruits meet for repentance:
And think not to say within yourselves, We have Abraham to our father: for I say unto you, that God is able of these stones to raise up children unto Abraham.
And now also the axe is laid unto the root of the trees: therefore every tree which bringeth not forth good fruit is hewn down, and cast into the fire.
— Matthew 3:8-10

They answered and said unto Him, Abraham is our father. Jesus saith unto them, If ye were Abraham's children, ye would do the works of Abraham.
John 8:39

For he is not a Jew, which is one outwardly; neither is that circumcision, which is outward in the flesh:
But he is a Jew, which is one inwardly; and circumcision is that of the heart, in the spirit, and not in the letter; whose praise is not of men, but of God.
— Romans 2:28-29

? Describe the truths that are being proclaimed in I Thessalonians 5:21 — "Prove all things; hold fast that which is good," and in Matthew 7:1 — "Judge not, that ye be not judged."

Which verse speaks about judging teachings and which refers to judging persons? Why are both of these truths important to remember when contrasting the different Reformed views concerning the Covenant of Grace and its members?

Doctrinal Distinctives	Baptist Denominations	Conservative Evangelical and Presbyterian Denominations Netherlands Reformed	Protestant Reformed
Number of Covenants pertaining to man's salvation	Two Covenants	Two Covenants	Two Covenants
Covenant Presentations	View 1 — p. 357 (without the shaded outward covenant relationship to in the Covenant of Grace)	View 1 — p. 357	View 1 — p. 357 (Excepting the Covenant of Works and God the Father as representative of the Trinity)
The *Unbreakable Aspect* of the Covenant of Grace	The Covenant of Grace	The inward relationship to (or essence of) the Covenant of Grace	The inward relationship to (or essence of) the Covenant of Grace
The *Breakable Aspect* of the Covenant of Grace	None	The outward relationship to the Covenant of Grace	The outward relationship to the Covenant of Grace
Only the *Spiritual/Elect Seed*	In the Covenant of Grace	In the unbreakable, inward relationship to (or essence of) the Covenant of Grace	In the unbreakable, inward relationship to (or essence of) the Covenant of Grace
The *Natural/Baptized Seed*	None	In the breakable, outward relationship to the Covenant of Grace	In the breakable, outward relationship to the Covenant of Grace
Regenerational Views	Personal, experiential regeneration and conversion Sketch A — p. 365	Personal, experiential regeneration and conversion Sketch A — p. 365	Dormant Regeneration Sketch B — p. 367

COVENANTS AND MAN'S RELATIONSHIPS TO THEM

Christian Reformed	Free Reformed	Canadian or American Reformed (Article 31)	Arminian/Free-will Denominations
Three Covenants	Three Covenants	Three Covenants	Three Covenants
View 2 — p. 358	View 3 — p. 359	View 4 — p. 360	Arminius' view of the covenants — p. 344
The Covenant of Redemption, and the inward relationship to the Covenant of Grace	The Covenant of Redemption	The Covenant of Redemption	None
The outward relationship to the Covenant of Grace	The Covenant of Grace	The Covenant of Grace	The Covenant of Redemption The Covenant of Grace
In the Covenant of Redemption and inward relationship to the Covenant of Grace	The Covenant of Redemption	The Covenant of Redemption	The Covenant of Grace (With those who chose to believe; "election" based upon foreseen faith of individuals)
In the outward relationship to the Covenant of Grace	Both the elect and baptized are included in the same offer in The Covenant of Grace	Both the elect and baptized are included in the promises of The Covenant of Grace	The Covenant of Redemption (with all mankind)
Presumptive Regeneration Sketch C — p. 369	Personal, experiential regeneration and conversion Sketch A — p. 365	Covenantal Regeneration Sketch D — p. 370	Decisional Regeneration — p. 345

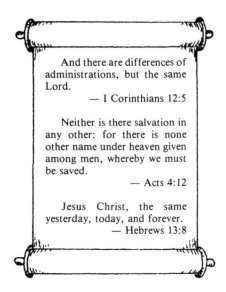

And there are differences of administrations, but the same Lord.
— I Corinthians 12:5

Neither is there salvation in any other: for there is none other name under heaven given among men, whereby we must be saved.
— Acts 4:12

Jesus Christ, the same yesterday, today, and forever.
— Hebrews 13:8

God's wonderful Covenant of Grace was revealed to sinners already in Paradise immediately after man's fall. It has been proclaimed through all ages, and it shall be presented to fallen sinners until the end of the world. While the same covenant or way of salvation (with the same blessings of the forgiveness of sins and right to eternal life through the same Covenant Head or Savior, Jesus Christ) has been and will be revealed throughout all ages, God has not always revealed and administrated His covenant in the same form. Four different modes of revelation, or forms of administration, of the same Covenant of Grace are spoken of in Scripture.

The four different forms of administration of the Covenant of Grace are as follows:

1. *The Particular Form* from Adam to Abraham — During this period there was no formal covenant, no sacrament administration, no special sign or seal to one set-apart group of people. While God revealed His grace personally to particular persons in the generations of Seth, no formal covenant revelation or administration was established.

? Dispensationalism is a belief that originated in the late 1800's. It teaches that God tested man, and that man was to respond to God, in different manners during different dispensations (time periods).

How is this belief different from believing in one Covenant of Grace being revealed in increasingly richer forms of revelation and administration?

Why is this distinction very important?

2. *The Patriarchal Form* from Abraham to Moses — God established His covenant more formally with Abraham and his seed. To them were given the sign of circumcision and the promises. All the natural seed were circumcised and placed in an external relationship to the covenant in distinction from all other families on earth. Yet all were not included internally in the essence of the covenant. The saving blessings of the covenant were given to some, but not to all — to Isaac but not Ishmael, to Jacob but not Esau.

3. *The National (or Sinaitic) Form* from Moses to Christ — God formally established His covenant with the nation of Israel on Mount Sinai. God set apart the nation of Israel from all other nations on earth. Under this national covenant, Israel's church and state became one. God gave them His laws — moral, civil, and ceremonial. The passover sacrament was added to that of circumcision.

Wherefore the law was our schoolmaster to bring us unto Christ, that we might be justified by faith.
— Galatians 3:24

We know that the national (law) form was an administration of God's Covenant of Grace for the following five reasons:

THE NATIONAL (LAW) FORM — A FORM OF ADMINISTRATION OF THE COVENANT OF GRACE	
Reason	Example Text
1. All the **ceremonial laws** concerning sacrifices, washings, priesthood, and tabernacle all pointed to, and were fulfilled by, Jesus Christ.	For the law having a shadow of good things to come, and not the very image of the things, can never with those sacrifices which they offered year by year continually make the comers thereunto perfect. — Hebrews 10:1
2. The sacraments (which included bloodshedding) all pointed to the Savior.	And almost all things are by the law purged with blood; and without shedding of blood is no remission. It was therefore necessary that the patterns of things in the heavens should be purified with these; but the heavenly things themselves with better sacrifices than these. — Hebrews 9:22-23
3. The gracious introduction to the **moral law**.	And God spake all these words, saying, I am the LORD thy God, which have brought thee out of the land of Egypt, out of the house of bondage. — Exodus 20:1-2
4. The moral law was given to increase the consciousness of sin and convict of guilt; to work need and place for Jesus Christ and His grace.	For the earnest expectation of the creature waiteth for the manifestation of the sons of God. — Romans 8:19
5. The moral law was given by the Mediator, Jesus Christ.	Wherefore then serveth the law? It was added because of transgressions, till the seed should come to whom the promise was made; and it was ordained by angels in the hand of a mediator. — Galatians 3:19

● **Ceremonial laws** — Israel's Old Testament religious laws which pointed to, and were fulfilled by, Christ

● **Moral law** — The Ten Commandments

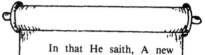

In that He saith, A new covenant, He hath made the first old. Now that which decayeth and waxeth old is ready to vanish away.

Then verily the first covenant had also ordinances of divine service, and a worldly sanctuary.
— Hebrews 8:13; 9:1

And for this cause He is the Mediator of the New Testament, that by means of death, for the redemption of the transgressions that were under the first testament, they which are called might receive the promise of eternal inheritance.
— Hebrews 9:15

These three forms of administration that pointed to and promised Jesus Christ, which looked forward to His perfect salvation as Head as the Covenant of Grace, can be distinguished from the last form of revelation. The final form is the fulfillment of the types and promises of the former. Scripture speaks of the first three forms as the old, and the fulfillment as the new, covenants or testaments. The Old Testament was the promise, the New Testament was the fulfillment, but, both form one complete revelation, Word, Savior, Covenant Head, and covenant.

4. *Ecclesiastical* (*Gospel* or *New Testament*) *Form* from Christ to the end of the world — the revelation of the Covenant of Grace in its final form is the richest and most gracious form of revelation in the following ways:

a. God's grace is revealed *most directly* — not through types and prophecies, but in actuality and fulfillment (John 16:13-15).

● **Ecclesiastical** — Referring to a worldwide church

? Do the Old and New Testament dispensations differ in plan or way of salvation for man? If not, in what way *do* they differ?

b. God's grace is revealed *most richly* — the Holy Spirit is poured out in all fulness (Acts 2:1-4, 14-18).

c. God's grace is revealed *most widely* — covenant relationship is no longer limited to one family or nation, but God's church includes people from all countries, tribes, and languages on earth (Matthew 28:19-20; Revelation 5:9).

The four forms of administration of God's Covenant of Grace can be pictured in the following manner; note how each form of administration from Abraham on has both its external, outward, breakable, and natural seed relationship; and its internal, inward, unbreakable, and spiritual seed relationship to the Covenant.

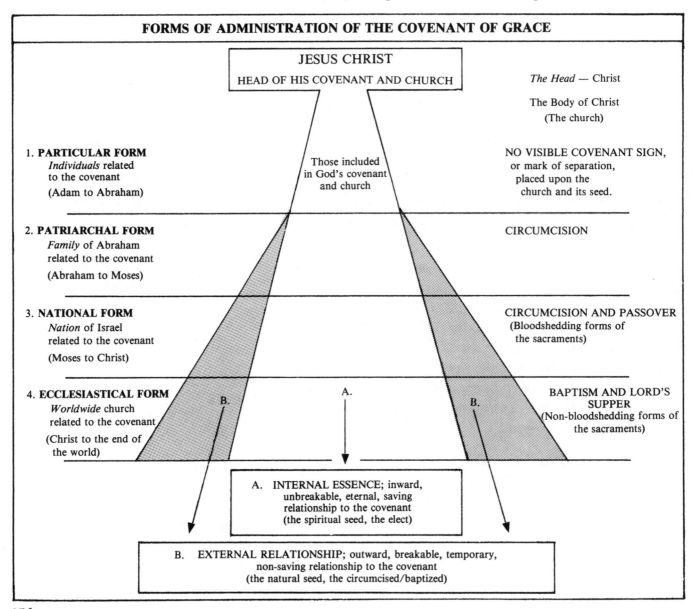

FORMS OF ADMINISTRATION OF THE COVENANT OF GRACE

JESUS CHRIST
HEAD OF HIS COVENANT AND CHURCH

The Head — Christ

The Body of Christ
(The church)

1. **PARTICULAR FORM**
Individuals related to the covenant
(Adam to Abraham)

Those included in God's covenant and church

NO VISIBLE COVENANT SIGN, or mark of separation, placed upon the church and its seed.

2. **PATRIARCHAL FORM**
Family of Abraham related to the covenant
(Abraham to Moses)

CIRCUMCISION

3. **NATIONAL FORM**
Nation of Israel related to the covenant
(Moses to Christ)

CIRCUMCISION AND PASSOVER
(Bloodshedding forms of the sacraments)

4. **ECCLESIASTICAL FORM**
Worldwide church related to the covenant
(Christ to the end of the world)

BAPTISM AND LORD'S SUPPER
(Non-bloodshedding forms of the sacraments)

A. INTERNAL ESSENCE; inward, unbreakable, eternal, saving relationship to the covenant
(the spiritual seed, the elect)

B. EXTERNAL RELATIONSHIP; outward, breakable, temporary, non-saving relationship to the covenant
(the natural seed, the circumcised/baptized)

God's Covenant of Grace is eternal. The essence of the covenant will be realized in its fullest extent in heaven. There, God will dwell with His people and they will commune forever with Him. There, no sin or separation will interrupt their eternal fellowship. There, the rich promises of the Covenant of Grace will be fully experienced by all true believers without end.

God's Covenant of Grace is most rich and gracious! In the Covenant of Grace, through Christ its Covenant Head, God grants more to His children than they lost in their first covenant head, Adam, in the Covenant of Works. This gracious truth is shown in the following chart.

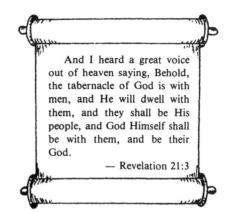

And I heard a great voice out of heaven saying, Behold, the tabernacle of God is with men, and He will dwell with them, and they shall be His people, and God Himself shall be with them, and be their God.

— Revelation 21:3

MORE RECEIVED IN CHRIST THAN LOST IN ADAM	
In the first covenant, the Covenant of Works, Adam lost for his children:	In the second covenant, the Covenant of Grace, the "second Adam," Jesus Christ, gained for His children:
1. An earthly Paradise	1. A heavenly Paradise
2. A humanly uncertain righteousness	2. A divinely-certain righteousness
3. Rule over earthly creatures	3. Rule over all things
4. Close communion; God with man	4. Oneness in communion; God inseparably joined to man in Jesus Christ
5. The love of God toward a loving and responding person	5. The grace of God; love toward rebellious sinners

For as by one man's disobedience many were made sinners, so by the obedience of One shall many be made righteous.

Moreover the law entered, that the offence might abound. But where sin abounded, grace did much more abound.

That as sin hath reigned unto death, even so might grace reign through righteousness unto eternal life by Jesus Christ our Lord.

— Romans 5:19-21

Not by works of righteousness which we have done, but according to His mercy He saved us, by the washing of regeneration, and renewing of the Holy Ghost;

Which He shed on us abundantly through Jesus Christ our Saviour;

That being justified by His grace, we should be made heirs according to the hope of eternal life.

— Titus 3:5-7

The depth of God's grace in the Covenant of Grace is unfathomable. What an indescribable blessing it is to be cut off from Adam and the broken Covenant of Works with its results, and to be implanted into Jesus Christ and the Covenant of Grace with its promises! God's grace is His wonderful, one-sided work of love toward sinners who deserve condemnation instead of salvation. Rev. Hellenbroek defined the Covenant of Grace as "the way by which God through Christ becomes the property of the sinner and by which he in turn becomes the property of God."

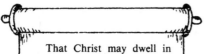

That Christ may dwell in your hearts by faith; that ye, being rooted and grounded in love,

May be able to comprehend with all saints what is the breadth, and length, and depth, and height;

And to know the love of Christ, which passeth knowledge, that ye might be filled with all the fulness of God.

Now unto Him that is able to do exceeding abundantly above all that we ask or think, according to the power that worketh in us,

Unto Him be glory in the church by Christ Jesus throughout all ages, world without end. Amen.
— Ephesians 3:17-21

● **Presiding** — Directing; leading; ruling

● **Defendant** — The person on trial against whom a charge has been laid

Is this your deepest longing and desire? Grace is a free gift of God; therefore, we must ask it of Him. Are you prayerfully and diligently using His means of grace? This is the channel through which He delights to give and strengthen His grace in the hearts of lost sinners. Was the prodigal son, the Canaanitish woman, Bartimeus, or anyone who pleaded as an unworthy sinner with the Lord for His grace ever disappointed?

God is a God of grace. His Covenant of Grace testifies of this truth. He is a God that delights to show mercy.

Imagine a judge **presiding** over the trial of his enemy, one who had slandered his name, mistreated him numerous times, and frequently fought against him. As the trial proceeded it became obvious to all that the **defendant** was guilty.

In suspense, the courtroom hushed to hear the judge's sentence. The judge sentenced his enemy justly, with a fitting three-year prison sentence for his crimes, to begin immediately.

However, after sentencing the criminal, the judge made a startling announcement. "I wish to officially proclaim," he stated, "that I will fully pay for this man's sentence. This man is free."

Would not such a scene reveal a rich depth of gracious love in the heart of this judge toward an undeserving and guilty sinner?

The Covenant of Grace testifies of a far deeper fountain of grace than the previous example. It reveals an infinite ocean of gracious love toward guilty, condemnable sinners.

In comparison to this story:
— How are sinners' crimes against God much greater?
— To pay the full sentence for the crimes of His people, what far higher price did Jesus need to pay?

The Covenant of Grace testifies of the greatest love and forgiveness ever shown. It also speaks of justice being fully paid. How? What double responsibility does this proclaim to us?

CATECHISM MEMORIZATION
Questions from Rev. A. Hellenbroek's *Divine Truths* — Chapters V and XI

1. Since God can have no communion with a sinner, how is it possible that He predestinated some members of the fallen human race unto salvation?

   To be consistent with His holiness and justice in salvation from eternity, God requested His Son to intervene as mediatorial Surety between Himself and His people by giving Himself as the ransom price for sin. This Divine agreement is properly called The Covenant of Redemption or The Counsel of Peace.

2. What is the Counsel of Peace?

   The eternal will of the Father to redeem the elect through Christ's suffering and death, agreeing with the will of the Son to offer Himself as Surety for the elect.

3. Has this agreement existed between the Father and the Son from eternity?

   Yes. "I will declare the decree; the Lord hath said unto Me, Thou art My Son, this day have I begotten Thee. Ask of Me, and I shall give Thee the heathen for Thine inheritance, and the uttermost parts of the earth for Thy possession" (Ps. 2:7-8). "And I appoint unto you a kingdom as My Father hath appointed unto Me" (Luke 22:29).

4. What must we consider in this Counsel of Peace?

   Two things: (1) the agreeing parties and (2) the work of each party.

5. In what respect did the Father reveal Himself in the Counsel of Peace?

   As a sovereign Lord, who deals with His Son concerning the ransom for the elect, which He was not obliged to permit.

6. In what respect did the Son reveal Himself in the Counsel of Peace?

   As Redeemer and Mediator who obliged Himself to pay the debts of the elect.

7. What was the work of the Father in the Counsel of Peace?

   The Father demanded that the Son fulfill all the requirements necessary for the redemption of the elect, which was the Father's eternal will. "And this is the Father's will, which hath sent Me, that of all which He hath given Me, I should lose nothing, but should raise it up again at the last day" (John 6:39).

8. Did the Father also make a promise to the Son in the Counsel of Peace?

   Yes, He promised Him an elect seed over which He would be Head and King. "I pray not for the world, but for them which Thou hast given Me" (John 17:9).

9. Has the Father done anything else in the Counsel of Peace?

   Yes, God the Father has confirmed the promise to His Son by means of an oath. "The Lord hath sworn and will not repent. Thou art a Priest forever after the order of Melchizedek" (Ps. 110:4).

10. What was the work of the Son in this agreement?

    Christ accepted the demand of the Father and assumed complete responsibility to fulfill this demand for the elect. "Then said I, Lo, I come, in the volume of the book, it is written of Me, I delight to do Thy will, O my God: yea, Thy law is written within My heart" (Ps. 40:7-8).

11. Is there anything else the Son of God did in the Counsel of Peace?

    Yes, He required in return that the elect be His inheritance. "Ask of Me, and I shall give Thee the heathen for Thine inheritance, and the uttermost parts of the earth for Thy possession" (Ps. 2:8).

12. Was there another covenant to replace the broken Covenant of Works?

    Yes, the Covenant of Grace.

13. When was that Covenant established in time?

    Immediately after the fall. "I will put enmity between thee and the woman, and between thy seed and her seed; it shall bruise thy head, and thou shalt bruise His heel" (Gen. 3:15).

14. What is the Covenant of Grace?

    The Covenant of Grace is the way opened up in Christ Jesus by which God becomes the property of the sinner, and the sinner in turn becomes the property of God (Jer. 31:33).

15. With whom is the Covenant of Grace established?

    With Jesus Christ as its Head, and all the elect who are comprehended in Him.

16. What does God require in this covenant?

    That which God requires — faith in Jesus Christ — He also promises to give to His elect.

17. What does God promise in the Covenant of Grace?

    Grace here, and eternal life hereafter. "Believe on the Lord Jesus Christ, and thou shalt be saved" (Acts 16:31).

18. Did believers during the Old Testament dispensation also partake of all the essential benefits of the Covenant of Grace?

    Yes. "Jesus Christ the same yesterday and today and forever" (Heb. 13:8).

19. How does a sinner enter into this Covenant of Grace?

    God first comes to him when He kindly and beseechingly invites him with much earnestness and uprightness and solves all his difficulties. (II Cor. 5:20; Ez. 33:11; Isa. 55:2).

CHAPTER 9

Part I. Chapter Review

1. Name God's covenants concerning:
   a. Nature and man's temporal state —
      1. _____
      2. _____
   b. Man's salvation and eternal state —
      1. _____
      2. _____

2. Compare the Covenants of Works and of Grace. For each, include the following: the representative head, work accomplished, result, those included, and principle of application used.
   _____
   _____
   _____

3. Name and define the two aspects of the Covenant of Grace:
   a. _____
      _____
   b. _____
      _____

4. Name five titles of Christ's official position in the Covenant of Grace:
   a. _____ d. _____
   b. _____ e. _____
   c. _____

5. Describe the work of each divine Person in the Covenant of Grace:
   a. God the Father — _____
   b. God the Son — _____
   c. God the Holy Spirit — _____

6. All the requirements and promises of the Covenant of Grace are fulfilled in, and freely given to, the elect by Jesus Christ. Why? _____
   _____
   _____

7. How is Arminius' presentation of the Covenant of Redemption different from all Reformed teachings? _____
   _____
   _____

8. According to Arminius, how does a person enter the Covenant of Grace?
   _____
   _____

9. List four scriptural reasons for a two-covenant rather than a three-covenant view regarding man's salvation:
   a. _____
   b. _____
   c. _____
   d. _____

10. Explain how the Covenant of Grace is both:
    a. Unbreakable — _____
       _____
    b. Breakable — _____
       _____

11. Explain how both of the following groups are related to the Covenant of Grace:
    a. Only the spiritual, elect, saved seed — _____
       _____
    b. The natural, baptized, unsaved seed — _____
       _____

12. State four benefits of an outward relationship to the Covenant of Grace:
    a. _____
    b. _____
    c. _____
    d. _____

13. How can the blessing of an outward relationship to God's covenant and church be:
    a. Overvalued? — _____
       _____
    b. Undervalued? — _____
       _____

14. Describe the following regenerational views:
    a. Personal, experiential regeneration — _____
       _____
    b. Decisional regeneration (Arminius) — _____
       _____
    c. Dormant regeneration — _____
       _____
    d. Presumptive regeneration — _____
       _____
    e. Covenantal regeneration — _____
       _____

15. Name the four forms of administration of the Covenant of Grace:
    a. _____   c. _____
    b. _____   d. _____

CHAPTER 9

Part II. Deepening Your Insight

1. Why are all covenants God makes with man, in reality, covenants of *grace*?
   _____
   _____

2. While similar in many respects, how is God's Covenant of Grace from eternity and His decree of election different? _____
   _____
   _____

3. For Jesus Christ, the Covenant of Grace was actually a covenant of *works*. Why?
   _____
   _____
   _____

4. Explain how repentance, faith, and obedience are both "conditions" to be found in, and benefits freely given to, the elect in the Covenant of Grace: _____
   _____
   _____

5. How would you respond to those favoring a three-covenant view because of:
   a. Scriptural references to God establishing His Covenant of Grace with the elect? _____
   _____
   _____

   b. Scriptural references of conditions to be met by those that are included in the Covenant of Grace? _____
   _____
   _____

6. Why is an external relationship to God's Covenant of Grace and church both a great privilege and responsibility? _____
   _____
   _____

7. How do the following covenant views differ from each other?
   a. The Baptist view and View 1 — _____
   _____

   b. View 3 and View 4 — _____
   _____

8. Describe both the inward- and outward-working graces and fruits that Scripture requires before one may view himself, or speak of others, as being saved.
   _____
   _____
   _____

QUESTIONS

Part III. Biblical Applications

1. Which verse or verses in the following chapters refer to God's Covenant of Grace from eternity? Write out the appropriate portions:
   a. Zechariah 6:_____ — _____
   b. II Timothy 1:_____ — _____
   c. Galatians 3:_____ — _____
   d. Isaiah 42:_____ — _____

2. How does Acts 22:27-28 illustrate two different manners of attaining citizenship, and how does this apply to an outward relationship to God's covenant and church?
   _____
   _____
   _____

3. Read the following scriptural portions. Quote the verses which show how misery, deliverance, and thankfulness were personally experienced in the lives of each:
   a. Mark 2:1-12 — _____
   _____

   b. Acts 16:27-34 — _____
   _____

   c. Acts 9:1-22 — _____
   _____

Part IV. From the Writings of our Church Forefathers

In your own words, explain the meaning of the following quotations:

1. "There is no reason to be given for grace but grace" (Ralph Venning). _____
   _____
   _____
   _____

2. "God does not choose us for faith, but to faith. We are elected to holiness, not for it" (Thomas Watson). _____
   _____
   _____

3. "The first degree of grace is the desire for grace" (William Fenner). _____
   _____
   _____
   _____

CHAPTER 9

Part V. From the Marginal Questions

1. How does the teaching of the Covenant of *Grace* exalt God to the highest and abase man to the lowest?

    _____
    _____
    _____
    _____

2. What rich security is lost by those who deny the truth that nothing depends upon man, but all upon Christ, as Head of the Covenant of Grace?

    _____
    _____
    _____
    _____

3. How is the blessing of opportunity different from the blessing of fulfilment? How does this distinction apply to outward and inward covenant relationships?

    _____
    _____
    _____
    _____

4. Does Scripture permit us to speak of a tree as being good, or as having a good root, before it brings forth good fruit? Does Scripture permit us to speak of persons as being regenerated before they bring forth the fruits of spiritual life? Why not?

    _____
    _____
    _____
    _____

5. Do the Old and New Testament dispensations differ in plan or way of salvation for man? If not, in what way *do* they differ?

    _____
    _____

EXTRA CHALLENGE QUESTIONS

Part VI. Your Selection from the Marginal Questions

Write out and respond to two marginal questions that interest you which have not been previously asked in this chapter's question section.

1. Question: _____
   _____

   Response: _____
   _____
   _____
   _____
   _____
   _____

2. Question: _____
   _____

   Response: _____
   _____
   _____
   _____
   _____

Part VII. Project Ideas

1. Research and study the reasons for teaching a two- and a three-covenant presentation regarding man's salvation. Stage a debate between these two viewpoints.

2. Present a panel discussion on the various covenant views studied. Use overhead transparencies and strive to make your presentation very informative.

3. Construct a chart which clearly displays the similarities and differences between the Covenants of Works and Grace.

4. Design a simplified chart which shows how the requirements and promises of the Covenant of Grace are fulfilled in Christ and include the elect as recipients in Him, as their Covenant Head.

5. Draw a poster which portrays and teaches the differences between the views of personal and experiential, decisional, dormant, presumptive, and covenantal regeneration.

10

The Mediator
The Natures of Christ
The Names of Christ

The Rock of Ages stands unmoved
And is forever sure;
Through every tide of time and strife
Salvation is secure.

No tongue or pen can ever tell
The richness of God's love;
He sent His one and only Son
To earth from heaven above.

May each of us then learn to see
Our misery and cry
To Him who can deliver us
And lift us up on high.

FROM OUR REFORMED DOCTRINAL STANDARDS

Belgic Confession of Faith

Article 18 — Of the Incarnation of Jesus Christ

We confess, therefore, that God did fulfill the promise, which He made to the fathers, by the mouth of His holy prophets, when He sent into the world, at the time appointed by Him, His own, only-begotten and eternal Son, who took upon Him the form of a servant, and became like unto man, really assuming the true human nature, with all its infirmities, sin excepted, being conceived in the womb of the blessed Virgin Mary, by the power of the Holy Ghost, without the means of man, and did not only assume human nature as to the body, but also a true human soul, that He might be a real man. For since the soul was lost as well as the body, it was necessary that He should take both upon Him, to save both. Therefore we confess (in opposition to the heresy of the Anabaptists, who deny that Christ assumed human flesh of His mother) that Christ is become a partaker of the flesh and blood of the children; that He is a fruit of the loins of David after the flesh; made of the seed of David according to the flesh; and fruit of the womb of the Virgin Mary, made of a woman, a branch of David; a shoot of the root of Jesse; sprung from the tribe of Judah; descended from the Jews according to the flesh; of the seed of Abraham, since He took on Him the seed of Abraham, and became like unto His brethren in all things, sin excepted, so that in truth He is our **Immanuel**, that is to say, God with us.

Article 19 — Of the Union and Distinction of the two Natures in the person of Christ

We believe that by this conception, the person of the Son is inseparably united and connected with the human nature; so that there are not two Sons of God, nor two persons, but two natures united in one single person: yet, that each nature retains its own distinct properties.

As then the divine nature hath always remained uncreated, without beginning of days or end of life, filling heaven and earth: so also hath the human nature not lost its properties, but remained a creature, having beginning of days, being a finite nature, and retaining all the properties of a real body. And though He hath by His resurrection given immortality to the same, nevertheless He hath not changed the reality of His human nature; forasmuch as our salvation and resurrection also depend on the reality of His body. But these two natures are so closely united in one person, that they were not separated even by His death. Therefore that which He, when dying, commended into the hands of His Father, was a real human spirit, departing from His body. But in the meantime the divine nature always remained united with the human, even when He lay in the grave. And the Godhead did not cease to be in Him, any more than it did when He was an infant, though it did not so clearly manifest itself for a while. Wherefore we confess, that He is **very God, and very man:** very God by His power to conquer death; and very man that He might die for us according to the infirmity of His flesh.

Article 20 — That God hath manifested His justice and mercy in Christ

We believe that God, who is perfectly merciful and just, sent His Son to assume that nature, in which the disobedience was committed, to make satisfaction in the same, and to bear the punishment of sin by His most bitter passion and death. God therefore manifested His justice against His Son, when He laid our iniquities upon Him; and poured forth His mercy and goodness on us, who were guilty and worthy of damnation, out of mere and perfect love, giving His Son unto death for us, and raising Him for our justification, that through Him we might obtain immortality and life eternal.

Heidelberg Catechism

Questions and Answers 1, 12-19, 29-34, 47-48

Q. 1. What is thy only comfort in life and death?

A. That I with body and soul, both in life and death, am not my own, but belong unto my faithful Savior Jesus Christ, who, with His precious blood, hath fully satisfied for all my sins, and delivered me from all the power of the devil; and so preserves me that without the will of my heavenly Father, not a hair can fall from my head; yea, that all things must be subservient to my salvation, and therefore, by His Holy Spirit, He also assures me of eternal life, and makes me sincerely willing and ready, henceforth, to live unto Him.

Q. 12. Since then, by the righteous judgment of God, we deserve temporal and eternal punishment, is there no way by which we may escape that punishment, and be again received into favor?

A. God will have His justice satisfied: and therefore we must make this full satisfaction, either by ourselves, or by another.

Q. 13. Can we ourselves then make this satisfaction?

A. By no means; but on the contrary we daily increase our debt.

Q. 14. Can there be found anywhere, one, who is a mere creature, able to satisfy for us?

A. None; for, first, God will not punish any other creature for the sin which man hath committed; and further, no mere creature can sustain the burden of God's eternal wrath against sin, so as to deliver others from it.

Q. 15. What sort of a mediator and deliverer then must we seek for?

A. For one who is very man, and perfectly righteous; and yet more powerful than all creatures; that is, one who is also very God.

Q. 16. Why must He be very man, and also perfectly righteous?

A. Because the justice of God requires that the same human nature which hath sinned, should likewise make satisfaction for sin; and one, who is himself a sinner, cannot satisfy for others.

Q. 17. Why must He in one person be also very God?

A. That He might, by the power of His Godhead, sustain in His human nature, the burden of God's wrath; and might obtain for, and restore to us, righteousness and life.

Q. 18. Who then is that Mediator, who is in one person both very God, and a real righteous man?

A. Our Lord Jesus Christ: "who of God is made unto us wisdom, and righteousness, and sanctification, and redemption."

Q. 19. Whence knowest thou this?

A. From the holy gospel, which God Himself first revealed in Paradise; and afterwards published by the patriarchs and prophets, and represented by the sacrifices and other ceremonies of the law; and lastly, has fullfilled it by His only begotten Son.

Q. 29. Why is the Son of God called **Jesus**, that is, a Savior?

A. Because He saveth us, and delivereth us from our sins; and likewise, because we ought not to seek, neither can find salvation in any other.

Q. 30. Do such then believe in Jesus the only Savior, who seek their salvation and welfare of saints, of themselves, or anywhere else?

A. They do not; for though they boast of Him in words, yet in deeds they deny Jesus the only Deliverer and Savior; for one of these two things must be true, that either Jesus is not a complete Savior; or that they, who by a true faith receive this Savior, must find all things in Him necessary to their salvation.

Q. 31. Why is He called **Christ**, that is, anointed?

A. Because He is ordained of God the Father, and anointed with the Holy Ghost, to be our chief Prophet and Teacher, who has fully revealed to us the secret counsel and will of God concerning our redemption; and to be our only High Priest, who by the one sacrifice of His body, has redeemed us, and makes continual intercession with the Father for us; and also to be our eternal King, who governs us by His Word and Spirit, and who defends and preserves us in (the enjoyment of) that salvation, He has purchased for us.

Q. 32. But why art thou called a Christian?

A. Because I am a member of Christ by faith, and thus am partaker of His anointing; that so I may confess His name, and present myself a living sacrifice of thankfulness to Him: and also that with a free and good conscience I may fight against sin and Satan in this life: and afterwards reign with Him eternally, over all creatures.

Q. 33. Why is Christ called the only begotten Son of God, since we are also children of God?

A. Because Christ alone is the eternal and natural Son of God; but we are children adopted of God, by grace, for His sake.

Q. 34. Wherefore callest thou Him our Lord?

A. Because He hath redeemed us, both soul and body, from all our sins, not with gold or silver, but with His precious blood, and hath delivered us from all the power of the devil; and thus hath made us His own property.

Q. 47. Is not Christ then with us even to the end of the world, as He hath promised?

A. Christ is very man and very God; with respect to His human nature, He is no more on earth; but with respect to His Godhead, majesty, grace, and Spirit, He is at no time absent from us.

Q. 48. But if His human nature is not present, wherever His Godhead is, are not then these two natures in Christ separated from one another?

A. Not at all, for since the Godhead is illimitable and omnipresent, it must necessarily follow that the same is beyond the limits of the human nature He assumed, and yet is nevertheless in this human nature, and remains personally united to it.

10

THE MEDIATOR

Sin produced a separation between God and man. It broke the Covenant of Works and destroyed the relationship of peace, friendship, and communion which man had with God in Paradise.

From man's side, no **restoration** of relationship (of fellowship and favor) with God was possible. God is perfectly holy and righteous — He cannot tolerate sin. The Lord is also perfectly true — He cannot lie. God had said, "In the day thou eatest thereof (from the Tree of the Knowledge of Good and Evil) thou shalt surely die" (Genesis 2:17b). Man's original and actual sin makes deliverance by man impossible.

● **Restoration** — The state of being re-established or brought back to the former condition

What is impossible by man, however, is possible with God! God graciously provided a perfect **mediator**, One through whom God and man could be fully **reconciled**. This mediator is the Lord Jesus Christ. As the second Adam, as the head of the Covenant of Grace, He provided full satisfaction and payment for man's sin.

● **Mediator** — One who attempts to bring two disagreeing parties into agreement

● **Reconciled** — Agreed; settled; restored union and friendship after separation

Scripture speaks of, and pictures, Christ's work as mediator in numerous passages. The following is one example:

After the death of Korah, Dathan, and Abiram, the people of Israel continued to rebel, saying to Moses and Aaron, "Ye have killed the people of the LORD" (Numbers 16:41b).

Upon witnessing this, we read: "And Moses said unto Aaron, Take a censer, and put fire therein from off the altar, and put on incense, and go quickly unto the congregation, and make an atonement for them: for there is wrath gone out from the LORD; the plague is begun. And Aaron took as Moses commanded, and ran into the midst of the congregation; and behold, the plague was begun among the people: and he put on incense, and made an atonement for the people. And he stood between the dead and the living; and the plague was stayed. Now they that died in the plague were fourteen thousand and seven hundred, beside them that died about the matter of Korah" (Numbers 16:46-49).

How was Aaron a type of Christ, as mediator, when he stood between the dead and the living? Why are we only safe, when standing behind Jesus Christ and His sacrifice?

How do the following aspects of this story all point to Christ's work as mediator:
— The high priest
— Fire from the brazen altar
— The incense
— Making atonement

? How is a similar lesson pictured in the first Passover in Egypt? How does the blood of the lamb portray Christ's work as mediator for His people?

The Bible speaks of the following three types of mediators:

1. *A messenger (or mediator of communication)* — One who relates the thoughts of one party to another, as Moses frequently served as God's mouthpiece to Israel

2. *An advocate (or mediator of intercession)* — One who pleads the cause of another, as Moses often did for the sins of the nation of Israel

3. *A peacemaker (or mediator of reconciliation)* — One who pays the price for, and reconciles disagreeing parties; one who atones to make peace, as Judah offered to pay the full price so that Benjamin could be freed

The following chart illustrates how the Lord Jesus Christ serves as Mediator between God and His people in all three of the previous manners:

And the LORD said unto Moses, Thus thou shalt say unto the children of Israel.
— Exodus 20:22a

Pardon, I beseech thee, the iniquity of this people according to the greatness of Thy mercy, and as Thou hast forgiven this people, from Egypt even until now.
And the LORD said, I have pardoned according to thy word.
— Numbers 14:19-20

Now therefore, I pray thee, let thy servant abide instead of the lad a bondman to my lord; and let the lad go up with his brethren.
— Genesis 44:33

JESUS CHRIST SERVES AS MEDIATOR OF:		
1.	Communication; as Messenger	I will raise them up a Prophet from among their brethren, like unto thee, and will put My words in His mouth; and He shall speak unto them all that I shall command Him. — Deuteronomy 18:18
2.	Intercession; as Advocate	Wherefore He is able also to save them to the uttermost that come unto God by Him, seeing He ever liveth to make intercession for them. — Hebrews 7:25
3.	Reconciliation; as Peacemaker	Neither by the blood of goats and calves, but by His own blood He entered in once into the holy place, having obtained eternal redemption for us. — Hebrews 9:12

How much more shall the blood of Christ, who through the eternal Spirit offered Himself without spot to God, purge your conscience from dead works to serve the living God?
And for this cause He is the Mediator of the New Testament, that by means of death, for the redemption of the transgressions that were under the first testament, they which are called might receive the promise of eternal inheritance.
— Hebrews 9:14-15

To be the mediator of sinners, this person must be God, human, and perfectly sinless — all in one person. No other could fully satisfy God's attributes, reconcile God with sinners, and deliver others from sin and its results.

The mediator *must be God* for the following four reasons:

THE MEDIATOR MUST BE GOD	
1.	*To support His human nature in order to bear the full wrath of God against sin.* Any mere creature would have collapsed under, and been consumed by, God's anger against sin.
2.	*To give an infinite value to His work.* No mere creature could ever finish paying the eternal price required for sin, nor could he ever pay the price for millions of sinners. As an eternal and infinite Being, only God could fully pay sin's price in a short time.
3.	*To have the power to lay down His life and power to take it again.* No mere creature has the right to enter into death for others, for creatures do not have disposal of their own lives, since they cannot take them up again. Justice will not allow death to reign over the innocent.
4.	*To apply the righteousness earned to sinners.* No mere creature would be able to apply life to others, to place new spiritual life into spiritually dead sinners.

The mediator *must* also *be truly man.* He must be human for the following three reasons:

THE MEDIATOR MUST BE HUMAN	
1.	*To satisfy God's justice.* The righteous justice of God required that the same human nature that sinned must pay the penalty for sin. This human nature included both soul and body — for both had sinned.
2.	*To be able to suffer and die.* To be able to physically suffer and die, one must be human. Neither God nor angels could suffer in both body and soul and die.
3.	*To be man's second covenant head, kinsman, redeemer, and high priest.* To be the second Adam — placed under the law, a near kinsman, and tempted in all points as we are — He must be human.

To be a mediator for lost sinners, this person must not only be God and human, but He must also be a *perfectly sinless* person. This is true for the following three reasons:

THE MEDIATOR MUST BE PERFECTLY SINLESS	
1.	*To pay the full price for guilty sinners.* One with debts himself could not pay for, nor redeem others. If He had any sin, He would also be guilty and in debt to God.
2.	*To earn eternal life for sinners.* Eternal life is the reward for perfect obedience. If the Mediator had any sin, He could not restore that which the first Adam lost. A sinner cannot be a **surety** for another.
3.	*To enable His human and divine natures to be united in one Person.* The divine nature could not take upon, and be united to, the human nature if the human nature was not perfectly sinless.

The only acceptable mediator to reconcile sinful human creatures with their holy, divine Creator is one that is God, human, and perfectly sinless — all in one Person!

As God, the Mediator would present God manward and as man, the Mediator would present man Godward. God and man would be eternally united in one sinless Person — the perfect Mediator!

No mere human being can be his own mediator with God for the following three reasons:

NO PERSON CAN BE HIS OWN MEDIATOR BECAUSE:	
1.	Everyone is born with the guilt and pollution of original sin.
2.	Everyone commits actual sins in thoughts, words, and actions.
3.	No one can bear the full wrath of God against sin nor make satisfaction for his own sin.

And the angel answered and said unto her, The Holy Ghost shall come upon thee, and the power of the Highest shall overshadow thee: therefore also that holy thing which shall be born of thee shall be called the Son of God.
— Luke 1:35

For He hath made Him to be sin for us, who knew no sin; that we might be made the righteousness of God in Him.
— II Corinthians 5:21

Who did no sin, neither was guile found in His mouth.
— I Peter 2:22

For such an high priest became us, who is holy, harmless, undefiled, separate from sinners, and made higher than the heavens.
— Hebrews 7:26

● **Surety** — One who is responsible or accountable for another; one who agrees to pay for the damages caused by another

? How do the following verses contradict those who teach that man can save himself through doing good works?

And if by grace, then is it no more of works: otherwise grace is no more grace. But if it be of works, then is it no more grace: otherwise work is no more work.
— Romans 11:6

Knowing that a man is not justified by the works of the law, but by the faith of Jesus Christ, even we have believed in Jesus Christ, that we might be justifed by the faith of Christ, and not by the works of the law: for by the works of the law shall no flesh be justified.
— Galatians 2:16

A father once offered to serve as mediator for his son, who had been convicted of not paying a debt worth several thousands of dollars.

The judge listened to the father's offer and proceeded to examine this possibility. However, upon investigation, it was revealed that the father also had several large debts with no savings.

Due to his own debts, the father's offer to serve as mediator was not acceptable to the court.

How does this story illustrate the truth that any creature not perfectly sinless could never be an acceptable mediator between a holy God and sinful people?

No other creature, neither **saint** nor angel, could be our mediator. This is true for the following reasons:

NO OTHER CREATURE (NEITHER SAINT NOR ANGEL) CAN BE OUR MEDIATOR, BECAUSE:		
	A Saint:	An Angel:
1.	Is born with the guilt and pollution of original sin	Cannot satisfy God's justice which requires that the same human nature which sinned must pay the penalty for sin
2.	Commits actual sins in thoughts, words, and actions	Cannot physically suffer nor die — the penalty for sin
3.	Stands in need of a mediator to make satisfaction for his own sins	Cannot be man's second covenant head, kinsman, redeemer, or high priest
4.	Could never bear or satisfy the full wrath of God against sin	
5.	Could never give an infinite value to his work	
6.	Does not have the power to lay down, and to take up, his life again	
7.	Cannot apply the righteousness earned to sinners	

For these reasons, Scripture strictly forbids us to trust in, pray to, or worship saints or angels. Jesus Christ is the only Mediator — God, alone, may be prayed to, worshipped, and trusted.

How do the following scriptural examples illustrate the truth that neither saints nor angels may be worshipped?

Peter at the home of Cornelius

And as Peter was coming in, Cornelius met him, and fell down at his feet, and worshipped him.
But Peter took him up, saying, Stand up; I myself also am a man.

— Acts 10:25-26

● Saint — A regenerated person; a child of God

For there is one God, and one Mediator between God and man, the man Christ Jesus.
— I Timothy 2:5

And to Jesus, the Mediator of the new covenant, and to the blood of sprinkling, that speaketh better things than that of Abel.
— Hebrews 12:24

? Why would God's saints and angels despise and hate the very thought of being a mediator for lost sinners?

? How do the charts on the previous pages confirm the truth of Acts 4:12 and I Timothy 2:5?

Neither is there salvation in any other: for there is none other name under heaven given among men whereby we must be saved.

For there is one God, and one Mediator between God and man, the man Christ Jesus.

Paul and Barnabas at Lystra

? How do the first and second commandments forbid us from attempting to worship God through saints, angels, or images of them?

Then the priest of Jupiter, which was before their city, brought oxen and garlands unto the gates, and would have done sacrifice with the people.

Which when the apostles, Barnabas and Paul, heard of, they rent their clothes, and ran in among the people, crying out,

And saying, Sirs, why do ye these things? We also are men of like passions with you, and preach unto you that ye should turn from these vanities unto the living God, which made heaven, and earth, and the sea, and all things that are therein.

— Acts 14:13-15

John on the Island of Patmos

And I fell at his feet to worship him, And he said unto me, See thou do it not: I am thy fellowservant, and of thy brethren that have the testimony of Jesus: worship God: for the testimony of Jesus is the spirit of prophecy.

— Revelation 19:10

398

Two passengers were once talking together in a crowded train car. They were discussing the foolishness of believing in Christianity by relating cases of hypocrisy, corruption, and public sin in the lives of several Christian people they had known.

As the talking and laughing grew louder, several other passengers could not help but overhear this mockery, also. Finally, a young man turned to the loud mockers and said, "You have been telling story after story about the failings of Christians. I am a Christian. The faith of true believers is not based upon other Christians — it is founded upon Jesus Christ. I challenge you to now speak about His faults and sins!"

The passengers were suddenly privileged with a quiet ride. Later, several went up to the young man to individually thank him for his fitting correction.

How does this story illustrate the truth that only Jesus Christ, and not saints, can be worshipped and trusted as our mediator?

To be saved, sinful man required a mediator who was God, human, and perfectly sinless — all in one person. Where could such a person be found? No angel or man could ever have thought of a way in which God and sinners could be reconciled.

But, blessed be God! He presented His Son — One who was God, took upon Himself the human nature by being born from Mary, and lived a perfectly sinless life. Jesus Christ — God's justice was fully satisfied in His obedience and death, and God's mercy was fully glorified in His suffering and dying for guilty sinners.

All of Christianity hangs upon the one, only, perfect Mediator — Jesus Christ. Is He your hope, desire, and life?

But while he thought on these things, behold, the angel of the Lord appeared unto him in a dream, saying, Joseph, thou son of David, fear not to take unto thee Mary thy wife: for that which is conceived in her is of the Holy Ghost.

And she shall bring forth a son, and thou shalt call His name JESUS: for He shall save His people from their sins.

Now all this was done, that it might be fulfilled which was spoken of the Lord by the prophet, saying,

Behold, a virgin shall be with child, and shall bring forth a son, and they shall call His name Emmanuel, which being interpreted is, God with us.

— Matthew 1:20-23

For He hath made Himself to be sin for us, who knew no sin; that we might be made the righteousness of God in Him.

— II Corinthians 5:21

With parting tears, a father approved of his son's desire to bring the Word of God to a primitive, dangerous, cannibalistic tribe. To reach them required several days of traveling by air and land, as well as three days of hiking over rough trails. Rejection and death loomed as a distinct possibility. Yet, the son desired to go.

What moved this son to leave his life of comfort and peace, and his father to support his plan to go on such a dangerous, faraway mission? Was it not a love for the souls of these heathen people?

Jesus' willingness to fulfill His Father's plan reflects a far greater sacrifice than this example. Name several ways in which this is true. What moved God the Father and God the Son to approve of, and undertake, such a mission? What does this reveal to us of the love and grace of the one and only Mediator between God and man, and of God who designed the plan of salvation by grace?

? What is meant by Jesus' active and passive obedience? Why are both necessary when providing full satisfaction for His people?

? What rich doctrines and comforts are denied by those who do not base their entire salvation upon the satisfaction of the Mediator, Jesus Christ?

Christ's satisfaction as Mediator is personal, actual, and complete, as shown in the following chart:

AS MEDIATOR, CHRIST'S SATISFACTION IS:		
1.	*Personal*: for His elect church, His children	I am the Good Shepherd: the good shepherd giveth his life for the sheep. — John 10:11
2.	*Actual*: taking place in time; actually paying the full price for sin and earning the right to eternal life	When Jesus therefore had received the vinegar, He said, It is finished: and He bowed His head, and gave up the ghost. — John 19:30
3.	*Complete*: paying the full price for the salvation of His church	By the which will we are sanctified through the offering of the body of Jesus Christ once for all. For by one offering He hath perfected for ever them that are sanctified. — Hebrews 10:10,14

THE NATURES OF JESUS CHRIST

The Lord Jesus Christ is both God and man in one sinless Person. As God, He always had a **divine** nature. Through His birth on earth, He also took upon Himself a human nature — both body and soul.

God reveals Jesus' divine nature in numerous references throughout Scripture. These can be grouped under the following two headings:

1. References which **ascribe** divine *names, attributes, works, and honors* to the Lord Jesus

2. References of *personal testimony* to Jesus being divine

Examples of various scriptural references under these two headings are provided in the following charts:

- **Divine** — God; belonging to God alone

- **Ascribe** — To credit, refer, attribute, or assign to

JESUS CHRIST IS DIVINE
for the Bible ascribes to Him:

1. DIVINE NAMES — Names that can only be given to God

a. For unto us a Child is born, unto us a Son is given: and the government shall be upon His shoulder: and His name shall be called Wonderful, Counsellor, *The mighty God, The everlasting Father,* the Prince of Peace. — Isaiah 9:6	c. In His days Judah shall be saved, and Israel shall dwell safely: and this is His name whereby He shall be called, *THE LORD OUR RIGHTEOUSNESS.* — Jeremiah 23:6
b. Behold, a virgin shall be with child, and shall bring forth a son, and they shall call His name *Emmanuel,* which being interpreted is, *God with us.* — Matthew 1:23	d. In the beginning was the Word, and the Word was with God, and the *Word was God.* — John 1:1

2. DIVINE ATTRIBUTES — Attributes of God alone

a. **Omnipresent**	For where two or three are gathered together in My name, there am I in the midst of them. — Matthew 18:20

? Those who deny Jesus' divinity, deny His ability to be our Mediator. Why?

- **Omnipresent** — Everywhere present; being in all places at all times

- **Omniscient** — Being all-knowing; having a perfect knowledge of all things

- **Omnipotent** — Almighty; all-powerful; having unlimited power

- **Immutable** — Unchanging; eternally the same

b. **Eternal**	In the beginning was the Word, and the Word was with God, and the Word was God. The same was in the beginning with God. — John 1:1-2
c. **Omniscient**	But Jesus did not commit Himself unto them, because He knew all men, And needed not that any should testify of man: for He knew what was in man. — John 2:24-25
d. **Omnipotent**	I am Alpha and Omega, the beginning and the ending, saith the Lord, which is, and which was, and which is to come, the Almighty. — Revelation 1:8
e. **Immutable**	Jesus Christ the same yesterday, and today, and for ever. — Hebrews 13:8
f. All divine attributes	For in Him dwelleth all the fulness of the Godhead bodily. — Colossians 2:9

3. DIVINE WORKS — Works that only God can do

a. Creation	All things were made by Him; and without Him was not any thing made that was made. He was in the world, and the world was made by Him, and the world knew Him not. — John 1:3,10
b. Providence	The Father loveth the Son, and hath given all things into His hand. — John 3:35

c. Forgiveness of sins	But that ye may know that the Son of man hath power on earth to forgive sins. — Mark 2:10a
d. Preservation of the saints	And I give unto them eternal life; and they shall never perish, neither shall any man pluck them out of My hand. — John 10:28
e. Resurrection and final judgment	For as the Father raiseth up the dead, and quickeneth them; even so the Son quickeneth whom He will. For the Father judgeth no man, but hath committed all judgment unto the Son. — John 5:21-22
f. Glorification	Who shall change our vile body, that it may be fashioned like unto His glorious body, according to the working whereby He is able even to subdue all things unto Himself. — Philippians 3:21

? Why can each of the works and honors listed only be given to God?

4. DIVINE HONORS — Honors that can only be given to God

a. That all men should honour the Son, even as they honour the Father. He that honoureth not the Son honoureth not the Father which hath sent Him. — John 5:23	d. The grace of the Lord Jesus Christ, and the love of God, and the communion of the Holy Ghost, be with you all. Amen. — II Corinthians 13:14
b. And again, when He bringeth in the first begotten into the world, He saith, And let all the angels of God worship Him. — Hebrews 1:6	e. Grace be unto you, and peace, from Him which is, and which was, and which is to come; and from the seven Spirits which are before His throne: And from Jesus Christ, who is the faithful witness, and the first begotten of the dead, and the prince of the kings of the earth. Unto Him that loved us, and washed us from our sins in His own blood, And hath made us kings and priests unto God and His Father; to Him be glory and dominion for ever and ever. Amen. — Revelation 1:4b-6
c. Go ye therefore, and teach all nations, baptizing them in the name of the Father, and of the Son, and of the Holy Ghost. — Matthew 28:19	

? When Jesus confessed to be God, equal with His Father, why would He be relating either a grand truth or great blasphemy? Which did Caiaphas and the Jews believe? If a person denies the divinity of Christ, why can he not be saved?

JESUS CHRIST IS DIVINE Personal Testimonies Given By:	
a. God the Father	And lo a voice from heaven, saying, This is My beloved Son, in whom I am well pleased. — Matthew 3:17
b. God the Son	But Jesus held His peace. And the high priest answered and said unto Him, I adjure Thee by the living God, that Thou tell us whether Thou be the Christ, the Son of God. Jesus saith unto him, Thou hast said: nevertheless I say unto you, Hereafter shall ye see the Son of man sitting on the right hand of power, and coming in the clouds of heaven. Then the high priest rent his clothes, saying, He hath spoken blasphemy; what further need have we of witnesses? behold, now ye have heard His blasphemy. — Matthew 26:63-65
c. God the Holy Spirit	And John bare record, saying, I saw the Spirit descending from heaven like a dove, and it abode upon Him. And I knew Him not: but He that sent me to baptize with water, the same said unto me, Upon whom thou shalt see the Spirit descending, and remaining on Him, the same is He which baptizeth with the Holy Ghost. — John 1:32-33
d. Angels	But while he thought on these things, behold, the angel of the Lord appeared unto him in a dream, saying Joseph, thou son of David, fear not to take unto thee Mary thy wife: for that which is conceived in her is of the Holy Ghost. — Matthew 1:20
e. Prophets	Now all this was done, that it might be fulfilled which was spoken of the Lord by the prophet, saying, Behold, a virgin shall be with child, and shall bring forth a son, and they shall call His name Emmanuel, which being interpreted is, God with us. — Matthew 1:22-23
f. Apostles	Then saith He to Thomas, Reach hither thy finger, and behold My hands; and reach hither thy hand, and thrust it into My side: and be not faithless, but believing. And Thomas answered and said unto Him, My Lord and my God. — John 20:27-28

A group of people once met in London for an English Literature conference. In his opening message, the president included the following remarks:

"Ladies and gentlemen, what would you do if Milton would walk into this room?"

"Ah," answered one. "We would give him a standing ovation!"

"What would you do if Shakespeare entered?"

"We would arise and crown him master of literature and song!" another responded.

"May I ask you," said the president, "what would you do if Jesus Christ would enter this room?"

After a period of silence, one reverently responded, "We would fall on our faces and worship Him!"

How does this answer reveal that Jesus is more than a mere human being, more than just one who is to be respected and admired for his personal achievements?

? How is Jesus much more than merely being the best man which ever lived or the best example to be followed?

The Lord Jesus is not only divine, but he also took upon Himself our human nature — both soul and body. Scripture testifies of Jesus' human nature in many places. The chart on the following page presents several examples:

? What rich doctrines and comforts are missed by those who deny Jesus' humanity?

? Those who deny Jesus' humanity, deny His ability to serve as our Mediator. Why?

JESUS CHRIST'S HUMAN NATURE
Revealed in the Following Examples in which Jesus:

a.	Was born	And so it was, that, while they were there, the days were accomplished that she should be delivered. And she brought forth her firstborn son, and wrapped Him in swaddling clothes, and laid Him in a manger; because there was no room for them in the inn. — Luke 2:6-7
b.	Matured	And the child grew, and waxed strong in spirit, filled with wisdom: and the grace of God was upon Him. — Luke 2:40
c.	Was hungry	Being forty days tempted of the devil. And in those days He did eat nothing: and when they were ended, he afterward hungered. — Luke 4:2
d.	Slept	But as they sailed He fell asleep: and there came down a storm of wind on the lake; and they were filled with water, and were in jeopardy. — Luke 8:23
e.	Was tired	Now Jacob's well was there. Jesus therefore, being wearied with His journey, sat thus on the well: and it was about the sixth hour. — John 4:6
f.	Ate and drank	And they gave Him a piece of a broiled fish, and of an honeycomb. And He took it, and did eat before them. — Luke 24:42-43
g.	Was sorrowful	And saith unto them, My soul is exceeding sorrowful unto death: tarry ye here, and watch. — Mark 14:34
h.	Experienced pain and suffering	And being in an agony He prayed more earnestly: and His sweat was as it were great drops of blood falling down to the ground. — Luke 22:44
i.	Died	And Jesus cried with a loud voice, and gave up the ghost. — Mark 15:37
j.	Was buried	And when he knew it of the centurion, he gave the body to Joseph. And he bought fine linen, and took Him down, and wrapped Him in the linen, and laid Him in a sepulchre which was hewn out of a rock, and rolled a stone unto the door of the sepulchre. — Mark 15:45-46

Jesus' human nature included both a human body and soul. Man sinned with both soul and body and therefore Jesus had to **atone** for both. Jesus suffered in both:

a. *Soul* — "Then saith He unto them, My *soul* is exceeding sorrowful, even unto death: tarry ye here, and watch with Me" (Matthew 26:38).

b. *Body* — "Who His own self bare our sins in His own *body* on the tree, that we, being dead to sins, should live unto righteousness: by whose stripes ye were healed" (I Peter 2:24).

Jesus' soul and body were truly human and yet sinless. This was possible because Mary, a human, was His mother; and God was His Father. Due to God the Holy Spirit's creating of Jesus' human nature, Jesus was born without original sin. Jesus did not have a human — a descendant of Adam — as His father. As a divine Person, He could do no actual sin. Jesus was a perfectly sinless Person in both His divine and human natures.

The Lord Jesus always had His divine nature. He always has been God, and always will be. From eternity to eternity Christ is God. He did not always have His human nature, however. He **assumed** His human nature from the virgin Mary approximately 2,000 years ago.

● **Atone** — To make payment or satisfaction for

> And the angel answered and said unto her, The Holy Ghost shall come upon thee, and the power of the Highest shall overshadow thee: therefore also that holy thing which shall be born of thee shall be called the Son of God.
> — Luke 1:35
>
> Behold, a virgin shall be with child, and shall bring forth a son, and they shall call His name Emmanuel, which being interpreted is, God with us.
> — Matthew 1:23
>
> In the beginning was the Word, and the Word was with God, and the Word was God.
> The same was in the beginning with God.
> — John 1:1-2

● **Assumed** — To take upon oneself; to take on

The two natures of the Lord Jesus can be clearly seen in numerous scriptural accounts. Read Luke 8:22-25:

Now it came to pass on a certain day, that He went into a ship with His disciples: and He said unto them, Let us go over unto the other side of the lake. And they launched forth. But as they sailed He fell asleep: and there came down a storm of wind on the lake; and they were filled with water, and were in jeopardy. And they came to Him, and awoke Him, saying, Master, Master, we perish. Then He arose, and rebuked the wind and the raging of the water: and they ceased, and there was a calm. And He said unto them, Where is your faith? And they being afraid wondered, saying one to another, What manner of man is this! for He commandeth even the winds and water, and they obey Him.

How can we distinctly observe Jesus' human and divine natures in this history?

Years ago, the Queen of England liked to take walks near her castle in Scotland. She liked to dress as an ordinary woman and walk alone — with a servant following some distance behind her.

One day, when the queen was walking alone with her servant trailing her, she came upon a flock of sheep herded by a shepherd boy. The boy shouted, "Get out of the way!"

The queen smiled and stepped to one side until the sheep had passed. Then she continued on her way. In a few moments her servant came along. He told the shepherd boy that the queen had just passed.

"Oh," said the shocked boy, "I did not know that she was the queen. She did not look like a queen to me!"

When dressed as an ordinary woman, did the queen cease to be queen?

The Lord Jesus' divinity was often hidden behind His humanity. How does Isaiah 53:2 speak of this truth when it states, "He hath no form nor comeliness; and when we shall see Him, there is no beauty that we should desire Him"?

And the Word was made flesh, and dwelt among us, (and we beheld His glory, the glory as of the only begotten of the Father,) full of grace and truth.
— John 1:14

And without controversy great is the mystery of godliness: God was manifest in the flesh, justified in the Spirit, seen of angels, preached unto the Gentiles, believed on in the world, received up into glory.
— I Timothy 3:16

But when the fulness of the time was come, God sent forth His Son, made of a woman, made under the law.
— Galatians 4:4

But made Himself of no reputation, and took upon Him the form of a servant, and was made in the likeness of men.
— Philippians 2:7

● **Finite** — Limited

Jesus Christ has two natures, but He is not two separate persons. He is one Person with both a divine and human nature. The one divine Person assumed a human nature and now has both natures. He is one, single, individual Person, but He possesses all the essential qualities of both the divine and human natures.

The two natures of Christ are distinct from one another — the divine nature stayed divine and the human remained human; and yet, Christ is one Person, not two. This fact cannot be fully comprehended nor explained by man. The doctrine of Christ's natures, two distinct natures and yet one Person, is similar in mystery to that of the Trinity — three distinct Persons and yet one God. Neither can this mystery be fully understood by **finite** man.

The following five mistaken understandings and false teachings have taken place in church history regarding this doctrine of Christ's natures:

1. *The denial of Jesus' divine nature* — Certain groups in early church history, the **Socinians** during the Reformation, and the **Unitarians** and other modern liberal theologians today, have taught that Jesus was not divine, but only human. This false teaching denies the numerous verses that ascribe divine names, attributes, works, and honors to Christ, as well as the testimonies of His divinity found in Scripture.

- **Socinians** — Followers of the Socinus brothers, who taught that Christ was only human, but after His death was exalted to participate in God's rule and power

- **Unitarians** — Deniers of the Trinity; believers in one transcendent God and in Jesus only as an excellent human example to follow

2. *The denial of Jesus' human nature* — the **Gnostics** in early church history and other groups later have denied Jesus' human nature. They teach that Jesus was divine and that His human nature was only a form through which He revealed Himself. This error denies the scriptural references of Jesus' conception, birth, development, suffering, death, burial, etc. According to this teaching, Jesus, as a Person, did not actually experience these things; they only happened to the human form He was using.

- **Gnostics** — Believers that the soul and spiritual aspects of man were good — created by a "good god," and that man's physical body was evil — created by an "evil god." Jesus was only spiritual. He descended upon and used a human body for some time and then departed, but He was not human

3. *The denial of both Jesus' human and divine natures* — The **Arians** in early church history and the Jehovah's Witnesses today teach that Jesus was created as neither God nor man. He was created as the highest creature — above the angels but below God. This belief denies the scriptural references to both Christ's divinity and humanity.

- **Arians** — Followers of Arius (fourth century A.D.) who taught that Jesus was the first and highest of all created beings, neither God nor man

4. *The denial of the unity of the two natures in the Person of Christ* — **Nestorius** taught that the two natures of Christ were not united in one essence or person in Christ. Jesus was a union of two persons in one. This union was similar to human marriage — two distinct persons becoming one. They are bound together in one union, but remain two separate persons. The Nestorians viewed Christ as two different persons who were morally agreed and bound together in purpose and action. This error denies the scriptural teachings that the Mediator must be God and man in one, sinless Person.

- **Nestorius** — Appointed Bishop of Constantinople in A.D. 428, he taught that Jesus was actually two persons — closely bound together, yet remaining distinct persons

— The head of a large monastery in Constantinople (A.D. 378-455), who taught that Jesus' two natures were not distinct, but intermixed in His Person

---

The Council of Chalcedon
A.D. 451

Concerning the natures of Jesus Christ the Council ruled:

"That after His (Christ's) incarnation the unity of His Person consisted of two natures, which are without confusion, without change, but also without division, and without separation."

---

5. *The denial of the distinctiveness of the two natures of Christ* — **Eutyches** taught an opposite error from that of Nestorius regarding Jesus' natures. Eutyches taught that the two natures were intermixed into one — into a new God-man nature. This teaching denies the distinctive characteristics of both the divine and human natures. It also produces various confusing and mistaken ideas, such as Christ's being everywhere-present in His human as well as divine properties. This error falsely degrades the divine nature, mixing it with the human; and wrongly exalts the human nature, mixing it with the divine.

The Council of Chalcedon met in the year A.D. 451, to examine the teachings of both Nestorius and Eutyches. It condemned both teachings as false and concluded that Scripture teaches the following regarding Christ's two natures in one Person:

The two natures of Jesus Christ are:

a. Without division and without separation (against Nestorius)

b. Without mixture and without change (against Eutyches)

The mixing of Jesus' two natures has led to several strange and incorrect teachings and practices. Two of these are:

1. The Roman Catholic Church, by mixing the two natures of Christ, teaches the worshipping of Jesus' human nature. It practices the bowing before, and worshipping of, bread (a wafer) which is "changed into" the body of Christ.

2. The great reformer, Martin Luther, also failed to clearly see the scriptural teaching of the distinctiveness of each of Jesus' natures. He believed that Jesus' human nature mixed with the divine and became everywhere-present after His ascension. From this view, he taught that Jesus' body attached itself to the bread served at the Lord's supper — coming in, with, and under the bread.

How did these errors in teaching and practice develop from not maintaining that Jesus' natures are without mixture and change?

"If Jesus was God living in heaven and then was born as a person on earth, He did not remain in heaven as God during His time on earth, did He?" a student asked her teacher.

"What type of work does your father do?" her teacher asked.

"He's a policeman," she answered, quite surprised at the question.

"When your father leaves his home and is working as a policeman, is he no longer father of your home?" her teacher asked. "Of course he remains your father at home. So Jesus remained God in heaven. God is everywhere in His divine nature, even when taking upon Himself a human nature on earth."

While this illustration is helpful to picture Jesus as being both and not one or the other, why is it much more difficult to comprehend Jesus' two natures in one Person than a father holding two different positions as one person?

"Pictures of Jesus Christ are forbidden by the second commandment," Sandra stated.

"They are not," Mike retorted. "We have all kinds of books and Bibles with pictures of Jesus. Pictures of Jesus do not picture Him as God, but only as human."

After discussing this question for some time, they brought it to their father.

"Well," their father said, "the two natures of Christ may never be separated or divided. They are inseparably joined in one Person — Jesus Christ. Jesus cannot be thought of or pictured as only human — He is both."

"Some people reverence or idolize pictures of Jesus," their father continued, "and even if Jesus' human nature could be separated from His divine, this would still be wrong, for we may not worship and adore Jesus as human, but as a divine Person."

How is the question of whether pictures of Jesus are permissible or not, related to the doctrine of His natures?

? Is it right to have pictures of Jesus and not to consider them as special? Why would any picture of Jesus need to be special? Is it right to have any picture or likeness of God?

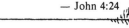

Thou shalt not make unto thee any graven image, or any likeness of any thing that is in heaven above, or that is in the earth beneath, or that is in the water under the earth:

Thou shalt not bow down thyself to them, nor serve them: for I the LORD thy God am a jealous God, visiting the iniquity of the fathers upon the children unto the third and fourth generation of them that hate Me;

And showing mercy unto thousands of them that love Me, and keep My commandments.

— Exodus 20:4-6

God is a Spirit: and they that worship Him must worship Him in spirit and in truth.

— John 4:24

THE NAMES OF JESUS CHRIST

More than two hundred names are given to the Mediator, Jesus Christ, in Scripture. Each of these names is rich and important, for each reveals some aspect of His person, natures, offices, states, or works.

Jesus' names include the following, and many more in Scripture:

? As human beings, we need names to distinguish ourselves from others. But no one is similar to Jesus Christ. Why then, has He given Himself so many names in Scripture?

THE NAMES OF THE MEDIATOR	
Jesus	Angel of the LORD
Christ	Root of David
Son of Man	The True Vine
Son of God	The Bread from Heaven
Lord	Rose of Sharon
The LORD our Righteousness	Lamb of God
The Mighty God	Lamb without blemish
The Everlasting Father	Lamb that was slain
My Lord and My God	Bridegroom
Emmanuel	Good Shepherd
The Only Begotten Son	The Rock of Ages
The Almighty	The Rock of Salvation
Creator of All	Rock and Fortress
Upholder of All	The Spiritual Rock
Alpha and Omega	The Surety
The Beginning and the End	The Great High Priest
The First and the Last	The Chief Cornerstone
The Word	Savior of the World
The Word Made Flesh	Messiah
Express Image of God	The Light of the World
The Brightness of His Glory	The Light of the Gentiles
Lord of Lords	The Bright and Morning Star
King of Kings	Dayspring from on High
Lord of All	Holy One of God
Prince of Peace	Captain of our Salvation
King of the Jews	The Deliverer
King of Glory	The Lion of the Tribe of Judah
The Way	The Ensign of the People
The Truth	Author and Finisher of Faith
The Life	Lord of the Sabbath
Wonderful	Just One
Counselor	Jesus of Nazareth
The Faithful and True Witness	The Foundation
Messenger of the Covenant	The Resurrection and the Life

Peter was deeply troubled by the frequent misuse of God's Name, especially that of the Lord Jesus, by two of the men he worked with at a gas station after school. Peter liked his work, but hated the **profanity** he heard. The men were much older than he was, and he didn't know how to answer them. He was afraid of trying to warn them.

One afternoon, their swearing was unbearable. Peter spoke out before he realized it and said, "Mr. Meyer, I know you love and think much of your wife. How would you feel if I used her name in a joking way or when I was angry?"

Mr. Meyer stared in silence at Peter. "That's how I feel when you misuse the name of Jesus Christ," Peter explained. "His name is most precious to me."

Peter's earnestness, honesty, and politeness made an impression upon Mr. Meyer. "Sorry, Pete," he responded. "I'll try to watch it."

Those who love God, love His Names. Do you? Are you willing to sacrifice your own name and honor for Christ's?

● **Profanity** — Swearing; the misusing of God's name; irreverent language

? When speaking with another about the misuse of God's name, how are the following important?
— My previous behavior
— My sincerity
— My timing
— My attitude

The two most commonly used names for the Mediator are "Jesus" and "Christ." "Jesus" is the Mediator's personal name, and "Christ," His official name.

The name "Jesus" is the Greek form of the Hebrew name "Jehoshua" or "Hoshea." It means "Jehovah (the LORD) saves."

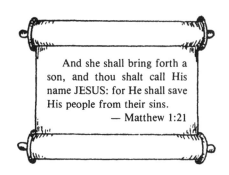

And she shall bring forth a son, and thou shalt call His name JESUS: for He shall save His people from their sins.
— Matthew 1:21

God's salvation is frequently defined as "delivering a person from the greatest evil and making him a partaker of the greatest good." What does this mean?

Three people bore the name "Jehoshua" (Joshua) or "Hoshea" (Hosea) in the Old Testament. Each is a type of Jesus — one as Prophet, the second as Priest, and the third as King.

1. Hosea the son of Beeri — the prophet (Hosea 1:1)

2. Joshua the son of Josedech — the high priest (Zechariah 6:11)

3. Joshua the son of Nun — the king or commander of the people (Joshua 1:1)

How is the name "Jehovah saves" a fitting and significant name for a prophet, priest, and king?

Why is it a most fitting name for the Lord Jesus Christ?

The Mediator was named "Jesus" because He would "save His people from their sins." Jesus is a complete Savior — He saves His people. As "Jesus," the Mediator not only *earned* salvation for, but He also *applies* salvation to, the hearts of His children.

If Jesus had only earned the right and offered salvation to His church, each person would have rejected it. As totally-depraved sinners, they would have freely chosen, with all men, for self, sin, world, and Satan. They, too, would have chosen to continue serving self instead of turning to God.

If Jesus only earned the possibility of salvation for, but never almightily applied salvation to, lost sinners; why would no person ever be saved?

But blessed be God! Jesus is a complete Savior. He not only merits, but also applies, salvation. Through His Spirit, He plants new spiritual life in the hearts of His children and makes them willing to turn to God in a way of repentance, faith, and obedience. The Savior is named "Jesus" because "He *shall save* His people from their sins!" What a richly gracious Savior is Jesus! Is He your Savior? If so, then He also is your Lord. Your deepest desire will be to know, love, and serve Him increasingly. Is this your heart's desire? He must become your Savior, shall it be well with you.

What rich truth and comfort is missed by those who deny both the totalness of salvation by grace and the name "Jesus"?

Some years ago, a Russian nobleman was traveling by sleigh in the Russian interior. Late in the afternoon he stopped at an inn and asked for a fresh team of horses to carry him several miles further to the next station, where he intended to spend the night. The innkeeper begged the nobleman not to do it, for the wolves would be out before he arrived at his destination. The man, however, was determined that he could make it, and drove off with his wife, little daughter, and personal servant.

Being only halfway to their destination, the frightening sound of the baying of wolves was heard. The man yelled to his servant to drive faster, but soon it could clearly be heard that the wolves were gaining on them. If the wolves would overtake and kill the horses, all would be killed.

With the wolf pack now very near, one of the horses was loosened into the forest. The poor animal rushed madly through the trees, and the wolves were diverted onto its trail. It was soon killed and eaten, and the pack began closing in on the travelers again. A second horse was loosened and more time was gained.

But with only two remaining tired horses, their speed was slowed. Their destination was near but they would not make it. The first wolves could now be seen approaching at full speed.

"Nothing can save you, but me!" the nobleman's servant exclaimed, and before the man had time to prevent him, he jumped from the sleigh. In a moment the wolves were upon him. The two panting horses continued on with the sleigh and arrived safely at the nearby inn.

The love of this servant for his master was very noble and touching. In what ways is it a picture of Jesus? Of the name "Jesus"? In what ways does the love of Jesus to save sinners transcend the love of this servant?

How will this nobleman view, and speak of, this servant for the rest of his life, do you think? How will those who have been saved by Jesus Christ view, and speak of, Him for the rest of their lives?

? Those missing the love of Jesus Christ in their lives, are missing the deepest love possible. Why? Why is the name "Jesus" most precious to those who have experienced something of His love?

415

- **Anointed** — To be chosen and set apart by having perfumed oil poured over a person

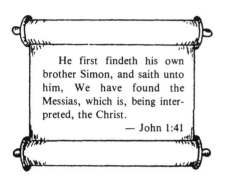

He first findeth his own brother Simon, and saith unto him, We have found the Messias, which is, being interpreted, the Christ.
— John 1:41

? Read of the anointings of both Saul and David to be kings over Israel in the following verses:

Saul - I Samuel 10:1

Then Samuel took a vial of oil, and poured it upon his head, and kissed him, and said, Is it not because the LORD hath anointed thee to be captain over His inheritance?

David — I Samuel 16:13a

Then Samuel took the horn of oil, and anointed him in the midst of his brethren: and the Spirit of the LORD came upon David from that day forward.

What difference is pointed to by Saul being anointed from a vial and David from a horn?

The New Testament, Greek name "Christ" is identical to the Old Testament, Hebrew name "Messiah." "Christ" means "The **Anointed** One." "Christ" is the Mediator's official name. In the Old Testament, persons were anointed for serving in one of three offices — that of prophet, priest, or king.

EXAMPLES OF OLD TESTAMENT ANOINTINGS FOR A:	
a. Prophet	And Elisha the son of Shaphat of Abel-meholah shalt thou anoint to be prophet in thy room. — I Kings 19:16b
b. Priest	And thou shalt put upon Aaron the holy garments, and anoint him, and sanctify him; that he may minister unto Me in the priest's office. — Exodus 40:13
c. King	And he arose, and went into the house; and he poured the oil on his head, and said unto him, Thus saith the LORD God of Israel, I have anointed thee king over the people of the LORD, even over Israel. — II Kings 9:6

In Scripture, oil is a type of the Holy Spirit. A person being anointed with oil pictured the following two truths:

1. Being *ordained* by God (appointed, chosen and placed) into an office

2. Being *qualified* by God (given the necessary abilities) for the office

Christ was *ordained* by God *from eternity* to serve as prophet, priest, and king for His church. He was *qualified* by God *in time* for His work.

Christ's qualifying was necessary for His human nature only. No qualifying work was necessary for His divine nature, for it is infinitely perfect in itself. The Holy Spirit qualified the human nature of Christ by giving Him unlimited gifts of wisdom, power, and holiness. These gifts revealed themselves in Christ's teachings, miracles, and sinlessness, as shown in the following chart:

CHRIST'S HUMAN NATURE QUALIFIED FOR HIS WORK		
Gift	Revealed	Example Text
a. Wisdom	Christ's teachings	For He taught them as one having authority, and not as the scribes. — Matthew 7:29
b. Power	Christ's miracles	And He said unto them, What things? And they said unto Him, Concerning Jesus of Nazareth, which was a prophet mighty in deed and word before God and all the people. — Luke 24:19
c. Holiness	Christ's sinlessness	For such an high priest became us, who is holy, harmless, undefiled, separate from sinners, and made higher than the heavens. — Hebrews 7:26

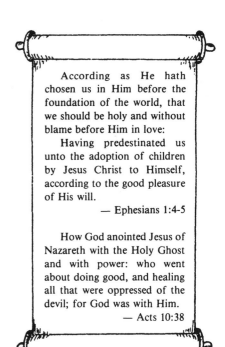

According as He hath chosen us in Him before the foundation of the world, that we should be holy and without blame before Him in love:

Having predestinated us unto the adoption of children by Jesus Christ to Himself, according to the good pleasure of His will.
— Ephesians 1:4-5

How God anointed Jesus of Nazareth with the Holy Ghost and with power: who went about doing good, and healing all that were oppressed of the devil; for God was with Him.
— Acts 10:38

The Triune God was involved in the anointing of Christ in the following ways:

1. God the Father — The Anointer

2. God the Son — The Anointed

3. God the Holy Spirit — The Anointing

Christians also bear the name of Christ. They also become a partaker of Christ's anointing as prophet, priest, and king. How does Question and Answer 32 of the *Heidelberg Catechism* describe the Christian's involvement in Christ's anointing?

Heidelberg Catechism — Question and Answer 32

Q. But why art thou called a Christian?

A. Because I am a member of Christ by faith, and thus am partaker of His anointing; that so I may confess His name, and present myself a living sacrifice of thankfulness to Him; and also that with a free and good conscience I may fight against sin and Satan in this life: and afterwards reign with Him eternally, over all creatures.

? How are true Christians anointed to be prophets, priests, and kings? How are they to exercise themselves in these offices?

417

How do the names "Son of man" and "Son of God" speak of Jesus' two natures?

Three other well-known names of the Mediator are:

1. *Son of Man* — Jesus frequently referred to Himself by this title. The name expresses His humanity — the birth, sufferings, death, and resurrection of His human nature.

2. *Son of God* — This name refers to Christ in the following three ways:

"SON OF GOD" REFERS TO CHRIST'S:	
a. *Birth* — speaking of the origin of Christ's human nature as divine	And the angel answered and said unto her, The Holy Ghost shall come upon thee, and the power of the Highest shall overshadow thee: therefore also that holy thing which shall be born of thee shall be called the Son of God. — Luke 1:35
b. *Offices* — as the Messiah, God's promised heir and representative	Of how much sorer punishment, suppose ye, shall he be thought worthy, who hath trodden under foot the Son of God and hath counted the blood of the covenant, wherewith he was sanctified, an unholy thing, and hath done despite unto the Spirit of grace? — Hebrews 10:29
c. *Divinity* — as the eternal Son of the Father	All things are delivered unto Me of My Father: and no man knoweth the Son, but the Father; neither knoweth any man the Father, save the Son, and he to whomsoever the Son will reveal Him. — Matthew 11:27

3. *Lord* — This name testifies of Christ in the following manners:

"LORD" REFERS TO CHRIST AS BEING:	
a. *Human* — referring to Him in a polite and respectful manner	And behold, there came a leper and worshipped Him, saying, Lord, if Thou wilt, Thou canst make me clean. — Matthew 8:2
b. *Natural owner* — having natural ownership or authority	And if any man say aught unto you, ye shall say, the Lord hath need of them; and straightway he will send them. — Matthew 21:3
c. *Supreme, divine owner*	For unto you is born this day in the city of David, a Saviour, which is Christ the Lord. — Luke 2:11

If a person claims to believe in Jesus as his Savior, must he also believe in Him as his Lord? Why? How will this reveal itself in the fruits of his life?

In biblical times, a faithful servant was trained to watch his master's hand and mouth. If the master wanted to communicate a request or command, he often would signal for this with his hand or speak a short order.

The faithful servant did not want to miss any command, request, or statement from his master. Therefore, his eyes and ears were looking and listening with anticipation. In this way, he waited upon his master.

Is Jesus your Lord and Master? If so, then your deepest desire is to wait upon Him with anticipation. Are you looking and listening for Him in your life? Is the fact of your poor servanthood a burden to you?

Jesus Christ is the one and only Mediator between a holy God and sinful people. He is God and man in one sinless Person. He bears numerous precious names.

Is He your Mediator and Savior? Do you love His names — Jesus, Christ, Son of man, and Son of God? Do you honor and serve Him as your Lord?

All of Scripture points to this Mediator — Jesus Christ. The Old Testament is full of prophecy and the New Testament, of fulfillment regarding Him. The chart on the following page provides some examples of this truth.

Jesus Christ is the central theme of the Scriptures; is He the center of your life?

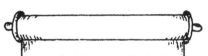

Behold, as the eyes of servants look unto the hand of their masters, and as the eyes of a maiden unto the hand of her mistress; so our eyes wait upon the LORD our God, until that He have mercy on us.
— Psalm 123:2

Wait on the LORD: be of good courage, and He shall strengthen thine heart: wait, I say, on the LORD.
— Psalm 27:14

Neither is there salvation in any other: for there is none other name under heaven, given among men, whereby we must be saved.
— Acts 4:12

For unto us a child is born, unto us a son is given: and the government shall be upon His shoulder: and His name shall be called Wonderful, Counsellor, the mighty God, the everlasting Father, the Prince of Peace.
— Isaiah 9:6

Yea doubtless, and I count all things but loss for the excellency of the knowledge of Christ Jesus my Lord: for whom I have suffered the loss of all things, and do count them but dung, that I may win Christ.
— Philippians 3:8

JESUS CHRIST — THE CENTER OF SCRIPTURE

Old Testament Promises	Events in the Life of JESUS CHRIST	New Testament Fulfillments
And I will put enmity between thee and the woman, and between thy seed and her seed; it shall bruise thy head, and thou shalt bruise His heel. — Genesis 3:15	**Born as a human being**	But when the fulness of the time was come, God sent forth His Son, made of a woman, made under the law. — Galatians 4:4
But thou, Bethlehem Ephratah, though thou be little among the thousands of Judah, yet out of thee shall He come forth unto Me that is to be ruler in Israel. — Micah 5:2a	**Born in Bethlehem**	Now when Jesus was born in Bethlehem of Judæa in the days of Herod the king, behold, there came wise men from the east to Jerusalem. — Matthew 2:1
Behold, a virgin shall conceive, and bear a son, and shall call His name Immanuel. — Isaiah 7:14b	**Born of a virgin**	Now the birth of Jesus Christ was on this wise: When as His mother Mary was espoused to Joseph, before they came together, she was found with child of the Holy Ghost. — Matthew 1:18
He is despised and rejected of men; a man of sorrows, and acquainted with grief: and we hid as it were our faces from Him; He was despised, and we esteemed Him not. — Isaiah 53:3	**Despised by the Jews**	He came unto His own, and His own received Him not. — John 1:11
Rejoice greatly, O daughter of Zion, shout, O daughter of Jerusalem: behold, thy King cometh unto thee: He is just, and having salvation; lowly, and riding upon an ass, and upon a colt the foal of an ass. — Zechariah 9:9	**Triumphant entry into Jerusalem**	Took branches of palm trees, and went forth to meet Him, and cried, Hosanna: Blessed is the King of Israel that cometh in the name of the Lord. And Jesus, when He had found a young ass, sat thereon; as it is written. — John 12:13-14
And I said unto them, If ye think good, give Me My price: and if not, forbear. So they weighed for My price thirty pieces of silver. — Zechariah 11:12	**Sold for thirty pieces of silver**	And said unto them, What will ye give me, and I will deliver Him unto you? And they covenanted with him for thirty pieces of silver. — Matthew 26:15
He was oppressed, and He was afflicted, yet He opened not His mouth: He is brought as a lamb to the slaughter, and as a sheep before her shearers is dumb, so He openeth not His mouth. — Isaiah 53:7	**Silent during His trial**	And the high priest arose, and said unto Him, Answerest Thou nothing? What is it which these witness against Thee? But Jesus held His peace. — Matthew 26:62-63a
I gave My back to the smiters, and My cheeks to them that plucked off the hair: I hid not My face from shame and spitting. — Isaiah 50:6	**Hit and spit upon**	And some began to spit on Him, and to cover His face, and to buffet Him, and to say unto Him, Prophesy: and the servants did strike Him with the palms of their hands. — Mark 14:65
They pierced My hands and My feet. — Psalm 22:16b	**His hands and feet pierced**	Then saith He to Thomas, Reach hither thy finger, and behold My hands; and reach hither thy hand, and thrust it into My side: and be not faithless, but believing. — John 20:27
And they shall look upon Me whom they have pierced. — Zechariah 12:10a	**His side pierced**	But one of the soldiers with a spear pierced His side, and forthwith came there out blood and water. — John 19:34
They part My garments among them, and cast lots upon My vesture. — Psalm 22:18	**Lots cast for His garments**	And when they had crucified Him, they parted His garments, casting lots upon them, what every man should take. — Mark 15:24
He keepeth all His bones: not one of them is broken. — Psalm 34:20	**No bone broken**	But when they came to Jesus, and saw that He was dead already, they brake not His legs. — John 19:33
And He made His grave with the wicked, and with the rich in His death. — Isaiah 53:9a	**Buried with the rich**	And when Joseph had taken the body, he wrapped it in a clean linen cloth. And laid it in his own new tomb, which he had hewn out in the rock: and he rolled a great stone to the door of the sepulchre, and departed. — Matthew 27:59-60
For Thou wilt not leave My soul in hell; neither wilt Thou suffer Thine Holy One to see corruption. — Psalm 16:10	**Arose from the dead**	He is not here: for He is risen, as He said, Come, see the place where the Lord lay. — Matthew 28:6
Thou hast ascended on high, Thou hast led captivity captive. — Psalm 68:18a	**Ascended into heaven**	And it came to pass, while He blessed them, He was parted from them, and carried up into heaven. — Luke 24:51

CATECHISM MEMORIZATION

Questions from Rev. A. Hellenbroek's *Divine Truths* — Chapter XII (Parts 1-2,4)

1. Who is the mediator of the covenant of grace?
The Lord Jesus Christ. "For there is one God, and one Mediator between God and man, the man Christ Jesus" (I Tim. 2:5).

2. Is He only a Mediator of intercession or also a Mediator of reconciliation?
Christ is also a Mediator of reconciliation. "Who gave Himself a ransom for all" (I Tim 2:6).

3. Is Jesus Christ the true Mediator and Messiah who was to come?
Yes, because all that was prophesied of the Messiah is fulfilled in Him.

4. How must we personally come to know Christ as Mediator?
(1) In His names; (2) In His offices; (3) In His natures; (4) In His states; (5) In His benefits.

5. What are the two most common names of the Mediator?
Jesus and Christ; the first, a Hebrew, and the second, a Greek name.

6. What does the name Jesus signify?
Savior. "Thou shalt call His name Jesus, for He shall save His people from their sins" (Matt. 1:21).

7. What does it mean to save a person spiritually?
To deliver a person from the greatest evil and to make him a partaker of the supreme good.

8. How does Jesus save His people?
By meriting and applying salvation to them.

9. Can we separate Christ's meriting from His applying of salvation?
No, for Christ applies salvation to all those for whom He merited it. "By His knowledge shall My righteous servant justify many, for He shall bear their iniquities" (Isa. 53:11).

10. Does this application of salvation depend on ourselves?
No, but it depends on the powerful operation of divine grace.

11. What does the name Christ signify?
Anointed.

12. What is the name of Christ in original Hebrew?
Messiah. "We have found the Messiah, which is, being interpreted, the Christ" (John 1:41).

13. How many parts are included in Christ's anointing?
Two parts: His appointment to, and qualification for, His mediatorial office.

14. Who has appointed and qualified Christ as Mediator?
God the Father.

15. When was this appointment made?
From eternity. "I was set up (or anointed) from everlasting" (Prov. 8:23).

16. In which nature was He appointed?
In both His divine and human natures.

17. When was He qualified as Mediator?
In the fulness of time.

18. In which nature was He qualified?
In His human nature, for no qualification could take place in His divine nature.

19. Why is His appointment called an anointing?
Because Old Testament men were ordained and installed to important offices by anointing.

20. Why is Christ's qualification called an anointing?
Because when anointed, God infused into such persons the qualifications necessary for these offices.

21. How is Christ anointed or qualified?
With the Holy Ghost. "How God anointed Jesus of Nazareth with the Holy Ghost and with power" (Acts 10:38).

22. What gifts of the Holy Spirit are particularly communicated to Him?
Wisdom, power, and holiness.

23. How did Christ manifest His wisdom?
In His teachings (Matt. 7:28-29).

24. How did Christ display His power?
In His miracles. "A prophet mighty in deed and in word" (Luke 24:19).

25. How did Christ reveal His holiness?
Through His sinlessness.

26. Did Christ have original sin?
No. "That holy thing which shall be born of thee" (Luke 1:35).

27. Did Christ have any actual sins?
No. "Which of you convinceth Me of sin?" (John 8:45).

28. Could the Mediator have any sin?
No, for one who is a sinner himself cannot satisfy for others. "For such an high priest became us, who is holy, harmless, undefiled, separate from sinners" (Heb. 7:26).

29. How many natures does Christ have?
A divine and human nature. "God was manifest in the flesh" (I Tim. 3:16).

30. Is Christ truly God?
Yes. "This is the true God and eternal life" (I John 5:20).

31. Which of the three Persons in the Godhead is He?
The Second Person, the Son. "But when the fulness of time was come, God sent forth His Son, made of a woman, made under the law" (Gal. 4:4).

32. Is Christ a real man?
Yes. "The man Christ Jesus" (I Tim. 2:5).

33. Of how many parts does His human nature consist?
Of two parts, soul and body.

34. Was Christ's soul part of His Godhead?
No, for He suffered in His soul and the Godhead cannot suffer. "My soul is exceeding sorrowful, even unto death" (Matt. 26:38).

35. Why was it necessary for Christ to be God?
(1) To support His human nature in bearing the infinite wrath of God and (2) to give an infinite value to His merits (Isa. 63:1-3).

36. Why was it necessary for Christ to be a man?
To be capable of suffering and dying.

37. Are the two natures of Christ united?
Yes, they are united in the Person Christ Jesus.

38. How was this unity accomplished?
By the divine Person assuming the human nature to Himself. "He took upon Him the form of a servant" (Phil. 2:7).

39. Is Christ's Godhead changed into His human nature?
No, He continues to be God.

40. Are the two natures of Christ intermixed so as to become one nature?
No, they remain two distinct natures, even after their union.

41. Do these two natures constitute two persons?
No, for they are united in one Person.

42. Are any divine attributes transferred to His human nature?
No, each nature of Christ retains its distinct properties.

CHAPTER 10

Part I. Chapter Review

1. What is a "mediator"? _____
   _____
   _____

2. Name and define the three types of mediators mentioned in Scripture:
   a. _____
   _____
   b. _____
   _____
   c. _____
   _____

3. To be a mediator between God and man, this person must be:

   a. Truly *God*, for the following reasons:
      1. _____
      2. _____
      3. _____
      4. _____

   b. Truly *human*, in order to:
      1. _____
      2. _____
      3. _____

   c. Perfectly *sinless*, because:
      1. _____
      2. _____
      3. _____

4. Why can a person never serve as his own mediator with God?
   a. _____
   b. _____
   c. _____

5. What is meant by Jesus' satisfaction being:

   a. Personal? _____

   b. Actual? _____

   c. Complete? _____

6. Jesus' divine nature can be proven from verses which ascribe divine _____, _____, _____, and _____ to Him. Scriptural examples of personal _____ of this fact can also be used to establish this truth.

7. Jesus' human nature included both a human _____ and _____.

8. Regarding the unity of the two natures of Christ, the Council of Chalcedon ruled, on the basis of Scripture, that Jesus' natures are:

   a. _____

   b. _____

9. "Jesus" is the Mediator's _____ name and it means _____. _____ is the Mediator's official name and it means _____.

10. Christ was ordained by God from _____ in both natures. He was _____ by God in time in His _____ nature only for His _____ nature needed no qualifying.

11. In the qualifying of His human nature, Christ received the following three gifts which revealed themselves in the following manners:

Gifts:	*Revealed in His:*
a. _____	_____
b. _____	_____
c. _____	_____

12. List three ways in which each of the names "Son of God" and "Lord" refer to Christ:

Son of God	*Lord*
a. _____	a. _____
b. _____	b. _____
c. _____	c. _____

CHAPTER 10

Part II. Deepening Your Insight

1. Why could God never be satisfied with a mediator who was less than God? _____
_____
_____

2. Why was it necessary for Jesus to have a human soul as well as body? _____
_____
_____

3. How does the Jehovah's Witnesses' teaching regarding Christ deny both His divine and human natures? _____
_____
_____

4. Describe how Martin Luther's mistaken teaching about the Lord's Supper is connected to his wrong idea regarding the two natures of Jesus Christ _____
_____
_____
_____

5. Why do totally depraved sinners need a Mediator that not only earns, but also applies salvation?
_____
_____
_____

6. Why would Jesus' divine nature require no qualifying work? _____
_____
_____
_____

7. How are Christians to serve in their anointed offices of:
   a. Prophet? — _____
   _____

   b. Priest? — _____
   _____

   c. King? — _____
   _____

QUESTIONS

Part III. Biblical Applications

1. Explain how the following verses speak of Jesus' satisfaction for sin being personal for His children:
   a. Matthew 1:21 — _____
   _____
   b. Ephesians 5:25 — _____
   _____

2. Name the divine name, attribute, work, or honor being ascribed to Christ in the following verses:
   a. Revelation 1:8 — _____
   b. Matthew 28:20 — _____
   c. Colossians 1:16 — _____
   d. Luke 10:22 — _____
   e. Matthew 25:31-32 — _____

3. Write out a verse from the following chapters which teaches that Jesus' two natures are both in His one Person:
   a. John 1: ____ — _____
   _____
   b. I Timothy 3: ____ — _____
   _____

Part IV. From the Writings of our Church Forefathers

In your own words, explain the meaning of the following quotations:

1. "Christ is the living Bible" (Thomas Manton). _____
   _____
   _____
   _____

2. "He suffered not as God, but He suffered who was God" (John Owen). _____
   _____
   _____
   _____

3. "It is a destructive addition to add anything to Christ" (Richard Sibbes). _____
   _____
   _____
   _____

CHAPTER 10

Part V. From the Marginal Questions

1. What is meant by Jesus' active and passive obedience? Why are both necessary when providing full satisfaction for His people? _____
    _____
    _____
    _____
    _____

2. Those who deny Jesus' divinity, deny His ability to be our Mediator. Why?
    _____
    _____
    _____
    _____
    _____

3. As human beings, we need names to distinguish ourselves from others, but no one is similar to Jesus Christ. Why, then, has He been given so many different names in Scripture? _____
    _____
    _____
    _____
    _____

4. If Jesus only earned the possibility of salvation for, but never almightily applied salvation to, lost sinners, why would no person ever be saved?_____
    _____
    _____
    _____
    _____

5. If a person claims to believe in Jesus as his Savior, must he also believe in Him as Lord? Why? How will this reveal itself in the fruits of his life? _____
    _____
    _____
    _____
    _____

EXTRA CHALLENGE QUESTIONS

Part VI. Your Selection from the Marginal Questions

Write out and respond to two marginal questions that interest you which have not been previously asked in this chapter's question section.

1. Question: _____
    _____

    Response: _____
    _____
    _____
    _____
    _____
    _____

2. Question: _____
    _____

    Response: _____
    _____
    _____
    _____
    _____

Part VII. Project Ideas

1. Draw a poster which portrays Jesus' work as Mediator — as Messenger, Advocate, and Peacemaker. Include several supporting texts for each.

2. Design a chart which clearly shows why the Mediator had to be God, human, and a sinless Person.

3. Write a paper on scriptural proofs of Jesus' divinity. Enlarge the list of proof texts given in this chapter with several other examples.

4. Construct a mural which contrasts the views of those who deny: Jesus' divine nature, Jesus' human nature, both divine and human natures, the unity of the two natures, and the distinctiveness of the two natures.

5. Research and present a panel discussion or debate on Jesus' two natures in His one Person.